The Well-Tempered House
Energy-Efficient Building For Cold Climates

Editor **Rick Wilks**
Assists **Brian Marshall**
Illustrator **Vilnis Lucs**
Conference Coordinator **Mark A. Craft**

The Well-Tempered House
Energy-Efficient Building For Cold Climates
Robert Argue

Publisher **Renewable Energy in Canada** 415 Parkside Drive, Toronto, Canada M6R 2Z7

Researched, written, printed
and bound in Canada
First Printing

Canadian Cataloguing in Publication Data

Argue, Robert, 1950-
  The well-tempered house

Includes selections of papers from a conference on
energy and housing held in Fairview, Alberta,
June 10-12, 1979.

ISBN 0-920456-25-1 bd.   ISBN 0-920456-26-X pa.

1. Dwellings — Energy conservation. 2. Solar
houses — Design and construction. 3. Solar
heating. 4. Dwellings — Energy conservation —
Catalogs. I. Title.

TJ163.5.D86A75   696   C80-094180-2

Renewable Energy in Canada is a
registered non-profit organization dedicated to the dissemination of information
about renewable energy sources,
technologies and related environmental
concerns.

In 1722 Johann Sebastian Bach completed Part I of *The Well-Tempered Clavier,* a collection of pieces written to demonstrate the versatility of an evenly-tuned keyboard.

So too, a well-tempered house can be achieved by understanding and balancing its various components.

Introduction

The Well-Tempered House presents the state-of-the-art of energy-efficient building in cold climates. This book was produced with two very specific objectives: To describe the construction of low energy-consuming shelters in cold climates; to integrate information on conservation and passive solar heating.

The following pages should combine, to maximum advantage for the homeowner, contractor or architect, the various elements of energy-efficient building. Our goal has been to describe the design or modification of a house so that it will perform as an efficient, conserving, comfortable and affordable unit. To achieve these objectives the emphasis is on several key factors: The elements that determine how the basic design of a house functions, what materials are used and how it is constructed.

Today's house, rather than requiring an enormous input of outside energy to function, can be made to be nearly self-supporting. Passive solar heating — using the sun to its best natural advantage — is one important approach. The second significant strategy documented is that of super-insulation. This approach concentrates on conservation first. The house is built within a heavily insulated, air-tight shell. It makes use of passive solar heating while minimizing the total window area.

The Well-Tempered House, in five sections, presents a "how-others-do-it-successfully" look at super-insulation and passive solar heating. It provides the information necessary to temper your own home and will direct the reader to sources for the tools and materials required.
The five sections are:
The Primer introduces (or recapitulates) the art of energy-efficient building and presents an overview of the various components and how they can best be combined.
The Proceedings of the Fairview Conference on Energy and Housing was an exciting conference that brought together many of the top designers and builders in North America to discuss their concepts and projects.
The Survey presents 14 examples of well-designed and built homes which combine the features discussed throughout the book.
The Access section provides an annotated list of titles and information on how to obtain hard-to-get components.
The Appendix presents weather data and material characteristics that will be useful in choosing designs and materials.

Much of the burgeoning field of appropriate housing is still in the developmental stage. New theories and approaches are conceived and implemented, sometimes to become part of the conventional wisdom, in other cases requiring still more refining. The absence of a complete set of hard and fast rules leaves room for different and innovative approaches. The Survey Section and Fairview Conference speakers reflect some of the varying, and sometimes contradictory, concepts currently being examined.

There is more than sufficient knowledge to make energy-efficient building work for you. Housing can be comfortable, bright and not the financial drain that so many homeowners face. These qualities are attainable, on the condition that we are prepared to alter many of our traditional attitudes and approaches. Such change is not only affordable, it would also work to halt the financially and ecologically destructive path we currently follow.

Anyone building today that does not incorporate energy-efficient features is doing both themselves and future generations a disservice. Today's houses may be described as "thermal slums" — there is no reason to produce more.

Robert Argue
June, 1980
Toronto, Canada

Contents

Building the well-tempered house

Primer

Introduction to super-insulation,
passive solar heating
and other energy-efficient techniques.

Introduction

The following section provides an illustrated survey outlining all aspects of energy-efficient building.

A house is one of the largest energy wasters today. Its size, shape, the materials used, design and quality of construction all affect its energy use. Few houses have been or are currently constructed to make wise use of these factors.

It is now possible to build a house that requires only 10 per cent of the energy needs of today's typical home. Many of the techniques require simple planning and common sense. These include quality construction, south-oriented windows and high levels of insulation. Others stipulate new methods or techniques, such as air-to-air heat exchangers or thermal shutters.

The Primer discusses each aspect of energy-efficient building and presents the methodology for putting it all together.

Home as Shelter

Historically we have constructed our homes as a defense against the elements. We've endeavored to create mini-climates that bear little relation to the external environment. This approach explains the uniformity in North American house design. Whether in the Maritimes, California or Inuvik, the commonalities of house design persist. If one location is too cold we install a larger furnace; if too hot we add air conditioning; if too dark we use artificial light. Humidity, temperature and air circulation can all be controlled to suit owner preferences. This is a classic example of a "technical fix"; in this case a mechanical device is added to solve a problem.

Similarly, the siting and orientation of a home is determined more by short-term economics than prudent energy-efficient construction. Little attention has been paid to modifying the architecture and design with respect to the specific site. The past abundant supplies of cheap energy have been primarily responsible for perpetrating these conditions. Now it's primarily expensive energy which is motivating the search for more appropriately designed and built houses.

But energy-efficient design encompasses much more than increased insulation in the attic and a well-tuned furnace. While these improvements are necessary for older homes, it is the aspects of new housing construction that are being questioned and re-examined. The new issues in house construction have become the size, shape, siting, interior layout, construction design and the materials used in the building. Also, because it is so inextricably linked, the home's relationship

with the natural environment must be considered. Rather than shut out the outside world, it makes good sense (economic and environmental) to make use of, and to account for, effects of the sun, wind, vegetation, slope and ground.

"To be happy at home is the ultimate result of all ambition" Samuel Johnson

A house is a shelter environment that we manipulate to work for us. It affords us

protection from the natural elements and, through its design and content, our lives. Ideally, a house should be able to accommodate many different moods and lifestyles, while at the same time not over-burden us with its operation, maintenance, and mortgages. And a house should be comfortable.

Comfort involves much more than merely the air temperature within the house. It's an experience based on the relationships between temperature, humidity, air movements, radiant energy, the clothes we wear, our internal thermometer, our activity and personal preferences. Comfort is affected by the temperature of the walls, floor, by the air at our feet, and the air at our heads. It is affected by the activity we are engaged in, the colours of the room, and whom we are with.

Convection, Conduction, Radiation

To understand the energy flows within a house it is important to understand the different modes by which heat moves. These are: convection, conduction and radiation. As a fluid (air or water) is heated it will rise, causing cooler fluid to replace it. In turn, this fluid becomes heated, thus setting up a convection current. This principle is used in thermosyphon systems. Passive hot water heaters or mass (Trombe) walls transfer heat to storage or to the room being heated by convection.

Convection conduction radiation

Air, pipes, kettles or any object in direct contact with the heat source will, if cooler than the source, be heated by conduction. Some materials obviously conduct heat better than others. Copper does this quite well and so is used in a solar collector to transfer heat. Polystyrene conducts very poorly and so is used as an insulator.

Lastly, a heat source will transfer heat by radiant energy. Higher temperature heat sources emit shorter and more intense radiant energy. The energy received by the earth from the sun is radiant energy. A wood stove will heat a room by radiant energy.

In addition to source, colour influences radiant energy. Darker colours both emit and absorb more radiant energy, while lighter colours will reflect and emit less. Flat black is used on solar systems for its absorbing qualities; while aluminized mylar or foil is used as an insulator because it reflects radiant energy. An understanding of these principles should result in a more appropriate use of colours, textures and materials in building and designing.

Direct contact with cold surfaces will reduce comfort levels. But even being in sight of a cold surface will make you colder, and not just psychologically. You are constantly exchanging radiant energy with everything around you. You gain energy if it is a high temperature source, such as a radiator; but you lose (and feel cold) if it is cooler than you. That's why uninsulated walls and windows can create discomfort, even if the air temperature is adequate.

Site

The site and how the building relates to it is a critical determinant in the calculation of energy consumption. The most profound effects, and the ones the individual has least control over, are the macro-climatic (regional) factors of degree days, design temperature, wind, hours of bright sunshine, and the total solar insolation. Other factors which can have an enormous effect on the energy consumption of a house are micro-climatic. These include the topography of a site, the sun path, specific wind regime, vegetation, soil and the placement of other buildings.

Macro Climate

Before designing a house an intensive study of the region's macro climate should be undertaken. While there is nothing anyone can do to control the elements, a sound understanding of the climatic personality is quite important.

Temperature is one of the primary considerations; specifically, the factors of degree days and design temperature. Degree days is a measurement of the extent of cold temperature. The term refers to the number of degrees per day that fall below a given level (65°F, 18°C). While degree days determine the total energy that will be required to keep warm; the design temperature indicates the worst temperature conditions that may be expected on any day (99 per cent of the time). This figure is used to size the heating system required.

If degree days may be seen as the enemy, then the hours of bright sunshine and total solar insolation are the major weapons in a defensive arsenal. The hours of bright sunshine, especially during winter months, provides an indication of how much sunlight can be expected to stream in those south-facing windows. Most regions receive substantial light in February and March, whereas November and December are cloudy and alternative means of heating must be found.

While data on hours of bright sunshine provides an important indication of the energy available, the figures on total solar insolation allow more detailed calculations. To date, most data has been collected for solar radiation on a horizontal surface. Information is becoming available for solar radiation for various slopes and aspects (see Appendix). Of special interest to house designers is the insolation on a vertical slope (90 degrees), as this determines the energy gain potential of windows. A vertical surface receives direct, bright sun radiation, diffuse radiation (from the rest of the sky) and reflected radiation. If water, ice, snow or a bright surface enhances reflection, it can increase the radiation striking a vertical surface by up to 30 per cent.

Micro climate

The micro climate consists of those aspects of a building site that the owner/designer can have the greatest influence on. The ideal site, the one that readily comes to mind when dreaming of the acme of solar homes, has a south-facing slope and is sheltered by coniferous trees on the north. It has complete access to the sun (as well as a view for miles and miles over rolling hills) and perhaps a flat area well-suited for a garden.

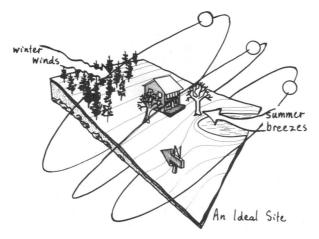

An Ideal Site

The south slope helps to ensure two things: it makes it more difficult for neighbours or nature to block your view of the sun (especially important in winter when it is low on the horizon); and it makes it easier for the north side of the house, the face that loses heat, to burrow into the side of the hill. Building into a hill helps temper the heat loss from the north side of the house as well as protect it from any unfavourable winds. At the same time it allows maximum exposure of the south face of the house.

This best-of-all-possible houses would be about halfway up the hill, out of the wind, but above the cold and mist that settles in the valley below. As additional protection from winter's heat-grabbing winds, coniferous trees would be placed about the north and west side of the house. (A good wind screen can reduce a home's infiltration heat loss by up to two-thirds.) Deciduous trees, which lose their shading leaves in winter, would be planted on the south side. A preferable option would be to employ a fast-growing, flowering vine that produces an abundance of edible seeds.

But of course this personal vision of bucolic contentment is not everyone's dream, nor can it be a general solution to an energy-depleted society. Many of the optimal (and less than optimal) homesites have been bought up by far-thinking people. The challenge lies in utilizing less than ideal sites in an energy-wise fashion.

For those many people who are stuck with a north slope or live as part of the vast majority in urban or suburban dwellings, there are still many energy-conserving measures that may be taken. A south slope can be "faked" by having the house set on the north side of the lot. This allows maximum control of access to the sun (although care should be taken so that a neighbour's sunshine is not blocked). One could also place earth-berms on the north and side faces of the house to simulate underground sheltering effects.

A growing number of municipalities have ensured that new subdivisions will have the lots laid out to allow a maximum number of houses a clear, southern exposure. Height restrictions of any object to the south of a house are based on the distance from the base of the house and will ensure that sun rights will be guaranteed over time.

To sum up, the following modifications to a site will boost a home's energy saving potential:
— minimize the northern exposure
— maximize the southern exposure
— provide shelter from the prevailing winds of winter
— allow shade in the summer
— make prudent use of the materials around the house: earth, rock, vegetation can all be used to advantage

Building exterior

The shape of a building is a major determinant in its energy consumption patterns. A dome minimizes exposed surface area, but gives no preference to the northern or southern exposure unless the structure is imbedded in a hill. A rectangle is the configuration most often used, usually with a long east-west axis. (This maximizes the southern exposure and provides a shallow house for easy heat and light distribution.) If the north side cannot be buried or bermed, then often the roof will slope down to the north. This allows more southern exposure during the winter and minimizes the east and west exposures during the summer (thus preventing overheating).

A house with fewer protrusions has less surface area. A two-storey house will have a smaller surface area than a one-storey house with the same floor area. However, because it is generally easier and cheaper to insulate ceilings than walls, a one-storey house can have as small a heat loss as a two-storey structure of the same total floor area. Attached houses, such as duplexes or townhouses, share common walls and consequently have significantly smaller heat losses.

Size

The larger the building, the more energy it takes to keep it warm. In relative terms, the larger the building the less energy per unit volume is needed. However, it is in absolute terms that you pay your heating bill. One large building with five units is more efficient than five little houses, but one small house is more efficient than a large one.

Today's average house is considerably larger than those built twenty years ago. We now include extra "single-purpose rooms" that are rarely used and separated rooms that at one time served many functions. Open plan arrangements and multiple-function rooms can give smaller houses the feel of being extremely spacious, while being efficient.

Orientation

As discussed, the most important consideration when orienting a house is the southern face. Most of the home's natural light and natural heat will enter through south facing windows. Due south, or solar noon, is the optimum direction for solar collection, but variations on this can be successful. As a general rule, it is preferable to orient a passive solar heated house east of south (15 to 20 degrees) rather than west of south. Oriented to the east it will heat up in the early morning, the period of maximum demand. By avoiding the west there will be a reduction in afternoon overheating problems.

There is a great deal of tolerance for non-optimal orientations. South slopes facing 15 degrees east or west of due south receive virtually 100 per cent of the radiation of a due south slope. Thirty per cent off south means a loss of under ten per cent. Even a south-east or south-west orientation (45 degrees from due south) will receive 75 per cent of the optimum sun. With this in mind, it is easier to make the sometimes necessary compromises or alterations that local conditions may demand. An eyesore (a junkyard or highrise) or a beautiful view may dictate the final orientation. The sun tables in the Appendix will help determine what penalty those rolling hills or dead cars extract.

Slope

Once the orientation of the house has been determined, the next step is to decide the size and the slope of the glazing. Both these aspects are influenced by the purpose of the glazing (to allow light into the house directly, protect a mass wall, or define a greenhouse), the materials used, and the design of the house. Generally, the glazing should maximize winter sun (for heating) and minimize summer sun (to prevent overheating). Controversy exists over the issue of sloped surfaces versus vertical surfaces for achieving this.

The advantages of sloped over vertical glazing are:
— it optimizes direct and diffuse radiation
— it can be aesthetically pleasing
— it receives summer sunlight (for greenhouses)
— it is useful as a skylight
The disadvantages of sloped glazing are:
— it is harder to construct and weatherproof
— it tends to overheat in the spring and fall
— it loses reflected radiation in the winter

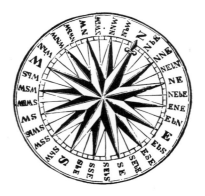

Building Interior

Designing the interior layout of a house is also an exercise in defining a lifestyle. Given a 20′ x 35′ two-storey shell, the possibilities and variations are numerous. Design and lifestyle considerations include decisions as to whether or not to construct many small rooms, or leave open spaces; design two stories, one and a half, or splurge on a cathedral ceiling. How many bathrooms and where? In addition to personal taste considerations, here are some energy-conserving rules of thumb:

— Design open spaces for rooms used all the time. The kitchen, eating and living rooms are used daily. An open plan allows free air, light and heat circulation.

— Design closed spaces in rooms used occasionally. It makes no sense to heat a spare bedroom if it is only used once a month, so there should be design provisions for sealing it off from the heating system and the rest of the house. Bedrooms don't need to be heated during the day.

— Place cold rooms on the north side. Rooms that don't require heat, such as the laundry, storage, closets, stairwells, workshops, etc., should be located on the north side of the house. This acts as an extra buffer to the colder north wall.

— Place rooms used in the morning to the east and south. In the winter it's pleasant (depending on personal tastes and hours) to have the sun stream into the bedroom. The light and added heat are good wake-ups. Kitchen and eating places that are placed to the east will also be bright and warm.

— Daytime living places should be to the south. Living rooms, work rooms and any other rooms used during the day will receive light and heat during the day if placed on the south side.

— Locate the fireplace (if you need one!) or chimney in the interior. A fireplace or chimney on an exterior wall will lose a lot of heat to the outside. If it's placed on an interior wall any heat loss will be to the house.

With two-storey houses uncomfortable (and inefficient) temperature stratification can occur as heat will naturally rise to the second storey, especially if there are large open stairwells and other spaces. Concentrating on the glazing on the bottom floor will help to even the heat out. Circulating fans, through duct work or vents between floors, will also help to even the heat distribution.

These suggestions are indications of what may be done to maximize heat and light. Lifestyle preferences may dictate a different approach.

Interior considerations with direct-gain systems

Sunlight or heat may fade or degrade fabrics used in a passive solar home. Direct gain systems, with their large window area, are most likely to cause problems with curtains, floor coverings and upholstery. In addition, consideration has to be given to the properties of materials, for example, will they act as a conductor or insulator of heat?

When they are used in windows, fabrics should have a minimal loss of tensile strength and resist heat, dust and pollution. Acrylics, nylons, glass and polyester have these properties. Upholstery fabrics should resist fading and be durable. Acrylics, wool, silk, cotton, linen, and nylon are appropriate. Flooring material should be determined by its abilities to either conduct or inhibit floor heat, depending on whether or not the floor is used as a thermal mass. Fading properties and resiliency are also important.

Floor coverings do not generally add to energy conservation, and in some cases can make matters worse. Tiles or sheet flooring do not affect the heat flow of a floor. Medium to heavy carpeting on a basement floor will marginally reduce the energy demand of a house by adding R2 to the floor. However, if carpeting is placed over a heated floor slab, the energy loss can be substantial, by increasing the downward flow of heat.

Insulation

It's almost redundant to suggest that insulation is of primary importance in developing the well-tempered house. Though this much is basic knowledge, there are a great many questions concerning the specifics (which insulating material would be most suitable, how much to use) that do generate some controversy. This section will explore the questions of why to insulate, where to insulate most effectively, as well as examine the various types of insulation and heat loss areas of the house. Shutters and window insulation (movable insulation) are discussed in a separate section.

A well-insulated house reduces the heat demand and permits any energy added to the house to be used to maximum advantage, whether the source of this additional energy is sunlight through windows, people, lights, machines, a fireplace or the furnace. Using adequate insulation means:
— reduced total outside energy requirements (thereby lowering fuel bills)
— warmer (and more comfortable) walls and floors
— increased value of internal heat gains
— being able to use a smaller furnace/wood stove/solar system
— a cooler house in summer
— a quieter house

Insulation is measured in R-values. This is a measure of the insulation's resistance to heat loss. The higher the R-value, the greater the resistance and the more effective the insulation. R10 is twice as good as R5, R20 twice R10. Various materials are rated and compared by the R rating per inch of material. Thus, the important consideration in determining insulation value is not the thickness, but the R-value that thickness provides. The new unit of insulation is RSI. One unit of RSI equals approximately 6 units of R.

The Insulation Sweepstakes, or How Much Is Enough, When Is Too Much

Over the years, Canada Mortgage (CMHC) has established minimum standards for insulation. Of course, most builders, in order to reduce front end costs, use these minimum standards as their maximum. These standards have become obsolete due to "conserver consciousness" and the rising cost of conventional fuels. There has always been a "leading edge" of owner-builders who have insulated their homes to unheard-of extents (often to the amusement of their neighbours). Now their efforts have been by-passed by the insulation sweepstakes! A *minimum* standard for a well-tempered house these days should be in the neighbourhood of R30 walls, R50 ceiling, R15 below grade, R20 floor over a crawlspace. These values will go up and down depending on local climate and energy costs.

Heat Loss

Through radiation, convection and conduction, a house experiences heat loss. Each area of a house presents its own problems and solutions.

The Attic

Attics normally account for 10 to 20 per cent of the heat loss in a conventional house. A large percentage of the loss is due to air leakage through holes and cracks. An air-tight, well-insulated ceiling (see Infiltration) will not have a substantially higher heat loss than any other part of the house.

Attics are now being packed with large amounts of insulation, R40 and higher. Super-insulated houses, such as the Saskatchewan Conservation House, have attic insulation of R60 to R80. Fortunately attics do not normally present logistical problems because it's relatively easy to install loose fill or batt insulation in the ceiling area. It takes approximately 19 inches of fibreglass batts to equal R60.

Masonry walls

Masonry walls (brick or cement block construction) are best insulated on the outside, thus allowing the thermal mass of the wall to be used as heat storage for the house. Thermal mass used within the house can alleviate severe temperature fluctuations within the living space and reduce summer cooling and winter heating needs. This is of special importance when incorporating a passive heating strategy such as a large south-facing window area.

Several options are available in insulating masonry walls either from the exterior or the interior.

Framing and strapping: Insulation can be applied to new cavity walls framed on the exterior or interior spaces. On the exterior, either rigid foams or rigid or batt fibreglass sheets can be installed between studs or strapping, then a new sheathing can be affixed to the strapping.

Adhesion: Rigid boards of insulation can be affixed to existing walls employing adhesives such as mastics. Problems might arise from differential expansion and/or shrinkage. Furthermore, as an exterior application most rigid foams need to be rasped or roughened if a layer of stucco (protective shell) is to be applied. (Alternatively, chicken wire can be used as lathing to support the material.)

Tracking systems: Several tracking systems have been developed in order to affix rigid insulation to exterior walls. One of the major advantages of employing such a system is that thermal bridging across studs or strapping is, for the most part, eliminated. The channelling strips are mechanically affixed directly to the existing wall with the insulation then applied over top.

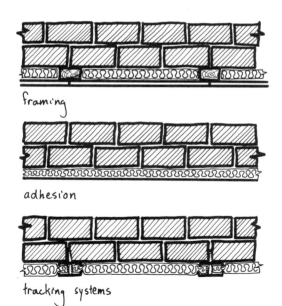

framing

adhesion

tracking systems

Insulating masonry walls

Frame Walls

Frame walls are the predominant construction technique employed in Canada and the United States. As thermal efficiency has become an important component of home construction, several alternative framing details have been developed to replace the standard 2 x 4 construction (which only allows R12 of fibreglass). To provide a larger cavity for installing insulation, some builders have begun to use 2 x 6 studs in wall framing. These studs can be placed at 24-inch centres thereby allowing the builder to maintain costs at a competitive level. This allows an R20 wall.

The insulation on stud walls should also be improved by strapping on rigid insulation or batts on the exterior/interior of the wall. Often 2 x 2 or 2 x 3 strapping is placed horizontally in 25-inch centres. Rigid insulation or batts are secured between the strapping.

The concept of double stud walls has been used as a means of alleviating thermal bridging while increasing the wall cavity. In the Saskatchewan Conservation House the exterior walls were constructed of two independent wall systems with an air gap separating the partitions. The cavity in the walls was filled with 12 inches of fibreglass insulation with an R-value of 40. An added advantage is that the vapour barrier can be affixed to the first inner wall. All plumbing and electrical work can then be accomplished without poking random holes through the barrier.

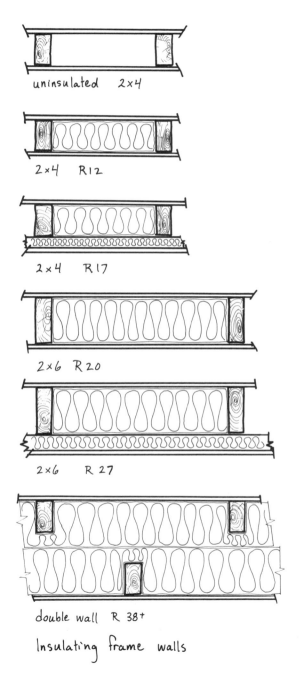

uninsulated   2x4

2x4   R12

2x4   R17

2x6   R20

2x6   R27

double wall   R 38+

Insulating frame walls

strapping in front of the
vapour barrier

Insulation Types — Advantages and Disadvantages

Type	Advantages	Disadvantages	Best Applications
Fibreglass (Batt and Loose)	— low cost per R — relatively non-flammable — resistant to moisture damage — no settling — comes in most sizes and quantities	— awful to handle — respiratory difficulties	— cavity walls — attic space
Fibreglass (rigid)	— light, easy to handle — breathes, permitting vapour to pass through — resistant to moisture damage — relatively non-flammable — low cost per R — can be used as exterior sheathing	— needs strapping for application to outside walls — compressible	— shutters — exterior walls — roofs
Cellulose	— recycled materials — low cost per R — small particles blow into most cavities — resists air flow — not affected by normal water-vapour	— absorbs heavy moisture — settles — possible fire problems if retardant not properly applied	— blow in existing cavities — attics
Urea Formaldehyde	— high initial R — low flammability — non-settling — fills cavity	— high vapour permeability — linear shrinkage leads to low R effectiveness — environmental problems; formaldehyde can emit gas	— cavity walls
Expanded polystyrene (Beadboard)	— cheapest foam — breathes — easy to use — moisture resistant	— low R value — flammable — not a vapour barrier — degrades under exposure	— insulating exposed floors — ceilings
Extruded polystyrene	— waterproof — vapour barrier — high R value — low outgassing	— u.v. degradation — flammable — costly	— exterior or interior of masonry walls and foundations — sheathing — under slabs

Basements/Foundations

Basement or foundation walls can be responsible for up to 25 per cent of a house's heat loss. Most of the heat escapes through the walls and is carried away. Insulation can be installed on the inside or outside of the foundation. Insulation applied to the outside keeps the mass of the foundation within the heated space of the house. Generally speaking, two inches of rigid insulation providing a value of R15 is adequate. In extremely cold climates this should be increased. Another strategy for insulating below grade foundation/basement walls, espe-

Type	Advantages	Disadvantages	Best Application
Urethane	— high initial R — applies on irregular surface	— highly flammable — outgassing of fluorocarbons — high cost — diminishing R value	— coolers, etc.
Vermiculite	— fire resistant	— causes com- pression of other materials — absorbs moisture — high cost	— attics — floors

Insulation Qualities and Cost

Quality	Type	R/inch (average)	Cost
loose	glass fibre (blowing, pouring)	2.16, 3.03	low
	cellulose fibre	3.53	low
	mineral fibre	2.9	low
	vermiculite	2.3	medium
	polystyrene	2.88	medium
	wood shavings	2.6	low
batt	fibreglass	3.17	low
	mineral	3.3	low
rigid	extruded polystyrene	4.91	high
	beadboard (expanded polystyrene)	3.9	medium
	polyurethane slabs	6.06	high
	fibreglass	4.47	medium
foamed	ureaformaldehyde	2.5	high
	polyurethane	4.8	high
natural	earth beams underground — employ ground temp. approximately 53°F poor insulation sod roof hay bales 18″ of hay = 12″ of fibreglass		

cially for existing homes, is to place rigid insulation horizontally from the house. It should be about a foot underground, extend approximately two feet and slope downward away from the house for drainage. This insulation will prevent much of the heat from escaping the basement.

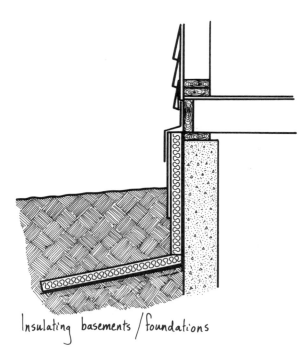

Insulating basements / foundations

Slabs

A concrete slab should be insulated underneath. At least two inches of rigid insulation should be used. If the slab is used as a radiant heater the insulation should be doubled.

Types of Insulation

As anyone who has investigated purchasing knows, insulation comes in many sizes, shapes, qualities and costs. To help sort through the labyrinthine data, here are some of the characteristics to evaluate:

R-value per inch: This is an indicator of how much material is necessary to achieve a certain insulation level.

Cost: This is best evaluated by a dollar per R-value per square foot. This allows comparisons among the different types of insulation.

Quality: Whether it is rigid, loose or structural will determine where it can be used most effectively.

Permeability: Some insulation acts as its own vapour barrier, keeping out moisture, while other types of insulation require moisture protection.

Inflammability: Some insulation is flammable or will emit toxic smoke during a fire. Building codes require these types of insulation to be protected.

How Much Insulation?

Canada Mortgage (CMHC) has set standards of R20 in ceilings and R12 in walls. These standards are far too low. The extreme school of thought suggests that people should install more insulation than they think is necessary and as much as they can afford. This position is taken by those who advocate "zero-energy" house standards, with insulation values reaching as high as R100.

Regional considerations are important in determining how much to insulate. Obviously the harsher the climate, the more insulation is needed and the greater the savings will be. Energy costs are also important. Heating with electricity in Prince Edward Island can cost many times as much as heating with natural gas in Alberta.

Vapour Barriers

Vapour barriers are extremely important. Their proper use cannot be over-stressed. They serve two major functions: they reduce air infiltration, and therefore heat loss; and they protect insulation from moisture coming from inside the house.

As humid inside air travels from the house to the colder outside, the temperature of the air falls. The air starts to lose its ability to hold moisture and the relative humidity increases. At some point the dew point is reached, where moisture begins to condense, wetting the insulation and wood studs. This can cause deterioration and rot; and reduce the effectiveness of the insulation. Moisture enters the wall through air leaks around the vapour barrier, as well as permeating directly through the barrier via vapour pressure. All air leaks must be sealed and the vapour barrier used should have a low permeability.

A vapour barrier is placed in the *warm* side of the insulation to prevent moisture from getting through. For this reason the barrier should remain intact, as any perforations will negate its effectiveness. Should the vapour barrier be broken (as is apt to happen with certain jobs such as installing electrical facilities), it must be completely re-sealed.

Electrical outlets are the most common perforators of vapour barriers. If it is unavoidable to place outlets in an outside wall, the vapour barrier must be continuous around the outlets and any perforations should be well sealed with a good caulk. Special boxes (polypan) are also available that reduce infiltration. These problems can also be overcome by using

a double stud wall system or a stud wall with strapping with the wiring through the interior wall, in front of the vapour barrier. As long as two-thirds of the insulation is exterior (on the cold side) to the vapour barrier, the remaining one-third insulation may be on the interior. The dew point will occur outside the vapour barrier and condensation problems will be avoided.

Some of the common problems with vapour barriers are:
— small perforations
— breaks for plumbing and wires
— seams
— corners and joints
— around window and door frames
—- chimneys and vent areas
— sill plates and where walls meet ceilings

A thick (6 mil) polyethylene sheet is commonly used. A barrier this thick will take a lot of beating without being perforated. All joints are taped or caulked and all perforations sealed. The barrier should be made continuous past joists and wall partitions, and caulked directly to window and door frames.

Other types of vapour barrier include:
— craft-backed fibreglass
— styrofoam (extruded polystyrene)
— foils (aluminum)
— vapour barrier paints
These are not as effective as a thick poly vapour barrier since it is harder to make them continuous, they damage easily and do not make an effective air barrier.

Thermal Bridges

A thermal bridge allows heat to "short-cut" from a hot area to a colder one. A common thermal bridge in a well-insulated house are the studs in the walls. A six-inch thick wall can be insulated with R20 batts; however, the studs will cover about nine per cent of the wall area. Because wood has an R-value of only R1.25 per inch, the wall is only insulated to R7 where the wood is. This problem can be decreased by ensuring that there is no direct connection from the inside to the outside. This can be done by having two sets of stud walls separated by a gap. Alternatively, horizontal strapping can be attached to the studs to minimize contact points.

Thermal Mass

Just as windows can act as solar collectors, the house itself may serve as the solar storage. The mass of the house, contained in bricks, walls, furniture and concrete floors, can soak up excess heat, releasing it as the temperature drops. Passive solar systems, which operate at much lower temperatures than active solar systems, can effectively utilize the mass distributed around the house.

The temperature of the mass within the house rises throughout the day, heated by direct or scattered sunlight, or by a rise in temperature in the room. By late afternoon this temperature rise peaks and levels off. The air temperature of the house starts to fall in the evening and the mass, now at higher temperature than the room air, radiates the heat that was collected during the day. The building interior, because of its large mass, is slow to respond to exterior conditions, creating a "thermal-lag effect".

Temperature Swings

A well-designed house will go through a regular cycle of temperature swings through the day and night. The temperature range is affected by many characteristics of the house and the climate. Minimizing these swings will make for a more comfortable home, although fluctuations of 8-10°F are quite tolerable (comparable to a thermostat set-back). Poorly designed houses (referred to as "a half solar house") with large south-facing glazing, but inadequate thermal mass, can have enormous temperature swings, sometimes in excess of 50°F.

The following characteristics help to determine the extent of temperature swings:

Amount of mass: the more mass within the house, the smaller the swing, although houses with excessive thermal mass and insufficient insulation may create walls that are always a few degrees below the comfortable temperature.

Type of material: some mass absorbs heat more quickly, thus reducing the temperature swing. For example, water absorbs more quickly than concrete due to convection. Mass with greater exposed surface area will reduce temperature swings. The colour of the material will also determine whether it absorbs (dark colours) or reflects (light colours) radiation.

Position of material: mass placed in direct or diffused sunlight is three to four times more effective than mass in reflected light.

Amount and type of glazing: the amount of sunlight that is permitted to enter the house must be matched with adequate mass.

Insulation: well-insulated houses lose heat more slowly. It is therefore much easier to overheat a super-insulated house.

The proper application of thermal mass will help to prevent excessive temperature swings. It will also be an aid in cooling, as the thermal mass can be used to advantage in the summertime to help store the cool night air. Some systems prevent overheating by venting to an isolated storage. In this way there is more control over the system and more even temperatures can be maintained.

Types of Mass

There are three major uses of thermal mass within a house: as part of a mass-wall system; throughout the house as part of the direct gain system; as isolated storage of a thermosyphon or hybrid system.

Mass-wall storage

A mass-wall system (also known as a Trombe wall) stores energy directly behind the glazing. The storage medium is usually either a concrete wall or a water wall. About 80 per cent of the energy captured by the system is absorbed and conducted into the wall. The air between the glazing and the wall is also heated (up to 150°F) and vents at the top and bottom of the wall allow the heated air to rise up and into the room behind it. Cooler house air flows in the bottom vent. The heat entering the wall slowly works its way through the width, with the mass storing the heat. The greater the conductivity of the material, the greater is the optimum thickness, and the greater the efficiency. The thicker the wall (the more mass) the less the potential temperature swing will be. However, beyond the optimum thickness the overall performance decreases since too much heat radiates back outward and less heat makes its way through to the house. A brick wall should be 12 inches thick (± two inches); a concrete wall should be 13 inches thick (± three inches). A water-wall, because of its faster absorption due to convection, requires an average thickness of six inches or more.

Thermal Mass Qualities

Materials	Heat Capacity Btu/ft³/°F	Advantages	Disadvantages
Water	62.5	— cheap — accessible — can be placed in many and varied containers	— heat stratifies in larger tanks — cannot be employed as a structural wall — freezing protection may be necessary
Concrete	31.7	— easily employed as structural or partition walls	— difficult to retrofit (loading problems)
Rock	32	— easily installed in existing basements — attractive in fireplaces	— needs large amount of space — loading problems
Drywall	20.3	— provides typical wall structures	— low heat capacity — minimal storage
Phase Change	9500 Btu/ft³	— occupies less space — stores at lower temperatures	— degrades with use — expensive
Brick	24.6	— easily employed — aesthetically acceptable	— low heat capacity

Direct Gain

In a direct gain system the sunlight enters and is absorbed directly by the living space. About the only objects in a house that are not used as thermal mass are people. (We have a self-regulating cooling mechanism and will not store heat.) Everything else is fair game: tables, chairs, walls, fireplaces, etc. However, it's interesting to note that some objects will do more harm than good. Wall-to-wall broadloom over a concrete floor or curtains covering a solid wall will render potential sources of mass ineffective. The total mass within a building will depend on many factors including its size, thickness, specific heat and placement.

Some common sources of mass within a space include:

interior partition walls, made of 4-inch to 8-inch thick concrete, stone or brick. The thicker walls should be used when there is contact with direct sunlight.

concrete floor slab, well-insulated underneath (R20) and finished with brick, tile, or another conductor of heat. If in direct or diffuse light the floor should be a dark colour.

partition walls are sometimes filled with scrap drywall or water-filled containers to increase the mass.

drywall (can be extra thick or double-layered)

all furnishings (i.e. of low mass) within the room would be of lighter colours.

Generally speaking, there should be 30 to 60 BTU/°F-ft² (600 to 800 KJ/°C-m²) of mass in relation to the glazing area. This implies 30 to 60 pounds of water or 100 pounds of concrete for each square foot of glazing.

A conventional frame house contains enough mass to prevent overheating as long as south-facing window area does not exceed six to eight per cent of the floor area. The better the house is insulated, the lower the percentage of glazing required.

Indirect Storage

In a thermosyphon or hybrid system indirect storage is used. A rock-bed storage, isolated from the rest of the house, is commonly employed. As in air-type active solar-heating systems, a rock-bed storage consists of:

— *a container* insulated to at least R25
— *duct-work* connecting the container with the collection source and the living space
— *controls and fans* (where required)
— *rocks* ranging in size from one to two inches in diameter (preferably round and of uniform size). One to two cubic feet of rocks for each square foot of glazing is a common size.

A hybrid system is most often used in conjunction with an attached greenhouse. As the temperature in the top of the greenhouse rises, the controls switch on a fan which vents the heated air into the rock storage. The system is reversed when the house or greenhouse temperature falls.

Without this venting-to-storage feature most greenhouses, even in winter, require venting to the house or the outside to prevent overheating. An isolated storage allows more occupant control over the temperature of the house. It also has the advantage of being able to be connected with other systems, such as a wood burning furnace or stove. Heat collected from an efficiently burning furnace can be stored in an isolated storage for later use.

A disadvantage of the hybrid system is the added controls and fans required to operate it. Not only are they an increased expense, but they require maintenance and power for operation.

Windows

"Through windows we review the world"

Windows, perhaps more than any other aspect of a well-designed house, require extreme care in planning, installation and usage. Too often the design and placement of windows is determined solely by aesthetics. Houses, both rural and urban, often have their picture windows face the street or road (sometimes the ugliest of views). Little thought is given to the prevention of heat loss through windows or to achieving optimum heat gain. Besides affording a view of the outside world, windows can bring light, heat and fresh air into the house. Care should be taken to ensure that they do not lose excessive energy, or gain too much. A combination of correct sizing and positioning, shading and insulation techniques and appropriate construction methods will ensure that windows are being used to their maximum energy-saving capacity. A discussion of these determinants follows.

The Optimal Source — Natural Light

Natural light, with its full spectrum, should be harnessed whenever possible. Rooms can be positioned and laid out to maximize the use of natural light. The following suggestions will allow the builder-renovator to get the most from this natural energy source:
— south-facing windows will receive the most direct light
— windows facing east receive morning light
— windows facing west receive afternoon light
— north-facing windows receive direct light only in the summer months
— transparent glazing lets in direct light
— translucent glazing diffuses light
— light decreases in intensity in deeper rooms
— lightly coloured walls help scatter light, increasing intensity

Windows as Heaters

Windows in a well-designed house can become principle heating sources. The majority should face south, be properly sized, air-tight and have night-time insulation. The objects are to:
— maximize heat collection
— minimize overheating
— minimize heat loss by conduction and infiltration

Effects of orientation

In Canadian climates, north-facing windows are the worst heat losers, while south-facing windows can gain more heat than they lose.

East and west windows will gain heat in the morning and afternoon respectively.

Both orientations, especially the west, tend to increase any overheating problems, as they are difficult to shade in summer.

All windows, regardless of orientation, should have insulating shutters or curtains when they are not in use.

Effects of size

Obviously, the larger the window the greater its capacity for heat gain or loss. A conventional house may have a window area that is equivalent to 10 per cent of the floor area. They would be randomly distributed around the house, regardless of orientation. A solar-designed house has the windows concentrated on the south, with few, if any, to the north. The south side may have at least 70 per cent of the window area.

Exactly how much window area is required before encountering the problems of extreme temperature swings in winter or overheating in summer is determined by the heat load of the house, the amount of thermal mass, and the climatic zone.

Generally speaking, well-insulated frame houses without increased thermal mass, should have south-facing windows comprising no more than seven per cent of the floor area. The relationship between greater window area and increased thermal mass is discussed in the section on Thermal Mass.

Effects of angle

Most windows used in passive solar houses are vertical (90 degrees). Of course, there are exceptions to this, most commonly in the form of skylights. Verti-

cal south-facing windows have many advantages including:
— greater potential for light energy in the winter (especially if enhanced by reflected sunlight)
— less light energy in the summer, and more easily controlled by overhangs
— easy to construct
— easier to insulate

For these reasons, most people stick to vertical windows. However, the use of clerestories or skylights do have advantages that become important in certain situations.
— Clerestories or skylights can act as the principle "solar collectors" when the south wall is shaded by other buildings and the roof receives sunlight.
— They can be used to bring natural light and heat to the back (north side) of a house or on a top floor. This can be especially important for underground housing.

Windows as Ventilation

Traditionally windows have been used as ventilators; open a window and let in fresh air. There are a number of problems with this method, and more people are installing fewer opening windows or even separate ventilators (openings that are only used for fresh air). Operable windows cannot be sealed as well as fixed windows. This means added heat loss through infiltration.

Several commercial windows are now on the market which are very well constructed. Generally, casement and awning windows, that swing open, close with a good seal. Sliding windows are usually much looser. The use of weatherstripping around windows in the winter will help ensure that they remain airtight.

Ventilators and operable windows are used for a number of purposes:
— regular air changes (if not equipped with an air-to-air heat exchanger)
— exhaust smoke or other specific odors
— allow cooling breezes in the summer

Shading windows

There are times when it's necessary to minimize incoming solar radiation to prevent overheating or reduce glare. Curtains and shutters block the sun, but they also obstruct the view.

A simple solution is the overhang. Awnings, eaves and constructed overhangs can all block direct sunlight while maintaining the view. The goal is to shade the higher summer sun, while allowing the lower winter light direct entry to the house.

Shading devices can be affixed permanently. But be aware that the sun timetable runs ahead of the heating timetable. Overhangs, unless very shallow, will shade the windows during times when heat is most required (for example during February and March).

Movable overhangs, such as rolled awnings, or perennial shading, such as flowering red azalias, may be used. Deciduous trees are a common perennial shading device. During the summer they can block 95 per cent of the light coming through, while in winter, when the leaves are gone, they let the sun in. Unfortunately, they can still block up to half of the light, and seriously affect the working of a solar house.

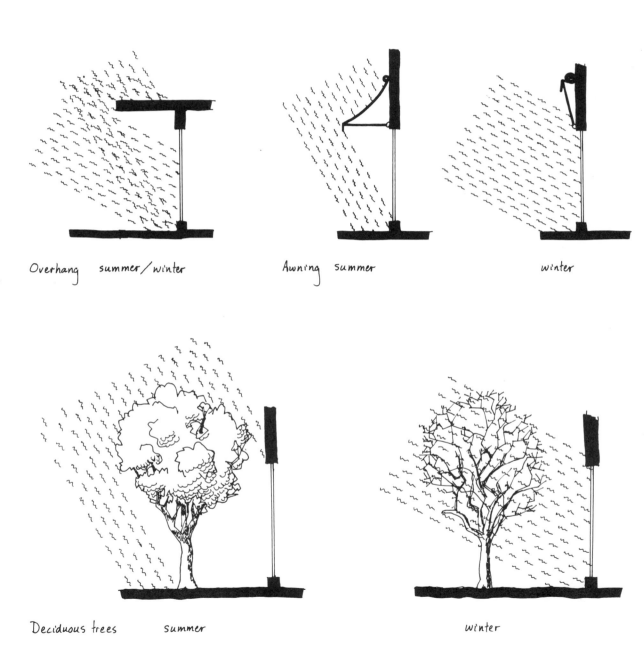

Overhang   summer/winter

Awning   summer

winter

Deciduous trees   summer

winter

Insulating windows

A double-glazed window has insulating properties of R1.7. Compared to a well-insulated wall of R30 or R40, windows can be a major source of heat loss. Windows may be marginally improved by the use of different glazing material and number of glazings. For example, triple-glazed windows insulate to R2.15. Making windows air-tight and ensuring that there is a thermal break between glazings will help improve their efficiency.

As discussed, the most substantial energy saving will come from the use of insulating curtains, shutters and shades. All windows, whether they face south, north, or straight up, will be considerably more efficient if covered up at night, or any other time they are not being used.

Curtains

Perhaps the easiest window strategy to implement makes use of insulating curtains. They are usually easy to install and operate. To maximize efficiency curtains should:
— be sealed along the edges, top, and bottom to prevent convection currents
— be reflective
— be thick (high R-value)
— be non-permeable (prevent water vapour from penetrating)

Sealing the edges of curtains can be accomplished by a variety of means including the use of tracks, magnetic strips, velcro, weighted bottoms, permanently sealed sides. An aluminized material such as mylar or nylon is often used to face a heavy fabric. The aluminized surface both reflects long-wave radiation and acts as a vapour barrier.

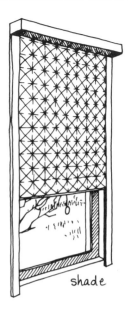

shade

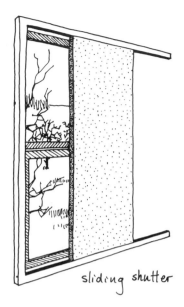

sliding shutter

curtain

Curtains, however, are not as effective as other systems. Even if the above efficiency-boosting conditions are met, a curtain will only add an insulating value of R1.25 to R3 to a window.

Shutters

A more effective strategy is the use of insulating rigid shutters. To perform efficiently they must have many of the qualities outlined for curtains, including sealed edges and a reflective surface. Shutters can achieve a very impressive insulating value, easily up to R10. However, shutters are hard to operate and require room for storage. Some are automatic but this generally adds to the cost, complexity of the job, and adds maintenance headaches. To date, most shutters have to be self-made, and so they come in an infinite variety. The common construction material is foam boards faced with wood and edged with weatherstripping.

hanging shutter

Shutters may be either inside or outside. Outside is difficult to operate, especially in adverse weather conditions. Inside shutters encounter the problems of condensation and frosting, especially if they are not well sealed.

Shades

A third category of movable insulation for windows is thermal shades. These shades roll up and down along side tracks which seal the edges. When rolled down many commercial shades expand, creating layers of air trapped between reflecting membranes.

Other strategies

Another approach being developed to further insulate windows is called "transparent insulation". This allows sunlight through the window, while at the same time having a high R-value.

An air gap between glazing helps to reduce conduction losses. Normally convection currents form if the air gap is too wide. The use of a convection suppressor between glazings, such as a *Honeycomb structure,* allows the gap to considerably widen without creating convection currents.

Radiation heat losses can be reduced with the use of a heat-reflecting surface. An extremely thin coating of a material that reflects infra-red radiation is generally placed over the inner side of the outside glazing, or on a thin plastic membrane placed between glazings. The advantages of transparent insulation is that it is working 24 hours a day reducing heat loss. Commercial development of these systems is just beginning.

Infiltration

Air leaking in or out of a house can account for 30 to 40 per cent of the heat loss in a typical house. Air changes are necessary; the process removes odours and excess humidity and provides fresh air. But most air changes are accidental and cannot be controlled. Air enters through cracks, around windows and doors, and other openings. Typically in new construction the air changes completely every hour, twice as often if it is windy. Besides the heat loss, exfiltration of warm moist air in a house can result in condensation and freezing problems inside the wall which can harm insulation and rot studs and joists.

A well-designed and built house is made as air-tight as possible. A continuous air-vapour barrier is installed and sealed at all seams and edges. All windows, door, sills, corners, electric and plumbing outlets, vents and pipes are sealed. A house can be made so air-tight that it requires open windows or forced ventilation to ensure adequate air changes. An air-to-air heat exchanger is a simple device that enables you to maintain a high level of air change, without the associated heat loss.

Like insulating, it is much easier to seal a house while building it than trying to patch up an old house. The following discussion will apply mainly to new construction, but it is also relevant to accessible areas within old buildings (such as attics). The information will also be of use to renovators.

Sources of Infiltration

Some of the spots where infiltration is most prevalent, and some of the methods of preventing the infiltration are cited below:

Sills: All sills should be well caulked. (Rolls of insulation can be placed between the sill and foundation wall.) This can be a major source of infiltration in older houses.

Attic: All joints and seams in the attic should be caulked (before re-insulating). Chimneys, duct work, light fixtures and other perforations should be sealed. (Note: insulation should not be placed within 3 inches of chimneys or recessed light fixtures.)

Doors: Doors should be tight-fitting and have good weatherstripping along the edges. There should be at least two doors leading outside, preferably with an "air-lock" between. If possible, situate doors in areas sheltered from the wind.

Windows: Windows should be sealed completely, tied in with the air-vapour barrier, and caulked from the interior. Fixed windows that don't open have less infiltration than movable windows.

Vents: Vents from bathrooms, kitchens and clothes dryers should shut tight when not in use. Better yet, use a re-circulating charcoal vent above the stove. The best method in an air-tight house is to vent through an air-to-air exchanger.

Fireplaces: At best fireplaces are an inefficient heat producer; it's much better to use an air-tight wood stove. The fireplace should have a tight, workable damper, and preferably an air-tight glass cover. An outside vent supplying combustion air minimizes the consumption of heated indoor air.

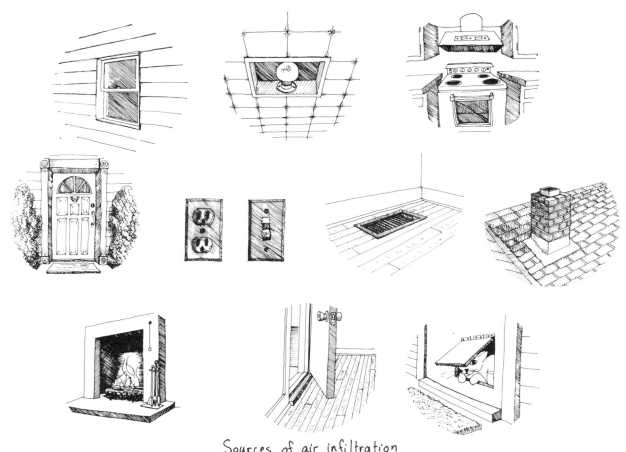

Sources of air infiltration

Source	%
Wall sill plate	25
Wall outlets (electrical)	20
Windows	14
Heating Ducts	12
Bathroom/Kitchen Vents	10
Doors	6
Fireplace	6
Recessed Ceiling Fixtures	5
Miscellaneous	2

Sources of Air Infiltration in Typical Housing

Furnaces: Furnaces exhaust a lot of heat up the chimney. A vent from the outside to the air-intake of the furnace will exhaust the outside air, rather than heated house air. The furnace can be installed in a separate air-tight insulated room.

Walls: The vapour barrier in walls often becomes perforated while installing wiring, fixtures and plumbing. All perforations must be completely sealed. The vapour barrier can be placed $\frac{1}{3}$ within the insulation, with activity occurring in front of, rather than through the barrier.

A double stud wall, or horizontal strapping over the studs, will allow this to happen.

Cats: Many cats have a habit of repeated entrances and exits during the winter-time, causing heat loss from the house every time a door is opened. Either change the cat's habits (though difficult) or devise a draught-free cat entrance.

Tools for sealing

The tools commonly used to seal a house include:

Caulking: Caulking should be liberally applied to all fixed joints, preferably from the interior. Caulk should have the ability of remaining elastic under extreme temperature and over time. Silicone is perhaps the best, and also one of the most expensive; butyl and acoustical sealants are also good.

Vapour barrier: There should be a continuous vapour barrier around the entire house. All seams and perforations should be sealed. The vapour barrier prevents air and moisture from leaving the heated space. The vapour barrier is always on the warm side of the insulation or at least within the insulation before the dew point is reached. This is generally no further than $\frac{1}{3}$ into the insulation. Six mil plastic is often used as it's an inexpensive, effective air-vapour barrier.

Tape: A good tape can be used to seal the vapour barrier seams and along any cracks. A polymeric foam is often used along sill plates and in window and door framing to both insulate and seal. Care must be taken to ensure that the foam doesn't offset the framing.

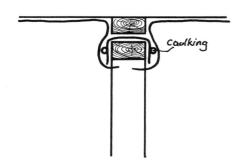

Continuous vapour-barrier through ceiling partition walls

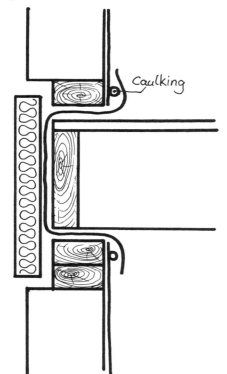

Continuous vapour-barrier past floor joists

Caulking Materials

Type	Relative Cost	Bondability	Durability	Best Application/ limitations
oil or resin base	lowest	good	poor	not for long term caulking
latex base	low	good	fair	some shrinkage
butyl rubber	low	good	fair	not for moving joints
polyvinyl acetate	medium	good	fair	shrinks and hardens
neoprene rubber	medium/high	good	good	concrete walls/foundations
silicone seal	high	good (not to concrete)	good	remains flexible/ not paintable
polysulfide	high	needs primer	good	can dry out
polyurethane	high	good	good	not readily available
hypalon	high	good	good	not readily available
polymeric foam	high	good	good	for sill plates and large holes
sub-floor adhesives	medium	good	good	for poly vapour barriers
acoustical sealants	medium	good	good	for poly vapour barriers

Weatherstripping Materials

Type	Relative Cost	Durability	Installation	Comments
adhesive backed foam	low	poor	easy	best on doors
hair/felt	low	poor	easy	will compact
foam with wood backing	medium	fair	easy	for windows and doors
door sweeps	medium	fair	easy	may drag on carpet
spring metal	high	excellent	easy	for windows and doors
rolled vinyl/aluminum	high	fair	medium	for windows and doors
door shoes/vinyl bulb	high	excellent	difficult	for doors only

Insulation is not a good air-vapour barrier. While insulating a house can reduce some of the worst air leakages, super-insulating will not appreciably reduce infiltration any further. Care must be taken in installing an air-vapour barrier, caulking all fixed joints and weatherstripping all movable joints.

Heat exchangers

As mentioned above, when a house is constructed to be air-tight, it may be necessary, and certainly desirable, to use an air-to-air heat exchanger to force ventilate. These simple devices exhaust the stale air through a series of parallel chambers. Fresh outside air is vented in through chambers parallel to the outgoing air. Heat from the outgoing air is transfer-

Sources of moisture in the home

Outdoor Temperature		Maximum Humidity Level	Desirable Humidity Level
°C	°F	%	%
-35	-31	20	15
-29	-20.2	25	20
-23	-9.4	30	25
-18	0	35	30
-12	10.4	40	40
-7	19.4	45	40
-1	30.2	50	40

Maximum relative humidity permissible to prevent condensation on a double-glazed window. Humidity levels 10-15% higher can be accommodated with triple glazing.

Source	Amount
Cooking	2.2 lb/day
Washing Dishes	1.1 lb/day
Washing Clothes	4.4 lb/week
Drying Clothes (in home)	26.4 lb/week
Bathing — showers	0.4 lb each
— baths	0.1 lb each
People	2.8 lb/person
Plants	1.1 lb/plant/week

Sources of Moisture in the Home

red through the thin walls (often plastic) to the incoming air. In this way 50 to 80 per cent of the heat contained in the outgoing air can be reclaimed. (The heat exchanger used in the Saskatchewan Conservation House is measured at 75 per cent efficiency.)

Humidity levels

At one point it was necessary to add humidity to a house in winter. Dry cold air infiltrated the house in great volumes and as it was heated, the relative humidity level fell. This not only caused furniture to dry out, but resulted in a level of personal discomfort. Today, with a well-built house, air infiltration is at a minimum. Now the humidity level in a house caused by breathing, showers, washing clothes and drying, etc. easily exceeds the comfort and safety levels. The excess humidity that condenses on windows and within walls can cause extensive damage.

The following chart summarizes minimum humidity levels before condensation appears on the inside of a double-glazed window. While some condensation is tolerable, excessive condensation can cause damage. In such cases you should: 1) reduce sources of moisture in the house; 2) vent moisture-producing rooms (kitchen and bath) as required; 3) induce ventilation through a dampered air vent to the furnace return air, or, if the house is very tight through a heat exchanger.

Internal Gains

All houses contain their own heating sources. People, lights, machines, appliances, water heaters, etc. all generate heat in a house. The average person is continually generating 100 watts of energy, more if he or she is involved in strenuous activity. Altogether, the internal gain of a typical house can range from 8 to 10 per cent of its heating needs.

The importance of internal gain has largely been ignored as it has traditionally been a small percentage of the total heat load. In the "well-tempered" house (a well-insulated and air-tight home) internal gain becomes more important, accounting for up to 30 per cent of a house's heating. This high percentage demands an understanding of the internal gain sources so that they may be put to a maximum advantage. The object is to make maximum use of internal gains in the winter and to minimize their impact in summer. To some extent, we do all of this naturally. We prefer salads to a hot meal in the summer, or dry on the line rather than use the electric dryer. Minimizing lights can also reduce summer's gains.

In the winter, the heat lost from appliances is heat gained for the house. But since electric heating is inefficient and expensive, we still want to minimize these gains. Natural or task lighting, dryers vented to the inside (if there is no humidity problem), and the use of efficient stoves and refrigerators all help to minimize electrical energy consumption.

The average family uses about 6000 KW-hr of electricity a year and almost that much again for hot water heating. The largest energy users are the refrigerator (1200 KW-hr), stove (1200 KW-hr), clothes dryer (900 KW-hr) and furnace fan (800 KW-hr). Hot water heaters are very inefficiently insulated and constitute a large heat loss area.

Source	kWhr
Dryer (1 hr/day)	5.0
Refrigerator (24 hr/day)	7.0
Television (3 hr/day)	0.6
Water Heater (24 hr/day)	3.6
Cooking (2 hr/day)	4.0
Lights (4 hr/day)	3.4
People (4 x 16 hrs/day)	4.0
Total Internal Gain	27.6 kWh/day

**Internal heat gains
(based on average winter conditions)**

Hot Water

Hot water is a big consumer of energy, typically accounting for 20 per cent of a house's energy in a year. (It is second only to space heating for energy consumed, and in a super-insulated house it can even exceed the space heating demand.)

There are four strategies to reduce the energy consumption of hot water:
— use a more efficient system
— reduce the use
— re-use the heat, or,
— change the supply

Increased efficiency

Generally hot water tanks are poorly insulated, resulting in much energy wastage. The stand-by losses of tanks is over 100 watts. To reduce this problem tanks can be re-insulated with 3 to 6 inches of fibreglass. The air-flow into the burner and chimney draft air for gas heaters as well as access panels and junction boxes of electric water heaters must be kept clear. Tanks set to a very hot setting lose more heat than those set lower; water tanks should be set lower than 50°C. Both water pipes from the tank should be insulated. Reducing the pipe diameter from $1/2$ inch to $3/8$ inch and reducing the length the pipes have to travel will save energy.

Reduction

Hot water use can be reduced through slight lifestyle modifications, and by making some technological adjustments. Common reduction practices include utilizing a rinsing dish for dishes or washing and rinsing clothes in cold or cool water. Technical changes can bring about a substantial reduction in consumption. A water-saver shower head can reduce by three quarters the hot water used while still affording a skin-tingling shower. A conventional shower lasts about 8 minutes and consumes about 8 gallons a minute. A water-reducing shower head can control the flow to under 2 gallons a minute while maintaining the pressure experienced. It will pay for itself in well under a year.

Re-use

It is possible to "re-use" the heat energy of hot water rather than send it down the drain. The simplest method is to leave water standing in basins and tubs until it falls to room temperature. More complicated systems use water-to-water heat exchangers to preheat cold incoming water with heated outgoing water. One such method uses a double tank. Cold incoming water passes through a tank that sits within a larger outer tank. The outer tank holds heated water that is being sent out.

Supply

Hot water can be supplied by a number of non-fossil, non-nuclear processes. A very common one is the use of wood heat. A copper coil in the firebox or flue of a wood stove can heat water in a nearby tank by thermosyphon action.

Solar systems for domestic hot water can be simple thermosyphon systems, breadbox water heaters, or active pumped and controlled solar systems. A commercially installed solar system will cost as much as $3000. If you are a do-it-yourselfer, an effective system can be built for less than one third of that.

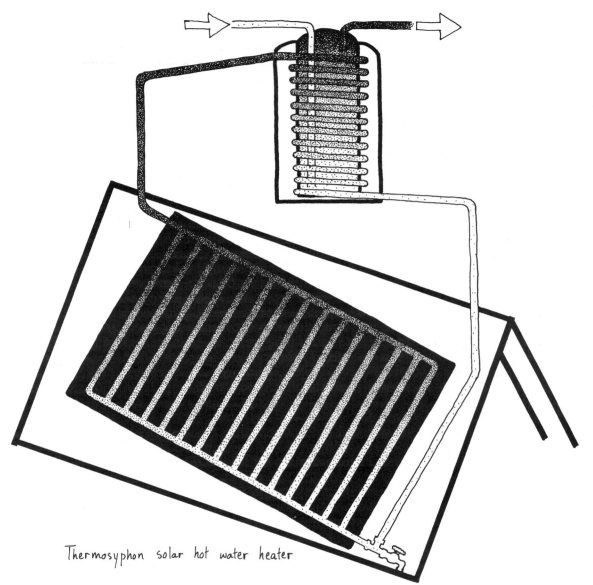

Thermosyphon solar hot water heater

Another method of preheating water involves initially allowing the incoming water to go through a free-standing uninsulated tank. The house will raise the temperature from around 45° to room temperature before it goes to the regular water heater tank. Of course, this takes energy from the house and puts it into the water. However, an energy-conserving house should have excess heat about eight months of the year and so this does become a practical method.

Cooling

Residential cooling has never been a big problem in most of Canada and the northern United States. For only a few weeks in the entire year are the days and evenings unpleasantly hot. Most discomfort is a result of poorly designed houses, so the proper design and operation of a home can do away with the need for most cooling. However, passive solar houses, because of their large window area, have a potential to overheat if care is not taken to avoid the problem.

There are three main approaches to cooling:
1) reduce internal gains
2) reduce solar gains
3) induce natural ventilation and make use of thermal-mass

Reduce internal gains

Any energy generated in the house helps to heat it. A few of the ways of reducing the internal heat are:
— vent whenever possible, i.e. dryers, stoves, etc. during the summer
— use minimum lighting
— minimise losses from the hot water heater
— insulate major appliances
— remember that a house full of people generates heat. Move your social life outdoors.

Reduce solar gains

Any effort to increase solar gain in the winter should have a corresponding summertime strategy for reducing solar gain:

Overhangs are used to prevent direct solar access but they can impede a window's performance as a collector if they extend beyond 12 inches.

Curtains and shutters can be used to prevent gains. They work best if they are closed in the day and opened at night.

Films/tinted glass reflect a large portion of the light, but winter collection suffers.

Natural ventilation

Ventilation can be used for three major purposes:
— Extract heat during the day
— Bring in cool air during the night
— Supply cooling breezes day and night

Extract heat

Mass wall: Vents at the bottom and top of a mass wall vented to the outside will reduce the temperature buildup. Vents at the bottom from the house vented at the top to the outside reduces temperature buildup while supplying a cooling cross-ventilation. Such a system may also be mechanically vented.

Direct gain: Venting should be possible at the top of any house to extract excess heat buildup. A vent stack will increase the effectiveness of natural ventilation.

Bring in the Coolth

When houses are opened at night in the summer they lose heat through radiation. The cooling of a house can be aided by ventilating with cooler night air. The thermal-mass within the house will store this coolth so it can be used in the day to prevent overheating.

During the day an unshaded or curtained glass wall that experiences significant heat gain must be vented. The energy of a vented sunspace can be used to induce a cooling cross ventilation.

Summer ventilation of a sun space

Back-up

Even the best-designed energy-efficient houses require some supplementary heat energy. How much is required depends on the weather, the design of the house, insulation, passive collection features, thermal-mass and how the house is used. Well-designed houses can reduce the "outside" energy demand to less than 10 per cent of a conventional house. But even that 10 per cent has to come from somewhere.

Traditionally back-up and supplementary heat is derived from oil, gas, electricity, wood, propane, and active solar systems. Supplementary heat refers to a source that can be intermittently added to the house depending on the requirements of the home and the availability of the heat. Active solar systems with storage and wood stoves are two common supplementary fuels.

Back-up fuels should be on call whenever necessary. They should be dependable enough so that an untended house will not drop below a certain temperature. The conventional fuels (oil, gas, and electricity) are commonly used as back-up.

An advantage of supplying supplementary or back-up heat to an efficient house is that little heat is required to maintain a minimum temperature. Energy-efficient construction reduces the need for large-scale equipment working to maintain temperatures. In the well-designed home heat storage or fuel storage can be smaller and the heating unit can be reduced considerably from conventional sizes.

Heat storage

An "active" heat storage that is thermally isolated from the house or environment is often used for supplementary heating. Generally a well-insulated rock-bed or water container storage capable of heating the house for three consecutive days is used. The heat is collected from either the house itself (i.e. ceiling ducting from a sun space), from an active solar system, or from a wood stove/furnace.

Supplementary and Back-up Fuels

Wood

Wood can provide inexpensive, efficient supplementary heat. The air-tight wood-stoves on the market can be used to heat an entire well-designed house. An old farmhouse might have burnt 30 bush cords of wood in winter, while today some houses are getting by with less than 2 cords in a heating season. By feeding heat from a wood stove into a rock storage, a greater degree of security can be obtained. The new combination of wood/oil furnaces can be used to provide both convenience and security. These furnaces rely on wood as long as they can maintain a pre-determined temperature. Below that level an oil burner cuts in automatically.

Wood is a renewable fuel (if managed properly) and can often be inexpensively obtained, especially if you are willing to put in a little work. Heating with wood, however, can be expensive if you live in an urban or suburban area and have to buy your wood. Books that discuss the types and characteristics of wood, wood safety and the variety of stoves being manufactured are commonly available.

Solar

Active solar heating systems can be used as a supplementary energy source, but this is difficult to economically justify on a well-designed house. The costs of a complete system are still quite high, and it would not be put to best use, since during sunny periods the house can take care of itself. In addition, even at best an active system cannot be used as a back-up and so some supplementary system is still required. As a solution some home-owners have installed an oversized domestic hot water solar system. The system will supply some heat energy during the heating season, as well as work all year preheating the hot water supply.

Oil

Oil as a back-up source of heat is best used in conjunction with a wood/oil furnace. An advantage of oil is that there is a supply maintained within the house, thereby reducing the peak-load demand on the oil companies. Other conventional fuels such as gas and electricity cannot avoid this problem.

Gas

Natural gas can be used as back-up in urban areas where piped gas is available. Canada (apparently) has a large supply of natural gas, but it is a non-renewable source and it's expensive (although cheaper than other conventional fuels). If many houses depended on gas as a back-up fuel only, there could be a very large demand a few times in the year, which could put a strain on the gas delivery system.

Electricity

Electricity is often used as a back-up energy source for well-designed houses. As far as the homeowner is concerned, it requires a minimum capital investment, it is a clean fuel, and it is convenient. The problem with electricity as a back-up is that it is the most expensive fuel as well as an inefficient source when taken as a system. Back-up is required in the depths of winter, on the coldest, cloudiest days and nights. The utility has to build the capacity to supply enough electricity at this time of greatest demand (peak load). But for 95 per cent of the year this equipment lies idle. A very inefficient and expensive system.

Whenever a back-up system is used, it will be a considerably smaller unit than those required for a conventional house. A well-designed and built house may only require one fifth of the installed capacity because of the lower heat demand brought by increased insulation and decreased air infiltration. Wood stoves are generally available in smaller sizes, but it can be a problem getting a small enough oil or gas furnace. Oversized furnaces waste a lot of energy with their constant on and off cycles. A solution to this problem is to purchase the smallest unit possible and use it to charge up a small rock-bed storage. This allows the unit to burn efficiently for a longer period of time.

Putting it all together

The development of an overall strategy for designing a house should follow certain basic principles. The interrelationship between the parts of a house is stressed throughout this book. By remembering that, it is then a question of balance, of trading one design feature against another. For example, it makes no sense to have a massive south-facing window area without a correspondingly large thermal-mass and shading devices. It makes no sense to super-insulate without also making a house air-tight.

To summarize, a house can be built so that each component interacts with each other part of the structure. The following qualities are universal to a well-designed house.

External

By adjusting the site, the orientation and the shape of a house one can minimise the exposed surface area and the chilling effects of winds.

A house can use vegetation and the ground itself to provide insulating shelter. The house is situated and oriented to have access to the sun (and does not block its neighbour's sun).

Interior

A house can be designed to maximise the control of heat flow and make the best use of internal heat gains. A house should contain sufficient thermal-mass to make use of all internal gains and solar input.

The skin

The skin of a house performs many critical functions. It:
— lets the winter sun in, through south-facing windows
— keeps the summer sun out, by the use of overhangs, vegetation, curtains or shutters
— keeps the heat in, through permanent insulation in the floors, roof and walls and through moveable insulation for window areas
— keeps the house air-tight, by the use of a continuous vapour barrier that is sealed
— provides a means for cooling and ventilation

Passive solar

The most critical factor that will determine the look and function of the house is the manner in which it maximises the passive solar heating potential. Four main approaches to solar houses are now commonly utilized.

Mass wall: sunlight passes through glazing and strikes a mass wall (whether brick, concrete, water, etc.). Heat enters the living space directly from vents through the wall or indirectly as the wall radiates heat. The wall acts as the storage unit.

Direct Gain: sunlight passes through glazing (windows) and enters directly into the living space, heating it. Storage occurs in the mass of the floor, walls, ceiling and furnishings. This is the most common approach.

Sun Space: sunlight passes through the glazing of a greenhouse, sunporch, etc. that is isolated from the main living area. Storage is in mass within the sun space or in the wall between the sun space and the living space.

Thermosyphon: sunlight passes through glazing and heats a collector that is isolated from the storage and living space. Heat circulates by convection to a storage area, where in turn it can circulate to the living area.

A fifth design strategy, *super-insulation,* concentrates on conservation rather than solar supply. A super-insulated house is one that reduces the heat load to an absolute minimum through various conservation practices. The majority of the required heat comes from internal gain and through south-facing windows.

Each system will vary as to the type and placement of collection, storage and heat distribution. What particular family type, how it is expressed, will be a function of climate (temperature, sunlight); the site; materials available; and the type of building desired.

Mass Wall

A mass wall solar system combines solar collection, heat storage and distribution within the same wall. The south wall consists of a glazed massive wall which both absorbs and stores the heat. Distribution of the heat to the house occurs through vents within the wall and through direct conduction through the wall to the house. The wall is sized so that heat absorbed during the day is radiated to the house at night.

Daytime operation

Sunlight passes through the glazing and is then converted to heat on the darkened surface of the wall. Temperatures on the surface of the wall will rise up to 150°F for solid walls, less for liquid walls. This heat conducts through the mass of the wall and also to the space between the wall and the glazing. Top and bottom vents allow a thermosyphon effect to transfer heat into the room, although the majority of the heat (80%) will be absorbed within the wall.

Night-time operation

A reflecting insulated curtain or shutter is placed outside the wall at night to reduce heat loss. As the temperature of the room drops, heat stored in the wall during the day heats the room.

Variables

Sizing

Sizing a mass wall depends on a variety of factors, the house size and heat load, the degree days, amount of sunlight, type of mass wall and orientation. A well-insulated air-tight house will perform well in Canadian climates with a wall area equal to 10 to 20 per cent of the floor area of the house. A reflecting surface (i.e. snow) in front of the wall and night insulation will improve the performance. In colder regions, and for poorly insulated houses, the area can be increased. For super-insulated houses the area can be decreased and will still supply half of the year's heating load.

It is generally preferable to have windows, as well as a mass wall, on the south side of the house. Windows supply instant light and heat to a room. As long as the window area is relatively small (i.e. under 5 to 6 per cent of the floor area) they will not interfere with the operation of the mass wall.

Wall thickness

The wall thickness is determined by the type of material used. Generally, a thermal lag, the time it takes for the "heat wave" to conduct through the wall, of about 8 hours is desired. Adequate time lag and storage will be provided by:
— a brick wall 12 inches thick
— a concrete wall (poured or block) 10 to 16 inches thick
— a water wall that averages 6 inches or more

Vents

Venting is usually required in colder climates. It helps to heat the house during daylight hours and reduces the temperature within the space (thus improving efficiency). Typically, vents occupy one per cent of the surface area of the house. They should be operable, either manually or automatically, so they open in the day

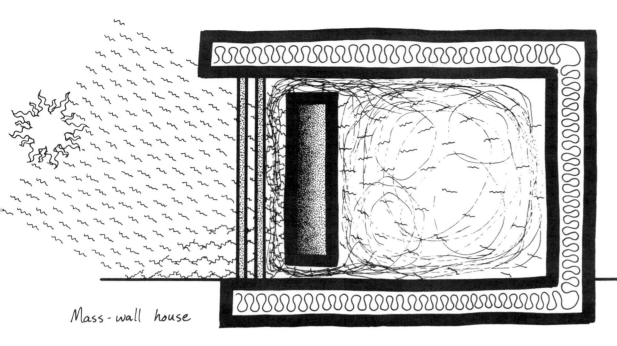

Mass-wall house

— vents at the top of the wall to the outside. Inlet vents can be located at the bottom of the wall either from the outside, or preferably into the house. The latter system can be used to create a strong natural ventilation of the entire house.

— curtains or shutters can be drawn during the day in summer to prevent overheating. If opened at night the mass will be cooled naturally.

Advantages of the mass wall

— the mass wall can be used to block an unsightly view or to act as a buffer from a noisy environment
— the house will experience smaller temperature fluctuations since sunlight is converted to heat and enters storage without entering the living space
— a house can be of conventional frame (low mass) construction since all the interior mass is in the mass wall
— a double-brick house, with access to the sun, can easily be retrofitted to a mass wall system with the addition of glazing

Disadvantages of a mass wall

— a mass wall can obstruct a good view and reduce natural lighting
— the house must conform to the architectural feature, both inside and out, of a mass wall on the south side
— a mass wall is more difficult to shutter as access is impeded by the wall

when heat is required but close at night. Night-time venting creates a reverse thermosyphon air flow, helping to cool the house.

Glazing

Any translucent or transparent material may serve as a glazing. Glass has the advantages of strength, a long lifetime, high transmissivity, and is of particular advantage if a view area (window) is desired within the mass wall.

Other glazing materials, such as fibre-glass, SDP, plastics, acrylics, etc., are lightweight and easy to work with. Spacing between the glazing and the wall should be 2 or 3 inches unless a larger space is required to accommodate an insulating curtain or shutter, or to provide access to the wall.

Shutters/curtains

A mass wall will lose much of its storage heat to the outside, even if there is a protective double-glazing. A curtain or shutter drawn at night can help reduce heat losses and substantially improve the efficiency of the system. Insulation on the outside or between double-glazing will eliminate condensation on the glass.

Cooling/venting

Like all passive solar heating systems, provision must be taken to prevent overheating and to allow summertime cooling. These provisions include:
— operable vents that can be closed when they are not required
— shading mechanism for summertime, including overhangs, deciduous trees, flowering runners, etc.

Direct Gain

A direct gain passive solar system utilizes south-facing windows to open the house up to the sun. The large window area accepts direct sunlight while the thermal-mass of the house (the floors, walls and any construction within the heat space) serves as storage. The thermal-mass in a well-insulated frame house is only large enough to store heat brought in by windows equivalent to 6 or 7 per cent of the floor area. If the window area is increased, then there is the need for a correspondingly greater thermal-mass.

Daytime operation

Sunlight enters the (preferably) double-glazed windows and is absorbed by the room, generating heat. Temperatures within the room will rise throughout the day; the area of glazing and the amount of mass within the room will determine to what extent this occurs.

Night-time operation

In the evening a reflecting, insulating curtain or shutter is placed over the window area to reduce heat loss. As the temperature of the room drops, heat stored in the mass during the day heats the room via conduction, convection and (mainly) radiation. Minimum temperatures are reached in the early morning when the cycle starts again.

Variables

Sizing of glazing

As pointed out earlier, the greater the south-facing window area, the more heat is gained by the house. However, a note

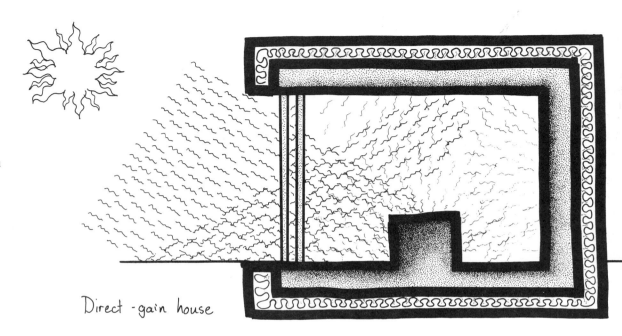

Direct-gain house

of caution. This can easily be taken to extremes if the amount of window area is in much greater proportion to the mass and heat load of the house. Serious overheating problems or inefficient dumping of excess heat will result. If there is adequate thermal-mass to absorb the heat, double-glazed south-facing windows provide a net heat gain to a house throughout the heating season.

A conventionally constructed frame house can accommodate approximately 7 per cent of the floor area as south-facing windows. Any more, without a corresponding increase in the mass, will result in overheating.

Thermal-mass

If the south-facing window area is to be greater than 7 per cent, then provision must be made for more thermal-mass than normal construction techniques allow. There should be 30 to 60 BTU/°F storage capacity for each square foot of south-facing window. That requires 30 to 60 lbs of water or 100 lbs of concrete per square foot.

Thermal-mass is about 4 times more effective if it's located in direct sunlight. Surfaces that have low mass and mass not in direct sunlight should be light-coloured to help scatter light uniformly. Mass should not be covered by insulating materials such as carpets and curtains.

Shutters/Curtains

As mentioned earlier, a properly sized double-glazed south-facing window provides a net heat gain throughout the heating season; that is, more heat is gained in the daytime than is lost at night. (In the dead of winter such windows will lose net energy, but will gain when averaged over the heating season.) The window's performance can be substantially improved by the use of insulating curtains or shutters. Of course, all windows, regardless of orientation, benefit from the use of insulating devices (see section on Windows).

Glazing type

There are many choices currently available for glazing, although glass, being transparent and long-lasting, is still to be considered preferable. Double-glazing with an air gap of $5/8$ inch is preferable. Triple-glazing provides better insulation, but reduces the sunlight transmitted. It should be used in colder regions.

Windows should be well-sealed (air-tight) and have no thermal bridge to the outside.

In some applications translucent glazing has the advantage of scattering light. This is useful in clerestorey applications and where the thermal-mass is distributed throughout the room. In these circumstances direct light tends to glare and produce "hot-spots" on the mass.

Cooling/Ventilation

Perhaps more than other passive solar heating strategies, a direct gain system has to be well protected from overheating. Some of the methods used to prevent summer overheating include:
— vertical glazing (90 degrees) which receives minimum sunlight in the summertime

— overhangs to shade the window in the summer while allowing access for the lower winter sun
— vegetation (deciduous trees, flowering beans, etc.) that shade windows in summer while exposing them in winter
— insulating curtains or shutters which can be drawn in the summer to reduce sunlight
— operable windows and vents to create convections in house.

Advantages of direct gain system

— a direct gain system is compatible with conventional construction practices; it cost no more to place windows on the south side
— a direct gain system can easily be architecturally pleasing. From the inside it allows a view of the world and it provides natural lighting
— a direct gain system is easy to shutter or to apply insulating curtains to, because of the accessible vertical glazing area
— a direct gain system is possible to retrofit by adding south-facing windows

Disadvantages of a direct gain system

— you may be locked into a not-very-pleasing view to the south
— sometimes ensuring adequate thermal-mass is difficult in a retrofit situation or in new construction
— a direct gain system experiences wider temperature fluctuations

Sun Space

A sun space solar system consists of a greenhouse, sunporch or other south-facing room that is attached to the house. This space acts as both the solar collector and storage area, and serves a useful function by transferring excess heat to the main house. The temperature within a sun space is generally allowed to fluctuate more than would be tolerable in a house, heating up in the daytime, and cooling off at night. In this way it acts as a buffer between the house and the outside environment. A sun space is often combined with a separate storage. Excess heat from the top of the sun space is ducted to an insulated rock-bed storage, to be used by the house as required.

Daytime operation

Sunlight enters through the glazing into the sun space and is absorbed by the mass within the structure. Heat is transferred to the rest of the house through the wall, vents (as in a mass-wall), or through doors and windows. Excess heat is stored in the mass within the sun space or ducted to a separate heat storage bin.

Night-time operation

At night a sun space cools slowly as heat is released by the mass within the space. If the wall between the sun space and the house is used as storage (i.e. a mass-wall) it will give heat to both the sun space and the house. Because a sun space is not normally a lived-in space, at night-time the temperature is allowed to drop. Insulated shutters or curtains will slow this process.

Variables

A sun space can be used for many purposes: as a sunporch, a sunroom, or more commonly as a greenhouse. A greenhouse, when properly designed and built, can heat itself through most of the year, will help to heat the attached house, and will be an economical way of supplying year 'round vegetables.

Location

The sun space is best located on the south side of a building that has access to the sun. In some locations it is only possible to attach a greenhouse on the east or west sides of a house. In such instances, the north (free-standing) wall and the remaining wall (west or east) should be well-insulated.

Mass

It is necessary to provide enough thermal-mass to prevent overheating on a clear day and to carry enough heat through the night. This is done using duct work and isolated storage, or the mass can be incorporated into the sun space itself. Some possibilities include:
—*masonry walls* between the sun space and the house
—*concrete floor*
—*water containers* (such as 45 gallon drums or painted conduit pipes with plastic liners)
—*rock-bed containers*
The north side, if massive, should be painted a dark red or blue. This will provide effective absorption of solar radiation while reflecting the part of the spectrum the plants like onto the plants.

Sun space house

Generally speaking, the more thermal-mass within a greenhouse, the smaller the daily temperature fluctuations. If only small fluctuations are tolerable, most of the mass should be within the sun space, especially in cold climates. In milder climates, or where the temperature is allowed to drop (say to 45°F) at night, then a separate storage can be used and more heat can be ducted into the house.

Connection with the house

A greenhouse can be connected to the house by a mass wall. The mass-wall will act as a temperature stabilizer and will help heat both the greenhouse and the house. Vents or windows in the wall will allow heat buildup in the greenhouse direct entry to the home. Glass doors will allow you to control the light and heat that enters the house as well as provide an entrance for people.

A hybrid greenhouse system is connected to the house via an intermediate heat storage. Heated air can be vented to a rock-bed or water container storage. The storage can be located under the greenhouse, or under the house itself (both allowing convection and low temperature radiant heating).

Cooling/Ventilation

One advantage of a greenhouse is that the temperature can fall or rise to an extent that would not be tolerated in a living space (depending on the plants growing.) But there are limits to what is acceptable in a sun space. One house that has a massive two-story glass sun space would commonly reach temperatures of 150°F on the second floor. Another greenhouse owner couldn't determine what temperatures were reached on a bright, spring day because the plastic thermometer had melted! Greenhouses, like any solar strategy, must be sized for the heat load and for the thermal mass. In the spring and fall, and especially during the summer, a sun space can produce excess heat, beyond the capacity of the house or storage. The problem is additionally complicated as a result of the angle of the glazing causing the structure to catch more summer sun. Four solutions to the overheating problem are:

— shading, using natural vegetation such as deciduous trees or vines
— the use of curtains or shutters to reflect the sun when overheating is a problem. The same shutters used to prevent heat loss during winter nights can be used to reduce heat gain during summer days.
— adequate ventilation to expel heat. The venting action generated by a greenhouse can be used to bring cool outside air from the north side through the house.
— using vertical or near-vertical slopes to decrease summer sun

Advantages

— a sun space is a good solution for existing houses as it can be easily attached to conventional houses that have access to the sun
— a greenhouse can serve the dual purpose of growing vegetables year 'round, thus reducing the need for tasteless and expensive imports, while supplying heat energy
— it creates a desirable living-space

Disadvantages

— the sun space is expensive if it's utilized as a heat source, and not as a greenhouse or additional household space
— lot line constraints may prevent the addition of a sun space

Thermosyphon

In a thermosyphon system the solar collection is isolated from storage. Hot air (or water) rises by convection to a storage unit located above the collector area. A thermosyphon system most closely resembles an active solar system, in so much as there is an identifiable solar collector and a separate storage unit. However, all the heat flows (collector to storage, and storage to space) occur naturally. When one mode is mechanically assisted with a pump or fan it is called a hybrid system.

Daytime operation

Sunlight enters the collection area where it is converted to heat. Heated air (or water) within the collector rises through ducts (or pipes) to the storage. Cooler fluid, from the bottom of the storage area, falls and displaces the rising heated fluid, creating a thermosyphon effect.

Night-time operation

Because the storage sits above the collector, the thermosyphon cycle will not reverse at night. The system automatically shuts on and off, and so requires no controls. Heat can be distributed to the space by natural convection when the storage area is below the space. Insulating curtains are not required for the collectors as they hold no heat. Only the storage requires fixed insulation to prevent heat loss.

Variables

Location:

The location of a thermosyphon system is controlled by a number of factors, the most important being:
— access to the sun
— location of the storage above the collector
— location of the space (preferably) above the storage

These three conditions will allow free-flowing thermosyphon action. Often, because of the configuration of the landscape or the design of the house, the above cannot all be met.

Variations on these suggestions include:
— a storage unit behind the collector. In this case provision must be made for preventing reverse thermosyphoning at night.
— hybrid systems in which one of the heat transfer modes is forced by pump or fans.
— a thermosyphon water heating system. The storage must be above the collector but may be placed anywhere in relationship to the house. Connection to a conventional water heater is by a pressurized water line.

Storage

For an air-circulating thermosyphoning system commonly used storage materials are rock-bed storage or containerized water storage. Storage can exist under slab floors, within or behind walls, in ceilings or attics.

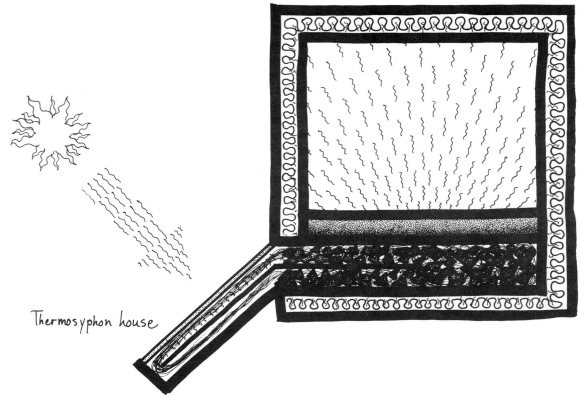

Thermosyphon house

Advantages of thermosyphon system

— it works automatically by natural convection
— does not require moveable insulation for collectors
— collection and storage are isolated from the living space. This helps to maintain level temperatures in the space and reduces overheating problems
— works well as a domestic hot water system
— conventional, low-mass building construction can be used

Disadvantages of thermosyphon system

— requires a fairly unique building site or house design for proper positioning of the collection and storage
— it can be a more expensive system since it requires the addition of collectors and storage that are separate from the design and construction of the rest of the building
— experiences added heat loss through piping or ducting runs

Super-insulation

A super-insulated house concentrates on reducing the heat demand to an absolute minimum. The majority of heat demand that remains is met by internal gains and by direct solar gain.

South-facing windows rarely exceed 6 per cent of the floor area. Conventional frame construction can be used and no additional thermal-mass is built into the house. The Saskatchewan Conservation House is an early example of a super-insulated house. By the end of 1979 there were perhaps 100 similarly designed houses in Saskatchewan.

Features

Insulation: The minimum insulation values used in some regions are R50 to R60 in the attic and R35 to R44 in the walls. Some houses are being built well beyond these standards. Special framing techniques are used which allow extra-wide wall cavities. Insulated doors and air locks are also used. Foundations and slabs are insulated up to R28.

Air-tightness: The greatest care is taken to ensure an air-tight house. Air-vapour barriers are made continuous through ceilings, floors and partitions. Any perforations and seams are caulked or taped. Great care is taken in the installation of electrical wiring and outlets, plumbing and vent stacks to ensure an air-tight seal. A double-wall, or strapping technique, allows the vapour barrier to be ⅓ within the wall. The vapour barrier is then out of reach of the trades: drywallers, plumbers, and electricians. Attic hatches are placed on the outside roof.

Because of the rigid standards of air-tightness, reducing the air change rate to as little as once every 20 hours or better, an air-to-air heat exchanger is used to ensure adequate ventilation without corresponding heat losses.

Windows: Windows to the north, east and west are reduced to a minimum. The majority of windows face south, but these rarely occupy more than 6 per cent of the living area. A 1500 square foot house would have a maximum of 100 sq. ft. of windows facing south. Windows are mostly of the sealed (unopenable) type. Any larger window area could lead to overheating and necessitate additional thermal mass. Windows are minimally double-glazed. Non-south-facing-windows would be triple-glazed.

Moveable Insulation: All windows, regardless of their orientation, should be protected with a reflective, air-tight insulating curtain or shutter. Shutters can be internal: in such cases they are easy to operate, there is direct access to them, but they are hard to store. In addition, they will cause some condensation and frosting problems.

Shutters can be external; they prevent condensation, but they're more difficult to operate and are exposed to weathering.

Shutters can be between two layers of glass; they prevent condensation, are protected from weathering but they are not as accessible.

Advantages of super-insulated house

— a very constant temperature can be maintained, overheating is prevented
— it results in a very quiet, comfortable, draft-free house
— it works extremely efficiently, reducing energy demand by 90 per cent or more over conventional houses
— can be built with careful application of conventional building practices

Disadvantages of super-insulated house

— the reduced window area is too enclosed for some people and reduces natural light levels
— it requires some unconventional (but not difficult) building methods, and very high standards of insulation
— it is difficult (and expensive) to retrofit an existing house to the required standards for a super-insulated building, although externally re-insulated homes are working successfully.

Underground Houses

Underground houses, also known as earth-sheltered houses, are becoming a popular approach to building energy-efficient housing. It is not the insulating properties of earth (it is actually a poor insulator), but rather its moderating qualities that make underground housing attractive. Ten feet below the surface the temperature fluctuates between 42° and 55°F, depending on the location. This fluctuation has a lag of several months behind the air temperature. Four inches of rigid insulation (such as styrofoam) will help maintain comfortable temperatures inside the building, although some designers are building "zero-energy" underground houses with 6 inches or more of styrofoam.

Water-proofing is an extremely important consideration for underground housing. A well-designed, dry site and good water-proofing should provide an adequate seal. Bentonite, a natural clay, Bituthene, a rubberized asphalt, and other built-up membranes are good water-proofing materials.

The most commonly used building materials for earth-sheltered houses are reinforced concrete and preserved wood. The ideal site affords a southern exposure, while allowing the other elevations to be covered with earth. Properly designed earth-sheltered homes can be bright, airy living places and should receive most of their required heat energy from internal gains and through the south-facing windows.

Double-Shelled Houses

The double-shelled house is a variation of the super-insulated house. Recently the concept has gained much attention.

The basic plan calls for a house within a house. On the north-south plane there is a continuous loop of air between the two building shells. Air, powered by the sun, circulates around the shells. It is initially warmed by the sun in the south-facing greenhouse, then rises into the attic and falls between the shells on the north side. The air then passes through an insulated crawl space under the house where it gives up some of its heat energy to the ground and the mass of the house before entering the greenhouse space. At night this convective loop is reversed as the ground gives up some of its heat.

The theory is that the envelope of air circulating around the house protects the inner shell from the extremes of the outside environment. This type of house works well, but it is yet to be shown that it functions better than any comparable airtight, super-insulated house.

A typical double-shell house will have ceiling insulation of R40 and R12 (inner shell), a north wall of R27 and R12 (inner shell), and east and west (solid) walls of R27 or better. A combination of internal gain and direct-gain solar heating through the greenhouse will supply the majority of the heat load of the house.

Retrofit

As is evident from the previous sections of this book, building an energy-efficient house requires a re-thinking of traditional house design and construction. But most of us are locked into the reality of poorly designed and built homes and do not have the luxury of starting from scratch. Therein lies the challenge — to make an existing home as energy-efficient as possible while not exhausting both financial and time resources.

As a starting point there are many worthwhile changes that can be undertaken with any home. Some are minor alterations that can be done with a minimum or no structural change.

Minor Changes

Conservation

Lowering the temperature of the house, especially at night or when not at home, and in parts of the house that are not used much, will save energy.
Fireplaces should all have tightly closed vents that are kept shut whenever the fireplace is not in use. Glass doors reduce the volume of heated air that escapes up the chimney while the fire is burning.
Some slight attitudinal changes may help save energy. For example, putting on a sweater may help avoid having to turn up the thermostat.

Insulation

Upgrading insulation in the attic is usually the first step.

Walls are harder to insulate, but some cavity walls can be filled (cavities under 2 inches are usually not worth the expense of filling).

Basement walls can often be easily insulated, both from the inside and out.

All window areas should be double-glazed. Large glass areas should have insulating shutters or curtains; south-facing windows should be clear during the winter days and drawn at night. Insulating shutters can be a very cost effective way of saving substantial amounts of energy. The section on shutters discusses the options available.

Airtight

Before insulating, all cracks and holes should be sealed and patched. Properly sealed vapour barriers should always be installed on the warm side of insulation. Acoustical sealant or other non-hardening caulking should be used at all seams and joints.

The sill plate, where the wall meets the foundation, is a major source of heat loss, as are the electrical boxes and cracks behind baseboards of exterior walls.

All cracks, seams, etc. should be caulked from the inside of the house.

Weatherstripping should be used to seal off all doors and windows.

Vents to the outside (i.e. kitchen stove, bathroom) should be airtight when not in use. Re-circulating vents should be used whenever possible.

Major Changes

Insulation

During renovation, walls can be strapped from the inside, making then thicker to accept more insulation. At that time a proper vapour barrier can be installed.

Houses can also be re-insulated from the exterior, a useful technique if siding is to be attached. First an air-vapour barrier (if the house lacks one) is wrapped over the house on the outside. Joints must be overlapped and sealed and the barrier sealed to window and door casings. The walls are strapped, using horizontal and then vertical strapping to the required depth. The window and door casings are then built out to the new wall. Insulation (fibreglass batts work well) is placed and then covered with building paper. The new siding can then be applied (or the old siding reused if it was salvagable). This gives a continuous envelope of insulation and does not require changes in the side of the house.

Foundations can be dug up and insulated. One method is to dig a trench 18 inches deep around the foundation. Insulate the exposed foundation and install a horizontal rigid insulation (styrofoam). It should be 2 inches thick, extend 2 feet and slope slightly down and away from the house. Fill the hole and protect any exposed foundation insulation.

Caulk and insulate between floor joists against an exterior wall.

Insulate around the hot water heater (leaving top and air hole clear).

Airtight

During renovations it is possible to have access to normally inaccessible areas of high infiltration. Take the opportunity to seal these spaces. They include:
— along the sill plate and where the wall framing meets the foundation.
— corners where walls meet walls and walls meet ceiling.
— areas around piping, ductwork and chimneys.
— if the ventilation rate can be reduced below $1/10$ change per hour then an air-to-air heat exchanger is required. From $1/10$ to $1/3$ air change, ventilation has to be induced to maintain air quality. One method of determining this is to check for the formation of excessive condensation. If humidity-generating activities have been reduced, but there is still excessive condensation then a greater air change is required.

Mass-Wall

A mass-wall passive solar system is generally difficult to retrofit unless it meets certain characteristics:
— a south-facing wall (within 30° east or west of south) that has access to the sun during the heating season.
— the wall should be masonry or double brick to provide heat storage.

Such a south-facing brick wall can be fitted with double-glazed sheeting (glass, plastic, etc.). Vents are placed through the wall as in a conventional mass-wall system, or alternatively, existing windows can be employed for convection. Provision should also be made for insulating curtains or shutters for night-time use.

Direct Gain

It is possible to increase the passive solar heating for any house by increasing the south-facing window area if the view, noise, and shading allow it. Provisions must be made for overhangs or other summer sun protection as well as for additional thermal mass if a large window area is installed.

Sunspace

A sunspace solar system, such as a greenhouse, is perhaps the best retrofit solar strategy. The expense for the addition of a greenhouse can be borne not only by the energy savings but also by the increased space (and increased sales value of the house), and the ability to grow vegetables year round.

Sunspace, in addition to requiring access to sunlight, must also be allocated adequate space within the lot. The south side is, of course, the ideal location as it offers protection for the north wall of the greenhouse and maximizes the tie-in with the house.

Thermosyphon

A thermosyphon solar system generally requires a specific site that allows the collectors to be placed below the storage and the space to be heated. Since the required configuration is seldom found in existing houses, its use as a retrofit strategy is limited.

The two thermosyphon systems that will have more widespread use are the thermosyphon domestic hot water system, and the "window-box" heater. The solar window-box heater consists of a collector placed against the south side of a house with the top feeding into the bottom of a window. A loop allows air from the room to fall to the bottom of the heater, become heated and rise into the house. Although no storage is provided, it is equivalent to the strategy of increasing the window area.

Fairview Conference

13 leading architects, builders
and planners discuss their
latest work and building techniques.

Introduction

The late 1970's might well be remembered as "The Age of the House". Suddenly attention was drawn to low cost, low energy housing — at least in the Western world. Reflecting this interest, the theme of *Fairview Conference 1979* (the first Fairview Conference) is energy and housing.

Our mandate was to not only discuss solar heated and super-insulated homes, but to extend the study of energy-efficiency to other pertinent areas. Our perspective was to encompass regionalism and the concept of regional housing; the use of alternate or indigenous building materials; methods of transforming the house from an energy-consuming entity to one that is virtually or entirely autonomous.

While at first glance it might appear unusual that a town in Northern Alberta's Peace River Region sees fit to make a contribution to energy-efficient and appropriate housing, Fairview turned out to be a remarkably suitable site. Our non-profit organization, *PeaceWorks,* worked closely with *Fairview College,* the co-sponsor and host of FC'79. The College provided reasonable and comfortable facilities in an informal atmosphere. An editorial in the *Lethbridge Herald* observed, "The planners of Fairview Conference would seem to be in the vanguard of the "brown-bagging trend", to put a name to it, and this is a very healthy development."

Whether the description is brown-bagging or grass roots or the conserver movement, there is a definite trend towards low cost, people-oriented, informal assemblies. It should be made clear that this conference is not a first or unique model. Paul Hanley and *Earthcare* have organized numerous conferences dealing with non-chemical agriculture and soil maintenance in Saskatchewan. The Institute of Man and Resources in P.E.I. has done much work, including their own conference on Ecological Agriculture. Groups all over North America have organized workshops and seminars on low energy housing.

The number of groups and individuals conducting such work, and the extent of their activities is staggering — and encouraging. Though individual contributions may seem quite small, the total consequence is enormous. Fairview Conference 1979 was another contribution to this important process.

To paraphrase *David Wright,* a true conserver is somebody who does it on his own. He doesn't talk about it. He doesn't give lectures across the country. He doesn't organize conferences. He is somebody who in his day-to-day life demonstrates conservation and, I would add, the principles of a conserver society. We trust, therefore, that by your actions, your contribution will be immensely greater than ours. We hope the information in this section will contribute to your success.

Mark A. Craft
Fairview, Alberta
March, 1980

Gordon Fearn

Gordon Fearn *is a member of the Sociology Department at the University of Alberta. He is an advocate of human scale technologies and decentralization. Among his current activities is an international learning centre in his native Newfoundland that will emphasize cooperative participation, self-directed learning and a self-sufficient environment.*

It is part of the human condition that we grasp for fixed features, for foundations and capstones, for boundaries and limits. We find security in the structures we create. We rarely define security in terms of process.

We are not very articulate with a flowing-stream concept of life. We tend to miss the significance of movement in our perceptions and understandings of experience. We label and categorize. We acquiesce as language structures our thought. Culture and society help in this patterned deception by encouraging our focus on the things and objects in our experience — encouraging us to miss the whole process of ebbs and flows that got us there, and here, in the first place.

The twentieth century, by such reckoning, has become a century of multiple jeopardies. Yet it is also a century of transition. In the words of Will and Ariel Durant in *The Lessons of History*, 1968, "We cannot be sure that the moral laxity of our times is a herald of decay rather than a painful or delightful transition between a moral code that has lost its agricultural basis and another that our industrial civilization has yet to forge into social order and normality."

What the Durants say is true for morals and history also may be true of society and its continuing transition. Glenn Seaborg, winner of the Nobel prize for chemistry in 1951, writing in *The Futurist* in 1974, suggests that "there are things that will have to happen, conditions that will have to prevail, given the physical limitations we face, but also given man's creativity and will to survive…The difficulty is not in predicting that we will arrive at these points, or even how we will arrive, but when, and how much disruption, deprivation, and destruction will take place in the interim."

On the Idea of Conservatism

The environment movement of the late 1960s predates the contemporary debate on conservation and the image of the conserver-oriented society. Two projects during the 1970s have been particularly influential: "A Blueprint for Survival," centered in England and published in *The Ecologist* in 1972; and "The Limits to Growth," sponsored by the Club of Rome and published in a continuing series of books — *The Limits to Growth,* 1972; *Mankind at the Turning Point,* 1974; *Reshaping the International Order,* 1976; and *Goals for Mankind,* 1977. Many authors, including those following, have the distinction of heralding the basic concerns which help to tie all of these works together: Barry Commoner, *The Closing Circle,* 1971; Paul Ehrlich, *The Population Bomb,* 1968; Buckminster Fuller, *Utopia or Oblivion,* 1969; E. F. Schumacher, *Small Is Beautiful,* 1973; Alvin Toffler, *Future Shock,* 1970; Barbara Ward and René Dubos, *Only One Earth,* 1972 — and numerous others, including several of those writing elsewhere in these proceedings.

Conservation here refers to the development of holistic and integrated strategies for achieving a sustainable future. So defined, conservation takes on meanings far beyond common dictionary statements. For example, once we realize that the conservation of scarce resources is the single largest source of such resources, we move toward a new concept of resource management. Furthermore, we add immeasurably to our concept of personal accountability when we realize that *human* resources, like material resources, are susceptible to depletion, and that human creativity remains the single greatest source of inspiration for achieving a sustainable future.

We talk about the conserver-oriented society when conservation is viewed as a societal alternative. Even here we pass beyond conventional meanings, for there is much more involved in this than an ideological shift from consumption to conservation. According to Cathy Starrs in *Canadians in Conversation about the Future*, 1976, "what is at stake lies beyond mere ideology — that at the most fundamental level, our ability to shift directions and to find more adequate ways of facilitating human well-being will depend upon a restructuring of our patterns of knowledge and on our ability to discover more adequate images of ourselves as full persons than those images by which our activities, values, attitudes and perceptions have been patterned."

Shifting directions involves looking at important questions in new ways. It is commonplace, for example, to view capital as wealth which, in one form or another, can be used to produce additional wealth. Wealth is defined in units of currency, such as dollars. But wealth can be defined in other terms. We are rapidly approaching the time when ideas of the mind, and human experience, will be viewed as the equivalent of capital. This is but another expression of the great transition facing civilization. It is visualized by King Hubert, writing in *The Canadian Mining and Metallurgical Bulletin* in 1973, when he says that "the epoch of the fossil fuels can be only a transitory or ephemeral event" — as Figure 1 suggests.

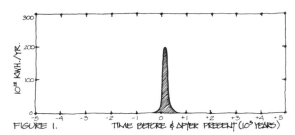

FIGURE 1.   TIME BEFORE & AFTER PRESENT (10⁹ YEARS)

Epoch of fossil-fuel exploitation

Defining wealth in new terms is also central in the argument of Amory Lovins in *Soft Energy Paths: Toward a Durable Peace*, 1977. Lovins notes that soft-energy technologies — such as solar and wind technologies — rely "on energy income, not on depletable energy capital." We are accustomed to pronouncements on the tens of billions of dollars required for the commercial development of hard-energy resources, such as coal, oil and gas, and nuclear energy. But billions of dollars so spent is "energy capital," or capital expended to exploit a diminishing resource. In contrast, "energy income" is that which is gained by exploiting a renewable resource. "Use of the renewable resources is equivalent to living on income; use…of the fossil fuels is equivalent to spending capital" — in the words of J. Bockris, writing in *Energy Research* in 1979. But thinking this way is fundamentally different from the thoughtways we take for granted. Thinking this way forces us to consider conservation in light of both the diversity of all available resources, and the totality of costs involved in their exploitation. When we do that, the conventional economics of capitalism may very well collapse. "Capitalism and growth as an economic philosophy may hence be one-time phenomena and terminate with the use-up of non-renewable resources" (Bockris).

When we focus on the ideas of conservation and the conserver-oriented society, we are using mind-capital to decipher the totality of our experience, including our thoughts about the future. Indeed, these ideas serve as a way to construct a bridge between the past and the future. A good idea has its own power — power which is particularly effective when persons are attracted to it for reasons which are both cognitive-intellectual and affective-emotional, that is, when both sides of the brain are stimulated. So it is that following the conservation ethic is far more than being conservation-minded or developing new technologies for recycling wastes. The conservation ethic is an emerging strategy for employing the mind and human experience as forms of social capital — as capital which transforms knowledge into process, and as capital which encourages risk. Thus, the ideas of conservation and the conserver-oriented society are attractive because they promise solutions to important problems, and because they serve as prototype expressions for those persons seeking both survival and quality in the pursuit of alternative lifestyles.

The Conserver Society

The concept of the conserver-oriented society has arisen not simply because it is the antithesis of the consumer-oriented society, but because its very introduction anticipates the growing debate on the future shape of social institutions. No longer can anything in the future be assumed. In particular, social institutions — the normative structuring of roles, relationships and social behavior — even now are being transformed so that the emphasis is swinging toward new stabilities to be found through diversity and change. These and related matters are discussed at length in three recent publications: Science Council of Canada, *Canada as a Conserver Society: Resource Uncertainties and the Need for New Technologies,* 1977; Lawrence Solomon, *The Conserver Solution: A Blueprint for the Conserver Society,* 1978; and Kimon Valaskakis *et. al., The Conserver Society: A Workable Alternative for the Future,* 1979. The last of these works explores the idea of the conserver society in more rigorous policy terms and, pursuant to the approach of the Club of Rome, suggests a multi-dimensional approach: "All too often we tend to view problems in a partial way. Faced with an energy problem, we come out, as a society, with a few energy-conservative measures. Faced with inflation we set up anti-inflation policies. Faced with unemployment we dig out our anti-unemployment arsenal. We do all this without realizing *(sic)* that the solution to the energy problem may actually increase inflation, the anti-inflation program may worsen unemployment, and the anti-unemployment policies may result in increased waste in energy and materials. The concept of the conserver society avoids such partial thinking by integrating as many aspects of the problématique as is humanly possible."

Institutional shifts are at the center of this new direction in thinking. For example, the conserver-society emphasis on total costing rests on an awareness that the market does not price all costs, but permits some costs to be externalized. According to the Science Council of Canada, this raises the "possibility for misallocation of resources. ...To the extent that costs are externalized and become social rather than private, or are deferred into the future, prices are lower than they should

be. ...The closer we get to the goal of total costing, the more apparent will become the high costs of our present ways of doing things." More apparent also will be the identities of those who are benefiting most from the high costs of maintaining the status quo.

But the institutional shifts now being debated are even more significant than new principles of accounting and accountability. We are all familiar with the increasingly strong tendencies toward centralization in society, seen especially in the corporate control of industrial production and in the regulatory power of the state. It is becoming clear, however, that corporations and states cannot increase the size and complexity of their operations forever, for as they do various inefficiencies creep in to circumvent basic goals. Decision-making based on clear information becomes overloaded based on misinformation. Centralization based on collective needs operating at one point in time becomes the reason for alternative strategies later, as hazards and vulnerabilities become apparent. Placing all the eggs in one basket is a recipe for disaster. Thus, many persons are arguing for decentralized and intermediate technologies such as the pursuit of soft-energy paths (Lovins) and localized ownership and management of resources and production (Schumacher). Such alternative conceptions offer an escape from vulnerability. In this respect, the Science Council notes that the principle of diversity recognizes "the normal statistical distribution of needs, roles, capacities, and incomes in a given population. ...Diversity, in the sense of decentralization, can conserve when it encourages responsible participation. The latter, and the sense of independence and freedom that

comes from self-reliance, can be additional positive values in themselves that should be weighed in cost/benefit calculations."

The contributions of Amory Lovins deserve additional expansion, for he is one of the few contemporary thinkers who discusses energy economics in the context of institutional structures. According to Lovins, the "distinction between hard and soft energy paths rests not on how much energy is used, but on the technical and sociopolitical structure of the energy system, thus focusing our attention on consequent and crucial political differences." Lovins discusses the nature of soft-energy technologies, in keeping with characteristics already noted in this paper, then he proceeds to convincingly make the point that the soft-energy path will allow more end-functions to be performed using much less gross primary energy, because energy conversion and distribution losses are virtually eliminated in the soft-energy scenario.

There is now no doubt that "the coming energy crisis," talked about for years, is upon us. It has come at a time when institutions are increasingly centralized and monolithic, but also at a time when there is increasing public awareness of the inequity and alienation which result from hard, capital-intensive technologies. Many persons are striving to gain a greater margin of self-sufficiency. Creative energies everywhere are rising. To illustrate, Figure 2 is based on projections by the Stanford Research Institute generalized to the Canadian population. While these projections are difficult to defend, they are presented as a possible summary of the course of future history. Without doubt, one of the metaphoric vehicles for such change will be the "obvious relevance to everyday life" of soft-energy paths, where soft technologies "use familiar, equitably distributed natural energies to meet perceived human needs directly and comprehensibly" (Lovins).

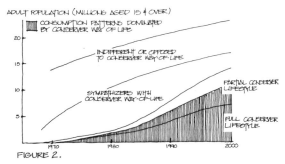

FIGURE 2.

Projections of changing consumption. From Stapenhurst, 1977

Conclusion

In Fairview, in the Peace River country of Alberta, with more than three hundred delegates assembled, one might think it difficult to see too far distant. Or is it?

The subjects of the conference — energy and housing — are not mere local fetishes. Toss in the world's exploding population, the life-sustaining needs of clean air, fresh water, food and shelter, and we have something of a definitive list of imperatives for human survival. By virtue of our interest in energy, we effectively deal with all of these subjects. So for several days in June, 1979, we can rightly consider Fairview as located at the centre of the global community.

In this brief paper, I have sought to discuss the conserver-oriented society as an image of the social future. The

conserver-oriented society is treated as a feasible response to non-renewable resource shortages, especially shortages of fossil fuels. In particular, the promise of soft-energy technologies is discussed as a strategy for human- and local-scale development and the pursuit of quality in life. I have assumed throughout that achieving the future cannot be assured, but I am open to the limits of the mind, and beyond, possible pathways to that future.

I end with the words of Kai Erikson, writing in *World Issues* in 1976-77: "I have suggested that human reactions to the age we are entering are likely to include a sense of cultural disorientation, a feeling of powerlessness, a dulled apathy, and a generalized fear about the condition of the universe. These, of course, are among the classic symptoms of trauma, and it may well be that historians of the future will look back on this period and conclude that the traumatic neuroses were its true clinical signature." Earlier in the same paper Erikson says: "A world without stable points of reference is a world in ruins for those who find themselves without the personal resources or the good luck to navigate effectively in it."

There can be no conclusion to an experience still in process. And yet, we must think and speak and act in ways that are more than tentative, in ways that involve risks, and in ways designed "to avert the thoughtless foreclosure of options" (Preston Cloud's phrase, quoted by Laurence Vigrass, 1978). Perhaps it is, then, that personal resources constitute the greatest renewable resource of all, and that achieving the future rests not so much on the rise and fall of fossil fuels, but on the courage and adaptability of

Homo sapiens — the distinctively human creative potential to forge social environments that rest in harmony with the natural world.

References

J. O'M. Bockris, "Economics, Political and Psychological Barriers to Building the New Energy Conversion Machinery," **Energy Research,** 3 (1979) 1-11.

Barry Commoner, **The Closing Circle: Nature, Man and Technology,** Knopf, 1971.

Will and Ariel Durant, **The Lessons of History,** Simon and Schuster, 1968.

Paul R. Ehrlich, **The Population Bomb,** Ballantine, 1968.

Kai Erikson, "Living in a World without Stable Points of Reference," **World Issues,** 1 (1976-77) 13-14.

R. Buckminster Fuller, **Utopia or Oblivion: The Prospects for Humanity,** Bantam, 1969.

Edward Goldsmith et. al., "A Blueprint for Survival," **The Ecologist,** 2 (1972).

M. King Hubbert, "Survey of World Energy Resources," **The Canadian Mining and Metallurgical Bulletin,** 66 (1973) 37-54.

Ervin Laszlo et. al., **Goals for Mankind,** Dutton, 1977.

Amory B. Lovins, **Soft Energy Paths: Toward a Durable Peace,** Pelican, 1977.

Donella H. Meadows et. al., **The Limits to Growth,** Universe, 1972.

Mihajlo Mesarovic and Eduard Pestel, **Mankind at the Turning Point,** Dutton, 1974.

E. F. Schumacher, **Small Is Beautiful: A Study of Economics as if People Mattered,** Blond and Briggs, 1973.

Science Council of Canada, **Canada as a Conserver Society: Resource Uncertainties and the Need for New Technologies,** Supply and Services Canada, 1977.

Glenn T. Seaborg, "The Recycle Society of Tomorrow," **The Futurist,** 8 (1974) 108-115.

Lawrence Solomon, **The Conserver Solution: A Blueprint for the Conserver Society,** Doubleday, 1978.

Frederick Stapenhurst, "Some Implications of a 'Conserver Society,'" **The Labour Gazette,** 77 (1977) 511-513.

Cathy Starrs, **Canadians in Conversation about the Future,** Environment Canada, 1976.

Jan Tinbergen, **Reshaping the International Order,** Dutton, 1976.

Alvin Toffler, **Future Shock,** Random House, 1970.

Kimon Valaskakis et. al., **The Conserver Society: A Workable Alternative for the Future,** Fitzhenry and Whiteside, 1979.

Laurence Vigrass, "Energy and the Conserver Society on the Prairies," unpublished paper, 1978.

Barbara Ward and Rene Dubos, **Only One Earth: The Care and Maintenance of a Small Planet,** Norton, 1972.

Alex Wade

Alex Wade *has been an architect for over twenty years. He specializes in the area of low-cost, energy-efficient, owner-built homes. He is the author of* 30 Energy Efficient Houses *and was a major contributor to* Low Cost, Energy Efficient Shelter. *He lives in Barrytown, New York in a house he designed and built for less than $1500.*

It is nice to be here in the centre of the world. I almost did not get here though. I called up our local travel agent to book my flight and she called back a couple of days later to say that she could neither find Fairview nor the place Tohilo. I had to explain to her that the latter was the Canadian postal code and not a town. (T0H 1L0)

I think it is remarkable that so many people are here. I was the keynote speaker for a regional conference on appropriate technology in Indianapolis sponsored by the National Science Foundation at which they were trying to get imput from the public. The public in Indianapolis was so interested that they had about half as many people there as you do here. So, when people tell you that you cannot get others interested in a remote location, I think you have certainly proved them wrong today.

My basic premises are that one can and should involve the average person in the building process and that the only way we are going to really exert a change in the consumer society is to, in fact, get people themselves involved in doing their housing. These concerns are expressed in the types of housing that I have been designing and in the three books with which I have been involved to date.

Over the past eighteen months, we have put together about ten houses that are each quite different in size and scope. They are mostly in the northeastern United States; a couple of them are in the midwest. They were obviously not designed for as severe a climate as northern Canada, so some modifications will be necessary.

One of the most efficient designs I have ever done is a solar shed house of about 1500 square feet. It is dug into a hillside and is a very compact shape so that there is minimum surface area exposed for the floor area involved. Our version of a cold winter, which would not bother you very much, is about two weeks of constant below zero weather with nights of -25°C or -30°C and daytime temperatures of about -15°C with no snow cover. Toward the end of that period, we checked this house at 10:00 one morning when the outside temperature was -23°C and found the inside temperature was +13°C. This house has no supplemental heat source and no insulating covers on any windows.

Two views of a compact 1500 sq. ft. house

A very tiny house probably was responsible for my new book. I call it the *Volkswagon* house. It is 24 feet square with a shed roof — very simple and easy to build. There are two small bedrooms in a loft and a compact bath, kitchen and living area downstairs. The original design had a greenhouse across the front. The owner, however, decided not to use the greenhouse but, rather, combine that area with the house proper.

The "Volkswagen" house

This particular house is not terribly energy-efficient since we included a number of big windows, but there is a view for miles out over mountains. To compensate for this we used some heavy, insulated shutters on the inside. It has a wood stove for back-up which probably will not be that heavily used.

Everybody liked the idea of that house but wanted one just a little bit bigger. So I designed a 24 foot by 36 foot salt-box-style house with south-facing greenhouse. This became the basic house about which I wrote the new book.

Basic salt-box style house

It sits on a concrete grade beam which is heavily insulated on the outside. It has a brick slab floor set in sand and a large masonry heat storage wall in the middle of the house through which a chimney flue is built at one end. The wall is positioned so that the sunlight from the skylights strikes it for a better part of the day. It also picks up heat from the small greenhouse in the front. This house has folding, insulating shutters that cover all of the larger glass areas at night.

Figure I is the first floor plan for this small, basic 24 foot square house which I have referred to as the Volkswagon house. It has insulating covers for virtually every opening. It has an airlock entrance and a compact bath and kitchen layout. The first floor has a small sitting area with folding doors that doubles as extra bedroom space. There is a combination kitchen range which serves as a heat source. Behind the range next to the bathroom is the washing machine. This was designed to be a basic, minimal house — to do the most with the least.

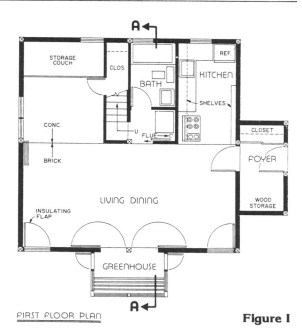

FIRST FLOOR PLAN   **Figure I**

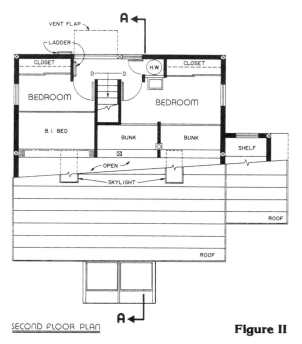

SECOND FLOOR PLAN   **Figure II**

The second floor of this house has two compact bedrooms with built-in beds (**Figure II**). The master bedroom has a double bed and there are two bunk beds in the other bedroom. We also have done this house in another version which has a steeple roof. In the steeple-roof version, we moved all three of the beds over to the north wall so that the beds are up in the air. This leaves all of the floor areas as usable space in the rooms.

That is the basic house design and we are now halfway through construction of the fourth version of it. We have designed quite a few variations. The north side in some plans has a car port where others have garages or workshops. One of the owners who is a gardener is doing the house with a full greenhouse across the south as well as a full north greenhouse across the back for various exotic plants that do not want direct sunlight.

Figure III is of a three bedroom house with a large living-dining area. The second floor of this house (**Figure IV**) has two bedrooms with a bath in the middle. All the plumbing in the house is concentrated in the centre next to a masonry heat storage wall to minimize the possibility of freezing.

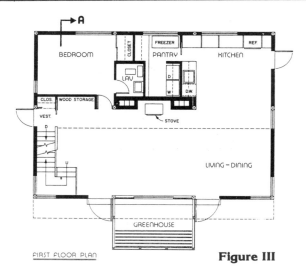

FIRST FLOOR PLAN   **Figure III**

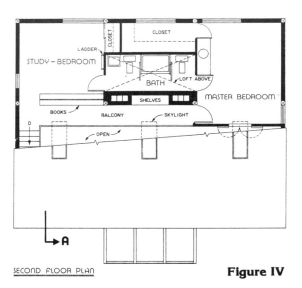

SECOND FLOOR PLAN   **Figure IV**

A great many of my clients are people who have low budgets and are trying to do a house with the least amount of money possible. But I also get clients who want to do an ecological design and have a fair amount of money and yet still want to get involved in the construction them-

selves. Instead of having a standard contractor-built house, they want something a little more exotic.

I also designed an expanded version of the basic house. The owners grow all their own food in a greenhouse which extends all the way across the front. This house was also expanded to the back where there is a workshop and a garage. It began with a salt-box roof that was extended down to form a symmetrical roof. The chimney is extended up all the way. They have installed collectors near the peak for a solar water heater.

An expanded version of the basic house

One of our most exotic houses has a two-story greenhouse with a duct system to circulate the heat into the house. It has a battery of solar collectors up on top, along with extensive window areas. On the very top is a roof deck from which you can see seven states on a clear day. To try to keep the house warm, we used a lot of earth berming. The whole first floor of the house has a berm around the north side and 30 feet further out is another wind break, mounded even higher. So there is a little artificial mountain behind the house to shield it.

A house with an extra large greenhouse

A small solar greenhouse is set into the middle of this house. It has a folding insulating shutter which comes down on the outside. The house also has a sauna on the second floor above the greenhouse. Sunlight comes into the greenhouse through a cut which is under the sloping seats of the sauna.

Off of the top floor is a sheltered roof deck. It is walled so that sun can get into it but not wind. It has a roll-up canvas top to keep off rain and prevent it from becoming buried under snow. It is a very nice place to be and there are even a few sunny winter days when the temperature on the deck is pleasant, since you are completely sheltered from the wind. We designed a window couch that projects out into a little bay-like window. There is a drop-down insulating panel that covers this at night so that you do not lose a lot of heat.

Two views of house with solarium and collectors

Sheltered roof deck

My editors, from Rodale Press, have been involved with my books. They have followed through with a number of the design features on their own house.

Details of the bathroom

"Please comment on insulating shutters: what types, style, storage, etc."

Generally, I use either urethane board or a styrofoam board covered with quite a variety of materials. I have done this in almost every conceivable fashion. Many people just leave the white styrofoam as is and use it as a friction-fit shutter. That is the very simplest way, but it would not be suitable for your climate.

I usually make a light frame around a urethane board and I try to arrange it so that it hinges up to the ceiling. For large areas, such as the window couch or the bay windows, the shutters simply hinge back against the ceiling and are dropped down on winter days and at night. You take them down in the summer.

The major problem with shutters is that they tend to be bulky and in the way. The greenhouse on one house I mentioned has an exterior shutter which folds up into the area above the greenhouse. But more often, storage is a major problem for such shutters. On several houses, I placed windows at the corners, and the shutters are side hinged so that they simply open against the adjoining wall.

Another promising technique I have used involves a product which I despise but which works well in this case — sliding glass doors. I bought the track for a four-panel-wide door, installed it on the outside of the wall between the house and the greenhouse, then put two doors in it. The doors can be slid back on the outside of the house. I also made insulating panels that fasten to the outside of the doors.

One can use shutters in three modes. Either they are closed as a glass door between the house and the greenhouse; in mild weather, they can be opened to allow heat to come in from the greenhouse; or in cold weather the insulating shutter covers can be added to the outside. This is an economical and easy way to get sliding shutters. Since they are on the outside wall (in the greenhouse) they are not taking up wall space in the house, nor are they interrupting the insulation or vapour barrier.

"What preservative do you use on your rough-sawn siding?"

I use a product called Cuprenal which comes as a pigmented stain. It is a little bit expensive with the pigment, but you can certainly add your own pigment to it if you wish. You have to mix it rather vigorously or it settles. Another major brand name which does not come with the pigment is Woodlife.

"What level of insulation do you use?"

I tend to vary the insulation level with the particular climate in which I am building the house. I have been using six-inch wall framing on virtually all of the houses. Since you get a lot more heat loss from the wind side of the house than on the other sides, I add a two-inch tongue-and-groove styrofoam layer on the north and west walls with insulating sheathing over it. I usually use just the standard insulating sheathing on the other two sides. When I move into more northerly climates however, I increase the insulation.

I have been using twelve inches of fibreglass in the roof, although for northern climates I have been adding a two-inch urethane board on top of the roof. There have been quite a few problems with sprayed urethane in the United States and a number of states have outlawed it, including my home state of New York. I do not use sprayed urethane, which I understand is used around here quite a bit. One of the major problems in doing a good insulation job on the houses is preventing air infiltration, and obviously the sprayed urethane makes a virtually airtight barrier; that can also cause you to suffocate if you do not allow for it.

On the skylights, I use a sliding urethane board shutter and I recess it into the ceiling. I also use extra urethane board insulation on the ceiling in the area where the shutter slides.

"What sort of fresh air intake and/or ventilation system do you use?"

In houses for cold climates that are well insulated and well sealed you can have a ventilation problem. I prefer to hook up a small fan for air intake and to use a carbon monoxide detector which can be valuable in a tight house. Carbon monoxide can sneak up on you and you won't know it has happened. Someone who has done an extremely thorough insulation job is much more likely to get into serious trouble.

"Do you have energy-use values for heating these houses?"

Most of them have not been built long enough to be properly monitored. Generally, they have wood-heat back-up, though some of them have radiant electric panels. The quantities of wood and the amounts of electricity used have been very minimal in all cases, but I do not have specific data.

"What insulating materials do you use for exterior masonry and under masonry floors?"

I put insulation down well below frost lines. Tests have supposedly shown that you really do not need insulation under the floor, but I have had to put it there. I use the urethane board. Depending on the climate, I use from two to four inches on the outside of the masonry.

"What is the cost per square foot of the houses?"

The solar shed with the angled wall had a total cost of $18.00 U.S. per square foot. It has fifteen hundred square feet in it. The owner acted as contractor and helper and did most of the final finish work. He contracted out the basic construction work, the well, the septic system, and the electrical service. That was an efficient and low cost house. The little Volkswagen house had a total cost of about $8,000.00 U.S. Most of the basic labour was hired, but the owner did the finish work on it. The house is 24 foot square with a loft of half that size. This means a cost per square foot of $9.25.

"Do you have any idea how many houses are being built based upon your ideas?"

I have had about 6000 letters and about 1000 people have ordered plans for the houses, but I do not know how many people went ahead and built them. I know that some have built houses directly from the book without buying plans because they called later with questions.

"What function does a greenhouse play in a solar house besides growing things?"

These greenhouses are all carefully positioned so they face south and in periods of bright sunlight you can get a significant heat gain from them. In cloudy, overcast weather, you get only a slight heat gain, but you have thoroughly minimized heat loss from that part of the house. Obviously, growing things is also a significant feature.

"Can bay windows be made so they lose no more heat than windows in a straight wall?"

Obviously the glass area of bay windows is greater than that of a standard window in a straight wall. Consequently, you are going to lose more heat at night or at any time the sun is not hitting the window. Conversely, if they are in a position where the sun hits them during the day, you are going to gain more heat. I provide a thorough insulating shutter cover.

"What type of insulation do you use with your post-and-beam construction and how is it supported in the walls?"

The basic construction of these houses involves six-by-six posts spaced 12 to 14 feet on centre. Between these, horizontally, I run two-by-sixes. They would be studs if they ran vertically, but in this case they are called girths because they go horizontally. They are two feet on centre and I put either fibreglass or styrofoam between them.

"Can urethane or styrofoam sheeting on outside walls trap moisture in the wood and cause rotting?"

Yes, indeed it can. It is important to get a tight vapour barrier on the inside of these houses. But don't forget to take into account temperature and humidity differentials because you may get a dew point in the wall and subsequent frost, particularly when you have fibreglass insulation. Not only can this cause rotting of the wood, but frost in fibreglass almost totally negates its insulating value.

I control this very carefully. I try to keep the wiring out of the outside wall, using either floor outlets or raceways on the outside wall. There must be a continuous vapour barrier over the inside of the studs. In addition, I am using sheet rock or a similar material, then I use a paint which is not permeable to vapour. You must be absolutely sure to keep vapour out of exterior walls. It is even more important in the ceiling because air tends to rise and moisture collects there. Do not put recessed electrical fixtures or other gadgetry into the ceiling because you are going to interrupt your vapour barrier. In addition, light fixtures recessed into a ceiling build up heat and can create a fire hazard, particularly when there is heavy insulation around them.

"Have you ever built a Trombe wall into a house? If so, how did you attach wood walls to the masonry to take into account the different co-efficient of expansion/contraction of the two materials?"

I have not done that specifically. I have done something similar on old houses that were faced with brick and I have never had trouble with expansion and contraction. This may have been because the wall was rather small and it was broken up with openings. If you ever use a Trombe wall, make sure that your brick is sitting on a solid, concrete foundation. I would attach it with metal ties to the wood framing; that way it would allow for some movement.

"What is your house like?"

It is thoroughly illustrated in *30 Energy Efficient Houses*. It is tiny. I designed it as a vacation cottage and wound up living in it purely by accident. It is not a desirable solar shape, being 11 feet wide and 20 feet long. It has a shed roof with a greenhouse on one side of it. Somewhat similar to the Volkswagon house only about half the size.

"What is the advantage of R20 insulation when windows are R2 and combustion air is needed for wood burning?"

It is fairly easy to make some sort of insulating shutters for windows so that they have an insulating value greater than R2. It is also easy to bring direct outside air into a wood burning appliance and put a damper on it so that it is closed when the wood burning appliance is not burning.

"Did you build a house for $1500.00?"

I just finished writing two books about that, and I could talk the rest of the afternoon on the different techniques that are involved. But I began my architectural work in a poor area of the country, where people did not have money to hire architects. I knew that if I was going to get any work doing houses (which is what I prefer) I had to figure out inexpensive ways to do them. That has been something I have been specializing in for 20 years. My house was the supreme test. It actually cost even less than $1500.00, I inflated the figure to account for inflation when I wrote the book. It actually cost me about $1100.00. It created enough attention that I was on the television program *To Tell the Truth*.

"How do you seal insulating shutters?"

I use a sponge neoprene, not the inferior type that one finds at hardware stores. The sponge neoprene is usually sold by

automobile supply houses or by good hardware suppliers. I use an eccentric cam twist latch that holds the shutter tightly against the neoprene.

"Do you have condensation problems using inside shutters?"

They have been rather minor. On some of the big ones, I have installed a small gutter with a tiny hole to the outside so that there is a weeping area. I try to use a wood such as cedar or cypress for the sills of these windows, one that will not be affected by the action of water.

However, you would have to be more careful in this area. I am sure that your condensation problems would be much greater because of the colder climate.

"Many of your houses have many nooks and crannies on the outside. Wouldn't this tend to be inefficient as they increase the surface area?"

Yes, indeed it would. Any time I add something like that I try to use an insulating shutter to cover the area where the projection joins the house. I do try to avoid things like that in the designs, but sometimes people are willing to cut a little more wood in order to have a house that has some distinction. If you will notice, the basic houses do not have any such projections. They are all compact, close-to-square shapes with the least surface area possible.

"Are there optimum angles for the south wall?"

Yes there are. The general rule of thumb on that is your latitude plus 15°. In my area that means about a 60° slope, but in

northern Alberta, your optimum angle is more nearly vertical. Also, in areas where you have a lot of winter snow cover, you get a great deal of reflection and vertical south glass is quite good.

"Why only a few windows in some of the south walls, instead of putting it full of windows?"

If you do not have something like a Trombe wall or other means of absorbing heat, then you are going to overheat the house. In addition, if it is a small, compact house and thoroughly insulated you do not need sunlight coming in many windows to heat it.

"How do you cool a house in the summer?"

I try to design as open a plan as possible for both heat circulation and air circulation in the summer. The first house I mentioned has small vents at ground level on the north side and more vents at the very top on the south wall, so in the summer you get a chimney effect. The warming of the air causes the air to rise across the front of the house where it is pulled out of the south vents, and cool air is sucked in from the north side.

"Have you done any work on multiple dwellings?"

I spent quite a few years batting my head against the multiple dwelling problem, working with various U.S. and New York State government agencies — all of whom made a mess out of everything because of conflicting regulations. For instance, we tried a Danish pre-cast concrete system, which in Denmark is an efficient way of building houses. But the agencies succeeded in showing that it was the most inefficient method possible in our country.

I wholly agree that with rapidly dwindling energy sources, high density housing is an area that should be looked at. However, the people I have dealt with are the sort of people who live a rather independent life and intend to grow all their own food. A lot of them are people who work at home, and so forth. They are a different class of people from those who would tend to live in an urban or semi-urban area in multiple dwellings. I have only had two or three requests for something like that.

"What are the systems used for heat storage other than masonry walls?"

Forty-five gallon drums with water in them make an economical storage system.

"Can you describe a sloping-glass detail guaranteed not to leak?"

That all has to do with who put it in and what kind of seal was used. Most sealants that one buys at the hardware store, including hardware store grade silicones, just do not do the job. You have to get a better grade sealant and you may have to specially order it. That is all there is to it.

You might get water-tight walls, but when you thoroughly weather-seal a house, and you make the house nearly airtight, you get pressure differentials between the inside and the outside so that water can literally be forced through the walls. It will come through a pin hole even if the pinhole is thoroughly protected from the weather. So I use an acrylic caulking

compound called Mono made by Tremco. It stays elastic forever, and it seals very thoroughly. It does not go on well unless it is warm, about 85°F. I keep it over a light bulb before I use it. I double seal the glass with that. I bed it in, and the material that goes over the outside is again sealed. I have had little trouble with leaks.

"What R values can be obtained in shutters?"

You can make a shutter as much as three inches thick. It is a cumbersome shutter, but I have done it such that when you use a urethane board with R8 per inch, you end up with an R value of 20 to 25.

"Where do you buy insulated shutters in this country?"

You don't. You have to make them. It is as simple as that. Various companies make patented roll up and roll down shutters. There is an outfit in Connecticut that makes a blind which has a pretty good R value. The problem is that all these things are disproportionately expensive compared to the cost of building them yourself. The commercial ones cost anywhere from $3.00 to $10.00 per square foot.

"How safe is the average home in regards to fire?"

Not very safe at all. One of the major causes of death in North America is by fire. Actually it has increased dramatically in the last two or three years. More people are heating with wood. Many suburbanites who had oil furnaces suddenly say they cannot afford the oil, buy a wood stove, set it on a wooden floor, never clean the chimney, and do other

dangerous and foolish things.

On virtually all of my houses I try to use a masonry floor and I have a masonry wall right in the middle of the house next to which the stove is placed. The framing is post and beam, so it is heavy timber. The floor between the first and second floors is open timber. There are no concealed spaces that could cause a fire. The outside wall has horizontal framing members which in effect make a fire stop every two feet. I use a spark arrester on top of the chimney. Most of my houses use metal roofs. They simply do not have a surface that will support fire.

"Given your basic premise of public participation in accomplishing energy savings, what is your estimation of the inhibiting factors in the infra-structure: legal, social, and economic? In general, what ways would you suggest these problems be overcome?"

The legal, social and economic problems have not been nearly as great as I had anticipated they would be. It takes some education and I think people have to be patient and work hard at this. There are certain areas where you are not going to be able to do things like this because they are not going to be accepted. If you go in the middle of a suburb of standard houses and try to build a house like I am recommending, it isn't going to be well received. This is not always the case, however; the basic house that I have talked about is in such a suburb and is being well received. I have considered the problem of acceptance and the basic house was designed to take advantage of as many of my ideas as possible while still carefully taking into account the sort of things that a bank wants to see in a house for resale ability.

"Are you aware of the Saskatchewan Conservation House and what are your thoughts on it for this climate?"

Yes, I am certainly aware of it and I commented on it somewhat in my latest book. I think that possibly the expenses of doing all the things that were done would override the benefits to the average person, but I certainly think a lot of the features are applicable. It is something that is worthwhile studying because you can pick and choose your features from it.

"Could you comment on insulating with earth? How much vapour barrier, etc.?"

Quite a few houses are bermed one full story at the back. The foundation wall is insulated to below the frost line with anywhere from two to four inches of urethane. Over that is a thorough vapour barrier which will keep out moisture. There is a perimeter drain.

"Why don't they paint houses black?"

Someone suggested that the trailer industry should do an energy-efficient trailer and paint the south side of it black. But if you paint an insulated wall, you are really not doing much. You are just increasing the surface temperature of the outside wall.

"What kind of glass do you recommend?"

For virtually all of my glazing, I use a standard, insulating glass door. This is double pane, tempered glass usually 45 by 76 inches.

Malcolm Wells

Malcolm Wells *is a long-time proponent of underground housing. He has designed and built dozens of underground homes, offices and businesses since the mid-sixties. He is the author of* How to Buy Solar Heating Without Getting Burnt, Underground Housing, *and is co-author of* Passive Solar Energy.

This is not as far north as I have been, because this morning I went a mile north of Fairview. *That* was as far north as I have been.

Just before I left Cape Cod, Massachusetts, I had a call from a friend of mine who works in the U.S. Department of State. He has known for some time that I have been concerned about possible U.S. intentions involving oil in the Middle East and whether we might go over there and try to take some of it for ourselves. He assured me that U.S. foreign policy now ruled that out completely and that the latest policy was for the annexation of Canada and Mexico.

Welcome.

Coming from where I do, I have become an expert in a lot of things — like ugliness and pollution and what architects do — things that you have not really begun to see here, even in your larger cities. We really do it right, down below. What has happened on the eastern seaboard of the United States is a picture of what is coming here in one form or another, unless you do everything in your power to stop it.

There are nice parts of New Jersey, which is where I am from, but the common conception of New Jersey is that it is polluted, asphalted, overpopulated, ugly, noisy. And it *is* all of those things. And those things are on the march; I see them coming here. New Jersey is what Alberta could become if Albertans are not careful.

Do not let what happened to New Jersey happen to this area.

For the first ten or fifteen years of my architectural life I ground out factories for a big company, all over the world. I destroyed forests and farms and thought nothing at all about it. I put in big heaters and big air conditioners and I made a lot of money. I did all sorts of research on office buildings and thought that I was doing pretty good stuff. For too long, I concentrated on tricky details — trying to get effects and textures and every once in a while using a little bit of greenery as a decoration on buildings. But most of it was just an attempt to get an impressive look here and there, with very little thought as to what architecture itself was all about.

But then I became smarter — or so I thought. My first office building in New Jersey was a shed-shaped building with almost no insulation. But it was covered with vines and surrounded by trees and shrubs and everyone still believes that it is a conservationist's building. It was thought that I did a great job there; it looks as though it is part of nature.

But of course it is not. It is a terrible, terrible heat waster. All the sewage goes away untreated into the river. The rainwater that falls on it rushes off down into another stream. The electric lights blaze away all the time. It is really bad stuff, and yet I got away with it and most architects can still get away with that sort of thing.

The green plant is the life system on this planet. All the land, all the oceans, are supposed to be covered with green plants. That is what I believe life is all about. And that is what architecture should be all about. And yet all of us who build or develop or design or engineer structures do nothing but destroy that very life principle.

So I began attemping to do a few things differently with earth berming and a better type of ground cover. It was a very timid approach at trying to do things a little better but I was amazed to see how well it worked and how widely accepted it was. And that gave me courage to take other timid little steps.

I visited Frank Lloyd Wright's underground theatre in Arizona on a hot June day in 1960. The inside of that open air, underground theatre was delightfully cool and I think that that made a little light bulb go on in my head. About that same time I went to visit an underground house in west Texas. The house is a concrete vault thirteen feet below the earth. Inside the vault there is a complete Cape Cod cottage with plastic flowers in the window boxes and electronic sunsets outside the windows. It really works beautifully, it uses almost no energy, it is silent and they never have to dust. But I thought it was horrible. I could not get out of there fast enough.

That was not what I would propose in the way of underground architecture. I realized that we needed sunlight and a little bit of outdoor exposure. I believe that the priorities should be these: living plants, then living people, then the machinery. This is about the opposite of what we have been doing up to this point. We see machinery on top of buildings, on top of land, with people inside of those horrible things.

So I began doing designs which illustrated that perhaps an underground house might not have to be sunless and windowless. I designed a museum, a World's Fair

building, a complete urban redevelopment. I even designed an underground airport which originally was to have taken up 70-square-miles of land for all the approach roads and fields and everything related to a giant airport, but by putting everything but the runways underneath, would have taken only seven-square-miles of land. But none of these things were built.

My early designs were based on the idea of trapping earth and water within a giant parapet on the roof of a building, which I now believe would have lead to all kinds of frost problems.

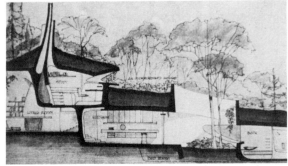

Early sketches of an underground home

Another near disaster was an underground auditorium in New Jersey. I was going to leave the natural rock wall exposed inside. It would have been a horrible heat loser and a damp place. In addition, the frost would have pushed the proposed parapet wall away from over the entrance. But, the good forces were looking over me and none of these things were built.

Since no one was having any of this, I decided to build an office for myself. I built two little square buildings facing each other across an open courtyard. They stood on a 59-foot-wide lot between a freeway and a sewer. The property had been completely asphalted over by a highway construction crew. So we started at zero and took it forward a little bit.

Since I wanted to grow mature New Jersey trees on the roof, I put a lot of steel in the concrete-slab roof. It is designed to carry 600 pounds per square foot. I did not want my first building to collapse. It stood up very well. We wrapped the entire structure in butyl rubber sheets. Butyl rubber is excellent material for wrapping underground buildings, but it is expensive. The cost is about 75 cents a square foot for the material, and the labour is quite high. But it is impermeable to water and is quite tough. One-sixteenth of an inch of butyl rubber, which is like inner tube material, will take a pretty sharp blow from the edge of a shovel without being cut and it is said to last forever. I have never had a leak using it.

After the office building was completed it was back filled and covered with mulch. Aside from a few cedar trees on top, we did not plant a single thing. The seeds that were in the mulch or that blew there or that were carried there by birds and other animals did all the landscaping. Each year it was a little bit different and it always seemed to get better. Beautiful summer greenness and, in the fall, riotous colours.

Wells' office with natural vegetation

On sunny days a skylight in one of the offices, four feet in diameter, provided all the light I needed to do my drafting. But on cloudy days it was not adequate. So I lined the inner walls of the skylight with aluminum foil, which costs 39 cents, using a bit of linoleum paste for the gluing. With this simple technique I got eight times as much light into that room and apparently eight times as much solar heat, because we did not have to use any other kind of heating until November of that year.

The first underground building was not insulated at all. I thought at that time that earth was the perfect insulator; I found out it was not. It is not, in fact, really an insulator at all, but it has wonderful characteristics which solve heating problems. It allows no air to penetrate the building, and it changes its temperature very slowly. My neighbour's roof, which actually was fairly well insulated, lost its

snow long before my uninsulated earth covered roof lost its snow. That does not really prove anything, because the heat loss from my building was far greater than my neighbour's, but it does demonstrate the thermally massive nature of all that soil.

Insulating the exterior of the house

My first proposals were concrete boxes set in hillsides. They would obviously be terrible heat bleeders. Any kind of a continuous indoor/outdoor architecture material, other than perhaps wood, really bleeds the heat. So it calls for a different kind of design. A better approach uses trellises instead of structurally connected overhangs, and wrapping the outsides of the structure with insulating materials.

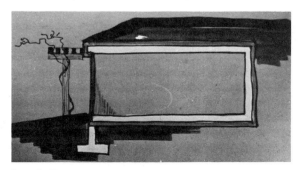

Insulation wraps the entire house

I had to retrofit my little New Jersey underground office with insulation on the ceiling. I also installed hinged, insulating shutters which are really effective. One inch of urethane was able to reduce the heat loss of that building by 50 per cent.

The architect's specialty is the false front. Nowadays we are pretty good at hiding things but somewhere, with every building, with every beautiful high rise in the city there is a garbage dump and there is a huge parking lot and there is an oversized electrical service coming in and there is smoke being produced somewhere. But we do not see those things. We go home and remember the fronts of buildings, even though we very often enter them from the other side.

There is, in the U.S.A., a strip mining mentality. Of course, in Canada you'd never see such a thing — Canadians take such good care of their land. But in the U.S.A. we farm the top soil away and we dig out the resources and dump them into the air. We build all over the surface of the land with utter disregard for all the life principles. None of the architects are studying biology. This is all due to the strip mining mentality and it is coming your way, courtesy of the U.S.A.

I believe the best approach is called sky-mining — using the earth to reduce the impact of buildings to whatever extent possible. We can then mostly get along on the renewable resources of the sky, which are rain, wind, oxygen, and sunlight. It is the way that the human animal is supposed to live on the planet. I am convinced of that, but we are a long way from it.

An early earth-covered house of mine is a north sloping shed with a large south side exposed. It uses the Thomason active solar heating system in which water simply trickles down black aluminum plates under glass then goes into a tank under the floor around which air is blown to warm the house. The house is timber framed. It has two inches of styrofoam which wrapped it entirely on all surfaces and it has about two feet of earth on the roof. During the great New Jersey winter of 1976, it burned no fuel at all.

The north-side of the house disappears under vegetation

Another recent project was in New York state, an office and lab for the New York Botanical Garden. It works surprisingly well, even beyond the solar engineer's predictions. It has external insulation, high thermal mass, solar heating, and window shutters which are religiously closed every afternoon when the sun goes down and whenever the sun is not shining. And it performs beautifully. All of the lighting in the building is daylight. The interiors are lighted by skylights and on each skylight there is a two inch thick, tightly fitted insulating shutter which is closed at night.

Wind problems can be solved using wind breaks. Structures do not have to be fully underground to cut out some of the devestating affect of the cold winds.

In southern New Jersey, there is a three storey library building which is not underground but has earth on the roof and a large earth berm on the north side up against three storey window wells which keep the wind from scouring a lot of the heat away from the glass surfaces. It also has exterior insulation and window covers and so on. That building was only approved by a very conservative board of freeholders because the Arab oil embargo had occurred the month before. It is just a big three storey box, but it performs pretty well. I was the design consultant and I recommended no parapets, but a deep mulch. A deep mulch will, in almost every case, completely keep the earth from eroding, providing the earth below the mulch is raked back to what is called its natural angle of repose, which angle you can get from any civil engineering handbook. I recommended that the building be covered with mulch and allowed to go wild.

But the architect was not quite ready to try that, so he put high parapet walls along the edge of the roof and used exotic, imported plants which require irrigation.

Earth-sheltered library

There are many incorrect procedures that are still being taught in the architectural schools. Continuous indoor/outdoor materials, great overhangs on north sides, heating pipes under the floor near the foundation where they bleed the heat away, wasteful fireplaces, we are still doing all these things. Even here in Fairview, I suspect.

We must start to use the free heat of the sun on the south side, use reflectors out of doors when there is no snow to bounce the light in, maybe use more efficient wood burning devices, earth cover, external insulation, put the heat pipes within the space that is to be heated so that when they do lose their heat, they lose it usefully — these things are terribly important and yet they are not being taught today. So it seems that *you* have to educate your architects. This is, in fact, the way it has always happened. We architects have to be kicked before we will move.

I always took my clients to the finest and most beautiful forest sites and told them to build there. Then I would go in and destroy the site for them and relandscape later. Now I try to get people to build on worn out sites that have been worked over for years — old parking lots, strip mines, eroded farm land. They are beautiful challenges and they cost less, too. You can have the pleasure of renewing land, of restoring it to life with architecture, instead of destroying it with architecture.

That is really what I think this is all about, far more than the energy savings. Energy is a good motive at the moment, and it gets a lot of people going, but much more than that is involved. The whole attitude of man toward the land has got to go back to the old ways.

Something else that is helpful is the idea of a very small building — something that people like Alex Wade are so good at. There is a stigma, though, attached to living in small houses which is going to be tough to overcome. Paradoxically, those people who can afford it will go on weekends and live in the very smallest of houses, provided they are floating. People will put up with the most uncomfortable conditions and will love it because it is a prestigious thing to do. Maybe we can somehow get across the idea that the alternatives are also prestigious and patriotic. Living in small spaces is a good way to save energy.

Another energy saver is the idea of a small window. The smallest window used, I believe, is the one that some of us have in front of our eyes hanging on our noses. By sitting very close to your eye glasses you can see giant scenes through them. Similarly, if you sit close to small building windows you can see giant scenes through them, just as you do through the windows of your automobiles. Windows therefore, do not have to be large and it makes great sense to keep them small, and all on the south sides of buildings.

Earth cover has a lot of appeal, as soon as people realize that it is not slimey and spidery and wet and crawly and full of death connotations. Earth covered buildings can be very appropriate, down to earth and full of mystery. There are many, many expressions. There are successful underground houses with swimming pools in the centre that act as its main thermal mass. I think underground houses are more appropriate and mysterious and have more potential for beauty than any other kind of building.

Underground swimming pool

But remember that earth is a heavy liquid which will always move when given a chance. I get a lot of planned proposals from people around the country and I find among them two frequent horrors. One is the feeling that concrete itself is an absolutely safe and perfectly strong structural material. Of course, it is no stronger than paper if it is designed improperly. A competent structural engineer or an architect must design for the tremendous earth pressures, especially in the north where you have frost pressures. The other thing I have found is that many people have designed into-the-hill, south-facing homes in which the bedrooms are way back in the hill with only one way out. There are going to be some real disasters if people continue to build them that way.

Fire is a problem in any building. We use so many plastic materials today that can produce toxic, noxious fumes, there must be adequate exits. Window exits, skylight exits, tunnels are three ways out.

Builders must comply with the building code. It was not written for nothing, and I do not think that it limits architectural design much at all. Everything in the code is there because of some horrible catastrophe and we do not want to generate any more of those things.

There are certain resource materials which are needed to build an earth-sheltered house. Butyl rubber is perhaps the most important. There is a companion product produced by some companies called EPDM. It is cheaper than butyl and reputedly works just as well. I believe that a material called Hypolon produced by Dupont will also work, and it is even cheaper. But butyl is the toughest material that I have found.

Bentonite is a clay that expands when it gets wet as all clays do, but it now comes in both bag form and panel form. Four-by-four foot sheets of corrugated cardboard are available between which a thin film of this clay material is placed so that it can be put against the walls of an underground building, overlapping the panels of course. This is completely waterproof when done property. It is not a vapour barrier, however.

Lightweight soil has been used for years in greenhouses and in a few other places where lightness of weight has been useful, but very seldom has it been used on earth covered buildings, where lightness of weight is also an important factor. Grace and Cambridges make all kinds of lightweight fill.

Gordon Schnieder in Oregon has produced several kinds of binders that he mixes with cellulose products and earth to get a nailable, insulating, waterproof, one-shot earth material. He feels that many buildings in the future will be built of his products. He calls them Cellusoil. Excess sawdust, newspapers or farm vegetable products might be profitably mixed with local soil, using Mr. Schnieder's methods.

Various underground houses

"Would you summarize the factors that make underground housing attractive?"

Today most people are concerned about energy prices, but in the long run we will learn to build underground because it will give us a much more pleasant world.

When I began considering underground structures back in the 1960s, I never thought about energy. I was thinking about runoff, wildlife, and green space as opposed to asphalt and concrete, and that is really what the former is going to give us.

"Are underground houses suitable in all climates, particularly the colder climates in this part of the world?"

I am very hesitant about saying an unqualified yes to that because I have been rather surprised by your frost depth and a lot of things that happen in the northern parts of the province. But I am convinced, if it is done properly, earth-covered architecture is appropriate almost anywhere. It does have many benefits.

"One of the aspects of underground architecture is the extra space that becomes available . . . more parks can be provided in densely populated areas, but in Alberta we have a great deal of open space. Would underground accommodation still be attractive here?"

You can have a lot of advantages with earth cover that people associate with places that are miles away. You can have the open space, the silence and the privacy so that you need not build one to an acre or three to an acre, but maybe twenty to an acre and still have all the amenities that you had hoped for: gardens, the whole business.

"What is the best material to use for mulch?"

Whatever you have. Mulch consists of any unwanted organic material, wood chips, hay, straw, chopped up newspapers, garbage; they all have various characteristics. I have found that perhaps the most ideal material to use in holding slopes is pine needles. I have found that the slope will not wash away at all.

"What is the angle of repose for most topsoil types?"

You would be safe in going two over and one up with almost any soil that has a bit of binder in it. But if you are really seriously interested, look at a civil engineering handbook. It has a table showing every soil's angle of repose.

"You must have encountered many institutional barriers. Are they diminishing with more underground buildings being built?"

I have not found that many. It seems to me that when people dare to do something, all the barriers melt away. That is probably not true for poor people. They seem to have insurmountable barriers. But if you have any kind of income at all and if you are really interested, I think you can make the barriers disappear. In every case, in my experience, that is what has happened. Years ago there were people who had terrible problems getting money for underground houses, but they did their homework, they completed their sketches and their heat loss calculations and their fuel savings and they went to bank after bank until they got their loan. It just depends on how serious you are.

"Do you have problems with vandals on your accessible roofs?"

I do not know if that will be a real problem or not. But that reminds me that you must put safety fences on the roofs of these buildings. They can be cleverly hidden among shrubbery, but you do not want little children falling off the edges of roofs, which they could very easily do. For a few dollars you can buy very cheap fencing and paint it with a mixture of black, brown and green paint so that you get sort of a natural colour, and put around some shrubbery. The fencing disappears and you can sleep comfortably.

"If we all use wood fuel, won't we live in a polluted desert?"

I don't believe that. A lot of woodburning experts are telling me that that will not happen. It might if we continue to use conventional houses, with poor insulation. But if we start to do things properly we will not use much wood.

"Please specify reflective materials for in and outside."

Inside I like cheap aluminum foil, with linoleum paste as the adhesive. It goes on easily. You spread the paste on the wall or on whatever surface you are treating, roll out the aluminum foil, smooth it with a sponge, and then a damp sponge washes away the excess paste. It goes on in a few minutes. For the outside there are plywood panels that come with aluminum sheets bonded to them but you can also make up your own reflective panels, probably using aluminum. White chipped stones, for instance, do not work as well because the building sees the shadow side of each stone. You really need something more like white paper, which happens to be an ideal type of reflective material for many of the parts of the solar spectrum, but it does not hold up well out of doors.

If you do use a reflective aluminum plate material on a roof for instance, perhaps below some high dormer windows, you do not want that metal plate to become a vapour barrier on the outside of the building. So it should be raised above the roof or ventilated so that vapour beneath the roof will not be trapped by the reflective plate or sheet.

"How does one keep dirt on sloped roofs?"

Well, first of all you should not slope the roof too much. But if you do slope it more than about one and a half or two in twelve, you should probably have cleats on the roof. The effect will be like a tire tread to hold that great mass of earth from sliding. Then the waterproofing can go right over the cleats. On the early New Jersey shed-roof house we ran long two-by-four cleats, not straight along the slope, but slightly diagonally so that there would be drainage, then draped the butyl sheets over the cleats. Sheets on cleat we call it.

"Do you know of any underground building which has escaped the eye of the tax assessor?"

How would I know of them? It is a good idea, though.

"What can be done to encourage underground buildings in areas with very high water table?"

Well, you must simply build above the water table, and that might mean building on the surface of the land and mounding earth over the building. You create an artificial hill and the wildlife and the plants love it. It does its job thermally and it is quite inexpensive. In that way you can build almost anywhere. Do not get down into the water table where you will be bound to rely on pumps if anything goes wrong.

"How do you ventilate or otherwise maintain fresh air?"

I have never found that to be a problem. Perhaps my buildings leak more than they should, but keep in mind that we do not use that much oxygen. I believe that we could all be sealed in a room for a long time before we would start to fall over. Of course, indoor plants will help a lot.

"How do you control humidity?"

I think one of the most delightful surprises about concrete and heavy masonry materials is their ability to absorb moisture. I know of an underground, uninsulated concrete building on the foggiest, dampest part of Cape Cod, in which the windows are left wide open all summer and the fog rolls in and out, and yet there is not the least bit of condensation or mildew or dampness in the house. It must be because that great mass of concrete absorbs the excess moisture, then in dry periods releases it. But you can get into trouble with mildew and related problems if you create unventilated conditions behind closets or in places where the wall may stay cool while the summer air is moist and warm. You must try to keep air moving through the buildings, or warm the walls, or let in some additional sunlight.

"Do you use post-and-beam in underground housing?"

I have used wood and it works very well. In Minnesota and, I understand, in Saskatchewan there are many timber underground buildings with treated wood foundations and wood walls. It seems to work well and I guess it has a lot of potential here where you have tremendous frost.

"Tell us about the necessity and methods of watering vegetation on roof slopes."

I believe that unless you have a vegetable garden on your roof you should not water it at all. The whole point of this kind of architecture is to try to conserve resources. You will find that if you do no landscaping at all, then natural vegetation will set up its own life cycle. The successful plants will thrive and the others will die and the cycle will go on until a balance is achieved. In a dry year, perhaps everything will die, but seeds will drop and mulch will hold the soil. The next year you will have another succession of plants. It operates perfectly, but you have to give them a chance. You must have a sufficient depth of earth on the roof or it becomes just a dry little desert.

"How do you eliminate the moisture generated by change in temperature?"

I think the concrete really does work in your favour. Except for perhaps the first year when the concrete is drying out, it really is a good moisture blotter. You must waterproof thoroughly on the outside, though. That is the key.

"How should one build a lawn on top of sand?"

If you have nothing but sand, you may have a tough time getting anything to grow unless you put a lot of mulch on top of it. Even so, there are plants that will thrive in that environment and I would suggest that you just let them grow.

"Have you encountered any special problems when trades people are involved in the construction of unconventional designs?"

Yes, cost. Most of us are frightened by the unusual and we have to be educated a little bit. But those barriers are falling away. A lot of contractors today are leading the architects in innovative design techniques. They would like to try these new things that are becoming so successful. If you work things out well in advance with the contracting people a lot of the barriers melt away.

"Please discuss cost efficiency of underground construction in initial construction costs and ongoing maintenance costs."

Underground structures are almost exactly comparable in costs to conventional, above-ground structures. The underground ones were about ten per cent higher a few years ago, but they are right in line now. The fuel savings, of course, are tremendous.

The exterior maintenance can be very low if you do the original work properly. Waterproofing has got to be done perfectly if you want to stay out of trouble. You have to be there and either do it yourself or watch the people who are doing it to make sure there are no little surprises left under the sheet, or any gaps or unglued places. Butyl rubber sheets, for instance, have a very strong memory. They do not like to be stretched, and if you stretch them too far while applying them, they will not like it, and will try to go back where they were. The glued seams might tend to open up. You have got to work with the material and be mindful of what it wants to do.

With earth covering, the building is not exposed to sunlight, which is a building's worst enemy in terms of deterioration.

"Is there a way of attaching styrofoam to a wall without using nails? And stucco to styrofoam?"

Yes, styrofoam can be glued to butyl waterproofing sheets. It can also be stuck directly to mastic waterproofings. It seems to go on beautifully without problems. I cover much of my styrofoam exterior with stucco, which is cement plaster on galvanized metal laths. Originally I used a lot of treated, wood blocking in the plane of the insulation to bolt the lath and the stucco to the structure. But I am finding that the stucco skirt that must come down over the first few feet of styrofoam can be lightly attached providing there is going to be earth fill against it. Once backfilling is done, the earth holds everything in place.

No one has asked yet about roots and rodents, but that is a common question. The roots apparently will not go through the waterproofing if the water is not getting through. They only want to go where the water is. I suppose that roots will in time try to get in between the layers of the styrofoam, into those nice, warm, moist places, and you should keep them out. I try to run the skirt of stucco from the surface down at least three or four feet so that it is deep enough to discourage most roots and most rodents from getting in there under the comfortable layers.

"What about the weed inspector who says you have noxious, if natural, weeds on your roof?"

There is a woman in Milwaukee named Lorrie Otto who has successfully defended several people in suits of that type in which neighbours have claimed that they were being damaged by wildflower landscapes. The tendency seems to be against the green lawn now, so that, at least in the United States, the legal precedent is in favour of the wildflowers.

"To what depths have you gone?"

I believe that we can go as far down as we wish, just as we can go a hundred stories up, providing the buildings comply with the safety codes. If the structures are adequate and the codes are complied with, you can go up or down as far as you like.

"At what temperature would butyl rubber be applied? Will it contract at cold temperatures?"

It will contract a little but it has enough give in it that that would not be a problem. Butyl must be applied at above freezing temperatures, but it is pretty tolerant in its ranges.

"Do you recommend that every aboveground house be multi-storey with at least one storey underground?"

The more you do the better. You can go a little bit of a distance with each of these things or you can go all the way, but the rewards are fantastic. And they are not all monetary, there are a lot of greater rewards I believe.

"What are the general principles or rules to follow in the construction of underground homes in matters like strength of walls, insulation and waterproofing?"

Number one is to keep the water out and number two is to make sure the structure is adequate. First you investigate the soil conditions and use straightforward waterproofing techniques in the proper way. Then you make sure that the building will carry the earth loads involved. You must not guess at structural matters. You must engage a structural engineer or architect, and that costs surprisingly little if you present your case to him or her properly. It really pays off.

Then, after waterproofing and structure, comes ventilation, proper fire exits, those sorts of things. But it is all straightforward, commonsense.

"In this part of the world, should we put insulation around the entire building?"

Oh, yes. We just learned a few years ago to put insulation on the outside of a building, and that is where it belongs. You must do it underground, too, because the earth can be cold and it can drain a lot of heat away otherwise.

"What are the specific characteristics of butyl rubber that make it better than, say, a 6 mil polyethylene vapour barrier?"

There are too many ways that polyethylene barriers can be damaged during construction. Butyl is a 60 mil material, much thicker, much tougher, and it is not subject to the deterioration that many polyethylene products are.

Jim Bohlen

Jim Bohlen *is a research and design engineer who has worked on projects ranging from building domes to the rocket design of guided missiles. He helped found* Greenpeace *and authored the* New Pioneer's Handbook. *Bohlen now lives at the Greenpeace Experimental Farm in British Columbia.*

In 1971 I started to write a book which was called *Low Energy Use Life-styles.* It was finished in 1972 and submitted to a number of publishers in Canada and the United States. The manuscript was returned numerous times but, undaunted, I waited for the energy crises, which happened in 1973. In 1974 the book was published because anything that was publishable in the area of energy use was put on the market at that time. It was then retitled *The New Pioneer's Handbook.*

In their desire to get the attention of the public, the publishers wrote on the flyleaf that I was living on a farm and practicing what I had written. I had no idea they had written it. When I saw the book I had terrible misgivings about maintaining credibility. So my wife and I went out and bought a farm and we moved onto it. I've been trying to follow the book ever since.

I'd like to discuss my environmental concerns in combination with what we have tried to do on the farm. I hope that it will all make sense to you. In my life I have gone from rockets to forest products and there is a lot of work in between. It may be interesting to some of you how I got from there to here. What I'd like to do is present a kind of history of how the Greenpeace Experimental Farm developed.

British Columbia is a beautiful province. We have such things as alpine meadows, in which there is very little air pollution. We have free flowing wild rivers. But we also have logging sites near those same rivers. I call them mining operations because sometimes the trees have been cut off of a vertical cliff. I don't believe there is any way that a tree planter is going to climb up and regenerate a rocky slope, unless he's half billy goat. You have to see it to believe it. All you see now is a grey cliff that was once covered with trees that were 80 to 120 feet high and about four to six feet in diameter and probably took a thousand years to get that way.

Logging operation

On Vancouver Island is a place called Nanaimo where smoke, ordinary water vapour, plus a few chemicals escaping from smoke-stacks, create a blanket of pollution almost every day which covers a distance of 25 to 30 miles in either direction and will actually go into Vancouver, which is about 40 miles away.

View of Nanaimo

Having these concerns and seeing what's happening to what is perhaps some of the most beautiful natural environment in the world, I tried to think of why all this occurs. And how am I a part of the problem? Basically I'm part of the problem because I read books; books require paper to be printed on. I use lumber for my house and I use energy to get from point A to point B. So some years ago I thought that the thing to do was to use as little of these resources as possible. And that was the beginning of the *Greenpeace Experimental Farm.*

The first thing to do was to find some land. On the way up to an oil spill in Alert Bay in 1971 I noticed that there was a nice little island called Denman Island which is protected from the heavy rains coming in from the Pacific Ocean by a range of mountains called the Beaufort range. The air from the Pacific Ocean deposits approximately 140-200 inches of rain each year on the west coast of Vancouver Island. About 120 miles further east, where Denman Island is located, we get about 40 inches of rain, which is comparable to a normal east coast rain regime.

The farm was carved out of the bush by hand and oxen in 1906. The whole farm was totally clear cut and the lumber skidded into the Georgia Straight and towed down to Vancouver for production into timber. The cedar which was left behind, and which in those days was not merchantable, was split up and rail fences were made of it. I guess that's not such an uncommon thing to find in the more remote parts of this country. An old logging road provides access to the property.

It is on this farm that we began our experiment of building structures that use minimal material.

We began by constructing a 16 foot diameter dome, adding to it a front porch and a cupola. We used wooden pegs to fasten the connections of the structural elements instead of nails or bolts. The design was inspired by children's Tinker Toys. The people who put the dome together had practically zero building experience, yet the frame was done in the course of about four hours. We covered the structure using hand split cedar shakes which we made from the logs we found on the property. (They had been cut in the 1906 logging operation.) The cedar logs were about four or five feet in diameter and had some rot on the outside, but the centers were as sound as they were when the tree was alive. A load test was provided by the first heavy, wet winter snow — which represents 30 to 40 pounds per square foot.

Building and testing the first dome

There was a king in Babylon named Hammurabi who developed the first building code in the world. It stated, "If a builder shall build a house and the house shall fall down and kill the owners, the builder shall pay with his life." It's good, isn't it? It eliminates a lot of problems. We've become more civilized since then.

From the experience that we'd gained in building this structure, we decided to build our house. We also decided that we would continue with the domes because we had had a lot of success with them, despite the fact that books had been written about how domes leak and have numerous other problems. We learned that domes don't leak, people build leaky domes. There's a slight difference.

We built two twenty-foot domes connected by a short passageway. They face slightly west of south and the natural shading of the trees, which are 80 foot high Douglas Fir, provide total shading in the summer and yet, because of our high latitude, we get full sun on the back wall of the dome in the winter. This was built in the days before thermal mass was any consideration. If I were going to do it again I'd probably have a thermal mass situation, probably a concrete floor.

Double domes on Greenpeace farm

Our domes are built on posts, in the Japanese fashion where the posts do not contact the ground directly. Instead, they sit on top of stones that have been rammed into the earth below frost level. The bottom of the post has been carved to sit on top of the stone. This is similar to Japanese tea houses. It makes a remarkably stable structure.

There are very few windows on the north side with extensive areas of glass on the south. In the middle of the house we built a brick wall, which separates what's nominally known as the living room from the bedroom, so that when we sleep our heads are against the brick wall. I had noticed that when sleeping the hardest thing to keep warm in a cold room is your head, unless you wear a stocking cap, and I'm not about to do that. I decided to try to store some heat in this wall, and it works fairly well.

We get snows in which it will start snowing and not stop until there's about a three of four foot accumulation. It's not dry, powdery snow, it's wet. It's so wet that about a week after it snows it's all gone. It just turns into water and runs away. But it makes everything beautiful. Trees are all covered with snow. Our whole driveway, which is about a mile long, is surrounded by evergreens. The snow gets so heavy on the evergreens that it pushes them all down across the driveway and there's no way you can get out. So we discovered an old technique — snowshoes. That's the only way we can get in or out after one of these snowstorms.

It is another reason why we could not put electricity back to our house. To install power lines would be disasterous in this kind of heavy snow situation, unless you want a fifty foot right-of-way through your trees. It would have cost about $8000 to go underground and we didn't want to spend that.

We had fully intended to use wind generators for electricity. But in 1976 I was connected with the Habitat Forum in Vancouver. There were supposed to be six operating wind generators and I spent a month before the windmills arrived making assessments of the wind potential. It wasn't too bad, averaging something like 8 to 10 miles per hour. According to the books I had read, you should be able to produce electricity.

The cheapest of these wind generators was in the order of $3000.00. We invited BC Hydro to connect up to our system and we would produce electricity for them. I was waiting with breathless anticipation, I would love to sell Hydro some electricity, instead of buying it from them. But I have to report that none of the systems produced any measurable electricity. In fact, one of the units, the verticle axis unit, had to be run by Hydro before it would even start, although I'm told now that that problem has been solved. But there are a lot of problems still remaining with wind systems. When you are dealing with these alternate technologies and something is not going to work you can tell it. If you have any experience with design engineering you feel in the seat of your pants that it's not the time to get involved in this technology. In 1976 that's what I felt.

On our farm we also discovered that since we're surrounded by eighty foot trees, we'd have to get above them somehow with the wind generator. It meant building a high tower and putting the wind generator on top of it.

So we settled for a Princess Auto Wreckers rebuilt truck engine generator and a Briggs and Straton motor. This unit has performed nicely for the last three years, and it has had to run a number of hours a day in order to produce the amount of electricity we need. The power is stored in two Caterpillar tractor batteries which give us a total ampere hour capacity of about four hundred.

Generator and battery system

The generator is so damn loud when it runs that you wished you'd plugged into BC Hydro. So we decided to see how little electricity we could get by on so that we wouldn't have to run the noise maker any longer than necessary.

Most of our lights are ordinary crane lights that you can buy in any department store. Each of them has a 15 watt, 12 volt bulb in it. It is part of our experiment of seeing how little light we actually do need. We started out with 25 watt bulbs in our reading lamps and found that they were practically burning a hole through our books because there was so much light. We cut down to 20 watts and then to 15 watts and found that that was pretty good. There's some fringe benefits from that kind of lighting. Because you can articulate it almost 360° and move it anywhere you want, I now, for the first time in my life, can find my socks in my beaureau drawer. All I have to do is open up the drawer, pull the light over, turn it on — and there they are! And they are both the same colour!

We also have the same type of lighting fixture above the sink, and it has the same value in being able to get into the kitchen cabinets to look for the little jar of herbs that you can't normally find.

Crane lighting system in the kitchen

How much electricity do we use? Over the last two years we've used an average of 2 kilowatt hours per week, or 8¢ worth if we were to buy it. That's for our entire homestead, and yet there is not one amenity that we do not have. We have HiFi, we have the occasional use of small appliances, we have all the lighting we need. If we had young children who were living with us I would imagine our consumption might be another kilowatt hour a week. So you can see, if you really want to or have to, you don't need very much electricity in your personal lifestyle.

We have a 25¢ composting toilet. (I hope there's no sales representative from Clivus Multrum listening.) We use a 5 gallon white pail which comes from A & W root beer. We fill that with rotting tree material, which we get from the floor of the surrounding forest and which is already almost composted. Every time we use the toilet, which is another 5 gallon pail inside of a hopper, we just take a layer of this humus and lightly cover the toilet pail so it looks like nobody used it.

A 25¢ composting toilet

The criteria we use is that you have to cover the toilet paper. That way it always looks like a nice earthen floor, so the aesthetics are acceptable as well. The hopper box is ventilated to the outside from the bottom. Air comes up between your behind and the seat and carries odors up the stack. Because of that feature, you don't stay there very long. But we discovered that it did not smell in any case, so last year we said to heck with the smell and we sealed off the vent and took in a library book.

The heating system: a Jotul 606

Both domes were equipped with chimneys. We're happy to report that after two winters, the only thing we need to heat our total of 720 square feet plus the 14 foot high ceilings is a Jotul model 606,

a small stove. We use approximately 3 cords of wood per year to do that, a mixture of Douglas Fir and Alder, which is a soft wood something like the poplar that you have here. Our cooking is done with a wood cookstove, which also heats our hot water.

The house is equipped with a muscle power water pumping system. Our pump, which was purchased from a company in Cincinatti, Ohio — the only place in North America where I could find such a pump, can either pump water directly into the sink or up into a storage tank which consists of an old used bathtub. This tank is in the attic, and the attic is only 18 inches above my head, yet we get a tremendous amount of water when we want it. You might think that you need 30 pounds of pressure, but we only believe that because in today's houses they use pipe that is so small in diameter that you do need 30 pounds of pressure to push the water through it. But when you put the water close to its point of use and use 3/4 inch diameter tubing, you get a tremendous flow. Those are the little things, the fine tunings that you learn.

There are about six of us living on the farm full time. We try to operate it as a sort of cooperative community. We do all the work in common, but we live our lives privately.

One dwelling was built by an 18-year old who never did much building before. It is a structure which we call an Eco-Cabin, which is basically an icosohedron with the bottom section cut off. Its structural elements consist of 12 2 x 6's, 10 feet long. Those 12 2 x 6's hold up a 4,000 pound sod roof. We have a beautiful grass crop on the roof every year. Now if

we could figure out how to get that kind of a grass crop on our fields we would have it made, because there is no fertilizer or anything else put on. However, we think that the wood smoke coming out of the chimney does deposit some nutrients on the roof and perhaps that's one reason it grows so well.

We try to use as many natural materials as possible in our buildings. In addition to using such things as cedar poles and cedar shakes, we have a small mill that works with our chain saw from which we make structural components out of Douglas Fir. At other times we try to use recycled materials, such as the automobile glass used in a prototype of the Eco-Cabin.

We are currently constructing our resource centre. It is a barn-type building equipped in such a fashion that it will serve as a laboratory. We expect to be doing research in appropriate technology relevent to our island and to the microclimate in which we are located. One thing we are including is a Farrolones-type, two hole composting toilet. Whether it works or not in our particular bioregion remains to be seen. However, we have an alternate use for that device. If it doesn't work, it is going to become a potato cellar. After all, you can't afford to experiment too much.

The barn is the familiar Dutch colonial design, but the very bottom portion of the roof, the part that overhangs the sides, is corrugated fibreglass which runs the whole length of the building on both sides. This allows natural light to come in onto our workbenches, which are also stretched out along the side walls.

Barn/Energy Centre under construction

The barn is where we are experimenting with wood-gas generators. We have a 1949 Ford tractor which now runs on wood gas. We next plan to set up a stationary wood-gas fired engine to run an electric generator and use a portion of the barn as the farm's energy centre. This will be where our preserving is done, where our freezing is done, where any equipment needing electricity is located.

Tractor that runs on wood gas

There are other types of appropriate equipment which will be be housed in our energy centre. One is a Stanley airtight cookstove. It works quite well. On very little wood it produces a lot of heat for space heating, for cooking, and heats as much hot water as one needs. Another is a Yanmar stationary diesel engine. This is a spark compression engine requiring no glow plug. You just wind it up and push a button and two valves and off it goes. It uses about one third of the fuel that a comparable gasoline engine requires.

Diesel generator for charging batteries

The Yanmar will be used to charge a bank of batteries which we recycled from a BC-Tel operation. You have to get to know the local BC Tel manager in order to get these. Like most things that are recyclable, in the beginning you get them for nothing. But the next time you come around, suddenly there's a service charge for taking them away. And then the next time you come to get them they tell you, "You're going to have to pay, you know. Let's see now, we've depreciated them over 14 years and they cost us $4000... well, they're going to cost you some money." And then the next time you go back to get them they won't be there at all because the manager's friend is going to be using them. So you see, when trying to get things on a recyclable basis the law of diminishing returns applies.

The garden is a very important part of our farm. It supplies us with most of the food we eat. We were forced to develop a tall fence because we have deer which we are reluctant to kill. We have deer that would win a high jumping contest. We started out with a fence about chest high — deer went over it. The next year we went up over head high — deer went over it. So the next year we went to about 8 feet — deer went over it. We're now up to 10 feet. And still I saw a deer do a standing high jump next to the fence — and almost make it, but not quite. So we stopped there, at 10 feet. But in order to get equipment in the garden to do work we have to be able to take the rails down, so we invented a simple device. It's just a loop of farm wire stapled to the post. We simply slip rails into it. It is a small appropriate technology thing, one that will never get into the newspapers, but it's handy for our region and it's cheap.

We are completely equipped with a solar heated hot water shower. This is simply a 45 gallon drum on a rebar stand that originally was used to hold fuel oil. There is a little old fashioned shower head coming out of the bottom of the drum, which is raised about 8 feet above the ground. This produces quite a spray of water. Now how do we heat the water? It's almost too simple to talk about. When we first started irrigating our garden, we had to use about 200 feet of black polyethylene pipe as a lead into the irrigation sprinkler. We noticed that when the water came out of that pipe initially, it would fry the vegetables. So we wondered what to do with all that hot water?

Shower stall fed with irrigation hose

That's when we thought about a shower. Now, before we start the irrigation system, we disconnect the black pipe, fasten it onto the drum, and pump all the hot water (about 25 gallons) into the oil drum and everybody takes a shower on a summer night.

That's the end of the Denman Island story, but I'd like to briefly mention some architecture which I think is appropriate to this area — another thing that I learned about at Habitat. It's called stackwall and basically consists of wood that is cut like cord wood and laid up like masonry blocks, with the butt ends facing to the inside and outside. The materials used are indigenous to almost all regions.

Stackwall construction showing corner detail

The system was developed at the University of Manitoba Civil Engineering Department where Dr. Al Lansdown is the principal investigator. He uses polyethylene as a vapour barrier and sawdust as insulation. The sawdust is treated with lime so that insects don't attack it. The corners are made of logs that have been Alaska milled and cemented. The logs are only cemented part way through each end and the intersices are filled with sawdust. The

reason for that is to avoid any thermal bridges to the outside. The R factor of a 2 foot wide wall is somewhere between 28 and 30, depending on how dry the logs are. I think this is quite appropriate for this area where you have a lot of poplar, a light density wood which has a better insulating value than a heavy wood like oak. Such buildings are virtually fireproof which is a great asset.

A distinguished visitor at the Habitat stackwall house

"Where can I buy a Greenpeace flag?"

At the Greenpeace office in Vancouver, 4210 West 4th Avenue, Vancouver, B.C.

"In stackwall, how do you handle shrinkage of logs as they dry out? What about insect damage?"

You should cut the logs approximately one year before you use them. Try to do your building in the summertime when the logs are driest and at their smallest dimension. If you're forced to do otherwise and build with wet logs, you're going to see chinks appear as the cement separates from the wood. In that case you will have to go outside and caulk it up. That's what the recommendation is from the Manitoba people.

What is the effect of insects? Remember that 2 feet is a lot of wood. It will take them quite a while. I've seen termite-infested garages made of 2 x 4's (of somewhat dubious construction) that have lasted 20 or 30 years.

"What is the maximum diameter of dome that is practical?"

If you build it out of 2 x 6's and want to allow for a 60 pound per square foot snow load, you could go to about 45 feet with no trouble.

"What problems are there in joining two domes? Is it better to build joining halls?"

The way we did ours was to put up one dome, look at it, and decide that it wasn't big enough, that we needed two. So we took a chain saw and cut a hole in the one dome, built another and pushed it near the hole, and cut another hole with the chain saw so the two of them mated. And then we worried about how to flash it from that point.

That proved to be a surprisingly good approach, because there's no way you could figure that out mathematically. However, I think it is better to build joining halls. It is more sophisticated and if you ever want to add another dome that's the way to do it.

"Do you have further details for building the Eco-Cabin?"

Yes. Write to the Greenpeace Experimental Farm, Denman Island, B.C. V0R 1T0

and ask for a copy of the Eco-Cabin plans. Be sure to enclose $3.50 to cover the publishing and mailing costs.

"What do you do for storage of food, i.e. refrigeration?"

For about nine months of the year, the climate on Denman Island is exactly like the inside of your refrigerator. It averages about 40° Farenheit. So if you have a good styrofoam insulated chest and set it outside that will work well. Freezing food can be a problem. However, after looking at what was involved in freezing food and in trying to keep it frozen, and in studying the amount of energy used, I decided that it is not worth it in most cases. I'd rather see you spend that amount of energy and money building a greenhouse which will produce fresh vegetables the year round — in our climate we can do that. We can lengthen the growing season so that we have fresh vegetables throughout the year, except perhaps during the month of December — and that is not because of the temperature, but because of the lack of light. We tried growing tomatoes in insufficient light one year and we got a tomato plant that was 10 feet high. But it had a stem on it a quarter of an inch in diameter and no blossoms or tomatoes. It was a lovely experiment, but one that you don't have to repeat.

"Tell us some more about what your future research will be about."

After working for the last four years on the farm and having primarily negative results in agriculture due to the capital expenditure needed to make it a viable commercial farm, we decided to look into different means of producing food naturally. Our first experiment was to pick one

field and plant it to hay using commercial fertilizer and another field which we left to grow naturally. From the first one we were not able to even recover the cost of the fertilizer. So there was no sense in continuing that project any longer. From the field in which we allowed that hay to grow we got very poor hay production — but we didn't lose any money. Its like going to Las Vegas and making the rounds of the gaming tables. When somebody asks you how you did you tell them you broke even. "You broke even? That's not bad." You say sure, it was easy. I didn't place any bets. And that's the same situation we found with natural farming.

So what we decided to do is to get into a new kind of agriculture which I hope will become much more widespread. It's called *agroforestry* and involves growing a forest that will produce food and lumber and will also produce fuel for your wood stove. Underneath the trees is a natural pasture for a variety of animals. It seems absolutely bucolic. No fertilizers, beautiful trees growing all around, you reach up and pick the nuts and fruits off the trees.

I'm 52 years old and I figure that it will take 40 years to establish this system. Fortunately there are a lot of young people working with me on this project. But I also keep reading about Helen and Scott Nearing living on their homestead. Scott Nearing is now 92. So, if I can live as long as he, I might get to see something.

While we are trying to establish an agroforestry programme we are trying to get recognition from the B.C. Department of Agriculture that this is a viable and necessary farming operation. If we can obtain such recognition, and I have every indication that we will, it will guarantee us farm classification for tax purposes. That's very important where we live. Denman Island is prime recreational land and if you do not operate a productive farm (which nobody there does, everybody is scamming the tax assessor) then you are subject to paying tax as though it were recreational land. On 40 or 50 acres this might be 3-4000 dollars a year in land taxes, which is more than most of us earn. If you can prove you operate a farm you would be paying $200-$300 a year.

We hope that our work in agroforestry will interest a lot of people who would like to see marginal land brought into production and also people who would like to get involved in agriculture that does not require large energy inputs in the form of fertilizers. If you've ever seen a west coast forest, just imagine how many nutrients and how much solar energy is going into growing those giant trees. It is phenomenal. A tree crop can yield as much as 300 cubic feet per acre per year, which is equivalent to a fairly good hay crop grown with fertilizer.

"What year did you build the two domes and at what total cost?"

The two domes were started in 1974 and finished in 1976. The total cost was $8,000, including the generator, batteries, and the composting toilet.

"What do you use for mortar in stackwall construction?"

I have never mixed the mortar, but I don't think there was anything special about it. It was just ordinary mortar.

"We have a composting toilet and have a terrible problem with flies. The toilet has been in operation for only 8 months. How long before this problem remedies itself?"

I was at the Audobon Centre in Maine two years ago and they have an operating Clivus toilet there. The Centre is a beautiful solar operation and the Clivus toilet was installed very nicely and was used by about 40 people who worked there. They also had a persistent fruit fly problem. It was about the only thing in the whole system that didn't work well. We anticipated having the same problem but one of the reasons we avoid it is that our buckets only hold five gallons, and two people fill up a five gallon bucket in about two weeks. The gestation period for fruit flies is, I believe, 13 days. So on the 14th day, we dump it into our composting hole. To amplify that a little bit, this is a nice system, we have two holes in the ground, each one being large enough to contain a year's waste. When one hole is filled, we cover the hole with dirt that came from excavating the second hole. Then by the time the second hole is filled a year later the first one is ready to be used as compost. It is safe too. We've had it analyzed by the Department of Health. We didn't tell them what it was, we just asked if this was okay and they said, yes.

"In the cordwood cement structure is wood preserver required to offset humidity absorbed by cement?"

I don't think so because moisture from the mortar is not sufficient to saturate the log. It requires an awful lot of water to saturate a log, approximately its own weight and the little bit of mortar which you just use at either end is not enough to cause problems. Someone else has

told me that stackwall houses do not rot if treated with bluestone dip.

"Could you grow black locust trees which give you, with bees, a honey production second to none?"

We thought of that, we found out that black locust is a very hard wood and makes excellent firewood. I don't know whether they would grow here. If they do, it is certainly worth investigation because it is a fast growing tree. The locust trees that have the thorniest spines are the ones the bees like the best because they're the ones that get flowers. However, there is a brand of locust tree that's thornless, and that might be more appropriate for fuel wood.

"What do you use for window sealants? Are you double or triple glazing your windows?"

Nothing works well as a window sealant except silicone. It is expensive, but worth it. It remains flexible down to 60 or 70 below zero. It is one of the few plastics that are environmentally appropriate. It doesn't break down in ultraviolet light.

"What can individuals do on a broader level to solve some of our problems?"

I think that the problem we're facing has more to do with attitudes than it does to do with technology. Human beings have lived on the earth in one form or another for approximately three million years. They have found ways to organize themselves into patterns that are based on the way they believe that they have to live. The way we are living now is based on the belief that there is an infinite supply of all goods coming from the earth. It is sort of a cornucopia approach.

China consists of approximately one fourth of the people living in the world. Prior to the organizational efforts of Mao Tse Tung and his followers China was the poorest, most degraded country on earth. A country that had for thousands of years stripped itself of all of its natural resources for the purpose of enhancing the glory of one or two thousand specially endowed people. We in North America and the rest of the world have attempted to become as endowed as those few thousand people in China. Because we are achieving that level of affluence, we are stripping the world a lot faster than the two thousand years the Chinese took to do it to their country. We'll probably strip it off in one or two hundred years. Therefore we have to reverse our perceptions of ourselves and our expectations. If our expectations are to be rich, we can be king for a day, but then we'll go into some kind of a decline. It is our choice.

Once we are committed to the idea that we have to restructure our society, we have to figure out how we are going to do it, and there are basically two ways. One of them is where someone else plans our decline for us and the other way is for us to do it voluntarily. I think the argument is basically just that. People who are interested in self-reliance are basically interested in the voluntary approach towards declining expectations. People who are going to sit back and continue to use as much of the fossil fuel reserves of the earth as possible, and who count on others to find solutions once the reserves are gone — those are the people who are going to have decline imposed upon them.

In answer to the questions that have been raised about expanding cities, the expansionist philosophy is that we will always expand. The people who are concerned with that philosophy are in power. The only way we are going to get rid of that philosophy is to kick them out. Theoretically, we can do that in our system of parliamentary democracy, but recent elections were an indication of how little anybody is concerned about the environment, about conservation.

Mike Kerfoot

Michael Kerfoot *is a solar designer and builder. He was largely responsible for the projects at the Yamnuska Centre in Seebe, Alberta (construction of solar greenhouses, solar water heaters and stackwall housing). He has conducted several solar and greenhouse workshops, and is currently a partner with* Sunergy Systems Ltd., *in Carstairs, Alberta.*

A lot of people don't recognize me because I did a very tragic thing a couple of weeks ago. I shaved off my beard. People have asked me why, and there are some valid reasons.

I had once been very much involved in energy-efficient housing and my own personal outgrowth was an extension of that concern. I had done some careful studies, supported by the National Research Council, on the effective insulating value of beards. If you live in Fairview, or other northerly latitudes this is an important concern. I discovered that you would reduce your facial heat losses by 2700 BTU per face area by having a beard.

Now this study took place when I was involved in energy-efficient housing. But now I am involved in energy-efficient solar housing, and that means there are other considerations.

First of all, it is very easy in these latitudes to receive 1850 BTU per square foot per day from the sun. If you do a careful study of your face, you find that you have about 1.5 square feet of face potentially coverable with beard. If you multiply the potential BTU by 1.5 square feet you find that you have the potential to receive 2775 BTU per face per nice day in Fairview.

That is a lot of energy in a real direct gain system. So I shaved.

I happen to live near a mountaineering institute where those in training are always doing push-ups and other exercises. A push-up is the most devastating thing I can think about, but I was tired of being humiliated by my mountaineering friends who bragged about the number of push-ups they could do. I weigh around 160 pounds and I go through about one foot of movement when I do a push-up. So that is about 160 foot-pounds per push-up. There are 778 foot-pounds per BTU so we find that that little bit of sunshine falling upon your face represents 13,493 push-ups.

Now I can share that with my mountaineering friends and tell them how many equivalent push-ups I am doing each day.

Examples such as these are useful because I feel it is important for us to realize the kind of energy sources available to us.

John Todd of the New Alchemy Institute has taught me to be very careful about what he calls the talk-to-do ratio. We have to be careful of how much talking we do compared to how much actual work we do.

Two years ago I had a chance to give a pleasant lecture to a relatively small group of people in Alberta on a topic of great interest to me, toilets. Not the ordinary flush-and-forget kind, but the composting systems.

After an hour and a half of vigorous discussion, we finished the session and I was standing off by a side door talking with a couple of people. An elderly gentleman came walking up the corridor and said *"Excuse me, sonny"* with a very pained look, *"Can you tell me where the washroom is?"* And I did not have a clue where the washroom was. We had spent an hour and a half talking about toilets and I did not know where the washroom was. That was a lot of unnecessary talk and an unfortunate lack of doing.

The most important thing with any of our activity is not so much the end we are seeking, because we usually do not have any idea what that end might be anyway, but rather what the process is. The process for us is very exciting. What we are seeking more than anything else is the ability to be simple. To do things simply has many implications such as decentralization, self-reliance and lack of vulnerability.

In whatever we do or try to do in this province we have to keep in mind the context in which we have to work. The great inflow of petro-dollars and the money building up in the Heritage Trust Fund, that giant piggy bank, has established a pretty effective mind set which has affected our social, cultural, and political modes. Politically, we think that we have it made. We are beginning to see heavy centralization of primary industry with a lot of the social ramifications. The major portion of our liquid fuels goes into transportation; moving goods about. It is important to recognize this; it has influenced a lot of our ways.

In housing in Alberta, a similar type of mentality prevails. There are large companies that put up a few thousand tract-style houses every year, without a great deal of responsiveness to environmental concerns, to energy savings, to material use. What they are selling is a lifestyle, Sierra-style living.

This is the infrastructure which promotes the lifestyles that we have right now. Our water systems, our electrical needs, our thermal needs, our sanitiation systems, all those tentacles are going out from this infrastructure, tentacles of irresponsibility because we do not, ourselves, take any responsibility for them.

Concerns with particulate contamination and carbon dioxide contamination due to our fossil fuel use are enough to make us look at alternatives. In front of us, under us, there are all kinds of energy sources. Direct utilization of the sun is possible in so many different fashions. There is the photosynthetic miracle. There are various forms of biomass conversion and hydrological cycles for hydropower. There are those things which are not directly related to the sun — geothermal or radioactive decay of the earth's core; tidal-power, certainly the oceans are big wave collectors which Britain and Japan are working on with some seriousness. The most exciting thing, though, is that we have a lot of options before us. We've been trying to explore only a few options.

In the area of housing, I think it would be useful to look at some other possibilities in terms of construction materials and methods. It is an important and humbling experience to go back to the lap of Mother Nature: take examples from how plants deal with their environmental imperatives, how a bird works with its environment. Perhaps more appropriate to Canada is the beaver.

In the far north, indigenious people such as the Inuit had an austere environment with which to contend. Ice and snow were the building materials. With that they evolved a shelter with a wonderful air lock system and convection loops. This can be very humbling when compared to the California ranch style houses that we try to implant in northern Alberta. Other people in other areas had different imperatives, different materials. The tepees of the plains not only reflected the kind of materials and environment at hand, but spiritual concerns as well. It was all integrated into their shelter. There is much from which we should learn.

It is obvious that any passive review always includes a few cliff dwellings, even though on closer examination they seldom orientate themselves in an optimum manner. Such dwellings utilized materials underfoot, the rock and the clay. The Pueblo dwellings responded very sensitively to where the sun was and to the annual climatic conditions.

Some people have mapped whole areas to determine the kind of clay materials that are underfoot which they might be able to use as building materials. With a Cinvan Ram you can squeeze the daylights out of soil. By adding a stabilizer when necessary you end up with building materials that are structurally sound.

Rammed earth house in Colorado

In this area of Alberta is a straw bale church near Sexsmith. The structure was made in the early fifties of rye bales, which we were told is the best material to use. It is stuccoed inside and out to protect it totally from the elements. Amazingly, the roof was just set on top of it, so the bales themselves were structurally utilized. Outside of Regina in Saskatchewan a few years ago they tore down a three storey hotel which was also made out of straw bales. And of course Greg Allen has done some good work with straw bale construction.

Straw bale church in Peace River Region

One of the alternatives displayed at Habitat in Vancouver in 1976 was the sulphur construction by the Minimum Cost Housing Group from McGill. We have done some sulphur work, just enough to be convinced that it really does stink. This material is very good: structur-

ally stronger than concrete, totally impermeable to water, and our stockpiles of sulphur are stupendous. We have millions of tons of that material. Syncrude produces 1500 tons per month. But hydrogen sulfide is given off so I think it would be important for long term health to coat the sulphur walls with silicone or some other coating. Sulphur is another indigenous, post-industrial material.

A lot of people have come to us enquiring about conventional log construction. I really think that logs are beautiful. If done extremely well, by the scribing method, it can be a tight building, much tighter than conventional construction. But they are still lousy insulators. To try to resolve this we conducted a ten-day workshop last summer on basic log construction. We developed a design technique which I would suggest that no one ever consider. It was a double wall structure, logs inside and out with a batt of insulation in between. That doubles your efforts of course, and log work at the best of times is a great deal of labour.

We have done a fair bit of stackwall construction, which we think is definitely appropriate for many areas. Some months ago we submitted a design proposal for a community centre to be located north of this latitude, near Fort McMurray. It was to be quite a large structure and its basic exterior construction was to be stackwall. There is a major infiltration problem if the log ends are left exposed. So I would say that it is important to put a heavy tar paper, 90 pound felt for example, over the exterior wall and then stucco the whole thing.

One thing nice about stackwall is that it is forgivable. When there is a two-foot wall

there is no need to worry about plumb lines and such. Being a foot out here or there is not too terrible.

Building the stackwall greenhouse

We have looked at some indigenous materials, things that are in front of us but which we so often neglect. We do not really need vinyl clad siding shipped from Japan. Many of our materials right here are most appropriate of all, certainly from an energy context.

I have been very much impressed and influenced by other people's work. My bias is towards passive systems and the many different possibilities of utilizing them. Peter van Dresser's work on the Sundwellings in New Mexico is an example which once again demonstrates that the old south-facing window, if integrated with adequate mass, can be a most efficient collector system.

After the last passive conference in San Jose, California, a few months ago, I was trying to escape from the city, via the usual 12-lane freeway. I left about 8:00 in the morning, which is of course the worst time possible. Driving along the highway I caught a quick glimpse out of the corner of my eye, on top of a hill, of a bunch of drums spinning around on top of a workshop building in what looked like a Savonius. I careened my car across six lanes and caused a forty-three vehicle crash up, but I did get to the top of the hill. I knocked on the door of the nearby house and an older gentlemen came out in his pajamas. In my embarrassment I explained that I was interested in his wind apparatus. After seeing my interest was genuine and sincere he started getting excited, took me out to his shop, and showed me his miracle Savonius — which turned out to be totally useless. Then his house started attracting my attention.

Savonius rotor powered shop

I started taking a closer look at it. By that time he was asking me what my interests were and I explained that I was interested in solar energy. He thought that was nice and that he would like to learn a little about it. Then he went on to tell me about his house, which has a bank of windows facing south, which is built on a thick concrete slab to directly connect itself to that incoming radiation, which has a very carefully considered overhang to prevent overheating problems. What in fact he was telling me about was a near perfect direct gain passive system. He built the house in 1958 and he thought it was a shame that we didn't know much about solar heating at that time.

There are many other fine examples of very simple direct gain passive systems. Simply let the sun come in on the concrete slab, but it is most important for us to assess what happens at night. Some areas, such as New Mexico, can count on mild weather and good radiation energy. They might not have to worry so much about night-time losses. But night-time losses in Canada can be quite incredible, and we have to do something about it. The very simplest thing is what Steve Baer of Zomeworks calls Nightwall. This is merely putting up beadboard against exposed glazed areas. We will look at other window insulation systems presently.

David Wright's houses are fine examples of direct gain houses. I recently visited one which incorporated a lot of mass. After talking to its occupants, I learned that the son of the family had an asthmatic condition which was so extreme that he previously had had to spend part of every winter in an oxygen tent. The asthma worsened during the winter be-

cause of the forced air heating system pushing dust around. However, during the first winter in their new house this problem did not arise. There was no need for an oxygen tent. That's exciting and that is important. It shows that passive systems have beneficial effects other than saving energy and money.

Steve Baer designed an airport terminal in Colorado which is a good example of a commercial endeavor: just a lot of windows and a lot of skylights facing south — how simple. But Aspen, Colorado, has a pretty cool environment, so he had to cover up those areas at night. In this case Steve used a couple of his own creations: beadwall for the vertical areas and skylids for the skylight areas.

Sometimes direct gain is not appropriate or suitable. People may live in an urban environment and not want to have neighbours peering in. Perhaps there is a brace of Picassos hanging on the wall which should not fade. There are many acoustic concerns. In such cases perhaps a Trombe wall would be more appropriate, even though it is normally less efficient and less effective than direct gain. Basically, we put a wall of mass up against the bank of south-facing glass. Of course, it excludes the view and excludes a lot of the sunlight. The majority of the heat simply warms the massive wall and the heat is conducted through the wall and radiates to the interior after a certain time lag. If vents are placed at the top and bottom of the Trombe wall, natural convection can be used to transfer heat.

I would like to say a word about the colour of Trombe walls. It is unfortunate that we paint everything black. I would rather that we make it more colourful.

The loss in efficiency is marginal, especially at the low operating temperatures involved, and I think the improvement in aesthetics is great.

Trombe wall workshop at Yamnuska

Trombe walls can also reverse thermosyphon, as can a water collector system. The solution to that is effective and simple. We hang a piece of Saran Wrap over one of the vents. It does an amazing job.

We enjoy working with drums. After all, this certainly must be the oil drum capitol of the continent. Forty-five-gallon drums filled with water provide a good surface for radiation and for convection. We use them in place of a Trombe wall, stacked next to our south-facing glazing. In our latitude it is essential to use some sort of insulating device across the glazing at night, beadwall or shutters or curtains.

We have looked at direct gain systems and at Trombe wall systems. Now let's look at isolated gain systems, which are probably best reflected in the Paul Davis

house that Steve Baer also built. In such a system the gain is in one area, heat is stored in another area, and heat is distributed to a third area — the living area.

We have done an isolated gain house using 500 sq.ft. of Acrylite glazing on the lower portion of the front of the house, behind which are 117 water-filled drums. We used a reasonable insulating curtain, the Ron Shores curtain from Snowmass, which has an insulating value of around R11 or R12. The curtain is exorbitantly priced, especially by the time our energy conservative government adds their duty and taxes. The back side of the house is bermed up so that twelve feet of it is underground. We used a metal roof with a good breathing space between the metal and insulation. The plan is open and we used air lock entrances. To increase the thermal mass we used a suspended concrete floor, which turned out to be cheaper than a conventional joist system. Certain rules of thumb say that mass which is in direct contact with the sun is three or four times more effective than that which is not. We do not really believe that from our experience. So I would say definitely try to hide mass anywhere you can in a house, any kind of mass.

West and south views of indirect gain and drum storage room

In this particular house we also installed a regular commercial *Clivus Multrum* composting toilet. We have fought an incredible amount of bureaucracy in this province in defense of the Clivus. We find it very exciting now that the Department of Agriculture of Alberta is monitoring this one. The Clivus saves a large amount of energy even considering the heat that is wasted up the stack. It is definitely cost competitive with a conventional septic tank and leach field system.

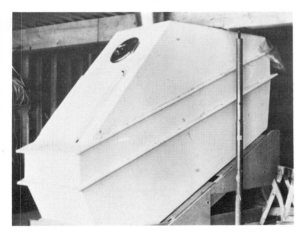

Clivus Multrum composting toilet

Greenhouses are of the greatest interest to us. The applicability, the appropriateness in this area is obvious. One greenhouse which we have spent a lot of time evolving simply involves a tank of water exposed to the sun in the bottom third of the greenhouse. The upper area is used as the normal plant growing area. The non-southern areas, east, west and north, are reasonably well-insulated to around R20. The thermal mass in the structure is around 20,000 pounds of water, not counting the soil beds. The growing bed is directly above the tank of water. The primary purpose of that tank is for heat storage. But we get more mileage out of it than that. We found that we can effectively sub-irrigate, not just by capilary action, but by evaporating water out of the tank into the more dense medium of the growing bed immediately above it. We could go away to New Mexico or Hawaii for a month's holiday and not need the neighbours to drop in to see how the plants are doing — they'll be optimally watered through out.

Integrated greenhouse home near Calgary

Helios Phoenix solar greenhouse

Drums stacked up along the back wall of a greenhouse may be totally inappropriate in our area. The light that we have available for photosynthesis in fall, winter and spring is marginal, so we should devise every means possible to re-direct more light onto the plant canopy, and try to use other means to store the heat. Some of the materials which we are using, such as aluminum foil, on our north wall to reflect more light on our plants can cause some plant anomalies. Thus far, most of our work has been done by architects and we have got to marry architects with agronomists for this type of work.

As architects, our major concern is to figure out a way to make a tight structure because we are approaching it from a thermal point of view. But we have to remember we are trying to grow plants and plants need carbon dioxide. If we should make it too tight then within an hour of operation after sunrise photosynthesis will nearly shut down because of the depletion of carbon dioxide. So we have to figure out ways to get carbon dioxide into that system. Of course, we can open the door, but that defeats all our hard work. People have put rabbits and fish or composting bins in their greenhouses. We have a great deal more to learn about that.

The value of insulating shutters cannot be too greatly stressed. Even the crudest and the most simple are important and effective, if they are manually operated. With aluminum foil, they become effective reflectors into the system. On large, commercial scales there are many systems available, but these are inappropriate and often inadequate for window insulation in a residence.

We have spent a couple of years playing with insulating curtains which has lead to a great deal of frustration, but perhaps the experience will turn out to be worthwhile.

Greenhouses sitting off by themselves seem to me pretty ridiculous. If there is ever the opportunity to integrate a greenhouse into a home, do it. A greenhouse is an efficient, effective thermal collection system. In our environment, we greatly appreciate having a humidifier, which the greenhouse effectively replaces. We appreciate having an air freshening unit, which the greenhouse also does effectively. It provides a psychological oasis — you have to attribute some kind of value to that. Of course, it is also a place to grow plants — some vegetables for the table and some flowers to enjoy.

Quanset-type structures with laminated beams are very common in this area and are easily converted into a commercial or community greenhouse. Insulate the northern half and there is an efficient and simple greenhouse. A greenhouse does not have to be in the backyard. There is no need to keep it small. Get ambitious and share it with the whole community. In Cheyenne, Wyoming, there is a 5000 sq.ft. greenhouse which is fully utilized by the "disadvantaged" group of the community.

The Ark at Spry Point, Prince Edward Island, is probably Canada's most well-known solar project. But even in that well thought out structure they learned what we all intuitively knew, that the direct gain passive systems as represented by their greenhouse was far more effective than the solar collectors which were built onto the building. The Ark has integrated many systems: sanitation systems, aquaculture as represented by the algae growing in fibreglass tanks, the horticulture of the greenhouse.

We have been looking at things in a piecemeal fashion like going into a department store and pulling out a pair of socks here and a t-shirt there. Somewhere along the line, our job is to integrate these in a stronger statement and that is very much our interest and our intent.

One example of such integration is in the United States. It hard to get excited about because it is in Davis, California — in California even if all the windows pointed north I am sure these would still be an excellent, passive gain system. Nonetheless, many things were integrated in this small energy-efficient community of about 80 houses.

Sunergy model home/office at the Calgary stampede

5000 sq. ft. community solar greenhouse

Village Homes in Davis, California

Tom Bender

Tom Bender *was the co-editor of* Rain: Journal of Appropriate Technology. *He has authored* Environmental Design Primer, Sharing Smaller Pies, *and* Living Lightly. *Bender is also the co-author of* Rainbook: Resources for Appropriate Technology *and he has been a major contributor to* Stepping Stones: Appropriate Technology and Beyond. *He is a former professor of architecture at the University of Minnesota, where he co-directed the Project Ouroboros experimental solar house.*

Sitting here for two days I've gotten a sense of perfect energy conserving architecture. First of all, it's spherical to have minimum surface for heat loss. It's underground to keep it from the extremes of the climate. It's good, solid construction, with no windows to lose heat. It's small and cozy, with little wasted space. It sounds remarkably like a coffin.

In focusing strongly on trying to get new things going — whether it's energy conservation or solar architecture (or something else) — we need to keep in perspective that there is a whole realm of other things we need to make a humane and harmonious world. In the next few minutes I will deal with architecture and solar design, and some of the implications to which they really lead.

I can suggest a few resources. Ed Mazria's new *Passive Solar Energy Book* from Rodale Press is the best source currently available on simple and effective solar design. It comes in two versions: a paperback and a professional edition, with about a $15.00 price difference. Get the paperback, then go to a library and photocopy the solar tables for your own latitude out of the professional version. If you can't find a copier that will take acetate, then just trace the guides in the back of the professional version. From that, you can make a sun mast to see where the trees and other obstructions will block out your sunlight.

Look into the *Ekose'a* home design, which has been developed in California by Lee Porter Butler. It seems particularly appropriate for this climate and offers excellent retrofit potential for the average ranch house. The design is an envelope system which has either a greenhouse or a vertical solarium on the south side that takes in the sun and heats the air. The hot air rises up through an attic over the house, is drawn down through a double wall on the north side, and back through a crawl space or a basement, using those spaces for heat storage. It is a gravity-powered convection loop which seems to work well. Looked at another way, it's a double shell house — the outer shell heated from the earth to the stable earth temperature of 45 to 50°F, and the inner shell needing solar or other heat only to boost its temperature from 45-50° to the desired inside temperature. It's an alternative to greenhouses or simple, direct gain. There are three good articles on it, one in *Better Homes and Gardens,* March 1979, and two in *Co-Evolution Quarterly,* Summer 1978 and Winter 1978-79.

Another resource is a two-part series of articles by Phil Henshaw in the April and May 1979 issues of *Rain* magazine. He talks about air currents in houses and using them in unconventional ways to make air convey heat into storage in safe, cozy places and to make cold air pump uphill and hot air downhill.

We just finished building our own house after many, many years of dreaming. It's not outstanding as a solar house, and I'd like to talk about why it is not. Our society's first reaction to discovering that we were, in effect, heating our houses with the windows open, was to close the windows — to insulate like crazy and try to keep the heat in. Energy conservation was the key word. Our second response was to look for a better furnace, so we turned to the sun. A third response, which our house represents, is to turn off the furnace, open the windows, and as much as possible, quit living cut-off from the rest of the world. We tried to minimize the amount of shelter — to provide only what we needed. The house is located on the Oregon coast. It's a seemingly benign environment, but we have about 80 inches of rain a year, a lot of fog, and 100-mile per hour winds in the winter.

Having spent a fair amount of time in Japan, Persia, and other parts of the world which have various living and building traditions, I have experienced the same frustration that earlier Western travelers have often mentioned when coming back from these areas. After experiencing other living patterns, going into a conventional European or American house leaves you incredibly stifled, cut off from the movement of air, from the seasons, from the natural rhythms of the sun and moon, day and night, storm and calm — everything which goes on in the world about us and which is a part of life. For instance, it's not an uncommon sight in Japan in the winter to see people wrapped up in a padded kimono, sitting on the veranda of their houses in the sunshine, with snow on the ground around them. The people keep themselves warm, not the buildings. They saved energy and saved a vital linkage between themselves and the rest of the natural world. I have found the same thing camping, traveling in various wilderness regions. It is really powerful and wonderful to be part of the "outside world," an experience that I hate to be cut off from.

What we're trying to evolve is basically a house which can maintain these linkages as much as weather conditions at various times permit. The south wall opens up almost entirely, turning the inside of the house into a porch open to the outside.

The overhangs and sun penetration are designed so that you are drawn to the edges between the inside and the outside — close to and not something very distinct from the outside.

Living area between inside and outside

Sleeping space catches sunrise and moonrise

We're trying to maintain contact with the rhythms of the day, orienting different parts of the house to the sun during the time they are used, not just designing for the technical efficiency of plumbing and mechanical systems. The sleeping space which is basically just a soft room at the edge of the living area, is oriented to the east for moonrise and sunrise; the living space is oriented to the south for the mid-day sun; the eating space is oriented to the west for sunset and sitting around in the evening. Try to think of other things which need to be brought together in a house beyond the technical considerations of closing sewage loops and getting away from use of non-renewable energies.

There's been a lot of talk here about material recycling and aesthetics and the cost savings involved. These are wise things to do when circumstances permit, but it is part of a larger question. We discovered that on the Oregon coast there are two things which are against material recycling. Number one is that anything you can get to recycle was probably built poorly in the first place, and is now rotten. Number two, if it was any good, somebody's already been there and gotten it.

It's not wrong to use new material. It's just important to make best use of what is available. Build permanently. Build well, so that the things used have an enduring value to people. It's not just for you to use but for the generations beyond you. The material is only one dimension of the process.

I have also had the misfortune of being able to compare the process of building totally with hand tools to building with the use of power tools. I built the house by hand without power tools partly because electricity wasn't available yet, partly because I had no power tools, and partly because I wanted to see what it was like to build peacefully and simply. The day after we finished building the house, it burned down. The second time we built with power tools and with friends' help instead of doing it ourselves.

Two views of Bender's Oregon House

We learned that the cost of labour in a house is not much compared to the cost of materials. Our house is about 1300 square feet. It cost about $17,000 for materials the first round, and I think that with paying people to help build it the second time, the cost was about $22,000 to $23,000. To me, it's worthwhile to take it slow, to use hand tools and to learn what twisted grain in wood means, what the difference is between green and dry wood, what it means to keep both your tools and your mind sharp, or what it means to be able to do a double mitre cut with just a hand saw instead of using

jigs and other devices. It's a really valuable opportunity when you take it. Power tools are fine, but they don't save you enough to make it worth missing the fun of doing something special by hand, whether it's making your own doors, a special window, or a handmade sink. Do it. It is something you will enjoy the rest of your life. It is certainly not putting money down a rat hole.

Our concern with solar energy is only the tip of an iceberg. What we're really talking about is the need and opportunity we have today to change the ways we do a great number of things. It's time to look at the ends which we seek instead of just the means. We've been looking at efficient transportation, for example, but transportation is only a means to get somewhere. Eliminating the need for transportation is much more effective than merely increasing the efficiency of transport.

Two-thirds of the land in urban areas, and a great amount of our energy and wealth, goes to the automobile. We have not looked at doing without it. We say, "O.K., we have the automobile, how do we accommodate it?" One city, Bologna, Italy, has been re-examining transportation during the last couple of decades. The city has eliminated automobiles from two-thirds of its streets, and has instituted free public transit during rush hours. The city has implemented planning policies which keep the workplace, homeplace, and funplace within walking distance rather than allowing segregated industrial parks, suburbs, and business districts. The city has tried, successfully, to minimize the need for the auto rather than to find ways to accommodate it. The city has extended basic thinking to many

urban institutions and systems. It has done more than any other city I know, towards achieving a humane place to live. *Red Bologna,* a book by Jaggi, Muller, and Schmid, documents what the city has been accomplishing. It's another resource.

Changes in land use can often increase the rewards our buildings give us. Once in Japan I was sitting in an abbot's residence, enjoying what I thought was a beautiful meditation garden outside, and suddenly an automobile drove through it. Between the greenery and a waterfall was a skillfully hidden driveway. We can make a great deal of beauty and peace with every little space when we clearly decide what we're really after. We can make a paradise where we are instead of driving far and wide in search of one elsewhere.

In Japan, one finds ingenious multiple use of space. In shoehorned urban areas, one member of the household may drive to work in the morning. The car goes out, leaving behind what was a garage but is now a shop. Other family members roll out the counters and open the shop for the day. It's one of many simple patterns of living-where-you-work which are traditional in many areas of the world. It can help us rediscover much simpler patterns to lessen the demands which we place on ourselves, our resources and the rest of the world.

We need to remember that not only is the resource squeeze pushing us towards simpler and less materialistic ways of life but that we gain quality in the process. A look at the size and variety of the larder of Glen Simmonds, a homesteader outside of Portland, would convince anyone that self-reliant patterns do not necessarily mean depriving oneself, but may be a means of providing oneself with a better quality of life. Glen was, years ago, the head chef at Antoine's, a famous French restaurant in New Orleans. He likes to eat, and he likes to eat well. There are lots of different kinds of carrots, and he likes good carrots. You can't buy those in the store — what you get there is what is easy to grow, package, store, and sell on a large scale. You can buy rubber tomatoes in a store, but you can't buy the good kind that Glen likes to eat . . . so he grows his own. And stores his own.

We're expanding the range of options which we have available to us. I'm not saying that everyone should live in an energy self-reliant house or not have an auto, or not eat meat. Some want to drive a Cadillac and are willing to eat beans to afford the Cadillac. Others like to eat steak and will drive a Volkswagon or ride a bicycle to have that steak.

If we consider sewage for a minute, we can get a sense of the range of options becoming available for various conditions and lifestyles. The Japanese have long produced a toilet which has a double flush. Depending on whether you have a lot to flush or a little, you turn the handle to the left or to the right and it flushes a different amount of water. The tank refills through a spout on the top which runs into a sink for washing your hands; the waste water from that is used to flush the toilet the next time. Water use is reduced more than 50 per cent with no loss in convenience.

Double flush toilet with top sink

In areas with existing sewers, reducing the water flow into the sewers using dams in the toilet tanks and using the sludge from the sewage plant for agricultural application at least gets the nutrients back on the fields and the water back into the aquifer instead of further polluting our drinking water. Five years ago people were up in arms at experiments such as this, and I remember some heated battles to prevent tests from being carried out. Yet this spring when I was in Indiana I overheard a farmer complaining bitterly that the neighbouring town would only haul sewage sludge ten miles, and he lives 15 miles out so he couldn't get any of it for fertilizer! So things are changing.

Another sewage option is what is known as a "honey dipper" — a tank truck which goes around and pumps holding tanks from low-flush toilets, providing a flexible alternative to the high cost, centralized sewage systems which are standard in many parts of the world.

A Japanese "honey dipper"

At another end of the sewage spectrum are compost toilets which are now legal in many areas and which eliminate the need for sewers, prevent pollution of drinking water, reduce water use, recycle nutrients onto food crops, and save money.

These examples illustrate what happens when we change our values and head off in a new direction and do as the Chinese have learned to do: put things together instead of taking them apart. One of the most beautiful examples I've seen of that is a Chinese pig pen. Over the pen is a grape arbor. The grape vines keep the pigs shaded and cool. The pigs eat grape leaves. The urine from the pigs water fertilizes the grape vines. More grapes and pork are harvested out of that arrangement than separately, and the waste and food problems of both resolve themselves. When you put things back together you get a lot more out than when you take them apart.

Once we begin to address our resources, we can look deeper at economics: systems which waste our wealth and resources and an alternative system that does what we want much more simply and effectively. I call this self-reliant economics.

We have to deal with interest rates. A society without massive material growth means a society with zero interest rates for loans and savings and investment, because there is no expectation of more physical wealth in the future with which to repay interest. As it is now, the interest rates are set by the most profitable ventures, which turn out to be highly exploitive practices of multinational corporations that bankrupt our resources, our country, and the wealth that should be our legacy to future generations. Particularly lucrative and exploitive foreign investments set corporate expectations for profits within our country, which in turn set interest rates throughout our economy. And high interest rates mean that the time horizon we look at shrinks. Any benefits or costs more than ten or fifteen years down the line we don't even think about any more because the other options of using our money now and getting more interest back on it overrides everything else. We have to have a longer time horizon than that — one which allows us to think about and build things of enduring value.

We have to deal with advertising. It's an incredible centralizing mechanism that affects how the whole productive sector of our economy operates. When I started talking about this a couple of years ago, people reacted strongly. They said any

control of advertising is restraint of free speech and advertising is necessary for our economy to operate. When we looked at it, we found that we are using public media — radio, TV, and postal services — for advertising which only the very wealthy have access to. Who can afford the $215,000 it costs for *one minute* of prime time network TV advertising? Is this free speech? Is this a wise and justified use of a public media?

The same is true of postal rates. In the United States there are very large postal subsidies for magazines and newspapers which contain up to two-thirds advertising. Is this a wise public policy to have?

The same is true also of billboards. They are being eliminated in a number of areas on aesthetic grounds. They can also be eliminated because of the adverse impact they have on local economies by supporting franchise, chainstores, and other centralized business practices which take money out of the local economies and really hurt the people at home.

Another thing we have to deal with is change in ownership of corporations and public monopolies such as utilities. We need to implement ways of getting more equity into the patterns and distribution of wealth. It's a question we no longer can avoid. There is no longer a hope for a "bigger pie to share", so we have to face the truth about our present distribution of wealth and take steps to correct it.

All this may seem a long way from solar houses, but we're already a long way into rethinking economics when we realize that the sun shining on our roofs is an energy income worth money that is wasted if it is not used, while fossil fuels are a savings

account of energy that is worth more tomorrow if we don't use it today!

The question was asked a bit earlier about what each of us can do to effect the necessary changes. I think a comparison to the nuclear power situation is quite *apropos*. Peter Van Dresser has said the claims of economics is basically fraudulent when we start digging into them, just as the claims of nuclear power proponents were found fraudulent five or ten years ago. The way we deal with such a situation is to dig into it, to investigate it and to find the reality underneath, then get that information out to other people. Use it as the basis for dealing with the politics of these things.

We must realize that the most knowledgeable people — the economists, bankers, investment analysts, political leaders, etc. — are really talking about *not* economics, but *finance*. They are not talking about the real expenditures of labour, materials and energy or the real costs incurred by a project such as the loss of other alternative uses of these resources or the resultant health and safety problems that may arise. Rather, they are talking about the *profitability* of a project — the tax and banking and business rules that determine *who* profits from the real work invested in a project. They do not talk about *who* profits from their "economics".

On the issue of cities versus rural areas, the latter are taxed to support urban areas. The same thing is true in distribution of services. These tax monies are used to provide services in urban areas and result in moving wealth from rural to urban areas.

The so-called *free*-trade economy which is the basis of our culture is different from what I would call a *fair*-trade economy. Free and equal people are not able to trade things, rather people and organizations with different amounts of power trade. Individuals are forced to compete alone against a monopoly. Farmers are a fine example of this. Individual farmers produce crops and sell them to a marketing organization which is controlled by a small number of food processors. The farmers also buy their fertilizer, seed, and other materials in monopolistically controlled markets — so they get squeezed at both ends. The power to determine the terms of trade is totally unequal.

When investigating these things, one looks into finance and money flows: franchises cause money to go out of neighbourhoods and communities and into major finance centers, central banks and corporate coffers. An incredible centralizing effect is caused by these institutional structures we've allowed to develop. The Institute of Local Self Reliance did a study on one of the MacDonald's hamburger franchises in Washington, D.C. and found that about 85 percent of the money which went into the cash registers of the franchise left the community. Even local bankers start rubbing their eyes and thinking twice when presented that information. They know very well what happens when the money recycles within a community rather than being exported. I think it's possible to get a fairly large constituency for important changes once we start documenting what's going on in these areas.

Getting back to real and sound economics will not lead to worse but to better conditions, particularly once we start

realizing that it is not just the material things that are important to our lives. Let's look, for instance, at some major qualitative differences in certain working patterns. Working for any large organization not only involves dealing with the day-to-day hassles evolving from the management of any large bureaucracy, but often it results in the necessary development of a countervailing union bureaucracy, and the resultant added frustrations of its organization behavior. I talk time and time again with people working in such situations who are virtually exploding with frustrations in their work environment.

Consider alternatives to this. Self-employment, for example, eliminates the split between labour and management. If you go a step further into self-reliance and start providing for more and more of your own needs, you're eliminating more and more of these conflicting roles which have developed. In self-reliant work patterns you get away from the division of producers and consumers. You're not having to argue for your wage or whether you should take an hour off and sit under a tree because it all comes out in your own balance sheet in the end.

Changing to simpler patterns can bring a lot of positive things. We're currently attempting to document this; we're examining a regional economy based on renewable energy, appropriate technologies, and patterns of self-reliance.

Peter van Dresser

Peter van Dresser *is a leading astronautic engineer. In the 1930's he was building solar water heaters and in 1958 he built his first solar-heated house. He works to develop practical methods to help individuals to preserve their natural resources and the best of their cultural traditions. He authored* A Landscape for Humans *and* Homegrown Sun Dwellings.

Many people are interested in what has been called the nuts and bolts of self-sufficient living and especially passive solar, of which we in New Mexico think we're the capital. I have particular concerns in these areas which have evolved over the past several decades and which have, in fact, been my concerns since the thirties.

I was active in the decentralist movement in the United States at the time, which in many ways anticipated the present environment and ecological movement. I am concerned about the evolution of our society in an ecologically viable direction. An important aspect of this is economic regionalization: the development of localities and regions which have the capacity to provide their necessities using flow resources, biotic resources, sunshine and so on. Thereby relatively small geographic limits can disengage themselves logistically from the gigantic overriding world complex of industry which has been rapidly evolving in the past few decades.

The reason my wife and I emigrated to northern New Mexico thirty years ago was because we felt this was a particularly fortunate region, in that it was classified by sociologists and economists as a backward, stagnant region. We now consider this to be a real advantage because it is neither the sort of terrain nor the sort of culture which is amenable to rapid development with big machinery, and the apparatus of big financial exploitation. It has resisted this type of development and it has retained its regional character, village-focused life and small-scale agriculture. There has, of course, been a terrible decline of the crafts and the original pattern of subsistence, but much of it is left and functioning. We felt

that within such a region the new concepts of biotechnics or appropriate technology could be applied at a scale at which they should be applied. The more we have lived in this region the more important we feel these intangible assets are — a cultural and social and economic matrix which actually encourages small scale development, rather than opposes it.

I have watched the growth of the movement towards personal self-sufficiency, homesteading, and supplying one's own needs. It is a reasonable and good movement, but I think we should be giving equal attention to the nuts and bolts of the social institutions that mold our economy and are forcing us into the extreme centralization that is occurring. These are man-made institutions and should be subject to our scrutiny and our study continuously. We should be thinking about political and business organization at the local level. We should strive for political entities on the order of townships and counties, or individual villages and corporate communities.

What concerns me is that the people who are looking for alternatives are looking for *personal* alternatives only. This is perfectly understandable as it is enough of a job to build a homestead and start to feed oneself. I have made my passes at this, too. My wife and I devoted a good deal of effort to personal self-reliance. But I think you must be involved in whatever can be done at the local and provincial and national level to modify, for instance, the government regulatory practices, the laws, the business practices, financial practices, tax practices, the codes of various kinds. Restrictive codes seem to be almost uniformly designed to favour a large centralistic organization and to make it very difficult for localist movements and regionalist economics to successfully evolve. This is my prime concern.

I have worked in passive solar. I have done a good deal of my own building and promoted some demonstration training programs in that field, which I think is important. But there is, I am afraid, in the ecological and environmental movement, a North American tendency to turn this work into another gadget package which will solve our problems. I am a little worried about this tendency.

Domes and methane generators and bicycle-powered devices and windmills are fine, but they are not an end in themselves. We have to think of a whole pattern of land use and the re-development of vital, smaller communities which contain within themselves small, diversified industries and which have the capacity to feed and supply most of their basic needs with reasonable skill and competence. This is a lot more than gadgetry. We have to have a whole new breed of fairly sophisticated small industries using local resources which are capable of supplying basic needs within our localities and our regions. The patterns for this type of development are still very vague. When you go to governments and talk about these things, it is difficult to present a convincing picture. We need to evolve this concept, be able to present it with good scientific and statistical evidence. It has been demonstrated that regional development is much more efficient than over-centralization. It is much sounder, it distributes the benefits to people much more broadly and it is real economics as opposed to a kind of psuedo-finance economics that is currently controlling many policies.

What I have learned about it is microscopic compared to the problem. It is an enormous problem. It is faced by all peoples of the world. I find that wherever I go — to each region, to each country — the people think that this thing is happening to them only, but it is happening everywhere. This is a global phenomenon.

When we examine our current energy problems, we see they are related to centralized systems. We are still at the stage in this energy business of attempting to develop a miraculous energy source that won't pollute and won't destroy and won't do a lot of damage, but will allow us to continue essentially the same social and economic patterns that we now have. I feel that the major energy comsumptive factor in our society is the logistic structure of the society itself; that is, the use of our land, the way our communities have clustered, the composition of our communities, the pattern of production and distribution, the over-specialization by remote regions which exploit slight agricultural advantages for mass growing of wheat or rapeseed or cotton, and the development of an enormously expensive transportation, distribution, and packaging system to allow us to profit from such slight regional differences. An enormous part of our social energy has gone into maintaining this machinery. Even the expenditures on war are not as great as the expenditures for the vast highway and transportation network and the constant movement that occurs within this system. Societal structures and maintenance of enormous, non-productive urban megapolitan centres, which are purely consumptive centres, is where the energy flows.

Compact, self-supplying regional economies can enormously reduce the energy requirements of our societies and can actually provide a higher standard of living, if you slightly revise the meaning of standard of living to include other amenities besides an excessive number of automobiles and so on. You can achieve high amenity and moderate to low energy societies by merely changing the logistics of our land use and our community patterns — that is a very important point.

We should be studying these things because I don't think enough analysis has been made. We do have the beginnings of an energetics analysis of society but it is, I think, still at the beginning. A very interesting book was written in the 1950's called *ENERGY AND SOCIETY* by William F. Cottrell (published by Greenwood) which does a very good job of analyzing the surplus energy projection of whole agriculture versus machine agriculture.

Most of our so-called economic studies really should be called financial studies. We have come to a point where we use the term economic viability when we mean financial profitability and all too frequently financial viability is economic catastrophe for a region. The more financially successful a project is the more ultimately damaging it is in terms of basic economics — the original meaning of economics being the study of the management of goods and commodities, not money.

Quite a while ago I began qualifying the term decentralization with the alternative term recentralization. Decentralization can unfortunately be interpreted as merely meaning further suburbanization: this is nothing but people going out to live in the country but still tied into the continental supply system. To achieve regional and local self-competency requires a degree of multiple recentralization but on a small scale. Fairly sophisticated local interlocking is needed. We will need to develop what we could call mini-industrial complexes. We can not just disperse people all over the landscape living in A-frames on mountains thinking they are building another society. We have to re-orientate and recentralize on a scale which is humane and which provides us with a multiplicity of small regions and sub-regional centres which I call micro-urban centres. This used to be the pattern of society and is indeed a perfectly normal pattern.

Many city planners claim that all the communities around a large centre are parasitic upon it; therefore, they should be included in the city to provide a bigger tax base. This, at least, is the rationale.

I used to work as a city planner and I am rather embarrassed to admit it. To the extent that the communities surrounding larger centres are dormitory towns and the work opportunities are concentrated in the central city you could say that they *are* parasitical. Until we develop truly organic communities which are genuinely self-supplying and self-competent in basic economic terms, the parasitic argument that the planners use has a certain validity and will prevail. I think the planners are amongst the hardest people to convince. They are part of the problem.

Unless the self-sufficient movement develops into organized communities, it will be ineffectual. We have to substitute for fairly sophisticated devices such as motor vehicles and television sets a sophisti-

cated organization which is organic. We can use relatively simple technology in most cases. I do not, for instance, foresee people making electric light bulbs as a cottage industry, but for the great bulk of our real needs relatively simple technology will be completely adequate if our organization is efficient. What we currently have is an incredibly inefficient organization in which we develop very elaborate technological devices to compensate for this overall inefficiency. So we have to develop a new concept of what sophisticated organization is. It is deceptively simple, but underneath it has its own type of scientific sophistication.

If we *had* developed our economics on a localized, energy-flow basis, giant corporations and giant projects like the Alaska pipeline would not be necessary. To manufacture electric light bulbs, moderate-size regional plants could be co-operatively owned. People are not going to be making light bulbs in their backyards or in cottage industries. There are hierarchies of centralization necessary but I think we have gone much too far in the direction of overcentralization. It is a question of balance.

A system of co-operatively owned regional plants will require study to determine what the optimum size is of various industries and so forth. There was some attempt made at this during the depression in the United States. There are hierarchies of concentration necessary, but a logical and efficient redistribution of the means of production and land use, and community re-organization would greatly reduce the need for vast plants.

The land taxing system is another debatable subject. Henry George advocated

this principle in the late 1800s. His thesis was that the value of land was created by the combined social effort of the surrounding community, and that those who held land and did nothing with it were profiting by the collective efforts of the community as a whole. Owners were able to charge high rents or sell the land at high values even though they did nothing with it.

Our taxing policy is the reverse. We let such people hold land at very low rates of taxation, and then we tax the improvements which penalizes the persons who make use of the land. George's thesis was that the primary revenues of the community should be derived from the rental of the land whose value they created. Whatever the person does on the land should not be taxed.

The argument is that this policy would stimulate economic growth. It is a decentralist policy which would stimulate the growth of many smaller communities and generate more revenues in the long run than the overdevelopment of certain places with land being held back speculatively for enormous profits. This is one of the things people should be thinking about nowadays.

I have come to the conclusion that the real factors shaping our economy are financial. Working in government and seeing government programs has made me skeptical as to their effectiveness in making any basic changes in the current patterns. Government functions because it receives a great deal of its support from large corporations. Government puts out token programs to help the declining rural communities, but such programs are generally ineffective.

People are probably justifiably suspicious of big government, but big government is the inevitable counterpart of huge business which really runs things. To undercut the powers of big government just puts us in the hands of big business. We have a Hobson's choice.

I think the current so-called tax revolt is a wholesome reaction against big government but unless we also work to develop true, regional autonomy, to simply cut down on government will not affect much.

My objection to most communist regimes is that they think they can simply take over the machinery of industrialism and by running it in what is supposed to be the public good, make it beneficial. I feel that the patterns themselves are inherently exploitive and will continue to create problems no matter what political regime runs them, whether it is done by profit-sharing capitalism or whatever. The very pattern of over-concentration and over-industrialization is exploitive and wasteful.

I could be classified as a federalist-regionalist. Once we achieve a mosaic of relatively non-exploitive self-competent regions, these can then federate into what is necessary to manage true world systems such as communications and scientific exploration. A world government that manages in detail the affairs of all peoples is neither possible nor desirable. I believe, as did Thomas Jefferson, in federation but only after the federated elements are in control of their own economics and are not dependent on exploiting other parts of the world for their survival.

In 1964, Rand mathematician Richard Bellman estimated that if all processes could be automated, then we would need only two per cent of the population to produce the goods needed for comsumption. As an ancient, dyed-in-the-wool decentralist, I regard such an idea with horror. It might actually be possible, but what are the other 98 per cent of the population doing? It seems to me, such an economy would be extremely destructive of the planet. The consumption of energy and irreplaceable materials — excessive use of things like copper, aluminum and the energy needed to keep these machines going — would be enormous. This would be inherently a destructive economy. I think the masses of people "liberated" from creative work would become psychological problems very rapidly.

There are claims that such a system would be enormously efficient in terms of recycling, avoiding waste and so on, but a lot hinges on the definition of efficiency in a situation like this. We have to think of the overall efficiency of an organism as a whole. Doxiadis coined the phrase "ecistical efficiency." Ecistical has the same root as ecology. It can be defined as the efficiency of an organism in supplying real human needs, taking into account the region, culture and local resources. This entails much more than simply the engineering efficiency criteria that we most frequently use.

I think the ecistical efficiency of such an organization as Bellman envisions would be extremely low, although the engineering efficiency might be very high.

To supply our basic needs on a regional basis implies regional housing, what is

called a "mature house culture" for a particular region. Coming from the adobe country, as I do, where we can build houses at amazingly low cost, I believe that one of the major solutions of regional housing in many parts of the world is rammed earth. In Greeley, Colorado, is the home of David Miller. This is a rammed earth house which was built in the 1940s and it is one of the handsomest houses that I have ever seen in my life. It is also solar heated. Miller has the most extensive library on rammed earth construction I have ever come across and he has travelled all over the world to accumulate it. Rammed earth is a universal material which has been used up as far north as the Arctic Circle in Scandinavia and northern Russia. It endures all kinds of climates and it is literally a no-cost, pure sweat-equity material. It is amazingly versatile, amazingly permanent, and it is acceptable in almost every building code. Obviously it does not apply to retrofitting houses, but if you are talking about developing a locally self-sufficient building industry, I think it has a tremendous future.

David Wright

David Wright *has been involved in alternative forms of architectural design since the early 1960's when he worked in several African countries with the Peace Corps. He specializes in microclimate design and natural heating and cooling methods. His houses are situated throughout the United States. Wright authored* Natural Solar Architecture.

It is a pleasure to be here in the land of the 10 pm sun. I have never been this far north and having these hours of sunshine is exhilarating.

Last night I was trying to get to sleep about 10:30 and it was still light. What amazed me was that there were people out mowing their lawns, and it kept going on and on. I finally went to sleep to the drone of lawn mowers in the distance.

This morning over breakfast, one of the people who live here tried to explain to me that those weren't really lawn mowers, but mosquitoes trying to get into my room.

When I received my invitation to speak in Fairview, I thought it would be a nice experience to get to see part of northern Canada. We received some weather data from the organizers and it was requested that we talk on topics relevant to northern Canada. Having very little experience with the area, I immediately turned to the weather data which is one of my base resources wherever I do work. When I started looking through this data it seemed to be pretty cold. It seemed to be pretty cold for a pretty long time. I came across the fact that one year there were eight inches of snow in August. This morning, even though it is only June, I noticed a little nip in the air and it felt like fall was on the way. So you had better begin to prepare your lawns for the next winter.

Alberta has a history of importing fruits and vegetables and nuts from the United States. This trend has been growing more rapidly in the past few years. I noticed at this conference you have quite a pick of the crop.

My good friends from New Mexico are here — some of the early pioneers and experts, people who five or six years ago were considered the lunatic fringe. I have noticed that in the intervening period we have moved from the lunatic fringe to the lunatic centre. We have even gained credibility with the United States Department of Energy, which is a major accomplishment for something as simple as energy conservation and passive solar energy applications. They are so much behind us now that they are probably very glad to have some of us up here this week representing the United States. They are not merely happy because we are here and might not come back, but they are happy because we are making the gasoline lines shorter in our home states.

The squeeze is starting to hit home in the United States. I wouldn't be surprised to see it start happening in Canada; do not think it happens just south of the border. It is going to happen all over. It is a change in economic consciousness. I just hope that they delay your long gas lines until winter so that you will have something else to do besides watch TV and curl. Sitting in gas lines is very entertaining and you get a lot of reading done.

The people in the grass roots movement and the passive solar field decided that the government is not necessary to implement energy conservation or the other changes we are trying to effect. As a matter of fact, if anything, the government is a hinderance. This is truly a grass roots movement and it is primarily you, and not the government, who is going to carry it forward. But in order for you to do this you have to stop talking about it and get on with it, to demonstrate by example. True activists in energy conservation are people who do it on their own. They don't talk about it. They don't go out and give lectures around the country, but in their day-to-day lives they demonstrate energy conservation.

We are using the term energy conservation, but what we really want to conserve is the environment. We are really becoming environmentalists, trying to preserve the world for generations to come. We are not just trying to save ourselves, not just espouse the viewpoint of a particular political party, not just solve this particular fossil fuel dilemma, but to save the earth for human beings to live on for a long time.

One of the things we have to do is learn to interact with our environment in an optimum way. One of the ways of achieving this is regionalism, and I agree with Peter van Dressers' philosophy very much. We must become regionally self-reliant, develop the talents and the resources available locally into systems and lifestyles which interact in an optimum way with the environment, which is to say, lifestyles which have the least possible impact upon the environment.

My particular specialty is architecture, what I call natural solar architecture. This does not mean merely heating buildings, but also ventilating, cooling, and creating life support systems. This is what architecture should be. As we start to understand how we interact with our environment, we will evolve new building forms. Habitats will change; they will have to change.

In the past, we simply took the wood stove and converted it into a gas furnace.

That wasn't very difficult, but you cannot merely insert a burner into a wood stove and call it a gas furnace. It will not work properly. Now we are trying to turn that gas furnace into a solar furnace or perhaps back into a wood furnace. And this, too, will not work properly.

Similarly, we should not expect to take a conventional structure and change it from a centrally heated house into a solar heated house. It can be done, but it takes modification of the architectural form. It is, of course, necessary to retrofit and to put vapour barriers in the right places, to use the right kind of insulation, to treat the house as a hot air balloon and so forth. This is energy conservation. This is necessary for the people who are stuck with a conventional style house — or stuck with conventional style thinking. But I feel that we have to evolve from building houses the way we *think* houses ought to be built, to building houses as they truly ought to be built to best interact with the environment.

That is what my business is. I belong to a company called SEA Group, *Solar Environmental Architecture Group,* in California. Our specific business is trying to evolve this appropriate architecture for each region. We fly all over the United States (we are working in 23 or 24 states at present) and try to develop the system of architecture that best suits that particular climatic area. That does not mean just weather, that means lifestyles, available materials as well as the way people build things and the way people perceive their environment. We also take into account the ways things were done in the past. The traditional input is often very valuable.

When we look at all these patterns in an area and consider the job to be done, we should come pretty close to what is probably the best architectural solution for that particular area.

People can do the same in their own regions, individually or as part of a group, as architects, as professionals, or as non-professionals. When people really start to think about these things, they can come up with a better answer than what they are doing now.

This is not to say that mistakes will not be made. Solar art today is very young. It is just starting to get on its feet; it is very enthusiastic and it doesn't always make the right moves. We are developing a new art and so we will make some mistakes. I think that some of the experts and the pioneers such as Malcolm Wells, Peter van Dresser and Jim DeKorne can testify to the fact that people do make mistakes.

I would like to talk about the fabulous man-made tree. It is a mechanical tree and is something that scientists and engineers could develop today. Technically it is quite feasible to produce an artificial tree that could utilize photosynthesis to produce leaves and fruit. But the fabulous man-made tree has a twist that makes it really quite wonderful. It is a hybrid with different kinds of fruit on different branches. The fruit even comes canned, already processed, which is a rather unique feature — probably the only thing that this tree does better than nature.

This example illustrates that we as mankind, technically advanced as we are, really have no need to involve ourselves with the things that nature does better. Let nature go ahead and do it.

Quite often people undertake tasks that we really do not have to do. They are often very expensive. They are mentally intensive and tend to drain us or to divert our attention from the areas with which we should be concerned. Nuclear energy is a good example of something with which we should not involve ourselves.

Similarly, it is not necessary to use high technology to heat and cool our homes and to heat our domestic hot water. It is important to use the energy that we are endowed with in the proper thermal regimes. It is ludicrous to use fossil fuels, like oil and natural gas, that combust at temperatures in excess of 1000°F, to make electricity and to pump that electricity to our residences and use it to heat water to 140°. That this is particularly foolish is made clear by the fact that the sun can do it for us most of the time.

Let me now consider three methods of domestic heating, or space conditioning. Sun energy came down to earth a long time ago and eventually was stored in the oil that is now underground. It got there by magic, as far as we are concerned. We now have oil wells that pump this depletable resource out of the ground. It is being depleted rapidly, believe it or not, and it is not going to be there forever. This oil is shipped to conversion plants where it is refined, polluting the atmosphere. That refined oil, in the form of house heating fuel, is transported by a cumbersome process to a house where it is held in a storage tank. When we need to heat the house, the oil is drawn into the inside where it is burned in a combustion chamber which is inefficient in itself, with

about 60 per cent of the energy going up the stack. The other 40 per cent of that heat energy is used to heat the house and to keep it about 20°C. Then the heat is lost to the environment through the weather skin. We can easily understand this system, as we have been using it for about 50 years.

The second method is an active solar system. An active system is cost-effective in some climates, but not very many. In this process, there is a flat plate collector that absorbs the sun's energy at its surface. When that flat plate collector gets hot enough, energy can be extracted from it and put into a storage tank. When heat is needed in the house, a little pump turns on to distribute the heat energy around the house to heat it up to 20°C. Finally heat energy, this time more directly from the sun, is lost through the weather skin to the outside.

Now we consider passive solar energy — a Trombe wall application. All we do is shape the building so that it acts as a collector. The home also serves as a thermal storage unit so that when the sun is available in the winter (when we need heat) the energy comes in and is stored in the mass of the house. Then it is distributed in the form of direct radiation from this same mass, heats the house to 20°C then the energy is lost through the weather skin. The same end result, but much simpler.

When we examine these options and think about the economics of it, either as individuals or in global terms, the passive solar alternative is a much more sensible way to go. I advocate passive solar energy as one way of helping to preserve our environment.

Once we begin to think in this manner we can come up with all kinds of possibilities. Of course, we have to carefully consider these and choose those that are appropriate to each individual and region.

We can learn a lot from the way a reptile, the snake, lives in entirely different micro-climates. Snakes in the tropics live in the trees because there is little thermal mass and good hunting up there. It is also shady and there is a lot of wind movement around them. They can keep their body temperature down in the thermal regime where they best function.

In the desert, snakes live underground for most of the year. This is particularly true at night when it gets cold in the desert and in winter. Snakes go underground because the earth's crust is more or less the same temperature all year around.

So should people begin to look at the natural patterns around them and decide if, for instance, in a given environment it makes sense to go underground. I think that going underground may be cost-effective in some environments, but not in all. Generally, underground construction is most cost-effective in more severe climates, either very hot climates or very cold climates. It is not sensible if the climate is fairly moderate.

Architecture should be shaped to best utilize the sunlight, to accept or reject the sunlight as needed. In the tropics we want very little thermal mass, and our buildings should be shaped more like an umbrella that is closed to keep out the sunlight. We do not want heat, either on the ground around the building or in the structure itself. Whereas in a northern or alpine setting, the house should be more like a collector, to trap and store heat.

This is rather abstract thinking, and may not seem relevant, but, since we do not yet know the answers, looking at some of these simple patterns may make certain concepts clear. In a northern situation, for instance, when the sun is available, the house should open up to let in all the sunshine possible. When the sun is not shining, the house should close. This is the beginning of the line of reasoning that pertains to the situation here.

Stated simply: build houses like a Thermos-bottle, with plenty of insulation but able to be opened towards the sun. When the sun is available in sufficient strength, the building can open up and take advantage of that. When the sun is not available, put in the cork and close up the Thermos-bottle house.

Design houses so that they use as little back-up heating as possible. When solar energy and energy conservation methods are used in this climate, it may mean the difference between ten cords and two cords of wood a year. The resident will not have to cut, haul, and burn as much wood.

Architecture ought to respond to the environment, particularly on the exterior. The interior can be divided into various use zones with various thermal regimes. A computer room, for instance, has to have much finer control than an area where the employees take their coffee breaks. A steno pool can not have direct sunlight pouring into it. There are a lot of internal considerations. But the outside of the building is different. Each side of the building can respond to the weather patterns around it. Rather than just build-

ing monolithic glass boxes, or totally underground buildings, perhaps we should take advantage of the various environmental inputs and utilize those for heating, cooling, ventilating or whatever is the task. I predict that we will start to see buildings that look like energy machines, rather than just places which keep out the weather.

Examing appropriate architecture from other regions may help us to discover what is appropriate for northern Canada. I had the opportunity to work in Saudi Arabia a few years ago. In some respects Saudi Arabia is much like northern New Mexico. It is not at all as I thought Saudi Arabia would be. The particular place where I worked is 9000 ft. high and gets cold in the winter. It even gets cold on summer nights. It is a mountainous region and rugged with not much timber left because the people have cut most of it for cooking and heating fires.

The type of farming and architecture practiced there has developed over a period of about 5000 years. The mountains are extensively terraced where the people engage in dry farming. These terraces were built over hundreds of years, using the local rock that was already in place. It works so well that they are still using the same methods today. Even though the country is extremely wealthy, they are building new terraces. But now they no longer do it by hand; they use bulldozers.

The residences make use of the native stone and are built on the worst sections of land, the most rocky outcrops. The roofs of the houses are layers of twigs. This makes a wonderful insulating, fibrous material. There is a vent in the roof for

cooling when it gets a little too warm, but most of the time the houses fairly well moderate the temperature. The overhead sun during the day strikes the earth in the roof and some of it radiates down into the living space. The stone walls absorb the short wave radiation of the sun during the day and conduct it through the walls. Because of the thermal lag of the massive stone structures, they radiate their heat energy to the interior throughout the night. The house is in almost perfect balance with the environment at all times, in this particular micro-climate.

In the same country of Saudi Arabia we find the same people, the same religion, the same economic system, the same government on the shores of the Red Sea. This area is only 60 miles away horizontally and 9000 ft. vertically, but it is an entirely different micro-climate. It is extremely hot and the temperatures rarely drop below 90°F. The clothing of the people is entirely different, they dress more like Navajo Indians rather than in the big robes that are normally thought of as Saudi Arabian.

Each climate has its unique characteristics

The Red Sea Saudi Arabians have a totally different architectural response to their micro-climate. There they use the local brush for their houses so there is very little thermal mass in the buildings. The houses and the ground around them are shaded by umbrella-like structures built to keep out the intense sunlight. Some structures are built with a thatch or palm throng fence around them. It is a rocky area and the fence shades the ground immediately around the structure. The earth mass, therefore, is not directly exposed to the intense sunlight.

Southern France has yet another micro-climate. There are buildings built about 1200 A.D. They are sheep houses which were needed because there is a lot of wind and it can get quite cold, even though the area is near the Mediterranean. They were extremely well-designed with arches which faced south-southeast. The back of the buildings were completely covered and had a kind of aerodynamic shape to take full advantage of the sun and to block the winds. The roofs were insulated with tiles and wood. The morning sunlight was able to reach to the back of the buildings in the winter, to heat and awaken the sheep. At night, the sheep were brought back in from the cold.

A friend of mine in southern France who is an architect has retrofitted one of these sheep houses in a clever way. He had put large sliding glass doors into the arches and insulated the roof so that the sun's energy that comes through is trapped in the mass of the building where it cannot readily re-radiate out. From a heating standpoint the structure is self-sufficient. He has also adapted a greenhouse that both heats and cools the building, and

provides all of the vegetables they use year round.

Massive arches of old sheephouses

No discussion of passive solar energy is complete without mentioning cave dwellings. In northeastern Arizona there are some appropriate cave dwellings, such as the Navajo National Monument. The settlement has a south-facing cliff which overhangs just enough to provide summer shading and yet let the winter sunlight into the dwellings. Up in the cliffs as they are, the houses are out of cold currents, out of the low spots, out of fog areas, up where they can take advantage of the sunlight.

Settlement built on a south-facing cliff

There is great thermal mass in these structures. In the fall, the sunlight begins to penetrate deep into the settlement — conducting into the large thermal mass. If they had had available things like Bead-walls, movable insulation and double-glazing they would not have had to use so much thermal mass. But as it is, the design works quite well. These people survived a rather long time, until they did away with some of their resources.

In nearby northwestern New Mexico are the cave dwellings at Pueblo Bonito. These dwellings are of an extremely sensitive design, one of the first solar collectors in architectural form. The settlement is once again set below a south-facing cliff, but in this case they do not use a cliff overhang for shading. They are, instead, in the wind shadow of the cliff to protect themselves from the blizzards that come in from the north-northwest. The cliff also acts as a reflector of the winter sunlight which comes in at a low angle. Some of this light is absorbed, some is re-radiated and some of it is reflected into the back of the structure.

This settlement used to be seven stories high. It was built so that each unit received sunlight. The building stepped down into a courtyard around a parabolic shape. Each unit had its own small courtyard which was exposed to the sun. Most of the storage units and the security rooms were underground.

One of the interesting things about this particular structure is that it is oriented east-southeast rather than true south. True south used to be one of the things that solar people insisted upon. However, in this particular climate, east of south is a better orientation for a couple of reasons:

in the winter, morning sunlight more quickly warms up the interior of the building; in the summer some of the western sun is blocked off. Since it is oriented more to the east, it is not getting as much exposure to the hot sunset. Victor Olgyay did some computer studies in the 1950's and found that the optimum orientation in Arizona is about 22° east of south. That happens to be the orientation of Pueblo Bonito. I am sure they had not read Olgyay when they designed and built their settlement, but they knew their environment extremely well and took optimum orientation advantage of this setting.

I like direct gain houses because of their architectual freedom and sculptural possibilities. I think it is also the most efficient method of trapping and utilizing solar energy. One of my favourite houses is the Karen Terry house in Sante Fe, New Mexico. I call it *Sun Step*. Karen calls it my house. It steps down a hillside. As far as I know, it is the first to do so.

Sun Step multi-level house

Because the house steps down the hillside it takes advantage of the various thermal regimes. The highest activity level is in the lowest, and coolest, part of the house — in this case the sculpture studio. In the middle level is the next highest

temperature zone, where living and dining take place. The bedroom and bathroom are in the upper level which is the warmest part of the house due to heat stratification and convection which carries the heat into the highest levels. The winter sun strikes interior partitions made of 45-gallon drums filled with water. These constitute the divisions between the levels so we have an internal water storage inside the walls themselves. The exterior walls of the building should be built like a thermos bottle and the mass should be as centralized as possible, away from exterior walls because that is where the heat loss occurs. When bringing solar energy into a building, bring it into the centre so that it is radiated to the interior spaces, and so that it is not lost through an outside wall.

We built movable insulating shutters that were designed to swing over the glass, but Karen never put them in since the house performs adequately. The coldest it ever got was about 56° on a winter morning after she had accidentally left open the outside door. She keeps the house warm by using a small pueblo-style fireplace.

The windows are all double-glazed using patio glass door replacement units. This is double-tempered glass. When they are bought in lots of ten or twenty, they becomes extremely economical. This kind of glazing is one of the best investments that can be made. It will last forever, whereas plastics eventually degrade.

Karen Terry's house is an adobe house. I like earth construction such as rammed earth or adobe. But there are other ways of holding earth together. Malcolm Wells has mentioned that Gordon Schneider is

working with an earth stabilizer that is going to be handy. Schneider is using cellulose additives. This is organic and is not energy intensive. Earth itself is an extremely low energy material. However, it cannot be used underground, rather cement blocks can be used. In the Terry house we used stabilized adobe, but if it gets wet it will deteriorate.

Insulating the exterior of the adobe

Exterior insulation was used. We simply applied rigid insulation to the outside of the adobe. There was a fallacy in New Mexico that adobe houses were warm in the winter and cool in the summer. In fact, the old ones were — when the walls were about three feet thick. But due to economics they started making them fourteen inches thick, and then ten inches, and even thinner. A ten-inch adobe wall is a poor insulator. It will store cold and it will store heat, but it will store the heat in the summer and the cold in the winter. It conducts from the inside to the outside. By putting insulation on the outside, the adobe then becomes internal thermal mass. The building once again can operate as a fly wheel.

We used polystyrene below grade because it is more resistant to absorption of water and we used polyurethane above grade because it will not fall apart if it freezes; there are heavy freezes and thaws in New Mexico. The insulation was wrapped with felt paper, then stucco was applied over it. We preserved a pueblo-style architecture and avoided a lot of annual maintenance.

A corrosion inhibitor was added to the water in the oil drums, the type of inhibitor used in industrial boiler systems. The plugs in the water drums must not be zinc because zinc and water create a battery which will cause the barrel to quickly rust out. We wrapped the drums with stucco mesh and plastered them with adobe plaster for aesthetic reasons. Steve Baer thought I was crazy because I was covering all those beautiful drums with mud, which is as odd a combination of materials as polyurethane and dirt. But it works.

The floors of the house are brick on a sand base. This, combined with the adobe walls and the water in the drums, creates a large storage volume in this house.

Karen had such good luck with her house that she built another one. The second one, however, is built into a hillside. She built it for speculation and hired me to do a plan. In researching the real estate

possibilities, she found that the formula was two bedrooms, two baths, 1500 sq.ft. — so that is what we built.

The house is called *Sun Cave*. It too works rather well. We sank it into a hillside to avoid the heat loss that would be imposed by the north winds. Building into a hillside provides a good profile and might be appropriate in northern climates. The storms blow over it and large heat loss areas are not exposed. The north is always the greatest heat loosing side of a house. By building into the ground we also cut infiltration dramatically, which is one of the greatest heat loss factors. This provides a profile that is responsive to the northern Alberta environment.

Sun Cave earth-sheltered house

We developed the concept of internal thermal mass even farther in this house. In a linear east-west house such as this, I like to put the interior mass wall perpendicular to the solar glazing so that the morning sun hits it from the east, the afternoon sun hits it from the west, and the energy is dissipated to the interior spaces as opposed to outside walls.

In Sun Cave, we used clerestory windows as a handy mechanism for getting the light and the heat into the back of the

house. Not only does this distribute the solar heat better, but it provides better summer ventilation. Another thing a clerestory does is scatter light throughout the building, thereby reducing the glare from the south glazing. These things are important when building a direct-gain house, or even a greenhouse-gain house, especially when there is a lot of direct south-facing glazing.

The back rooms are painted white. Once the energy is in the house and has changed wave lengths, everything does not have to be black. If you paint the rooms white the energy will, in fact, be more readily distributed to the thermal mass. This also provides a much better quality of light in those rooms that are toward the back. Rooms that are built into hillsides do not have to be dark and dank at all. They can be quite open and airy. As a matter of fact, most solar houses are more open and more airy and have a better link to the outside than most conventional houses. People who have the impression that underground or earth-integrated housing has to be dank and cold and cave-like are mistaken. There are many examples that show that it can be quite a refreshing and a secure environment.

My own house is on the west coast. There is a heavy prevailing wind so the house is sunk into the ground around a courtyard. It is oriented slightly east of south. I used earthberming; the earth that was excavated was used for berming around the building. It has a sod roof. This is another type of profile that I think will work in the north as long as it is made water tight.

This house was the first building which I designed to be a passive solar-cooled building. Movable insulation is important. In this case it is a pull-down shade of three layers of aluminum and one of polyester that is pulled down at night and during cold periods. It acts as a radiation barrier and is effective. Not only thick styrofoam achieves an appropriate R factor. Layers of aluminum or reflective membranes will provide effective insulation in most cases.

David Wright's earth-sheltered house with a view tower facing west

Solar collectors are integrated into the house itself. One of the reasons is for aesthetics. I feel that if we are going to develop a solar house, then it is certainly nice to do it alone and have it work. But I also feel that if we want to help solve the so-called energy crisis then we have to have impact on a lot of people; and if we want to have impact on these people then we have to satisfy the American middle class ideal. If we want the American middle class to accept alternatives, then we have to make such housing aesthetically pleasing. By having made an impact on the American middle class, we will also influence that portion of the world's population which looks to America for its ideals and lifestyles.

The only piece of building that sticks up above the landscape is the tower. The tower provides us with a magnificent view to the west. We used tinted glass in the tower to prevent overheating.

We tried to integrate the building as much as possible with landscaping. I think that if we are concerned about the environment, we have to start to blend in with the environment as much as possible. This house was an attempt to do that.

The sunlight comes in through a large bank of south-facing windows and is stored in the poured-in-place concrete walls. This also makes for a superb quality of light inside the house. It is simple, rustic, and economical — and quite pleasing.

The only auxiliary heat in the 1200 sq.ft. structure is one wood stove. During the first winter, I burned a total of 12 pieces of firewood in a 3200 degree day climate.

In other houses in the same area, we have used thermal stratification. Fireplace heat and solar heat are allowed to stratify in the structure, then we use a high efficiency fan to pull that energy down to store it under the floor in the back of the house. This is something that would be suitable in the north. When there is excess heat from solar or from wood heating within the building, collect the heat and put it into storage. Blow it through rocks or sand under the floor of the building; there will be radiant mass from which heat will come for a long time.

In Cody, Wyoming, is a house I call *Prairie Sun.* Such a house is quite suitable to northern Canada and uses radiant heating, passive solar, and direct gain. It has been in operation for two winters and it works extremely well. Night-time insulation is used to cover the windows. The house is crescent shaped. Bedrooms are placed to receive morning sunlight, but the main solar gain occurs in the living spaces. A lot of internal mass is used, as is earth berming. We wanted to go into the ground because of the strong blizzards and prevailing winds, but could not do so because of an 18-inch deep water table. We simply built the house above the water table and bermed all around it. We also shaped the building so the storms would blow over it and leave the solar windows and clerestory windows on the south face clear.

The house has a very simple plan. It allows a lot of light and provides some storage mass. The only auxiliary inside is a little pot belly stove in which they burn a cord and a half of wood during the winter in an 8300 degree day climate.

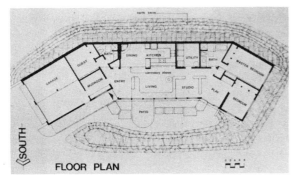

Earth-sheltered solar house in Wyoming

A high quality of light comes through the clerestory. This light is extremely important to the functioning of the house. The light strikes and is absorbed by the massive brick wall at the back.

In addition to massive walls, which can act as room dividers, to store and radiate heat energy, I would probably put a greenhouse on the south side in northern climates. The sun would still penetrate through the greenhouse, but there would be an extra buffer zone as well as something that is usable for year-round vegetable and flower production. A greenhouse in this climate would make a lot of sense. However, it must have movable insulation to prevent massive heat loss at night.

I have a fantasy which I call life support shelter or the steady-state solar house. We now have the technical ability, the materials and the knowledge to develop housing structures that are made out of low-energy regional materials such as stabilized earth. Cheap, light-weight membranes and some electronically controlled apparatus can be imported and used in a system which will grow all the food needed by the inhabitants, recycle all of their waste and water products, and generate their power. This is not done by magic, it uses technology that we have available. I have been saying for a long time that if given enough money and enough time then I could develop such a design. We now have a client who has advanced the money. Now I have only to complete the design. The only variables undetermined are the amount of money it will cost and the amount of time it will take.

The question has been asked, *"What can each of us do to effect the needed changes in society?"*

We are after self-reliance and, to a certain extent, independence from the central government. The means of obtaining these goals can be found in the people who are trying to break away from the established patterns. Other than starting your own little homestead, there are ways to work within existing political and economic structures to effect this autonomy we seek. Confronting the powers-that-be with economic and political arguments is one such way.

Fred Hoffman said in a recent New Mexico Solar Energy Bulletin that the military complex in the United States has a lot of money tied up and, hence, it is a huge investment by the people of the United States, although it is not particularly serving them in a positive, direct fashion and perhaps even acts in a negative manner much of the time. Hoffman suggests that one of the arguments that can be used for decentralization and self-sufficiency is a military one. He points out that as an intensively centralized economic and political entity we are quite vulnerable to enemy attacks. If, by using such arguments, we can convince the government that by conserving energy and by aiming towards decentralization we can better protect ourselves, then some of these agencies might work for us, behind our backs. That would be quite a change from having them working against us, behind our backs, as we are used to.

In fact, I understand that the United States Navy, and possibly the Air Force, have received instructions that by 1985 they are to have a certain number of new structures that are to utilize passive solar energy. This may mean that they will, inadvertantly perhaps, help us work towards decentralization. We may be able to considerably benefit from their work and multi-million-dollar investment.

Leslie Davis

Leslie Davis *was the supervisor of a crew that organized and ran a dozen solar greenhouse workshops throughout New Mexico from 1977 to 1978. She was a charter member of the* Solar Sustenance Team *which trained twenty teams from different States to conduct their own solar greenhouse construction workshops.*

I am from the southwestern United States. I come from a tradition of peoples who have used indigenous materials to create their shelters. Cave dwellings are an example of people choosing places that fit their needs. Large overhangs disallow the summer sun and north walls offer protection from winter winds. Yet, these configurations are such that the winter sun is allowed into the dwellings. It is vitally important that we understand some basic principles that our ancestors knew intuitively and took for granted, principles which we have forgotten and are now beginning to relearn.

One of these principles is to know and make the best use of the location of the sun in the sky during different times of the day and at different times of the year. In the summer the sun is high in the sky. At latitude 56° it gets up to about 57° at noon on June 21. That is the highest the sun gets in the sky. Also remember that the summer sun rises well to the north of east and sets well to the north of west. However, in the winter, on December 21, the sun at latitude 56° does not get any higher than 10° above the horizon and remains completely in the southern sky. There are two considerations — the height or altitude of the sun, and the azimuth of the number of degrees from south at which the sun rises and sets at a specific time of year.

At the spring and fall equinoxes, in March and September, the sun will rise and set at exactly due east and west, and it gets to be about 34° above the horizon at noon. Those are important pieces of information. People need it for any solar-tempered building that they design.

An attached solar greenhouse uses solar energy to provide household heating and to produce food. It is like adding a room onto one's house which is a producer instead of a consumer. It is not something that just uses heat, but is something that generates heat for itself as well as for the adjoining structure. Not too many rooms in our homes can do that.

For the most part I will consider retrofitting, taking an existing house and attaching a greenhouse to it.

I want to emphasize that the greenhouse does not have to face due south. About 30° either way is quite satisfactory and, if there is a choice, go somewhat to the east, especially in the high mountain regions.

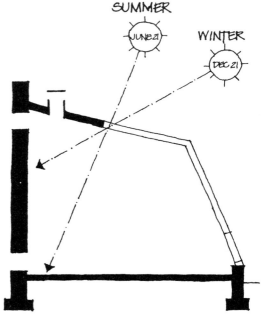

GREENHOUSE SUN ANGLES

When the greenhouse is on the south side of the house the south wall of the house is now the north wall of the greenhouse. The roof can be half opaque and half clear; a tilted shed-type greenhouse. It is what someone would build if you asked them to build a solar greenhouse in northern New Mexico and in most of the middle latitude areas of the United States. We will have to make some changes as we move farther north.

Designers must know where sun is in the greenhouse for two reasons: plenty of sun in the winter to heat the greenhouse and the house as well as to grow vegetables, and shading in the summer to prevent overheating. By using this half-and-half roof design, I get plenty of sun well up the back wall, yet in the summer that wall is completely out of the sun. The house is actually going to be cooler because of the greenhouse than it might have been otherwise. We are not just interested in heating, we are also getting involved in cooling.

We are also not just designing a greenhouse for thermal heat performance. We are interested in a place in which to grow things. Our engineers and architects who worry about thermal performance, insolation, and climatological data should talk to our gardeners. They have to be aware of what is planted and where it's planted in the greenhouse.

In the spring, summer and fall the sun is mainly in the front of the greenhouse and it is warm during the day and at night. Put hot-loving vegetables in front. Things like lettuce and other cool weather crops can survive better in the back where it is a little bit cooler. Tender plants like eggplants, tomatoes, peppers and cucumbers like the heat of the front and they will also shade the cool-loving plants at the back. You can shade the outside of the greenhouse with sunflowers.

Remember, however, where the winter sun is. It will shine far in the back of the greenhouse. Temperatures are colder than the summer, so things that need a lot of heat should go in the back of the greenhouse. Cool weather crops, broccoli, cabbage, spinach, chard, can better withstand the cool, high light conditions up in the front.

One of the most controversial areas in greenhouse design is the tilt of the front face. That seems to be *the* greenhouse question. But, it really doesn't make much difference. A lot of people have their own prejudices, but we have found that the tilt little affects the greenhouse performance and there are sometimes other considerations. In a greenhouse with a front face tilted back as far as 60°, for instance, it is hard to work inside and not bump your head on the rafters. It also tends to overheat in the summertime.

A vertical greenhouse, at the other extreme, has plenty of headroom in which to work and plenty of room for plants. But there must be some transparent roof area so that there is some sun in the summer, especially in the lower latitudes where the sun is close to vertical. If there was no glazing in the roof, we would have very little growing space since vegetables need direct sun. However, this means we will have more heat loss in the winter.

A vertical face should be suitable north of latitude 49° because during the winter the main solar gains are from reflection off the snow. In addition, the low winter sun will be able to go straight in. Sunlight transmits through glass according to the angle at which it strikes the glass. If the sun is normal, or perpendicular to the glazing, more of the light will pass through. As the sun gets away from perpendicular, some light begins to reflect. Glazing should be as perpendicular as possible to the winter sun, but not to the summer sun. The low winter sun is, therefore, another argument for a vertical face at this latitude.

A greenhouse design is a series of trade-offs among thermal performance, growing space, living space, the materials available, the money available and aesthetic considerations.

Designers must provide two kinds of ventilation. A greenhouse is a solar collector in which the glazing has been moved away from the back panel and put people and plants in between. But the heat which it generates still must get into the house. On a clear winter's day, even at latitude 56°, and even with cold temperatures, the greenhouse can be as hot as 80 to 90°F by 11:00 in the morning. Since the greenhouse does not need to be over 90°F, some kind of ventilation to the house is called for. This is a true passive system using convection currents in which hot air rises and cool air falls. A low vent and a high vent to the house is needed; doors and windows have proved to be one of the best combinations. A doorway provides plenty of height to set up a convection current.

By the same token, heat may need to be dumped in the summer although that is not always the case. Once again, a high vent and a low vent is needed. Place the vents so that the prevailing summer winds can come in at a low point and go out at a high point.

Top and bottom vents of attached greenhouse

Water-filled drums used for storage and as stands

Heat storage is another important element. Forty-five gallon drums of water make excellent storage which is needed in a solar greenhouse not just to keep that greenhouse from freezing in the winter, but to keep it from overheating in the summer. If the heat can be stored in thermal mass and not in the air, it does not get as hot in the greenhouse. Basically it is flattening out the diurnal swings of highs and lows. The greenhouse will lose heat rapidly as the sun goes down, the water drums start working. If the drums are 60 to 70°F and it is 35°F inside the greenhouse, they are going to lose their heat to the inside of the greenhouse.

Another use for water drums is as plant stands. Plants like bottom heat. If the roots are warm, they will grow faster. The drums provide that bottom heat.

Night-time insulation is another important consideration, especially in colder climates. However, it is not neat, simple, or easy. It is cumbersome and expensive. It can be put on the inside or on the outside. It can be a curtain, a roll-up shade or shutters. Many things are possible but none of them feel comfortable to me. It is difficult to put it inside because one has to manoeuvere around plants. Putting it outside is difficult because it is cold and windy. It has to seal well or a convection current is created that can thermosyphon out enough heat to make the insulation useless. In New Mexico we do not have to deal with such insulation, but I think Canadians are going to need to consider it.

Types of insulation include the curtains and shades I have mentioned, rigid foam, and things like *Beadwall.* Beadwall is Steve Baer's invention. It is basically two

layers of glazing to which a vacuum cleaner is hooked to blow styrofoam beads in at night, creating an insulating wall, and suck them out during the day. Glycerine is added to prevent the build-up of static electricity. It is a neat design, but it is expensive.

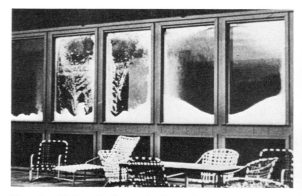

Beadwall insulating windows in operation

Perhaps Canadians should consider a solar greenhouse as a season extender, say from February to November, for growing things and for heating the house. If there are a couple of clear days or a clear, sunny week in January or December it may also get warm enough in the greenhouse to add heat to the house. Do not expect that it is going to be a heat collector or a food producer during the entire winter. Adopting this attitude can save the expense of night-time insulation.

Let us review greenhouse design elements. Design for the sun angles in both winter and summer. A protractor and some cross sections of a greenhouse on paper helps to determine where the sun is going to be in the greenhouse at different times of the year.
Ventilation: In the winter, get the heated air into the house; In the summer, dump it — provide high and low vents to set

up convection currents.
Storage: Provide plenty of thermal mass, water preferably or earth beds, rocks, a stone floor or a brick floor. What David Wright has applied to solar houses also applies to solar greenhouses.
Finally, there is night-time insulation, as discussed above.

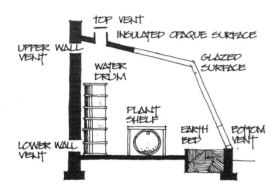

GREENHOUSE ELEMENTS

The Doug Balcomb house is considered to be one of the best performing passive solar greenhouse around. Designed by Wayne and Suzanne Nichols, it is a house built around a greenhouse. Temperatures in the living space are always between 68 and 72°F, summer and winter, night and day. They lit the fire in the woodburning auxiliary only a couple of times last winter.

The rock storage system is underneath the floor and the fan system is used to bring the heat down. The turret on the top is a vent that opens up in the summer as do the two doors in the front of the greenhouse, and the side, east and west entries.

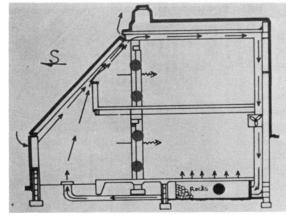

The Balcomb's passive solar greenhouse with a cross-section showing the rock storage

A thick adobe wall separates the greenhouse from the house. Mud is a good conductor of heat, although slow and provides great thermal mass. The dark adobe walls soak up heat all day long and about eight hours later, just about when its needed, it starts migrating into the living space behind. Because of this mass the greenhouse never over-heats. The plan of the house is triangular and is cut across by the greenhouse.

Greenhouses as integral parts of houses, or greenhomes, as some people are

calling them, are important to consider when building from scratch.

Bill Yanda started about six years ago with some money from the Four Corners Regional Commission in New Mexico to build greenhouses. Bill had a pit grow-hole on his property, and in the cold winter of 1971, when it was about -40°F things were growing in it. He was dumping heat in the middle of winter. So he decided to dig a hole on the south side of his house and put the grow hole there. But his brother-in-law, who is a builder, pointed out that his house would fall down if he excavated that close to it. Therefore, Bill decided on an above ground attached greenhouse. The reigning solar experts at the time told him that he could not use 80° and 90°F heat for space heating, but that it would have to be 160° or 180° or 190°F. However, subsequent greenhouses proved that to be wrong.

Eventually, and with further funding, we began working with Bill conducting greenhouse workshops and training people all over the country. We recently finished a training program in conjunction with the United States Department of Energy in which we trained 20 groups from across the country. We taught them not only how to build greenhouses and plant in them, but how to organize community workshops. Most of our experiences have been in lower income, rural areas. But we know that if you can sell it to middle America, you can probably sell it to anybody, so it is important that these things be aesthetically pleasing to a lot of people.

Midland, Michigan, has very cool, cloudy winters and shady deciduous trees in the summer. In the suburban area is a greenhouse which is architecturally integrated with the house. It is on the west side because the south side of the house was right at the property line. The north wall, therefore, is heavily insulated. The south wall is vertical and on the roof is a saw tooth arrangement of clerestory windows. This system allows a lot of light in the greenhouse. It is painted bright white inside to reflect the light because there is little mass except in the floor. I was in the greenhouse in the winter on a very cloudy day. The saw tooth arrangement and the white interior made it much lighter inside than it was outside. This greenhouse is done very, very well.

Something that a lot of people forget is that plants need light from all directions and by the very nature of an attached solar greenhouse you are taking away all of their north light. They must be given some in return. A little bit of east and west glazing helps, as do sawtooth or other clerestory arrangements. If you use a sawtooth arrangement be certain to carefully caulk the bottom of each "valley." This is the weakest point in such a design as far as leaking is concerned.

When attaching a greenhouse to a two storey house, build the greenhouse so that the top of it is above the floor level of the second storey of the house. Because of stratification, the hottest air in a greenhouse is at the top and hot air in the top of a room does not do very much good. Psychologically one feels warmer if the feet are warm, not if the head is warm. If that hot air is kept at the floor level, the resident will feel warmer than having that same hot air at the top of the room. With a two storey house make the greenhouse wall fairly tall, and install a vent so heat can go from the top of the

greenhouse to the floor level of the second storey.

The stratification can also be used to pull in air from lower levels and to cool the house when needed. In the previous example of a two storey house, such a ventilation pattern can be arranged by opening up further vents high in the second storey and vents low on the north wall of the first storey.

The narrower the greenhouse is, the more effective a heat collector it will be. As it becomes wider it becomes less efficient. Even with the low winter sun, a greenhouse which is too wide will not allow the light to reach halfway up the back wall as we desire. I would suggest a geometry of eight to 12 ft. in width and at least 16 ft. in length. Another problem with too wide a greenhouse is that even though the sun gets in, the warmed air has to travel farther to get back into the living area. The wider greenhouse is less efficient in heating the room behind it. Therefore, it should be longer than it is wide, approximately one and a half times as long.

Greenhouses are wonderful places to be — for children, for dogs, for cats, for people — and everybody ought to have one. My greenhouse produced enough heat to heat virtually all of my house most of the year and to heat at least the front two rooms for all of the year. It cools my house in the summertime, and has produced vegetables year round for my husband and myself. So it is certainly worth whatever trouble it takes.

"Please sum up good greenhouse design strategy in terms of orientation, glazing angle, and the storage of heat for Alberta latitudes."

First of all, you want it to be as much to the south as possible. I would say that anything within 30° of due south will work about as well as anything facing directly south. If you have a choice, go to the east and not to the west.

As for glazing angles, I am not totally sure what are the optimum angles for this latitude. I have only worked as far north as the Canadian border, but my guess is a vertical front face with a fairly steep, tilted roof that is partially glazed would make the best use of your sun angles.

"Can you limit the glazing to the vertical south side of a greenhouse and have the roof closed and insulated?"

We have done that in the northern parts of Michigan, Minnesota, and North Dakota where their winters are cold and cloudy, but those have had quite generously tilted front faces. You can do that with a vertical front face but you will have virtually no direct sunlight in the spring and fall, and especially summer. So it may not be your best option.

"What are effective ways to prevent big temperature drops and overheating?"

A proper design will take care of a lot of overheating. You want to be careful not to have a front face that is perpendicular to the summer sun; a 45° roof angle could cause problems, especially here. To temper the diurnal swings, (the high and low temperatures), have plenty of storage. We use water; it is the most effective medium for its volume, and 45-gallon drums are cheap. Because of your cold winters, you may need to put some antifreeze in the water in the drums.

"Would it be feasible to locate a swimming pool in a greenhouse?"

Yes, if you have the room and can circulate the water so that it does not become stagnant. It can be a good heat sink.

"Can you extend the growing season but avoid overheating by putting greenhouses on the east or west side of the house, and use the south side for say, a Trombe Wall or direct gain heating?"

You could, but the problem with east and west heating, especially in this climate, is that in the winter the sun is mostly in the southern sky. In the summer, however, because it rises so far to the north of east and sets so far to the north of west, the sun is mostly in the eastern and western skies. So if you built your greenhouse on the east or west side, it would get very hot in the summertime and it would not get warm at all in the winter.

"Would lack of light for plant growth be more detrimental here in December, January and February than the actual cold?"

Yes. The light is as much of a problem as the cold because of your low light levels. That is one of the reasons you should decide if it is worth trying to get through those months or to consider a greenhouse as a season extender.

"How important is reflected light to plants?"

It is very important and you want to bounce around as much light as you can. Anything that cannot absorb heat and be a heat sink should be painted a light colour and used to bounce that light around.

"Is there such a thing as an indigenous insulation material that is cheap, efficient and durable?"

Bruce Edwards of Wabasca tells me that the Cree Indian people, before the coming of boards for roofs, used to use sticks with clay and a three-quarter inch layer of spagnum moss, more sticks and clay, more moss, and so on; three or four layers like that. The clay served as a vapour barrier and the purpose of the spagnum moss was to insulate. This is what they did for hundreds of years to provide themselves with warm houses.

"Would you give us your analysis of glass versus fibreglass glazing please?"

I will not do an analysis for you, but refer you to chapter nine in the *Solar Greenhouse Book* from Rodale Press. I can give you some personal experience with the two products. We have been working in low income rural situations. Fibreglass is half the cost of glass, it doesn't get broken in a workshop, it goes up fast and easy, and you can nail it. Those are considerations that are important to us. As far as the plants are concerned it also diffuses the light which they like. Glass on the other hand is durable, but is harder to install.

"When designing a new house, are there problems in incorporating a greenhouse into the living space?"

I think there would be. Although it would perform better thermally, you may not want to dump all the humidity from your greenhouse into your living space. Particularly in a really cold climate. You have to be able to control that. In addition, if it is cold at night, you will want to close it off because the convection current will reverse and pull heat from the house. Humidity may not be quite as much of a problem. We built one in Louisiana, in the swamp, with removable panels for summer and flap vents all the way around the bottom and big dormers in the house. The greenhouse is cooling the house better than it has ever been cooled before, as well as heating it during the short heating season.

"When adding to an existing house how do you protect the existing wood frame house wall from humidity of the greenhouse?"

If not already treated, I would suggest you treat it. But don't use something that will kill plants. I would suggest copper naphanate.

"Another advantage of letting greenhouses freeze during severest winter is elimination of most viruses and some insect problems."

Of course, especially in this climate. If it is going to freeze anyway you might as well let your aphids and white flies go too. I don't do that however, I have too many perennials in my greenhouse and too many herbs. I have gone through two winters and taken plenty of food out of my greenhouse and my insect population has not been a problem because of my ladybugs.

"Would tin foil be of any assistance in the greenhouse?"

Yes, I can see some places where it might. I have used it in some back wall areas that don't get enough light. However, this winter I painted the top half of the north wall of my greenhouse, the adobe wall, white, and that did a much better job than tin foil does. I have also been told that reflected light from a reflective surface can be detrimental to plants.

"How would you deal with frosting of the glazing?"

That is going to happen, but if you double glaze it will not happen as severely. When it gets very cold you will have condensation on the inside that will frost up and it will rain in your greenhouse the next morning. I do not do anything, it is moisture in the greenhouse.

"What about a sunken greenhouse above the water table but below the general floor level so that you can integrate circulation with rock storage?"

I would agree with you on the rock storage. But in a retrofitting situation this can get very complicated and expensive. My own experience tells me to avoid complicated things and stay as simple as possible.

My first ideas about greenhouses for this latitude included sunken ones. However, I am now somewhat concerned about the frost problems this far north. Perhaps we should consider the idea of floating a greenhouse with no footing at all. Not having to worry about frost heave might outweigh the extra heat loss that you may

experience without the earth protection. Let me make it clear though, that if you can avoid frost heaving (one of the most important design adaptations for extreme northern climates is to sink the greenhouse perhaps three feet into the ground) it helps to decrease heat loss. If you have water table problems, you can use earth berming.

"What type of floor do you recommend?"

I would recommend something you can sweep. I am saying that as a gardener, not as a builder. It is nice to get those dead plants off the ground. Gravel works well, but it is difficult on your knees when you are planting and it is difficult to sweep and to keep clean. Concrete block, old broken tile, paving brick, adobe floors are all relatively easy to sweep and provide some heat storage.

"What is the incidence of injuries in these projects?"

There have been two injuries in four years and do you know who has been the victim both times? Me. They were purely accidental and it was better it happened to me than to an onlooker. This problem has come up recently with groups in urban areas and we have to be careful about liability. You have to stress safety because it could otherwise be a problem.

"What percentage of your workshop participants go on to show others how to build greenhouses?"

Thank you for asking that question. We have been able to document through the Solar Sustenance Team and the New Mexico Solar Energy Association that for every greenhouse that is built in a community in one year, there will be ten or eleven within the next year.

James DeKorne

James DeKorne *has been working with solar greenhouses and hydroponics for many years. He is currently experimenting with wind generators, grey water retrieval systems, composting toilets and wood-burning water heaters. De-Korne is the author of* The Survival Greenhouse *and a contributor to* The Solar Greenhouse Book.

A good many years ago when I was young and idealistic, I read *Walden* by Henry David Thoreau. I was very much taken with that book because it seemed to offer a kind of metaphor to living the good life. Although I am many years older now than when I first read it, I am still shamefully idealistic. I have endeavoured to try to live that kind of life with that kind of perspective. The only difference between Thoreau and myself is that I am married and I have two children. Thoreau was a bachelor, as far as we know he never even had a girl friend. I thought that if Thoreau's experiment could only be duplicated by someone of his exact temperament, it would be a pretty invalid kind of experiment. Those principles would work for anybody if they want to apply themselves to it. As the years went by, fate ordained that I should end up in El Rito, New Mexico. That was where my Walden pond was going to be.

A one-acre homestead was all that I could afford at the time. An altitude of 7,000 feet means that it is very, very cold. Even on summer evenings it cools off. There are probably only a few evenings in July that the temperature does not go below 50°F, so it is very difficult to raise tomatoes outdoors. The growing season for all practical purposes is only about 90 days.

In addition to this handicap, the rainfall over the last several years has only been about 11.75 inches annually. This means that in the summer we often cannot raise food without irrigation. My wife and I irrigate our crops with ditch water, and usually by the end of June or the middle of July the ditch is completely dried up.

Since my ideal was to be self-sufficient, to provide all of my own food, I realized that I would have to go to some other method of raising food. I could not rely on the outside conditions, so I would have to create my own growing space. Naturally my thoughts went to greenhouses.

In about 1971 when the *Whole Earth Catalogue* was popular, the authors mentioned the Llama Grow-hole, which was a pit greenhouse in New Mexico about 70 miles from where I lived. It was a season extender because it was built into the ground and the earth evened out the temperature. The creators were able to raise food, so they claimed, all year round. Immediately I thought that my greenhouse would have to be a pit greenhouse, that it was the only thing that would work.

Ironically, at this same time, Bill Yanda, whom I did not know then, was going through similar thinking. Bill was going towards the attached greenhouses whereas I was going towards the pit greenhouse. As it turns out, I am totally in his camp now. I would not even think of a pit greenhouse anymore, unless it was attached to the home. But there are difficulties in digging a hole right next to your house if you are retrofitting.

As mentioned, we have a low rainfall and a 90-day growing season and it is very difficult to raise anything outside. I wanted to create a little man-made eco-system to provide maximum output from a minimum input. That meant no fossil fuels, I could only work with natural systems.

My wife and I received no government grants and everything was done with our own money. But in my shameless idealism I had to pay some kind of tribute to Thoreau. I called our homestead *The Walden Foundation.*

The Walden Foundation in New Mexico

In those days, in 1973, there was little information about greenhouses. I am more of a poet than a scientist, but I knew that greenhouses had to face south. But if I had to face my greenhouse south, it would have been on a diagonal to my property line. It would have looked strange and I did not want that. I wanted it to be right along with the fence lines and along the driveway, so I faced it west. Despite the fact that this greenhouse, designed in 1973, did not use double-glazing and faces the wrong way, it still works well during the summer. However, it is not effective in the winter.

Along the west wall I installed a tank for water storage. Water storage is a good idea, but I thought rather than having 45-gallon drums in there not doing anything, I would raise fish in the water tank and do a double service. I could raise fish and heat the greenhouse at the same time. So that became part of the design.

Fish require that a certain water temperature be maintained and that the water be filtered. I realized that I would need power. In considering the power sources available, I decided upon a wind generator. The electricity would run pumps to cycle the water from the fish tank, through a solar panel, through a filter system, and back into the tank. It would be a modified active system running off the wind.

At the same time, I decided that hydroponics had a lot of advantages. I decided to try hydroponics, using a very simple technique. In a hydroponics system the plant receives its food in liquid form. The plant, instead of growing in soil, has its roots in gravel, perlite, or sometimes, even sawdust. This medium is just to hold the roots, all the food comes in the water solution.

I cut 45-gallon drums in half lengthwise and braised a tube on the bottom of each half, attaching a hose. On the other end of each half I placed a 5-gallon oil can.

Hydroponic growing and feeding system

To feed the plants, I lift the end up and solution runs out of the 5-gallon can into gravel, irrigating the plants from below. As soon as the 5-gallon can is empty, I put it back on the ground and it drains back down. It is, as I said, a very simple technique.

Sunlight is the energy input. It comes into the greenhouse. It also creates wind, and that produces our electricity. Starting up at the top we have aquaculture or raising fish. The water in which the fish live is very rich in nutrients and so we leach the nutrient rich water through compost, in which we are raising worms to feed to the fish. This water produces our hydroponic fluid which feeds the vegetables.

Aquaculture tank which feeds the vegetables

Our leftover vegetables are fed to rabbits. Why do I have rabbits in the greenhouse? The process of photosynthesis is a result of the action of sunlight, water and carbon dioxide. Carbon dioxide is probably the most important fertilizer that plants get. But since it exists normally in the air, we do not think of carbon dioxide as a fertilizer. We cannot readily raise the concentration level of carbon dioxide in the outside air. In a greenhouse, however, which is a closed environment, we can raise the carbon dioxide level. Studies have shown that, even in the winter when there is little sunlight, an increase of carbon dioxide level will, in effect, compensate for the low light level. I concluded that it was important to raise the carbon dioxide level in my greenhouse.

Rabbits fertilizing the air with CO_2

Of course, carbon dioxide is what we breathe out. We take in oxygen and exhale carbon dioxide. Any animals living in your greenhouse will be creating carbon dioxide. Hence, I used rabbits.

The rabbits provide the carbon dioxide which effectively fertilizes the vegetables. They also provide the manure which feeds the earthworms which feed the fish. Therefore, we have a complete cycle.

Rabbits also have a very fortunate breeding cycle. They come into heat about once every 30 days and their gestation period is also about 30 days. It seems that at any given time, if a rabbit does not have a litter, then more than likely she is in heat. You begin with three does and one buck and on the first of May you breed doe A. Then on the first of June doe A is giving birth and you are breeding doe B. On the first of July doe A's litter is ready to slaughter, doe B is kindling, and you are breeding doe C. In this manner it is quite possible in one year to produce about 400 pounds of protein if you have good breeding stock. You can produce even more if you have more rabbits.

Four hundred pounds is equivalent to raising a calf every year, at much less trouble and expense. It makes a lot of sense to keep your rabbits in your greenhouse, to provide carbon dioxide, and at the same time to provide protein.

However, remember that every eco-system is a local eco-system: what works in one area may not work in another.

There is a great deal of controversy about organic versus chemical methods of food production. Hydroponic gardening is generally done with pure nutrient salts that are manufactured by a chemical company, not by using a compost heap. In the old days, I believed that organic food was nutritionally different from the food raised with chemicals. I now feel that the nutritional difference is zero. Organic manures have to be broken down into their inorganic form before the plant can use them and the plant does not know the difference between an atom of nitrogen which came from a test tube and an atom of nitrogen which came from a compost heap.

Comparing different sources of nutrients

There are many good reasons for not putting chemicals on soil, but I'm not talking about soil, I'm talking about hydroponic growing bins which are filled with gravel. I tried making some organic hydroponic solution but I finally gave up on it because it was a lot of work. Every batch of compost that is used, through which water is leached to make the hydroponic solution, has a little different chemical composition from previous batches. That means you have to test it and you have to add nutrients to keep the solution uniform.

In 1973, when I first completed this greenhouse, I bought 50 pounds of Hyponex, which is a common hydroponic chemical. Today, in 1979, I still have about ten pounds left.

Hydroponic chemicals last much longer than chemicals used on the soil. One reason is that the chemicals are constantly recycled. What the plant does not use runs back into the container. It is not like pouring the solution on the ground where it leaches down into the water table and disappears. The solution is, instead, contained in a closed system. For that reason, hydroponics is efficient and conserves both water and nutrients.

We found that on about February 21st even though the weather was not getting any warmer, suddenly plants would start growing. Between February 15 and February 23 the plant growth would definitely increase. That was because there was more light. It was not the temperature, as it was still cold in the greenhouse, but the light level that made a tremendous difference.

To increase this light we tried experiments using reflectors. I found that during the early part of the growing season, around the end of February, reflectors would considerably boost the growth. But after the middle of March, the reflectors did not seem to make much of a difference. In other words, the light intensity was such that by mid-March, the reflectors did not add to it.

Even though we could increase the light intensity with reflectors, we could not increase its duration. At the winter solstice, we have ten hours of sunlight and at the summer solstice we have fourteen hours. If I could increase the amount of light during the winter by four hours, then I could theoretically have the growth equivalent to a summer's day.

I used the wind generator to this end, a 200 watt, *Wincharger.* I did not know much about wind-generated electricity and I thought that using a wind generator was just like turning on a switch in the house. I hung a flourescent fixture over the plants. To help keep them warm, I built a plastic tent around the tanks. I installed a time switch on the light so that for two hours before sunrise and two hours after sunset the lights would go on. That would increase my daylight to about fourteen hours. The only problem was that there was not enough wind to keep the batteries charged, hence there was not enough light.

A Wincharger and a Jacobs with a solar collector in the foreground

I also used a kerosene light to help keep it warm at night, and to provide carbon dioxide, which did help. But I finally gave up trying to grow vegetables in the winter.

The lack of wind also caused problems in the fish tank. Power from the wind was to be used to pump the water from the fish tank through a solar panel, where it would be heated. The water would also be treated in this manner. But during periods of insufficient wind, the pump could not function. I still believe that if you do have enough wind this system will work just as I had designed it.

Aquaculture is, theoretically, just as easy as raising chickens or rabbits. Because of the efficiency of a cold-blooded animal like a fish, almost all of the food it eats goes into putting on weight; whereas, about 90 per cent of what is fed to a warm-blooded animal is burned off as body heat. But there are a lot of problems with aquaculture. One of them is the susceptibility of tropical fish to disease. Another is their sensitivity to the water temperature.

One of my problems was that I used blue gill sun fish. Talapia is an herbivorous fish which is generally used in aquaculture. Since it is not native to the United States, the fish must be bought from special hatcheries and I could not afford that. I went to a nearby pond with a fishing rod and some worms and caught about 55 blue gill sun fish and I planted them in my tank. I raised worms to feed them, but it was impossible to raise enough worms, short of having a worm ranch. The fish were voracious. Soon my worm supply ran out, so I decided to forget about aquaculture.

There are other reasons to carefully reconsider aquaculture. Other than a cold water fish like trout, fish will not put on much weight below 70°F. Talapia, for instance, is a warm water fish and it cannot survive in water temperatures below 50°F. One good frost could destroy all of your work.

I feel that essentially the answer is to not think so big. Think more in terms of an aquarium, a 45-gallon drum that has been made into an aquarium. This would use thermostats and pumps to cycle water through a small solar panel to keep the water in the drum warm enough for fish. The other area of concern is aeration and filtration. What I have envisioned is the same system that works in home aquariums scaled to a larger size. I would suggest using components that can be run off a 12-volt generator.

Even though my pit greenhouse was not an unqualified success, I learned that I really like hydroponics. It is simple even if it sounds complicated. There are ten reasons why I favour hydroponics.

One of the myths about hydroponics (and I am guilty of perpetrating this myth) is that hydroponics will outgrow soil three to one. This is not true. Hydroponics merely provides an optimum feeding system for plants and because it is optimum the plants seem to grow bigger and faster and produce more fruit. But the same thing would occur in soil if you had the optimum conditions. Optimizing the growing conditions is reason number one.

Another advantage of hydroponics is that it conserves water and nutrients because everything is recycled. Thirdly, it is impossible to overwater or underwater your plants since they are being given just what they need. With soil it is much harder to know if you have overwatered or underwatered your plants. The nutrient mix in your soil is also unknown, especially if you are using an organic compost. If you use a hydroponic chemical mix, you know exactly what is in it. It is a perfectly balanced plant food and the plant is getting everything that it needs.

A fifth advantage of hydroponics is that it is possible to use low energy automation. It is also possible to utilize space in a greenhouse which otherwise would go to waste.

There is also a possibility that, since it is a liquid you are using to feed the plant, you could run that liquid through a solar panel and could keep it heated in the winter. It is well-known that if the soil temperature is, say 70°F and your air temperature is 40°F, then the plant reacts to the soil temperature and will grow very well. We cannot say that it will grow as well as if the air temperature were 70°F also, but we can compensate for low air temperatures by having a high soil temperature.

The eighth advantage is the possibility of using carbonated water as a carbon dioxide implementation. I did just that in an experiment I will discuss later.

Hydroponics is inexpensive. I have gone six years on 50 pounds of Hyponex.

The main advantage is that it is very, very efficient. Once a system is set up it almost runs itself. It is possible to design a system in which everything is done automatically, such as the one I am using now.

I might point out here that there are ways to maintain winter food production other than using hydroponics in greenhouses. We found that our chickens laid a lot more when they were given green food, so we fed them sprouts. We simply put oats or barley in a tray, sprouted them, and then fed them to the chickens. In this manner we found that we could amost equal our summer egg production during the winter months.

Sprouting feed for the chickens

We maintain our salad vegetables during the winter by growing them in aluminum trays on our window sill. We put the plants close together and obtain tremendous yields out of a small space.

I believe that vertical walls are the best for a greenhouse. They are the easiest to work with. If I were building in the north, then I would not even consider any other angle for a greenhouse wall. Because

Fairview is so far north, there is no advantage in having a tilted greenhouse wall.

I previously mentioned my CO_2 experiment. Carbonated water is nothing but CO_2 in water. I used club soda, which is carbonated water. Two tanks were planted with the same type of plants on the same day. I used the same sized seedlings and kept everything as identical as possible. The only variable was that one tank received a normal hydroponic solution every day, while the other tank received a normal hydroponic solution one day and a quart of club soda the next day.

The tray on the right received the Club Soda

The tank which received the club soda every other day experienced an 81 per cent increase in growth over the control tank. Using club soda is an expensive way to increase the carbon dioxide supply. But it is possible to buy carbonating pumps, which are used in bars and restaurants, to make carbonated water. These can be obtained from second-hand restaurant supply stores at a relatively low cost. I create my own carbonated water.

It is important to take into account the fact that carbonated water has a pH different from that needed by plants. After I have poured the carbonated water into the growing beds I must drain it out as soon as it stops fizzing. Using this technique I had no problem with the pH difference causing changes in my plant growth.

My initial system of watering the gravel bed was a very tedious manual way of doing it. But I had wanted to keep it as simple as possible and was not interested in automation. Another method is to use a timer and a pump. The timer would be set to turn on the pump at various times during the day to feed the plants.

I have been using a new system. There is a raised container of nutrient solution which has a drip spout to drip into a growing bin which is nothing but a long trough. This trough drains into another container at a lower level. In the lower container is placed a sump pump which is controlled by a switch connected to a float valve in the upper container. When the top container is filled with solution it drips the solution onto the plant bed and runs down the growing bed, irrigating the plants, and drains into the container at the end. As the nutrient solution in the upper container is depleted, the float valve lowers and trips the switch, which is connected to the sump pump. The sump pump pumps the solution from the lower container back to the upper container. As the fluid fills the upper container the float valve rises to shut off the pump.

But to make the system totally automatic I had to compensate for the solution that will either evaporate or be used by the plants. For this, I have installed a float valve in the lower level and another tank with water in it. Therefore, if the level of solution in the lower tank goes down, water is automatically added. As long as

the power does not go off, the plants can be perfectly fed and watered for extended periods.

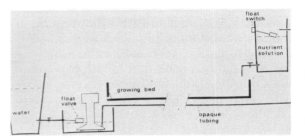

Automatic feeding hydroponic system

The pump in this system uses about 100 watts of electricity. It runs for 15 seconds, 8 times per day. Using a 30-day month, it runs about one hour a month, which is to say 200 watt hours. It would take five months to use one kilowatt hour of electricity. Where I live, one kilowatt hour costs 7 cents. I think that is an energy bargain. I think that is what you would call appropriate technology.

The man who developed this is Dr. P. A. Schippers of Cornell University. In his research greenhouse at Cornell he has developed some other useful techniques.

One technique uses 2 x 4's spaced about three inches apart with black plastic laid in between them to form troughs. Lettuce is planted in small pots which are simply placed in the troughs. He does not use perlite or gravel. The plants grow in the hydroponic solution itself. You can plant close together and the whole thing runs automatically. It is inexpensive, using mostly black plastic.

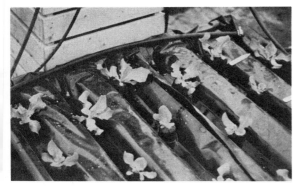

2 x 4 growing beds planted with lettuce

Dr. Schippers is from the Netherlands where there are more acres under glass than in the entire United States. He has received so many enquiries about his system, most of them sent by me, that he has in self-defense formed a little company to supply things like the switch and the pumps, which are sometimes difficult to obtain. He puts out a catalogue and he sells plans for building these systems, and supplies hints for using hydroponics.

In my greenhouse I adopted Dr. Schipper's system. I used the 2 x 4 idea putting the plastic on top and simply setting the whole thing on top of my drum halves. I used an old water heater which I salvaged from the dump for the upper container. I used the old faucets from the water heater and adjusted them to drip into the growing bed. For my lower container I used a plastic baby bathtub that I bought at a dime store. I have an evaporator cooler pump in the bathtub which runs off of my wind generator. It uses so little electricity that even my small wind generator can supply it.

2 x 4 system over steel drum halves

Another of Dr. Schippers' ideas was to nail some felt to 4 x 8 sheets of plywood. Two sheets of such plywood were nailed back to back to form an A-shaped structure and little strips of wood were nailed along the lengths. A tube along the top was installed so that there is a continuous drip coming down to moisten the felt. Dr. Schippers planted radishes along the wooden strips. Such techniques make use of vertical space, such as the north wall of a greenhouse on which, ordinarily, you do not grow anything.

A "radish wall" before and after

Another one of Dr. Schippers' techniques to make use of vertical space is shown by the *lettuce tree.* The lettuce is grown on PVC pipe in which holes have been cut. To me that represents an answer to the world food problems. If you can obtain that kind of production from that small a space, then it is an exciting possibility.

"Lettuce trees" before and after

I have become totally convinced that the attached greenhouse is the only way to go. In my pit greenhouse it would often be so hot in January that I would have to open up the vents. I may have just been splitting wood to keep my house warm and yet I was letting all of that excess heat from the greenhouse go to waste.

My house is a typical, northern New Mexico, Spanish-American, farm house. Every downstairs room has a door opening to the outside, all more or less to the south. Every room upstairs has a similar south-facing window.

I removed the porch onto which these doors and windows opened and replaced it with an attached greenhouse.

I extended the upstairs dormer windows so that they are now directly over the greenhouse roof. There are some trap doors built into the ceiling of the greenhouse so that I can direct air into the upstairs when needed.

Adding a solar greenhouse

These various openings provide 21 possible ways of venting this greenhouse. There are four dormer vents; each one of the dormer vents can be either vented to the outside by opening the outside dormer windows, or to the inside by opening the inner dormer windows. In addition to these eight ways of venting I have two outside doors, four inside doors, five cold air vents, plus vent stacks on the roof. This allows me to manipulate the greenhouse to get practically any temperature I want in any part of the house.

We find that we spend most of our time in the greenhouse. The psychological value of this is, in many ways, more important than the amount of heat or the amount of food we get out of it. It is very nice, when it is cold outside, to sit in a nice warm place where plants are growing. I do not want to put 45-gallon drums in my greenhouse because I do not like them. I am going to have a hot tub and a fairly large aquaculture tank.

Interior view of attached greenhouse

I am using the nutrient flow technique, using PVC drain pipe as my growing trough. It makes an inexpensive trough which does not leak. We have tomatoes and chili peppers growing in it and they are doing just beautifully. With this system my wife and I will be able to raise not only all our own fresh vegetables (with the exception of things like potatoes and carrots) but we will have enough left over to sell or to give to friends. We have more growing space than we need — but we love plants.

"What is Dr. Schippers' address?"

Dr. Schippers has guides explaining the techniques I've been talking about. While the catalogue is free, he charges a little for the guides, but they are well worth it. Guide #2 is called the *Nutrient Flow Technique* for growing plants. Guide #1 is *Hydroponic Growing of Houseplants the Simple Way.* His address is
Dr. P. A. Schippers,
Hydroponics Growing Systems,
P.O. Box 252, Calverton, New York, 11933.
Ask him for his catalogue.

"Can the heat provided by a compost pile be used in a greenhouse?"

Yes, very definitely. In Europe greenhouses are more popular than in the United States and Canada. A lot of people in France, Holland and other countries bring fresh manure into the greenhouse during the cold weather and compost it. The heat given off the composting manure, not to mention the carbon dioxide it also produces, really helps the plants.

"Do you have problems growing root crops such as carrots or turnips?"

No. All you need is a deeper tank. I have grown carrots, potatoes and radishes. Just make sure you have a tank deep enough to take it.

"Does your solution drip all of the time?"

Yes. Day and night.

"What are the growing solutions you use?"

I use two solutions. One is called Hyponex and I think the company/distributor is in New York. Any garden supply store can get it for you. The second one is Dr. Chatilers Solution which is produced in Florida.

"Fifty pounds of Hyponex in six years has now fed how many people?"

My wife, myself, and two kids. My nutrient solution requires a teaspoon of Hyponex per gallon of water. With my system, we therefore use 15 teaspoons every two weeks, which is how often you should change your solution.

"How much organic material have you produced?"

We should have weighed every thing we grew. Unfortunately we did not. But consider this: you can really supplement your diet with what you grow in your greenhouse. With a system as I just discussed I see absolutely no reason why you should ever have to buy lettuce or tomatoes or vegetables such as that. You should be able to raise it all in your greenhouse.

"Such chemical growing may seem good at first glance and I think it has potential, but it is not the cure-all it may seem, as we have a limited supply of these concentrated chemicals. If you take them all out of the soil, the soil will be quite infertile."

This is a very good point. This is the only criticism of hydroponics that I will accept as valid. I do not believe in putting chemicals on soil and I never, in fact, put them on my own soil. The reason for this is that eventually, if you do not put any organic matter back into your soil, the soil bacteria which are absolutely necessary for converting organic nutrients into the inorganic form which the plants can use will die out and soon you will have dead soil in which nothing will grow. We have been able to feed the world with chemical agriculture, but we are painting ourselves into a corner.

I have justified doing this with hydroponics because I am not putting anything on the soil, I am putting it in the gravel beds. But it is true that these chemicals are petroleum-derived and we know that we are running out of petroleum. This is a valid criticism of hydroponics or any kind of chemical growing. I justify it by noting that 50 pounds of nutrients solution will last over six years. I wonder how many gallons of gasoline you have burned in your car in the last six years? Have you obtained as good a mileage as I have with 50 pounds of Hyponex?

"How many square feet do you have in your greenhouse?"

My new greenhouse is 420 square feet, the pit greenhouse is 220 square feet.

"How do you germinate?"

I use what are called Jiffy Sevens. They look like thick, brown fifty-cent pieces. You put them in water and they swell up into a little round pot in which you put your seed. When the seedling comes up, plant the pot and all in the trough in your greenhouse. The roots will go right through the Jiffy Seven pot into the gravel bed. You can also plant seed directly in the gravel, but sometimes the seeds settle to the bottom and wash down to the end. You will be better off to use the Jiffy pots.

"What is the Hyponex nutrient balance?"

It is 7-6-19. Dr. Chatiler's Solution is close to that, too. You can get other brands with any nutrient balance you want.

Some disagree with my statement that plants get all they need from hydroponic solutions. All I can say is that we must be living in different sets of illusions. I used to be a rabid organic freak, but I am now convinced that there is no difference in the nutrients. Organically grown tomatoes and tomatoes grown with chemicals cannot be distinguished by any laboratory on the face of the earth. That is pretty good evidence. If there is a difference, it is small, so small that you cannot detect it. There might, however, be a difference. I don't know everything.

"What is your source of water, rainwater, city water, well water?"

Well water is the best for an organic mixture. Water that has been in the ground will have micro-nutrients which rainwater would probably be lacking.

With Hyponex and Dr. Chatiler's Solution you have a complete mixture so it does not matter. But do not use city water; it has a lot of chlorine in it. If you have to, let the water sit for about 24 hours to allow some of the chlorine to evaporate.

"Is there a book detailing the methods you just described?"

No. I have a book that describes my old greenhouse. There is nothing invalid in that book, but it does not have my new methods in it. I am writing a book at present and I hope it will be available in a short time.

"Do you use different nutrient solutions for different plants?"

This is a good question because some plants require different concentrations of nutrients. In general, plant food works just fine, but if you have some specialized plants that require more nitrogen or phosphorus, for instance, then you should gauge your nutrient solution to the type of plant you are growing.

"What can each of us do to effect the needed changes in society?"

It is an illusion to think that there is one panacea for all of our problems — that we are going to find one thing that is going to work in every case. There are many different things which work and I feel that what you choose depends upon your personality.

"What are *we* going to do about big government?" and "What are *we* going to do about the big corporations?" imply that *we all* must do it. That we all must agree upon a course of action. That would

mean that I could not do anything until you agree with me. My particular approach is to look at what *I* can do and not to wait for others to agree with me. To go out and try to do what I think is right. Perhaps by example, if I'm doing something worthwhile, I will influence others to begin their own work at their individual levels. If we wait until everyone agrees, then nothing will happen.

We have a problem in our own village in New Mexico. They want to develop a uranium mine not very far from us. One of the arguments used is that this will provide jobs for the community, since there is currently a lot of unemployment. "Jobs for the Community" is the rallying cry. So we can pollute our waters, we can have babies born with two heads and so forth, for the sake of jobs.

There must, however, be another way. People do have to have jobs, we cannot all live like Thoreau in the woods. Not everybody wants to do that and it is not practical.

I have been living on a homestead for 13 years now and I have found out by hard, personal experience how difficult it is to make a living. You have to have some cash income to live in an area such as northern New Mexico where there is very little work. Probably the main source of income in my village is welfare payments. I tried many different ways to make money and finally, a little over a year ago, I hit upon an idea that I thought would be a good source of income for myself and my family.

In Mexico, wood burning water heaters are manufactured. These appliances are common and just about every home there has a wood burning water heater in it. With the energy crisis in the United States and Canada, I thought that the time had come for the wood burning water heater to be revived.

I borrowed $3500, went down to Mexico, made contact with a couple of factories, and started importing the water heaters, never having done anything like that before in my life. I am not a businessman, but I taught myself to be one and I taught myself how to import.

The factory in Mexico is a beautiful example of what appropriate technology is all about. It is in a building that is about 350 square meters and it employs about 20 people, all using relatively simple tools. They have hydraulic presses which form various parts of the water heaters, arc welders, and so forth. It is labour intensive and provides employment for quite a few people.

In my village we have a rather large building which is now vacant. With a small investment, I thought that I might be able to get some of these simple tools, hire the manager of the factory in Mexico as a consultant, and start a hot water heater factory in our village.

That is what I am going to do. I am not going to wait for somebody to say "Why don't we do this?" We can, in this way, provide employment in the village for about twenty people, producing something worthwhile: wood burning water heaters which do not consume gas or electricity.

This is the kind of thinking that we have to begin. Everyone, I am sure, has an idea. I encourage you to try your ideas. Do not wait for a consensus, go out and do it yourself and you will be surprised how often you succeed.

Greg Allen

Greg Allen *is a designer and builder of solar and passive solar houses. While working as an engineer he was the design manager for Amherst Renewable Energies Ltd., manufacturers and installers of solar heating equipment. He is currently a partner with the Toronto firm of* Allen Drerup White, *designers, builders and consultants.*

We have covered such a large spectrum today that I am almost tempted to say that there is nothing left to say. But I know better. I am pleased to note that of all the topics discussed, one of the few that has not been covered is that of building your own solar collectors. It seems to have been the traditional topic of discussion for sometime with solar energy and renewable energy gatherings.

I think the fact that active systems are not being discussed is indicative of new directions that have been taken in recent years. Specifically I refer to the approaches that really do have a high impact and the potential for massive application now.

Unfortunately, our civil servants are busily trying to define solar heating systems in terms of solar collectors, complicated control mechanisms that fill half the basement of a house, and various other elaborate devices. However, I'm sure we have all witnessed several accounts of some very basic notions that work more effectively than these rather complicated items.

I believe that the general interest is really towards action. What can we do with our own homes at this point? And this can represent quite a diversity of lifestyles. We don't all have to be raisers of fish; we don't all have to become self-sufficient in the country. I don't believe that at this stage in history we are anywhere near developing that kind of society. We can individually aspire towards those goals and they can give us some kind of vision for the future, an inspiration to keep us working. But we have to recognize that we are in a transition period. What we do has to fit. We are going to have

paradoxes in our lives and we are going to have to live with them. That is something that I have always had to contend with. I have tried to resolve them, but everytime I thought I had resolved one, I had created another paradox.

I have become a lot softer in my approach and attitude. I thought that consciousness-raising in the environmental field could be effected by redesigning houses so that people would reconnect with the environment. I now think that was rather presumptious of me, particularly when a lot of the experiments that I was doing with these people did not always work. I now have a lot more humility and listen to the people I work with much more closely to try to understand how they perceive where they are going with their lives. I do my best to learn from the experiences that I have had, to take the best of those ideas and apply them to their situations. It is very important that we learn how to interact with each other. The process of developing new ideas is a synergetic one.

Initially my partners were going to live the good life. They went out and forged a homestead. They had a trout farm, they had a horse, the works. And they had poverty. They were building houses for other people, who were also poverty stricken. This was in southern Quebec.

They had little opportunity for getting out of this rut. No matter how far they moved towards personal self-sufficiency, it was always a marginal operation. They were still hooked to the automobile, still desirous of communicating with the world at large. There were taxes to pay and so on. They had to have some kind of economic base, so they tried to make it by building for other people who didn't have any money. However, without a cash flow in the community, it just doesn't work very well.

Homestead in southern Quebec

I suspect it is somewhat different in Alberta. I get the impression that there is a lot of money coming this way. If we took something like the Heritage Fund — but don't call it the Heritage Fund, call it an energy fund, that is where the money is coming from — and we put the surcharge on fossil fuels into a renewable energy fund, then the faster we consume our non-renewable energy, the faster we would get to a position where we don't need them any longer. I think that would be a harmonious way of dealing with the transition.

But back to my partners. None of them had been involved in any construction before. But they fell in love with wood. Their first house was not a solar house, but a wood stove is the sole heating source. It is a rather energy-efficient house because it utilizes compact construction. The common theme that has come out of everything that we have

done or considered is that building small makes a lot of sense. Making ultimate utility of the space we generate is the right approach, not building large, rambling structures.

In their first house built for a client, my partners used barn beams throughout the interior. I, too, constructed with barn beams. The final result is nice, but it creates problems when trying to get a vapour barrier seal over the beams, when trying to gyprock up to their edges, or when trying to debug them. There is a considerable set of arguments for not using them.

Using barn beams for interior construction

My partners had already begun using a lot of south-facing windows. There are a lot of solar houses around that I think were intuitively done. I've noticed a lot of houses that have large south windows. I don't think they were all by accident. I think people appreciate the fact that the sun does rise in the south and it is certainly nice to be inundated with sunlight during the day.

The first house that I ever constructed is

near Kingston, Ontario, overlooking the St. Lawrence, a very beautiful site. When I got to the site I found a rock escarpment dropping 8 feet. I thought, "My God, this is south-facing rock." It reminded me of the Pueblo Indian photos that we have seen. How could I make that work for me? I worked out a scheme in which the south part of the house had two floors with the sunlight coming into the greenhouse in the lower floor, spilling up against the rock face and running through the house. It has worked quite effectively.

At that time I was also convinced that a collector was a necessary adjunct. Up on the roof are collectors. The storage system was paraffin. I had to start with something exotic, which caused a lot of headaches.

This house sits on an 8-foot rock escarpment

This house itself is a stack-wood house. I hadn't realized that it was going to catch on. I was driving up to Ottawa one day, and there were several barns on route, but I couldn't believe that the stones could be that regular, so I drove up the lane and had a look at them. Lo and behold it was log. I talked to the farmer and he said the barn was 75 years old. There was no sign of decay. I was quite impressed. I had to try it myself. I believe it worked quite effectively.

It was rather a tricky house, built on a hexagonal grid. That was another presumption, that you don't have to build rectangular houses. For a while I thought that I'd change all the rules of construction. It worked all right, but it certainly involved a lot of labour and head scratching. It had pleasant effects, but it did add to the cost.

Fireplace wall construction

The fireplace was built right into the wall. At that time I felt circulating fireplaces were adequate. I don't believe they are any longer. I had to go to far greater measures to make a fireplace also do duty as a heat source.

Another one of my partners' projects

illustrates something not to do. The house is built on posts and the floor is difficult to insulate. There might be some solutions coming out of the Saskatchewan Conservation House on how to better insulate floors. But in this case they couldn't put fibreglass insulation down between the floor joists because the joists get soaked in the rain. And they couldn't simply protect them with a vapour barrier because when sill plates are put around the outside of the frame a lake is formed in the middle of the building. It is a really difficult problem. They had to put the insulation in after the house is constructed. In this case they put styrofoam in between the joists after the house was finished and tried to fit it as tight as they could. But there is enough air infiltration around the styrofoam that the floors are quite cool.

The challenge of a north-facing slope

This house was on a challenging site. My partners had a propensity for getting north-sloping sites. Again, this was not a solar house, but the south windows became a little larger.

We have always tried to encourage owner-builders to come to us. It is

enjoyable to work in conjunction with people who have done a lot of reading on the subject. There is a good dialogue on the possibilities for a house when the owners take on the construction (provided that they have some building skills). There is a better control over the construction quality.

One building that I designed is a rather strange configuration for solar heating. I was really audacious in my early efforts. The owner wanted a building based on Buckminster Fuller's notion of a cable-supported structure. We started the design in the beginning of September and they were moved in before Christmas. It was a very effective way to build. We built very large wall sections on the ground and hoisted them into place. There is a greenhouse on top of the garage. The greenhouse was an interesting notion, but it never really did get fully tried. Unfortunately, after the owner suddenly died the project was never quite completed.

Cable-supported house

The cables come down from the peak and support a floating platform. The structure was put up with telephone poles which formed a scaffolding which was used before we did the rest of the building. The system was fairly effective, but still rather audacious and hard to justify in terms of cost-effectiveness. It did provide an interesting space for the owners. I was even daring enough to put the great pyramid plexiglass dome on the top, and in the process doing a little more experimenting on the occupants.

A view of the skylight from the floating platform

In this same house one of the criterion was that it was to be built on a cliff, and that none of the trees were to be touched. This made it difficult to realize a solar structure. So we constructed a large, solar collecting device glazed on the southside. It is 24 ft. tall with a reflective surface on the north wall, and a salt pond. Salt ponds are a phenomenon that were initially observed in Israel. Because of higher densities of salt near the bottom of the pond, it means that the water is more dense and that the normal stratification (where warmer water rises to the surface and the heat begins to be discharged to the atmosphere) does not take place. Any solar energy that is absorbed at the bottom of the pool is retained by the water down there. The upper layers of water actually act as insulation. It is an anti-convection type of pond. Quite high temperatures are obtained at the bottom of this device. We devised means by which the majority of the light passing through the glass surface would be reflected downwards into a black painted pool in the bottom of this structure. When it was under construction, it created some unusual effects for the welders that were putting in some of the pipes. There were deformities in the reflective mylar, and they were getting scorching sensations all over their backs as the reflective concentrations were zeroing in on them.

Solar concentrator and salt-pond storage

Agricultural buildings are another project that we enjoy doing. We have built a solar heated stable and a solar heated pig barn. It is appropriate using solar energy in the agricultural industry.

Three years ago, I designed and built a house on Amherst Island in Lake Ontario which was an attempt to be the last word in solar heating in Canada. There is a big difference in approach between the New Mexico examples and what we have to do in Southern Ontario. There are large amounts of cloud cover and it is only one day in three when there is sun in the mid-winter periods. Solar has great limitations and the only way I could see of getting around that was to have extended storage and large areas to collect solar energy. Consequently most of the south walls are glass and there are reflective sky lights that actually concentrate light downward into the back portions of the house. The whole house is inundated with light which supercharges the building in a hurry.

Amhurst Island passive solar house

The north wall is metal roofing again. Metal roofs are on a lot of barns. They are incredibly practical, quick to put up, and they don't leak. Metal roofs are inexpensive and I really don't think that they are unattractive. One little peek hole to anticipate visitors is the only window on the north wall.

North view showing metal roofing

Virtually the entire front portion of the house is greenhouse. It is a 1200 sq. ft., compact, three bedroom house. The floor is concrete slab on grade construction. There is a massive fireplace in the middle. The idea was that the floor was going to get hot from sunlight falling on it, hot enough to transfer heat to the concrete. Water would then be circulated through the slab through pipes. Excess heat would be picked up by water circulated from the bottom of a storage tank (which was going to be de-stratified with baffles) which would cool the floor slab and transfer the heat into the storage. At night or when the building called for heat, the reverse would take place and there would be radiant heat in the building. However, what happened was heat went into the air and the low sun angle created a low transmission into the slab itself. That was really not a pronounced effect. The pronounced effect was that it was very warm upstairs. In fact, before it was completed in February the temperature was 120°F upstairs. I had created a live-in solar collector.

The southern wall (right) heightened to catch the sun

The curtains were also an attempt at a low budget solution to the insulating problem. Sealed air space with a reflective foil gets approximately an R value of 3.5. These curtains were reflective foil, but it is a tricky proposition to seal curtains. Another objective was to make them rather easy to put into place. This was done by one central pulley. It pulled the whole area over. However, I don't think it adequately seals. There is quite a drop coming off the glass. I think it would be more effective on a vertical surface to use something like a chain to weight the bottom of the curtain and use a zipper to seal the edges. I think then the technique would work.

The back-up heating was provided by the fireplace in which there was a water circulating grate. The fireplace had glass doors and water circulated from the storage through the grate (which was an old house radiator), thereby taking heat from the firebox area and putting it into the storage.

The sun angle by early summer is such that little light actually enters the house. The skylights and overhangs on the glazed areas were designed so the sun was concentrated in the winter and practically eliminated in the summer.

We haven't touched on active systems. An active solar heated building inspired by Nick Nicholson's work was done by my partners. As it was on a north sloping site, they had to make it quite tall to give the southern wall enough exposure to act as a solar collector.

The collector is of simple construction and is cost-effective. It is one of the few active systems that can be justified in terms of its cost. The building costs something like five cents a week to heat. They began with 2 x 6 framing, then increased its insulation by strapping. There are also large windows to the east and west. Such a house shows us that one should not go on the premise that one has to have a south facing hillside on which to build a solar house. Nor is it impossible to have extensive solar applications in the city.

The collector was built right onto the south wall of the building. It begins with normal wall sheathing, aspenite, and intake and outlet vents at the top and bottom of the wall. Then the wall is strapped. They next put up the sheet metal (taking care to allow for expansion in the seams), painted it black, and glazed it with fibreglass reinforced plastic.

Installing the collector system on the south wall

Concrete block plenum with temporary spacer strips

Rock storage was used, with concrete blocks as the end manifolding. I now believe that the only way to deal with rock storage is to actually use the advantage of stratification: move the heated air in at the top and take it out at the top. In this case they tried to make the flow lateral. They used concrete blocks to create the space to circulate air through the rocks.

Such are the internal workings of an active system. It is a rather simple one. I am doing a study right now for the National Research Council on solar controls and we consistently find that the simpler the system is, the more effective it is.

I try to avoid the subject, but that house on Amherst Island was built with hay bales, a tempting resource. I presume that most people when they were kids played in barns and built bale forts. That was my inspiration. It seemed a low cost approach to creating a highly insulated building. It is. But it is an incredibly labour-intensive process to put the stucco on.

My partners wanted to try it out on an art gallery. They used a concrete slab on grade with treated edge beams to distribute the load. They build trusses and hoisted them in place. Then the roof went up so that they could work with the hay bales no matter what the weather. They raised the hay bales off the ground to avoid any problems with ground moisture at the bottom (snow, water, run-off, etc.). The hay bales were then laid up between the trusses. 1 x 3 strapping was put up every couple of feet, top to bottom, and chicken wire was tied to that. The bales were stacked with staggered seams and

no special means of stabilization. The strapping holds it rigid until the concrete is on, at which point the bales are no longer needed for stabilization. The concrete that is used over the bales adds a fair amount of thermal mass to the structure. The hay bales also allow for contoured walls by simply putting them over one's knee, bending them into shape, and putting them in the wall.

Hay bale insulation being installed

It turned out to be a pleasant little building inside and out. It is not a solar building but is heated by one small wood burner. Some of the finishing touches include the contoured walls, skylight, and central staircase. It is a simple building, but it works exceptionally well for its purpose. The total cost was under $10,000.

Hay bale insulated art gallery

We did a project for some clients which was written up in Harrowsmith magazine. It was an old farmhouse which I think I would have written off, but I guess they had grown attached to it. There was a lot of leakage into the basement. That is a common phenomenom and a weak point in most houses. It can be detected by going along a sill plate of a house where the air being sucked in can be felt and the walls are freezing cold. These people decided to move the house onto new foundations, insulate the exterior of the foundations, and add a solar greenhouse to the south side.

Greenhouse addition above the rock storage

We extended the new basement to allow a little room for rock storage. I think that a reasonable approach to constructing a rock storage vessel is to do it in a wood frame and a plywood skin. The inlet and outlet duct areas can quite readily be framed. Low cost batt insulation can be used as insulative material. It is quite strong and integrates into the rest of the construction. This new extension was underneath the greenhouse.

The greenhouse floor was plywood. The notion was that air was going to be taken off the top of the greenhouse and put through the storage.

We worked out a simple device for this particular system to reverse the flow through the storage. The system consists of an air intake at the top of the house which goes through a wood-fired furnace. The fan from the wood furnace is on at all times to blow the air into the top of the storage and return the cool air to the house during the solar periods of the day — we are actually using the bottom of the rock storage to cool the over-heating that often occurs with a direct gain house. At night, a manual damper reverses the flow through the rock storage. Simply by using the damper there is both a heating and a cooling mode which combine to take care of the excessive gains and allows heat to be stored until it is needed.

I often think that Amherst Island is rivalling New Mexico in per capita solar houses. There are 3 now in a population of 300. One of the fellows who helped with the construction of the first one has built his own. He used drums filled with water under the crawl spaces as his storage, and ducted air from the peak of the house. He also uses exterior insula-

tion. I generally prescribe at least four inches of blue board, the true styrofoam for external applications below grade.

Water-filled drums and masonry walls add thermal mass

The window insulation used in this house was simply styrofoam panels inserted in the window frames. They are very displeased with this. Besides being rather difficult to place every night, there is an inch of frost built up on the windows. I suspect that conditions in the north would be even worse.

At one time I went through an active solar period in which I got into collector manufacturing. I thought that I would be able to stay on Amherst Island by creating a viable industry for the local population. So I set up a solar collector manufacturing operation. Well it didn't take long before we got into such nonsense as a large solar collector array which went onto a high school in Toronto. I believe it cost something like $60,000 for the steel work alone.

Collector supports on a Toronto high school

When I got to the site I saw something I couldn't believe. There was a large bulk head on the auditorium that was south-facing and a dark brown colour. I went over to it and found that it was hot. It was already an excellent collector. It could have been quite readily retrofitted with glazing and it would have performed quite adequately, but that was overlooked. The other thing that was overlooked, to my amazement, was that there was no insulation in the walls. I asked about it and found that the standard practice is totally uninsulated construction. And this was a recent school building.

This type of unconcern for energy conservation is not unusual. I did a study for a highrise condominium in Toronto. The insulation consists of 1 sheet of aluminum foil. Windows are single glazed. They have large exhaust fans that suck air out of the building so that it just about caves in. All seals have come off around the windows and the fan sucks in air around the floors and everybody turns the thermostats up to try to stay comfortable. It is really disastrous. It is typical of most of the construction that is going on.

I did another large solar installation on a shoe factory in Picton, Ontario, which I hope to see imitated in other applications. It is a flat roof air-type collector. The size of the collectors themselves is smaller than the size of the manifold ducts, so the object in large scale, active air systems is to minimize the manifolding ducts. In this case, the collectors actually acted as ducts and ran the full length of the building, and the air passes down the length. It worked quite effectively, however, there is a lesson to be learned here as well. First we must look at conservation, not solar applications. I insisted that before we undertook a solar installation for the building, energy conservation measures be implemented. By the time we had effected those measures, there was practically no heating load left in the building. So the collectors are just a lot of show for what they do.

Some of the more recent projects that I am doing demonstrate more effective approaches to the problems of solar applications and strategies for energy conservation in northern climates. In one case, we were given instructions that the building was to be designed like an Ontario farm house, but a very large version. I think it is about 4500 sq.ft. It wasn't possible to convince them that small is beautiful. They are well-to-do clients so we used some of their financial resources to put a large amount of energy conservation into the building.

On the south side of the house is a sun porch, which is traditional in farm houses. But below that sun porch, on a lower level, is a greenhouse which also provides heat to the main house. To me, this example proves that there is no one style that is appropriate for solar. There are definitely designs that work better than others, but I believe that people can effectively make use of many different forms. The farm house or salt-box style is particularly adaptable.

The house in question has practically everything in it — a hydroponic greenhouse operation, a sauna in the basement, a large workshop. It has two and a half stories: a main floor, a floor above that, then a loft above that.

The window insulators in this building use garage door hardware which are for large panels and which work fairly well to put large sections of rigid insulation into place. The walls are insulated to R45, ceilings to R50.

Saunas are a convenient way of using wood heat. They can act as a type of plenum to take hot air to rock storage or to deliver it to the house. Either a special wood-fired sauna stove or an ordinary wood stove can be used.

The reason a wood stove operates efficiently is because the predominant form of heat transfer is radiation. This radiant heat then gets absorbed by the surfaces of the room and that transfers to the air quite effectively because of an extended surface area. That is why the Jotuls and other stoves sitting in the middle of the room are highly efficient devices.

The same principle can be used by

putting the stove in a sauna, the walls of which act as extended surface areas to transfer heat and to elevate the room temperature. This heated air in the sauna is then transferred, by means of fans, dampers, and thermostats, to either the house itself or to a rock storage, depending on where the heat is needed. I think it is a nice complement to a solar heating system that uses a fan and a rock storage. It can also make wood heating a lot more convenient, because a day or two's heat can be stored simply by charging with the wood stove. An added advantage is that there is more efficient combustion and heat transfer when a wood stove is burned hot. That heat can be put into storage which improves the efficiency of the device.

I tend to prefer a direct gain building, perhaps with a greenhouse with a rock storage and forced air system because of the better control of air temperatures as well as the capacity to extend heating. In a simple direct gain building, unless there is a regular cycling of solar input, there is not going to be full use of the solar gain that can be obtained from a south-facing wall. Usually we go to a hybrid system in which there is a direct gain to the internal structure of the building mass elements, but in addition excess heat is collected at the peak of the building and is forced through rocks for longer term storage.

There is one solution which we use to derive high R values in walls. One of the objectives in a highly insulated wall is to run the vapour barrier inside of the services (wiring, etc.) to make a much easier and much better job of sealing. This can be achieved by strapping the frame walls. You can get an R30 wall with this construction. Then we do not have to

seal all round the electric boxes, which is almost impossible.

There is a heat pump system which I am trying to find someway of prototyping. It seems preposterous to me to use a heat pump to draw heat from the outside air because then, when the highest heat needs occur, we get the lowest performances in the device. It seems to me, better to put a heat pump on the storage side of a reversing damper on a rock storage. This would enable us to maintain exact room temperatures. We can put any excess solar gain or any excess heat in the building into thermal storage for later use. It would also work in reverse to enable us to take heat from the rock store even when the rocks are below room temperature.

"What about noise from metal roofs?"

I consider the noise rather musical. But insulating materials muffle the noise anyway, and I don't think it is a detrimental aspect of metal roofs.

"Do you use corrugated metal?"

I have been using ordinary, farm, metal roofing that has corrugated bumps which are necessary for sealing the edges and for rigidity to the structures.

"Would you recommend going to slab heating with solar heated water?"

Yes, I think radiant heating is a very desirable match with solar heating. It is a low temperature supply and it is the most efficient way of heating yourself because

you can actually drop the temperature in the room and still feel just as comfortable. Heat is absorbed directly by your body which is very comfortable. But I'm very reticent to do more liquid systems. I don't really like them, they scare me. I stick pretty much to air, even in a radiant slab. In a recent building we used an ordinary downspout for rainwater and set up a grid through the concrete floor slab and manifolded it into plywood at either end of the floor and ducted heated air through that. It worked quite effectively.

"Is there always a frost build-up problem with insulating shutters or windows? If so, what is the solution?"

Usually there is a build-up, but I think you could eliminate that if you could seal them adequately. One suggestion is to use a small removable vent, as you used to have in storm windows, to vent the space and reduce the condensation. I think that exterior shutters as in the Saskatchewan Conservation House, are the answer to condensation problems. But you have to have an overhang to protect it from the weather. Some systems use an overhead door and sliding track hardware very similar to accordian doors which run down the side of the windows. There is a rope that goes up over a pully and down into the building and a winch with which you crank the door up over top of the window areas.

"What is the R value of the hay wall?"

It never was measured, but I anticipated that it would be somewhere in the neighborhood of R30 to R40.

"Can we get or buy copies of some of your house plans, generalities if not specifics? I think houses should be suited to each individual site."

I agree very much. Not just to each individual site, but to each individual. I think it is a shame that we have this mass replication of bad buildings. I would rather see a variety of errors than one mass error. I feel strongly that this is still very much a learning process and that it is really worth your while to contact people who have used solar energy and have lived in solar structures. Then you can make decisions for your house. Do not simply duplicate another house.

"For a slab heat distribution system how much insulation should we use between slab and earth?"

It depends on the region. I would suspect around here that you'd probably want to put in at least four inches of polystyrene.

"Is there any problem with condensation when using a tin roof? If so, how do you ventilate it?"

I haven't experienced a problem. We have discussed it a fair amount because you notice it in barns. But I don't know if the same phenomenon would occur with a well-insulated roof. I usually leave a ventilating gap much the same as you would use in truss roof construction to create enough air flow to keep the humidity down.

Harold Orr

Harold Orr *is with the Division of Building Research of the National Research Council of Saskatoon. For two decades he has investigated insulation and the air-infiltration of residences. He was one of the forces behind the successful* Saskatchewan Conservation House *in Regina.*

I'd like to discuss the work we've done in Saskatoon, including work on the *Saskatchewan Conservation House.* I want to emphasize the words Saskatchewan Conservation House. I talk to a lot of people about the Saskatchewan Conservation House and they say *"Oh, you mean the solar house in Regina."* I *don't* mean the solar house in Regina. I mean the energy conservation house in Regina. I am very particular about saying that because when we got together as a committee (I don't know if you ever designed anything by committee, they say a camel is the result of a committee trying to design a horse and I can believe it) we were asked to design a solar house appropriate for Saskatchewan. Well, we have a few solar houses in Saskatchewan, but we don't have any that are appropriate.

I don't think there are any true solar houses appropriate to this area of the country. Now there certainly are some in other areas of the world. But here, it really isn't feasible to try to design a solar house. So we wrote back to the Government of Saskatchewan who was sponsoring this project and said we were interested in designing a conserving house that would be appropriate for Saskatchewan but we were not interested in designing a solar house. About three committee meetings later we got a reply to our letter. In the meantime we had been designing a conserving house and we had the house pretty well under way. The notice from the Saskatchewan Government said fine, go ahead and design a conserving house, but make it solar.

We can't win them all, so we put solar energy on the house. I think that perhaps the solar energy installation has distracted from the particular values of the house.

The thing that is very striking on the outside of it is the 160 sq.ft. solar collector, which is very noticeable. The first thing people see when they come in the door are the pumps that circulate the fluids through the solar collector. There is a big sign that explains the thermal storage tank. There is a control panel, complete with a handle that kids can turn and not do any damage. So people immediately think solar.

Then they get into the mundane things. There are windows with shutters on them. Beautiful carpet on the floor. But they cannot see the vapour barrier anywhere; they cannot see any insulation except for a mock-up of the wall which is not entirely accurate. Upstairs they can see a heating coil which is heated with solar energy. And so on all the way down the line.

Consequently people ask how much the solar system costs. There is $30,000 worth of hardware and that can just about be doubled for the labour putting it into place. So, there is $70 to $80,000 for the solar system. When we go back and try to calculate or estimate how much it costs to heat this house, we find that the amount of energy needed for heating is very, very small. Such calculations do not even take into account the internal gains, such as the heat from the people in the house.

The design loads in the Saskatchewan Conservation House are 11,500 BTU per hour at a design temperature of minus 40°F. It is about the same size as a 1100 sq.ft. bungalow with a completely finished basement. Such houses in Saskatoon are being designed with a heating load something on the order of 60,000 to 80,000 BTUs per hour.

One of our problems was how to buy an 11,500 BTU furnace. They only make them for trailers.

Tent trailers.

Small tent trailers. In any case, to heat this house with electric heat costs about $35 per year. We had a $70 — $80,000 heating system to provide $35 worth of heat, which doesn't make sense.

Some people came away thinking it was a failure because obviously the heating system isn't practical. They're right. That is what we tried to say when the project started, that the heating system wasn't practical. But the energy conservation *is* practical.

Saskatchewan Conservation House

It has a large amount of insulation in the walls, and we had to fight hard to get that put in because we were told that it wouldn't pay, that the law of diminishing returns applies. However, we finally prevailed with economic arguments, and put in R44 in the walls. I have gone back since then and had another look at it and wondered what would have happened if we had put more insulation in the walls and made it just a little bit tighter.

Suppose for example, we had doubled the amount of insulation in the house, how much extra would that have cost? I estimate about $2,500. And yet, if we had doubled the insulation we estimate that we would actually reduce the heating cost to zero.

A zero house is one which requires no heating and is an illustration of what might happen if we went to R80 walls, R80 ceiling, R50 in the floor, quadruple-paned the windows and provided even a little more tightness on the air barrier, which I think we can do today. You could eliminate entirely the $60,000 solar system. Any time I can invest $2,500 and get back $60,000, I feel it is a good investment. I am not suggesting that we should put R80 in the walls. But I think it is a better investment than putting $60,000 into a solar system that really isn't doing the job we want.

If people want a solar system, build the cheapest solar system that can possibly be built, people should scrounge the materials and build it themselves.

The University of Saskatchewan has been doing this quite effectively for solar grain dryers. They use a sheet of clear polyethelene on the outside and a sheet of black polyethelene on the other side and the sun shines through, heats the air and they use that air to dry the grain. It works wonderfully and it costs $150. They can dry a lot of grain with $150. At the end of the year they throw away the plastic, but the thing has paid for itself in about six months.

Now that's getting effective solar utilization. But putting this on a house is another story. In the Saskatchewan Conservation House we need heat only from December through February, about two and a half months of the year. There is no solar system that we could afford to put in and have sit idle for nine and a half months. It just isn't feasible.

The south-facing wall of the Saskatchewan Conservation House was designed to hold the solar collectors at the optimum angle, 78°. The result was that when we got snow, it collected on the solar collectors and it wouldn't melt off. We had to send a man up to shovel the snow off. In cold weather, it quite often snowed a little bit every day. It was quite a miserable job. Put your solar collectors vertically, the snow will fall off.

How do we design new housing for the Canadian Prairies and for the Peace River region? Someone has suggested we should start our houses by digging a hole, but I have some serious doubts about that. Farmers in our area may be smarter than we are. They dig a hole in the ground and call it a dugout, and expect it to fill with water. On the other hand, we dig a hole in the ground, put a leaky box in it and we call it a basement and expect it to stay dry. Then all summer we pour water all around it on the lawn. Talk about appropriate technology.

We have used energy unwisely because it has been so extremely cheap. We've been lead down the garden path. I'm certain that this is true in terms of electric heating of homes. In certain areas of the country electric heating of homes has been popular and is being pushed strongly. I suspect that the homeowner who is heating his house electrically is being subsidized by the power company. The actual cost of the equipment and amortization of equipment and the energy it takes to heat the house is likely about three times what the homeowner is paying for it. This is a cost that's being borne by the small user, the fellow that just lights his house and is trying to conserve energy. We can go a long way in reducing our needs for fossil fuels.

I had an enquiry from a lady one day who was very concerned about the energy crises, what could she do? She asked about solar energy and I suggested that active solar at that time wasn't a viable option but she should consider energy conservation. She asked about putting in a wind mill to generate electricity to heat the house. Finally I suggested that she bring her plans in an let me have a look at them. So she brought them in. It was a nice two bedroom house just for her husband and herself and her teenage daughter who was just about old enough to leave home. But it was 5000 sq.ft. I didn't have the heart to suggest to her that she should simply cut it down into about one third and she would save the biggest chunk of energy — not only for fuel but also energy used in construction.

I have a metric family, I have ten children. The house I live in is 1100 sq.ft. Yes, we're a little crowded. We have triple bunks in the boys' room and a few things. I could certainly use some extra room. But right at the moment, my house uses less energy than most of the houses of its vintage in Saskatoon. When I was building the house in 1964 I said I wanted full insulation in the walls, that was R10 at the time. The contractor told me that it didn't pay, that it would cost me money. I asked how much and he said $25. Because I put that $25 in I'm saving about $150 a year.

A professor at the University of Saskatoon built a low energy house with R44 in the walls and R60 in the ceiling. They moved in last November and his wife began complaining that it was awfully stuffy in the master bedroom. That means that that temperature must be getting warmer. So, he put a recording thermometer in the bedroom, turned the thermostat down at night, and watched the thermometer. It rose all night. Two bodies lying in bed provide enough heat to keep that room more than warm. They in fact, have surplus heat that they can use to heat the rest of the house. This was at -30°F.

R44 walls, R60 ceiling

From our work at the Saskatchewan Conservation House it appears conceivable today in this very severe climate that we can build houses that use 10 per cent of the energy of a conventional house. This may not reduce fuel costs by that much because one of the problems with natural gas and electricity is the way they are priced. If we use little or no energy we still have a basic monthly payment. As we use the next little bit of fuel we pay through the nose but as we use more and more, we pay less per unit. If we build a

cement kiln in the back yard and use it a great deal, we would get it cheap. We have the wrong mentality in terms of the way energy is sold.

Another problem we run into is the bureaucracy of taxes. If we build a low energy house, make our walls thicker to put in more insulation, and so forth, we immediately find that we're clobbered by the taxman. The taxman measures the outside of the house. We still haven't got any more space inside than the neighbour, but we've got a bigger house outside so we're paying higher taxes. For every inch added onto the house, it increases the tax load about one half of one per cent.

There are other peculiarities that we have in our laws. For example, if we build a house with thicker walls this often means we need a bigger lot for it because we're required to have certain clearances on the sides of lots. That means a greater cost for both the lot and a greater cost for the services. When it's all added up it may not encourage someone to put on more insulation or to go to an energy conserving house.

Our experience with the first low energy house, Solar 1, taught us not to go overboard with windows. Even on a cold day in January, if the sun shines, this house would overheat. But we can't store the energy. I think, frankly, that we can't afford to put in storage to store energy even if that energy is free.

The first series of low energy houses built in Saskatoon show a lot of variation — they looked different, they had different orientation, some used berming, some had greenhouses. But they all had the vapour barrier on the inside of the wall. There are some distinct problems with placing the vapour barrier there because it is very difficult to rely on the sub-trades to make sure that they keep the vapour barrier completely sealed and they don't puncture it with holes which they cover up before anyone notices. The houses of the second generation have the vapour barrier built into the middle of the wall. It is usually placed on the outside of the interior wall. I think it is better placing it there than on the inside, but I think that sheathing should still be placed on top of the vapour barrier.

Two super-insulated air-tight houses

We end up with a barrier that is out of the way of the electricians and the plumbers and the dry wall installers. Yet it covers the outside of the interior parti-tions completely plus it covers the outside of the floor joists. It can be sealed much tighter and much easier than the conventional placing.

Serious problems can arise without a proper, continuous vapour barrier. We saw an extreme example of an improper barrier in Churchill, Manitoba. The frost build-up in the attic was about five inches thick. It was in an apartment building and we estimated that for each apartment in the building there were 500 gallons of water which had turned to ice in the attic. When spring came, the ceiling fell in. I mention this because it brings up the point that all of this water was not from the outside, but from inside the house.

Excessive frost build-up in attic signals a serious air-leakage problem

Every bit of ice in the attic was from water which was evaporated in the house, either by humidifiers, from breathing, from cooking, from whatever is done in a house. It was carried by air up to the attic. For each pound of water in the attic it took 200 pounds of air to carry it there. At the end of the winter, we estimated that it had taken a million pounds of air to carry that much water up into the attic.

Think about that for a moment, if you have 5000 pounds of water, how much is it going to take to heat that? It takes a lot of energy to heat that from the outside temperature to room temperature. That alone is an indication of the energy loss in this particular building.

As important as insulation and vapour barriers is maintaining a good infiltration barrier. In Saskatchewan is the best insulated house anywhere, with R52 walls and R84 ceiling. I wondered if the owner had shares in an insulation company, but he said he just had a good buy on insulation. I suggested to him that he had more dollars than sense which turned out to be true. The house has essentially no air barrier at all. It is like insulating a wind tunnel. It doesn't help very much if you have a gale blowing through the center of it.

In 1975 in a standard 1100 sq.ft. bungalow, we could expect three areas to contribute approximately equally to the total heat loss. One third of the loss was through the windows and walls and ceiling, another third was through the uninsulated basement, the final third was due to infiltration. Combined, these three areas represent the total heat loss of an average 1975 bungalow. Since then Canada Mortgage has insisted that we insulate basements so we have reduced the heat loss of the basements by about a half. We have gone from R10 in the ceiling to R36, so we cut the ceiling loss way down. We have gone from R7 in the walls to R12 or higher and that has cut the heat loss in walls down quite a bit. So what happened was that by 1978 we ended up with pretty close to 50 per cent of our heat loss due to infiltration — because that had not been reduced. So it certainly is justified to spend $1000-1500 to help control infiltration. In fact, I think that we can justify spending more money on that because I know what the fuel prices are today, but they are not nearly as high as what they are going to be tomorrow. I would suggest that every dollar spent making houses more airtight is worth ten times as much as every dollar spent on adding more insulation to the house.

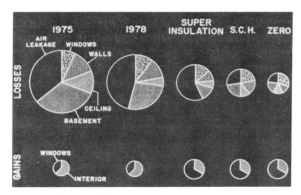

Heat gains and heat losses

Take the example I use of an older house. If I spend $25 in caulking compound and seal all the cracks and holes in the attic and elsewhere and make the house as air tight as possible, I estimate that I will save more on the fuel bill than I will with $200 worth of insulation.

One of the components of air leakage is the attic hatch, that little door up there which opens to the outside. It leaks air, so be sure the attic hatch is weather stripped. If the front door is weather stripped then the attic hatch should be weather stripped. Likely there is more leakage through an unweather stripped attic hatch than through an unweather stripped door, because the pressures on the attic hatch are greater than they are on the door.

Another thing not to do is to put an exhaust fan in a ceiling. It is almost impossible to seal around it and make it air-tight. I very rarely see one that is done properly. The caulking can come loose. There are motor brackets to caulk. The joints must be taped. The electrical box must be contended with — it just isn't worth it.

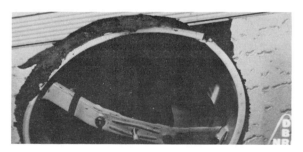

Exhaust fans are difficult to seal and sometimes require extreme solutions

The question arises of how tight is necessary. In one case, owners were having problems with condensation in the attic of their house. I had asked them to go up and caulk along the interior partitions, to seal it and make it tight, but they had left a little crack. It was about an inch long and it was just wide enough to slip a knife blade in, perhaps a sixteenth of an inch wide. And yet they got frost boil on the top. Now this might not seem too important, it is not going to cause any serious problems. But there was at least a pound of water there which means that there had been at least 200 pounds of air going through there. That is the problem, heated house air escaping.

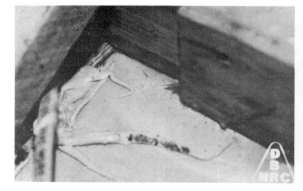

Small cracks can cause frost boils and therefore heat loss

Be careful to continue the vapour barrier right up to the bathroom plumbing stack. Simply pushing insulation around it is not adequate. If people do this without the vapour barrier being sealed, they find that the pink insulation turns gray. The same company that makes that pink insulation makes fibreglass air filters for the furnace. They are made by essentially the same process and the same machine. They do exactly the same thing if they are placed over a hole, they filter the dust out of the air. I don't know why one would want clean air in the attic, but this seems to be the way we do it. We stuff an air filter around the bathroom plumbing stack so that we have clean air in the attic.

Plumbing stacks are difficult to make air-tight; insulation is not adequate

The owner of a house who had this exact problem called me for advice. In his case the air coming through around the stack kept the roof surface so warm that no frost formed. Instead, frost had collected on the gable ends on this house. They could expect 20 gallons of water to run down from the gable ends through the wall system and wind up in the rumpus room in the basement. So I told them to seal up the holes around the plumbing stack. The first time I told them to do this they said they knew what to do. (Our conversation was over the telephone.) But the next winter they phoned back to say they still had the problem. So I flew up there and made an investigation.

What I found that they had done was to pile insulation higher around the plumbing stack. So what they had was exceptionally clean air in their attic, but they hadn't solved the problem. I told them to use something that is air-tight, to use caulking compound and polyethelene to seal it.

A major step in the progress of construction were the first houses that were built using a double wall system, when both walls were erected at the same time. I highly recommend this system. It has cut down the labour construction remarkably. We use $^5/_{16}$ inch plywood for top and bottom plates which hold the two walls together.

Our current method in new construction is to build an interior wall which has the vapour barrier on the outside and to place sheathing on top of that. We then build an outside wall directly on top of it while the inside wall is lying on the floor, then fasten the two walls together with a strip of plywood which is the thickness of the wall. This acts as a truss to hold the

walls in position and makes them tremendously strong. The method makes it easier to keep the walls straight as mentioned. It also keeps the vapour barrier out of the way, three and a half inches away from the sub-trades.

When the wall is in place we put R20 batts between the two walls from the outside. R12 batts are placed in both the outer and inner walls so we have two layers of R12 and a layer of R20 with the vapour barrier one third of the way into the wall system.

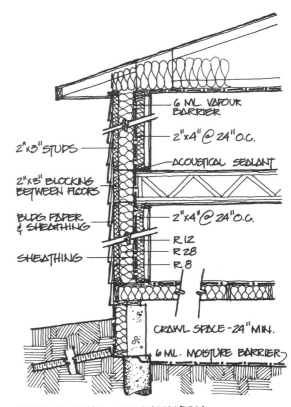

6 ML. VAPOUR BARRIER

2"x4" @ 24" O.C.

ACOUSTICAL SEALANT

2"x3" STUDS

2"x3" BLOCKING BETWEEN FLOORS

2"x4" @ 24" O.C.

BLDG. PAPER & SHEATHING

R12
R28
R8

SHEATHING

CRAWL SPACE - 24" MIN.

6 ML. MOISTURE BARRIER

DOUBLE WALL CONSTRUCTION

If the vapour barrier is put in the middle of the wall system, make sure that at least two thirds of the insulation is on the outside of the vapour barrier so that the vapour barrier is kept warm. The vapour barrier on the outside wall can be completely inspected before and after any electrical wiring is done, just before the insulation goes in. The owners can ensure they have an airtight house.

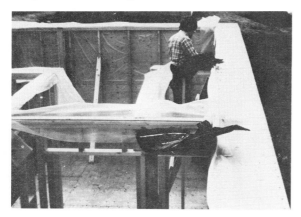

Sheets of poly are laid over all partitions

The double wall with plywood truss; inner wall (bottom) has poly on the exterior protected by plywood sheathing

Double wall in place

Interior of double wall; R12 and then the vapour barrier

Exterior of double wall; R20 and R12 outside the vapour barrier

In a retrofit situation I suggest insulating on the exterior. Strip off the old siding and wrap the house in 6 mil polyethylene. Glue this vapour barrier around windows and door frames to assure a good seal. Then put strapping on the outside which will hold the insulation. You can put in R28 insulation. Frame the windows to make them extend out a little farther. They will be set back into the wall, and it just looks like they are in a picture frame. It really is a nice architectural feature. The house is then covered with building paper and new siding.

The retrofit; first wrap the house in poly

Secondly, install the framing

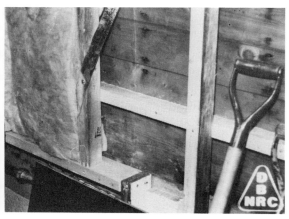

Thirdly, install the insulation and cover with building paper

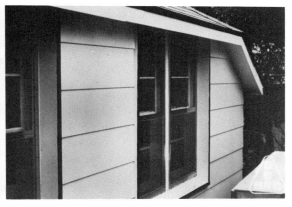

Attach the siding: note the sunken window

A new air-tight super-insulated house

The cost of the insulation, the vapour barrier, and the strapping is about $700 for a standard house. We estimate that it is possible to use this technique to reduce the energy consumption of a house by 65 per cent.

I suggest that people try to design their houses so that they use the minimum number of framing materials. Every extra 2x4 put in is a place that can't have insulation. That is the name of the game — insulation.

For foundations we are currently employing a grade beam and piles. The walls overhang the foundation by quite a bit to allow insulation to be applied to the outside of the foundation. I think that it is important to keep foundations warm, particularly concrete foundations. Certainly, it may be cheaper and easier to insulate on the inside, but if we are going to insulate the foundation well on the inside, it should have some small amount of insulation on the outside to protect it and keep it from getting so very cold.

The first really low energy house I worked on has been extraordinarily successful even though it has only R20 in the walls and R40 in the ceiling. The key is a tight air barrier and shutters on the windows. The power people are interested in the energy consumption because it is totally electrically heated, including hot water. They couldn't believe the results so they went in and recalibrated the meters, but the electricity consumed this January, which was extremely cold, came to $35.

"How do you seal a space between a masonry chimney and a ceiling joist?"

If you are building a new house, I would suggest that you use two firestops and that you set the firestops in such a way that they form a space which you can solidly pack with insulation. You can't really caulk it because the chimney has to move up and down.

"I noted that you suggested the use of electricity for heating in Saskatchewan and you probably do that for a reason. We use natural gas and we feel we lose a tremendous amount of heat up the chimney. Would you comment on that? I think our house is under negative pressure all the time with the heat going up the chimney."

You are exactly right. The chimney acts as an exhaust fan, which continually exhausts. If you build a tight house, as tight as we are building, there is some concern about fuel-burning-fired appliances because you may not have enough air to supply the appliances and the people too. A lot of people are putting in fireplaces. Fireplace stores are popping up all over the place. If you want to put a fireplace in a low energy house, there is one good way of doing it. Put a window in the wall where the fireplace would go, then go out in the yard and put your fireplace about two feet from the wall so you can look out the window. You look out the window and see the fire. The radiant energy can come in through the glass and you still have about the same efficiency as if it were in the house. If you put in an openable window you can reach out and throw the wood into the fireplace. Then you are not concerned with bringing combustion air into the house and having to seal the pipe. You are not concerned about sealing the chimney as it goes through the roof, and you are not concerned about keeping the heated house air from going up the chimney.

Let's go back to your gas furnace. I think you need to do the same thing to your gas furnace. If you are putting in a gas combustion appliance you need to isolate it from the house. This can be done — there are fireplaces with which you can do what I have suggested and you can do the same thing with your furnace. In my house, I am building a room that is air tight around the furnace. After the house is already built, it becomes difficult to do, but it can be done. I am very carefully sealing the air barrier around the chimney. I want to bring outside air into the furnace room so the chimney is totally isolated from the house. The indications are that this should reduce the energy consumption by about 20 per cent on a conventional house.

"You suggested that building solar-heated homes with thermal storage facilities is not economic on the Canadian Prairies. What are the main facts that prompt you to say "no" to solar, and briefly, what is the alternative that you suggest?"

The problem with solar is basically the cost, the investment in the hardware needed to collect the solar energy. If you invest a dollar in solar equipment, the return that you get is small. On the other hand, if you invest a dollar in energy conservation, your return on that same investment is likely to be two, three, as much as ten times as the return from investing it in solar. So the thing that we should be doing, particularly in terms of existing houses, is making the best use of

the energy that we need to buy for other purposes. For example, we're buying energy for cooking, for lighting our house and we're not going to change that very much. Also, of course, we generate heat ourselves. Windows that are on the south side also contribute energy.

Perhaps the most cost-effective thing a person can do in building a new house is simply to face it so that most of the windows face south. It doesn't cost you a penny to do that and the benefit is the free energy you get. If you can contain it in the structure to keep it warm, you have gained immensely.

It is entirely possible, with the technology that we have today, to reduce energy consumption in new houses by as much as 80 per cent. In existing houses, in certain situations, the likely saving is as much as 65 per cent. But it takes a very careful evaluation of where the energy is going, and particularly the one neglected portion of this is usually air leakage.

A house can be looked upon as a big chimney. Air leaking into the bottom of the chimney is heated and goes up and out the top. This is the problem. We need to stop the holes in the bottom of the chimney and to stop the holes at the top. By doing this, we can reduce the air leakage.

Now there are some potential problems that may occur because we've done this. One is that we may get higher humidities in the house. So now we need to control the moisture in the space, and we may provide increased ventilation for the house. But unless you build your house really tight, you will always have more than sufficient ventilation or leakage to

provide all of the ventilation requirements, and you can't easily control that.

"There are probably construction techniques and building designs that are associated with low energy building which are not well-known to most tradesmen. Would there be any merit in having the Saskatchewan Conservation House designers prepare a course of instruction that could be offered at a technical institute to young people who want to get into carpentry and other sub-trades in order to be able to build these kinds of houses?"

We are situated in Saskatchewan and this has been done in our province. We have been working with the trades schools there and providing information. We are also working towards providing not exactly constructional manuals, but details that show techniques of putting in vapour barriers and so forth, but I think anyone can do this almost intuitively if he knows what he's trying to achieve. We use polyethylene like most others, to make the house air-tight. If you examine the details of your house very carefully, and follow the path of the polyethylene so that every surface, including the floor, is completely covered, and every sheet of polyethylene that goes on is sealed positively to the adjacent sheet that carries on to the next portion of the house, your house will be tight. The only problem is that you have to think ahead before you start construction. People are often averse to doing this; they like to work with their hands and they get carried away in the spur of the moment. When they get to the point where they have to put in the air or vapour barrier, it is too late. They have not thought ahead. It is like painting yourself into a corner. But if you sit down and think about it carefully, practically any design will work.

All of the work is not done by one person but by a series of specialists working in particular fields, and your interest in making the house air tight is not shared by the man putting the electrical wiring in, or the man who is putting the plumbing in, or the one who is putting the drywall on. You have a half dozen other people who in their trades have a habit of trying to punch holes in the air barrier.

So we are trying to work on details that allow placement of the air barrier in a position where it is less likely to be attacked, and can be made much more air tight easily. It should also be pointed out that a conventional house design is likely to be more suitable for putting on an air barrier than most of the so-called low energy houses that are being designed with these funny shapes. These unusual shapes lead to situations in which it is extremely difficult, and sometimes impossible to make the thing air tight. We find some terrible details going ahead because the person is preoccupied with having a wall for the sun to shine on or having an air space so the air can flow up and mingle with air from other parts of the house. It can not be forgotten that if you are going to conserve any energy, the most important aspect of the house is that it has to be air tight.

"In respect to solar-heated homes and in particular, thermal storage, what is the practicality or value of storing heat from the sun in Trombe walls? Is the Trombe wall a practical heating facility in this part of the world?"

At the moment we don't have any firm data on this so I'm rather reticent to say whether Trombe walls are good or not. From the best information we have available, the suggestion is that if you build a Trombe wall and compare it to an equivalent area of normal glass wall, from a Trombe wall you'd expect more heat loss than you would from a conventional window. The reason for this is that while the sun is shining in and heating up the air space between the window and the Trombe wall, that air is going to get very hot, and you're going to have greater losses through the wall than if the sun was shining in and coming into some other portion of the building.

As soon as the sun goes down, you could expect a still greater heat loss than if you have a normal window because you have a heated surface directly in contact with that window.

Now let's look at the situation where you put a shutter on, first on the window and then the same shutter on a Trombe wall. Once again, you would expect greater heat loss from the Trombe wall than you would with a similarly shuttered window. If you put a Trombe wall in and put a shutter on it, it's possible that you can get some useful heat from the Trombe wall. However, if you have a window of the same size with the same shutter on it, the sun's energy will come into the house and will be absorbed by the interior partitions, particularly, interior floor units, and any other thermal mass such as furniture, which you have in the house and which combines a much greater surface area than the Trombe wall would have. Each surface has a lower temperature and radiates heat less quickly to the outside.

So it seems that if the Trombe wall costs you extra it just doesn't pay because the amount of energy you can store in any thermal mass that cost you money is not worth it. It is better to reduce your window area, which of course immediately saves energy losses from the space and such losses are likely to be greater than heat gains that can be made from larger windows.

"So the only advantage of a Trombe wall would be that it would moderate temperature swings?"

That is true, except that this is exactly what occurs in the thermal mass that you inadvertently build into the house. The tons of drywall that you put into the house, the tons of wood framing material, the ton or two of furniture you put into the house also do the same thing, but you have to put it in for other purposes. This thermal mass is just as effective as the thermal mass of a Trombe wall, and it is free.

Now it is distinctly possible that under some particular situations Trombe walls may be of some benefit. For example, if you had a house that was situated on a site where it was necessary, because of the siting or view, to place windows on the north or some other angle, and the view to the south is a garbage dump, then it may be advisable to use a Trombe wall.

"What do you know about a single component polyurethane foam for use around windows?"

It has some advantages and some disadvantages. It does make a very good seal if you get it in place between the window frame and the studs of the wall. Unfortunately, we don't usually use the studs as an air barrier and unless you seal your vapour barrier to the stud you have not gained anything because the air just goes around the other side of the foam.

There are other disadvantages in its use. One is that it has a tendency to expand in place as it cures. There have been some cases in which it pushed the window unit away from the framing and so made it impossible to open and close the window. This will not cause problems, however, with a sealed window.

If you are going to use it, use it judiciously. Use a narrow bead near the wall surface and don't try to fill the whole cavity with the foam or you can easily build up pressures that will push your window out of shape.

"Won't the insulation inside the vapour barrier be wasted in the system you recommend?"

The insulation on the inside of the vapour barrier is as effective as the insulation on the outside of the vapour barrier, as long as the vapour barrier is no more than a third of the way into the wall. In fact, if you divide your insulation up into individual small layers that are separated by air barriers it works better. If you build a wall with 2 x 6 studs and put in R20 batts, the studs act to conduct heat. We can calculate what the reduction in the insulating value is due to this phenomenon. However, if you actually measure a wall that has been built this way, you find that the numbers you obtain don't match the calculated values. What happens is that the vertical spaces on either side of the insulation allow air to rise on the warm side, cross over at the top, and fall on the outside thereby circulating air. This creates a convection cell in the wall

system. For an R20 wall it appears that you get a reduction of approximately ten per cent from the insulating valves which had been calculated.

When you divide the wall and place the vapour barrier inside the wall in the double wall system we have discussed, the insulation in the centre interrupts the air flow and eliminates the convection problem. Therefore we get a higher value for the overall wall insulation.

Paul Kurjata

Paul Kurjata *is a contractor and designer in northern British Columbia. He is the president of* Woodcraft Industries *in Dawson Creek, B.C. and a builder of energy-efficient houses for northern climates.*

In Dawson Creek we are basically building homes based on ideas worked out in the Saskatchewan Conservation House. We believe that this is definitely the most cost-effective way to save energy in our climate. Before such information was available, we were building staggered stud homes with double walls and we were careful with such things as thermal breaks, but we did not do a good job on the vapour barrier.

I would like to begin with an examination of a few typical section details of our current houses, then take a look at the total system including thermal shutters and air exchangers, and finally the different heating systems that we might consider. I'll also go through a few costs, ways to cut costs, new products, some financing problems and the relationships with builders, government and utility people.

Figure I is one of our conventional bungalows with a full basement on a footing. Note that I am illustrating a double wall system as a way to achieve R40 on a foundation. If we had used a concrete pad then it would have been important to isolate that pad from the ground to prevent significant heat loss, especially in a cold region such as ours. In the section in Figure I, we have used extruded polystyrene, R15 (**A**). This also keeps the frost from getting into the foundation and cracking it. We have to keep the frost away from drain tiles, because an energy-conserving structure can create problems that are not normally faced with conventional structures. By totally isolating the interior environment from the exterior, things like drain tiles and water lines are not receiving the benefit of the heat loss that would

normally keep the earth near the house close to room temperature. So we arranged the basement insulation to allow for some heat transfer (point **B**) to keep things from freezing.

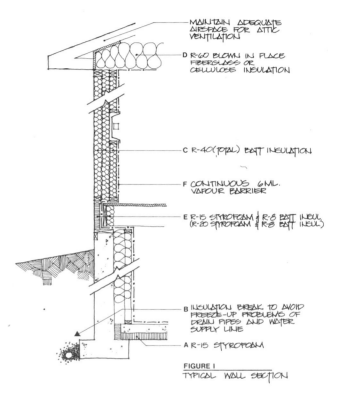

- MAINTAIN ADEQUATE AIRSPACE FOR ATTIC VENTILATION
- D R-60 BLOWN IN PLACE FIBERGLASS OR CELLULOSE INSULATION
- C R-40 (TOTAL) BATT INSULATION
- F CONTINUOUS 6ML. VAPOUR BARRIER
- E R-15 STYROFOAM & R-8 BATT INSUL (R-20 STYROFOAM & R-8 BATT INSUL)
- B INSULATION BREAK TO AVOID FREEZE-UP PROBLEMS OF DRAIN PIPES AND WATER SUPPLY LINE
- A R-15 STYROFOAM

FIGURE I
TYPICAL WALL SECTION

Point (**C**) illustrates the double wall system. We minimize thermal breaks between the inside and outside environments. Note the continuous vapour barrier. Where the roof joins the wall you maintain the R60 level right to the exterior wall line so there is no weak point in the system at point (**D**). Use a built-up cantilever truss or a similar arrangement.

As in all areas of the house, with the floor joist system we want to keep the thermal bridging to an absolute minimum. The floor joist is insulated from the exterior with R15 styrofoam (point **E**), although others might put in R20, depending on what there is for bearing.

Such a system also enables a really good job of maintaining a continuous vapour barrer (point **F**) which is absolutely critical to making this sort of system work, otherwise it is virtually impossible to do a good job of vapour barriering in this area. This is what is done with conserving homes in Saskatchewan. In this example, the interior wall has to be the bearing wall because the floor joists are resting on that wall. This allows those floor joists to be pulled in and to run batt insulation at the exterior end of them (point **E**), using a plywood plate to maintain a spacing. During construction, first lay the vapour barrier, put the plywood plate down, lay the floor joists down, then lay the sub floor. Be careful not to tear the vapour barrier.

The concrete foundation has been of standard construction. However, the preserved wood system is beginning to receive acceptance. More and more people, including myself, believe that when properly handled it is a good, permanent system. But I stress that it must be properly handled, especially when back filling granular materials so that there is absolutely no problem with water. Allow for the expansion in what appears to be the typically expansive clay sub-soil. Don't take short cuts with preserved wood. It is attractive in low energy housing because it is easy to manage a thermal system well and to maintain a continuous vapour barrier all the way

around the home.

In a preserved wood foundation (**Figure II**) we use a 2 x 8 exterior wall insulated to R28 with a 6 mil vapour barrier on the interior (point **A**). Others might consider strapping the interior with 2 x 3's on edge (point **B**) to achieve another R8. Greg Allen brought this idea up and it is one way to achieve high R values and maintain vapour barrier integrity. As well, such a system minimizes thermal cold bridging because there is only a $1^1/_2$-inch-square cross section where the 2 x 3 strapping intersects the 2 x 8 studs. This is acceptable, all things considered. I think this is more cost effective than the other methods we have discussed, at least from a builder's point of view.

This is a good system and there is no problem with thermal bridging. But allow some heat to get to the drain tile so that there are no freezing problems (point **C**). To illustrate this, I spoke to an engineer who did some work at Fort Nelson. An apartment had been backfilled to about three feet up a preserved system, which was sitting on a wood sleeper set up on graded aggregate. They had not insulated the bottom portion of the wall (which was covered by the backfill) as they had been instructed to do, because they knew that they had to get dome heat into the area where the drain tiles were. However, the water lines in the interior structure froze because it was quite cold in the bottom two feet of the wall. So they insulated and the next winter they had some chinooks in February and March. The snow melted and the water drained down. Since there was no heat getting to the drain tiles, all the water froze underneath the support system and heaved the whole apartment building, cracking all the gyprock. This is a

good illustration that little details need attention or there will be problems, perhaps major problems.

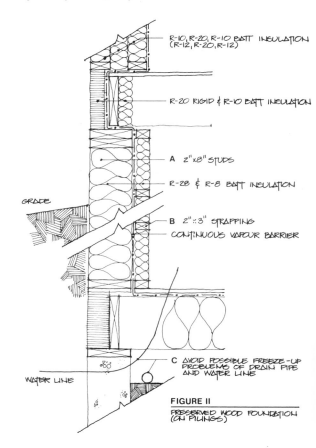

FIGURE II
PRESERVED WOOD FOUNDATION (ON PILINGS)

I personally favour trying to work with preserved wood on some kind of a concrete or wood piling system. I think it has more general application than trying to tie car ports and other structures to houses.

In **Figure III** you can see the vapour pan (point **A**) which is a good method of insulating and maintaining a continuous vapour barrier around electrical outlets. You can buy these from an outfit in Edmonton for about $2.00 apiece. They are an effective way of handling the problem. The vapour pans go in before the electrician does the wiring. The electrician will be pulling the wires through the pan, then the area around the wires can be caulked with accoustical type caulking. This method will pretty well eliminate any air leakage around the boxes.

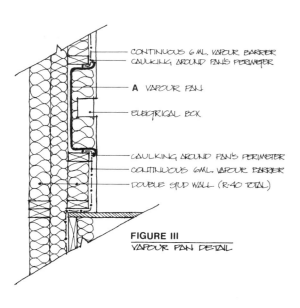

FIGURE III
VAPOUR PAN DETAIL

I can see that the system advocated by Harold Orr in Saskatoon has more integrity in the long run. The vapour barrier is placed within the wall itself, on the outside of the interior studs.

Figure IV illustrates the strapping system mentioned by Greg Allen as opposed to the doubled-up 2 x 4 exterior framing system. From a builder's point of view,

this appears to be a cost-effective way of achieving between R30 and R38 insulating values and also keeping the vapour barrier out of the way of sub-trades (**A**). It is worth a good, hard look.

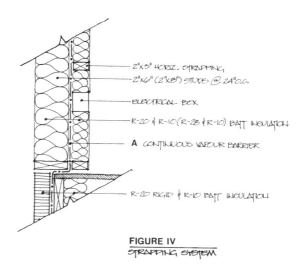

FIGURE IV
STRAPPING SYSTEM

There are four or five things that are important in order to make an energy-conserving structure work. We cannot afford to overlook any one of them because the system will break down.

Orientation. I won't get into cost, but I must stress that to make this situation work you must have proper orientation. Orientation is worth 33 per cent of the heat bill, so do it properly. This was well illustrated in the pie graphs that Harold Orr was working with.

Vapour barriers must be continuous and perforations absolutely minimized. Use a 6 mil vapour barrier instead of 2 mil. Use vapour pans and run caulking every place that two sheets of vapour barrier lap and do a good job caulking around the floor joist and other areas.

Thermal shutters have been discussed by a number of people. They are obviously the most difficult thing to manage in the system and there is no easy way to do it. The main thing is that it has to be tight. When closing the shutter there can't be any convection or there will be condensation problems and a breakdown of R values.

The system also uses *air-to-air heat exchangers.* The University of Saskatchewan in Saskatoon has prepared an excellent brochure on how to build them. What an air-to-air heat exchanger does in an energy-conserving structure is, first, maintain a comfortable relative humidity which can otherwise be quite high in a tight structure. The second thing it does is introduce fresh air at healthy levels. They are designed to change air once every four hours. A house such as we are describing usually has an air change only every 24 hours unless it has an air-to-air heat exchanger in place. The exchanger introduces fresh air at an acceptable rate and recaptures heat from air that you are exhausting. These systems work at about 80 per cent efficiency and are cost-effective. They can be built for $70 worth of materials and $30 worth of fans. It would cost from $400 to $500 for a contractor to do the job.

Super-insulation, the R40 and R60 values, are obvious to the system. I do not feel that it makes much sense to spend much money on introducing mass into a structure that is losing so little heat. Already the heat bill has been reduced by 90 per cent if we abide by the rules. Therefore it is hard to justify spending more money to get that other 10 per cent when we can burn a cord of wood to make it up.

One thing that I feel *is* worthwhile, is to save scraps of dry wall and discarded plastic bottles which can be filled with water and stored within interior walls or between floor joists. Over a year or two, 1000 gallons of water can be accumulated in the floor joist system. This means that the owner could leave a conventional house for two weeks in the winter and the whole system could break down, the electricity could be out, the worst blizzard could be blowing, and yet it would take weeks for this house to cool down because all this mass has to cool to 32° before the place is going to freeze. I think this is worth considering and that eventually we will be looking at homes which have only a wood heat auxiliary system.

The conserving features of the home in concert with the solar orientation and passive solar gain will provide 90 per cent of the heat required and we can look at wood heat to make up the difference. Right now we are all hung up on our pilot lights. We feel secure with them, and it is hard to get used to the idea that maybe they are not needed and not very good to have around in any case.

This whole system is cost-effective today. With cost of energy being what it is, the cost of financing so high, and inflation even worse it is worthwhile to lay out the extra $3,500 because there will be increasing savings each year. Next year, more money can be made on the investment. We find that these costs jive with the work that we are doing right now.

I will briefly discuss some of the heating system options which we are normally looking at today. We will consider natural gas, fuel oil, electric heating, and wood. Solar is assumed in this case.

In Dawson Creek, and I suspect in most of Alberta, natural gas is the most cost-effective way to go because the price of gas is so low right now. People have to make their own decisions as to what will happen with rates in the future, considering the fact that it is a non-renewable fossil fuel. It is so cheap relative to electricity that one cannot afford not to use it. So let's assume one has a natural gas furnace installed, the first thing is to try to seal the furnace space off from the rest of the home. This will eliminate uncomfortable drafts at one's feet. The second thing to consider is the type of gas furnace that works with electronic pilots and flue dampers. They reduce the draft going up the chimney plus they are safer than the standard furnace. The price is about $400 more than a standard furnace, but makes the house more efficient.

If one is forced to consider fuel oil, go to electric heat. Electric heat is especially worth looking at once energy consumption has been drastically reduced. Electricity does cost a lot of money, but electric heat is safe and there is no fresh air intake to worry about and no chimney. It is easy to install and is low maintenance compared to an oil system.

Wood is really attractive because it regenerates itself over a short period of time with proper cultivation. It is a radiant, comfortable heat. It has been receiving a lot of acceptance, even with people who are building right in Dawson Creek. Many are accepting air-tight burners in the basement and they are serious about using it. When one needs only one or two cords of wood to achieve 100 per cent of the heating needs, one can get excited about it. However, I believe that insurance

people don't like to see ducted wood heating systems because it can set up hot spots in the ducts, and they are potential fire hazards. Insurance people like to see a wood system as an auxiliary source which means it would not be ducted. A lot of people are considering wood and oil combination furnaces. I do not feel this makes a lot of sense, from many points of view. The initial cost is high and they are not all that efficient.

What about total costs? A double-wall home with R40 walls, R60 ceiling, good vapour barrier, wood casement windows, wood siding, asphalt roof, electric heat with wood back-up, an air-to-air exchanger in place and above average workmanship and finishing will cost about $52,000 at mid-1979 prices.

I have also priced out an attached solar greenhouse at $3,700. That breaks down to $1,700 labour and $2,000 for materials for a 20 x 30 ft. greenhouse with double-glaze glass and a grade beam on pilings. Although the heat gain benefits from a greenhouse may be marginal, I feel they are really an exciting thing in our region in terms of retrofitting, as well as being a great place to be in and a place to grow food in.

Regarding foundation costs, we have found that different people are making different claims for their systems. For instance, there is a Du-All Block foundation system coming out of Edmonton which is a wood cavity block that can be filled with concrete and rebar. It has attractive thermal characteristics. Or a preserved wood system or a concrete system as we have discussed may be considered. We are finding that it is quite hard to choose between the three when considering the finished costs. They come within five per cent of each other.

The obvious way to cut costs when building is to reduce the size of the house. This has been discussed again and again. Plan the home for later additions if necessary. This makes a lot of sense — the Europeans are masters at it.

Financing may be a problem. When looking at financing an extra $5000 with ten per cent down, the debt ratio will cause trouble. Work on bankers; credit union people are usually receptive. It is harder to get the banks to move since they wait for instruction from Canadian Mortgage. Bankers need to be convinced that there will be a saving of $500 each year on heating the home; therefore, that extra $500 can be used to build the home properly. It is a paying proposition and in the long run money can be made.

I want to touch on builder-client relationships. It is important to use a good contractor and to keep everything up front. Be positive all the way through, keep the lines of communication open, especially when dealing with government people and inspectors. In Dawson Creek we have good relationships built up with all these people and they are really supportive. They are as interested in the system as we are. Be fair with people at all times. It is hard for them to do their jobs if we come to them and say you have things all wrong. We must do our homework, do a good job on it, and they will see the light sooner or later.

It is extremely important to share our knowledge. When we have something which is important, it is better to share it — it might save money in the long run,

there might be something missing in the system that another person would notice. What we need are systems that work, that is the only way others will accept them. I feel good about what is happening. I think the future looks pretty good.

"Should airtight houses have smoke detectors?"

Yes, that is critical. I think Canadian Mortgage is insisting on them. Alex Wade also mentioned carbon-monoxide detectors.

"Does the $52,000 figure include the land?"

No, it does not include the land.

"Are wood/concrete blocks filled with a concrete rebar acceptable for structural strength for a full 8-ft. basement wall or greater for underground housing?"

Yes, all the problems have been worked out by various engineers. There is also a concrete panel or joist system. It looks to me like it is really attractive for underground shelter in our area, one which takes care of all the problems that have been brought up in the last couple of days. A good manual, if you are considering underground or earth-sheltered housing, is the book that is published by the people of the University of Minnesota (*Earth Sheltered Housing.*) It is an excellent book and will get you started on the right path.

"What system do you use to seal the bottom plate to the concrete foundation?"

At that point I try to wrap the floor joist system so the vapour barrier prevents air infiltration into the interior environment. You can use a number of sealing methods: running caulking, or fibreglass insulation; some people use building paper. It is worth taking some care to get a good tight seal under there to minimize problems in your crawl space. Also, it is important to bring the styrofoam (if you are working with styrofoam and concrete) up so it laps the floor joist system and you don't get a cold bridge into the corner of the concrete.

"What are you using or recommending for window covers, drapes, shutters, whatever?"

I am not recommending or using anything at this point. Everybody is going to try different things in Dawson Creek this year, and next year we will know. It doesn't look like there will be an easy solution.

"What shape is your styrofoam insulation in after the ground has settled?"

That is a good question. First of all, I neglected to mention that you have to protect the styrofoam from sunlight with preserved wood or asbestos board or something like that to below ground level. The second thing that you would probably want to do is use some sort of a nailer strip to keep the styrofoam from crawling up the wall with frost working on it. We nail in 2 x 4s half way up the floor joist system if it is possible or else on the wall, whichever works best for the situation. Although it has never happened to us, some people have observed this problem on commercial buildings.

"The building code requires moisture barrier between concrete walls and inside insulation below grade."

Now you have me there. You are probably right, I don't know my building code that well. I look at it when I am doing the job. That is a problem all the time. I guess it has to do with capillary action in the concrete. In light of what we are looking at now that might not apply.

"Talk about the need for large houses in this climate."

There are a lot of people talking about reducing space in our climate. We are really reluctant to give it up because winters are long and hard, we spend a lot of time inside in the winter. It is a difficult decision for you to make, to shave 200 or 300 sq. ft. off your living space. All things considered, you might have to do it. If you had a space like a greenhouse attached you could add to your interior space with a functional area. You might be willing to accept less space with a greenhouse to look forward to.

Another thing I want to touch on: the percentage of glazing you should have facing south to prevent the interior space from over-heating, and at the same time get full benefit from what sunshine there is. This works out to about seven to eight per cent of what they call total square footage, so if you have 1000 sq. ft. and a basement, you have 2000 sq. ft.; you will want 140 to 160 south-facing sq. ft. of glazing.

"How about electrical resistant cord in basement floor slabs? Who are the most credible window manufacturers? Do you manufacture your own doors?"

Putting electrical resistance cord or lines into the slab is probably a good way to go, but I don't know much about its efficiency. Radiant heat is comfortable but I think you definitely want R15 styrofoam around the slab because you are risking losing a lot of that heat to the exterior. You might, in fact, want to beef this up quite a bit. If you look at it in that context it might be less attractive.

Who are the most credible window manufacturers? I can't really say. Any good wood window with awning casement-type openers is effective. You can even look at doing some of your own weather stripping around the openers. If the product is deficient, say if it is a box window, you can caulk up the joint to bring it up to the standard that you need. Generally speaking, if you stay with a wood window you won't have that many problems.

We don't manufacture our own doors. Some people are advocating steel doors which are insulated to R10 or R15. I feel that you are splitting hairs. I think a steel door is difficult to handle from an aesthetic point of view. You can make a good impression on people with a nice front door so we usually indulge in that area. We don't use steel doors. The rationale is this: Three exterior doors at 20 sq. ft. apiece is 80 sq. ft. on a total 3000 sq. ft. exposed to weather, and you are talking about the difference of R13 for a steel type door to R3 for a built-up wood door.

We normally use a good, heavy, wood door with some design work on it inside and out. People feel good about it when they walk in. I think all things considered, that is at least as important as the marginal insulating benefit of steel doors. In any case, the most important thing in any door system is how you handle the weather stripping. You have to adjust it every year to keep the infiltration down.

Finally, I would like to say that although wood frame construction is what we can relate to right now, if you look at things from Peter Van Dresser's point of view, this is a pretty temporary solution to shelter. In the long term we have got to do some work using rammed earth and cinder blocks and things such as this because that is where the future will be.

It is hard for us to relate to that right now, but it would be good if some of us did some work in this field. Maybe building an out-building just to see how these things work in our region. It is important to begin such work in this region.

One of the first things Peter Van Dressser noticed when he arrived here was that trees were pretty scrubby. He thought that we should be cultivating our wood crop, which we are not doing because wood is still a vast resource up here. We should learn from people from other regions which have already gone down this road. It is important to keep all such things in mind as we plan our regional future.

Fairview Conference Sponsors

Solar Energy Society of Canada

Since its formation in October 1974, SESCI has grown into a national organization that is recognized as the principal forum for renewable energy activities in Canada. Contact SESCI, Box 1353, Winnipeg, Manitoba.

Grant MacEwen

Honorary Chairman. Former Lieutenant-Governor of Alberta and one of Canada's most popular historians, agricultural writers and ecological spokesmen.

Fairview College

Located in the town of Fairview, 564km northwest of Edmonton, the College offers educational programmes in agriculture, animal health care, turfgrass management, adult upgrading, vocational skills, automotive and heavy duty/diesel mechanics, business education, and apprenticeship trades: welding, carpentry, heavy duty mechanics, motor mechanics and beekeeping. It also provides a wide range of continuing education opportunities — such as this Energy and Housing Conference. Write Box 3000, Fairview, Alberta T0H 1L0.

Peaceworks

This non-profit organization works towards an integrated, comprehensive approach to steady-state economics and appropriate technologies. It advocates an understanding of the impact and implications of our activities in the narrow framework in which they occur. It encourages the use of local and renewable resources, including our human resources, to develop an approach to life that incorporates both the micro and macro prespective. Contact PeaceWorks, Box 1599, Fairview, Alberta.

Acknowledgments

Fairview Conference 1979 did not just happen. It grew out of the planning, scheming, dreaming and dedication of a small army of people. As with all group efforts, I have trepidations concerning the thank you's; I fear that some of the substantial contributions will be inadvertently overlooked.

I wish to thank all those who were not content to just make it happen, but persevered to achieve an unqualified success.

Lee Ellis — master of the well-tempered press release.

Mary Crunkilton — for a little bit of everything

Ross Knox — somehow, incredibly, transported everyone to and from the airports and got the money to the bank.

Richard Crack — lighting, sound system, stage, projections, audio and visual recording. He was assisted by Susan Crack, Tony Lesperance, F. W. Chan.

Paul Tatarewicz — whose promotion of renewable energy in Alberta has gone far beyond his role as host of CKUA Radio's weekly *"Solar Tutorial"*.

Gordon Fearn — moderator and "Edmonton front".

We can not possibly mention everyone on the Fairview College staff who contributed their time and energy. Special thanks to Dr. Fred Speckeen, Sandy McKenna, Charlene Doll, the kitchen staff, janitors, Mr. and Mrs. James Tait, Dave Vanberg and the grounds crew.

Other people and organizations helped in a variety of ways: Gerry Wright and Joey Skoreyko of the Faculty of Extension, University of Alberta; Ian Burn, Manager of Energy Conservation, Ministry of Energy and Natural Resources; Grant Notley, MLA for Spirit River-Fairview, and his staff; The Fairview Post; The Fairview and District Chamber of Commerce. We thank Mr. Grant MacEwen for his support.

The Proceedings section is dedicated to Ted Olson in recognition of his years of interest in, and promotion of, renewable energy and the well-tempered house.

Mark A. Craft
Conference Co-ordinator
Peaceworks

Survey

Details 14 superbly designed, energy-efficient houses.

Introduction

Thousands of energy-efficient buildings have been constructed across North America. In the following survey we examine 14 outstanding examples. The homes selected cover most climatic regions with cold climates, ranging from northern British Columbia to western New York State. They share excellent design strategies, they are well-insulated and they make use of passive solar heating.

It's important to keep in mind that it would be a mistake to make too much of regional characteristics as they relate to energy-efficient construction. It is still too early to determine what the most appropriate approach with each climatic region might be. However, certain procedures can be observed.

Cold, but sunny climates such as the Prairies suggest super-insulated houses that minimize the total window area. Milder and cloudier climates, such as Vancouver's, require less insulation but more glass area, in part to increase natural light levels. Houses built in central Ontario, Quebec and New York tend to compromise and so they're constructed with increased levels of insulation and a greater glass area. Hybrid storage or added thermal mass is used extensively to prevent overheating.

The most salient feature of these houses is that they all work well. Each follows its own approach to passive solar heating and efficient design with a successful end result.

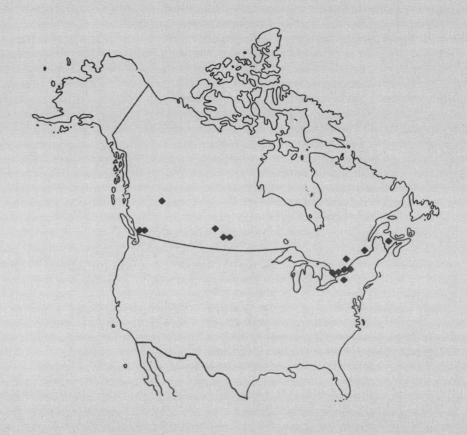

Cooper Greenhouse
Vancouver, B.C.

Designer/builder: Ken and Akkaporn Cooper
Date completed: March 1979
Size of greenhouse: 164 sq. ft.
Latitude: 49°N
Heating degree days: 5500 (°F), 3007 (°C)
Hours bright sunshine: 1784
Design temperature: 19°F, -7°C

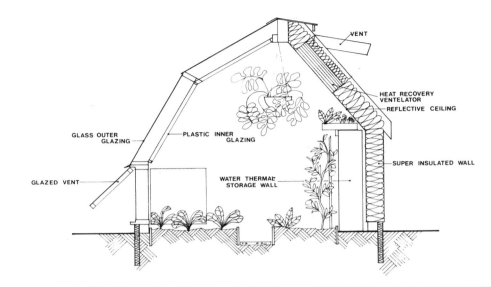

VENT
HEAT RECOVERY VENTELATOR
REFLECTIVE CEILING
GLASS OUTER GLAZING
PLASTIC INNER GLAZING
SUPER INSULATED WALL
GLAZED VENT
WATER THERMAL STORAGE WALL

Construction techniques: This is a detached solar greenhouse on an east-west axis. The south side is glazed; other surfaces are insulated with fibreglass to R22. There is a total of 163 sq. ft. of double-glazing, sloping at 30°, 60° and 90°. The lower (90°) glazed area uses flat fibreglass outer-glazing over Tedlar inner-glazing. The entire length opens as a vent. The 60° glazed area uses tempered glass over Teflon film (used for visibility). The 30° upper glazing uses tempered glass over Teflon film (to diffuse the sunlight). All non-storage interior surfaces are painted white or are covered with aluminum foil to reflect light onto the plants and thermal storage.

Thermal mass: There is 200 lbs of water along the north wall contained in dark blue tubes. The tubes are conduit pipes approximately 12″ in diameter. They are imbedded in concrete and have a plastic liner that holds the water. The dark blue (dark red would also do) allows high absorption of the sunlight, while reflecting onto the plants light of a usable wavelength. A pool on one end of the greenhouse holding 2700 lbs of water supplies additional thermal mass.

Operation: In the spring the greenhouse is used primarily for salad crops and to start seedlings for the garden. In the later spring, summer crops are planted such as tomatoes, peppers and herbs. In the early spring temperatures ranged from a minimum 50-57°F to a maximum 79-90°F. Cloudy day peaks would be a high of 68°F. In the summer the minimum temperature was 63°F and the top vents (and storage) prevented overheating. High temperatures were held 79-90°F. Plans call for the addition of night insulating shutters and a fan-operated heat recovery ventilation. Their effectiveness in improving winter performance will be monitored. Total cost for materials has been $1800.

Kitsun Housing Cooperative
Vancouver, B.C.

Designer: Atelier 2000
Solar systems designer: Solar Applications and Research Ltd.
Date completed: May 1979
Size of house: 8 unit townhouse, total 8,800 sq. ft.
Latitude: 49°N
Heating degree-days: 5500 (°F), 3007 (°C)
Hours of bright sunshine: 1784
Design temperature: 19°F, -7°C

Passive solar features: The south face of the building is a combination of mass-wall and direct gain systems. There are seven mass-wall units, each 145 sq. ft. for a total of 1017 sq. ft. The wall is 12″ concrete. Mass-walls were used for visual privacy and substantial protection from the street noise. Because of the busy (high profile) position of the townhouses the walls were painted dark tones of red, blue, brown and black. Double-glass is .5 m from the wall. Within that space a Thermal Technology Corp. R16 moveable curtain is used (one per wall). There is an additional 44 sq. ft. per unit (372 sq. ft. total) of south-facing windows, the majority angled 60°. Mass is contained in a quarter of a million pounds of exposed concrete in the north-south partition walls, and the concrete floor slabs. The walls are left grey; the floor slab is covered with red or black linoleum. Rotating Louvre shutters (skylids) are used to shutter the 60° windows.

Conservation techniques: The unit's exterior walls are wood frame with R20 fibreglass. The ceiling contains R35 fibreglass. The foundation has 2″ of rigid styrofoam. Non south-facing windows have roll shades made with five layers of aluminized mylar for a total insulating value of R16 (IS shades). The north (main) entries have air locks.

Operation: Each mass-wall unit has two thermo-syphon vent openings that heat the bottom floor (eating area) of each townhouse. The vent closures consist of rippled surfaced glass to increase natural lighting to the lower south side of the building. The insulating shutter is controlled manually or automatically, triggered by a small thermostat exposed to sunlight. There is a summer (cooling) and winter (heating) mode. The majority of the direct gain system uses Skylids® for insulation. Counterbalancing freon tubes, one inside, the other outside, operate the shutters automatically. Cross-ventilation is established using a first-floor north window and a ventilator (.4 x .6m) on the second floor, south side.

Other features: There is a freeze-proof passive solar water-heating system for heating domestic hot water. There are seven 93 sq. ft. collector arrays and one 62 sq. ft. array. Storage is in seven units of 100 gallons each and one unit of 60 gallons. The system uses a propylene glycol and water fluid and copper coil heat exchangers (Solar Systems Industries). Collectors are aluminum absorber plate, copper tubing, single acrylic glazing (Sol-Way Solar Engineering).

Back-up: Electric heat is used for back-up.

Performance: The solar gain is estimated to be 60 per cent of the heating load. Internal gains are estimated to be 15 per cent plus, with the remaining 15-25 per cent being met by the back-up. The estimated temperature swing on a clear, winter day is 8°F (4.4°C). The added cost of the direct gain, mass wall, domestic hot water and conservation systems was approximately $10,000 per unit. The solar component was sponsored by the National Research Council of Canada. Preliminary monitoring results indicate that back-up energy requirements can vary from unit to unit by as much as 1000 per cent. This indicates the importance of lifestyle and consumer habits.

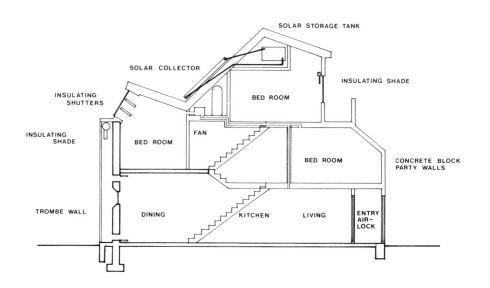

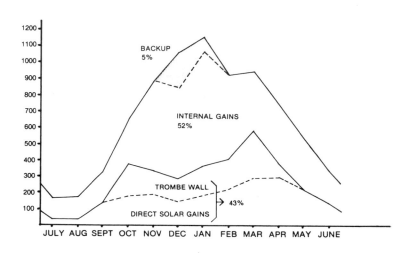

PREDICTED ANNUAL THERMAL PERFORMANCE OF KITSILANO COOPERATIVE HOUSING PROJECT BROADWAY & VINE, VANCOUVER, B.C.

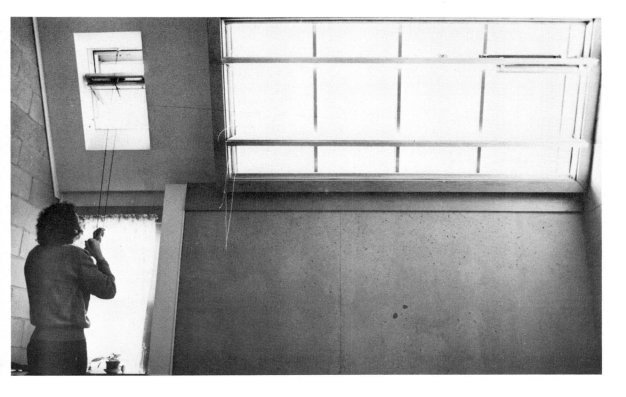

Automatic Skylids® and manual window-vent provide light, heat and fresh air

Schindler House
Tupper, B.C.

designer/builder: Gretel/Eric Schindler/Wood Craft Industries
date completed: December 1979
size of house: 2200 sq. ft.
latitude: 55°N
degree-days: 11,000 (°F), 6100 (°C)
hours of bright sunshine: 2122
design temperature: -38°F, -39°C

Conservation Techniques: This is a super-insulated, air-tight house. The walls are double-wall with an air gap for 12 inches of fibreglass batts (R40). An open-beam ceiling achieved with scissor trusses accomodates R60 fibreglass batt and cellufibre insulation. The trusses are built up at the exterior wall line to accommodate full R60 insulation at that point. The crawl space floor is insulated with R15 styrofoam. The interior of the foundation has R15 batts, and the exterior, R15 styrofoam. The floor joists are pulled in to accommodate insulation on the outside and a continuous wrap of 6 mil vapour barrier. The vapour barrier was caulked at all joints. Vapour pans were employed at all electrical outlets in the exterior walls and ceilings. There are air-lock foyers at both entrances to the home. The exterior doors are insulated steel. Because the house is air-tight, a counter-flow heat exchanger (à la University of Saskatchewan) is used to de-humidify and bring in fresh air.

Passive Solar Features: There are 150 sq. ft. of glass on the south side, representing seven per cent of the floor area. This includes a 180 sq. ft. solarium. All windows are double-glazed, with wood casement openers.

Back-up: The heating system consists of two air-tight wood burners in tandem with a 10 kw forced-air electric furnace. There is a Jotul #6 fireplace/wood heater on the main floor and a Blaze Princess fireplace/wood heater on the lower level. Hot water is provided by a 60 gallon electric tank; a wood hot water preheat system is set up in a thermosyphon with a water jacket installed in the Blaze Princess.

Performance: In the first two months of 1980 they burned ²/₃ of a cord of poplar. Electric heat consumption for the two months was $10.00. Without drapes the living areas on the south side feel cool at night so insulating shutters will be added.

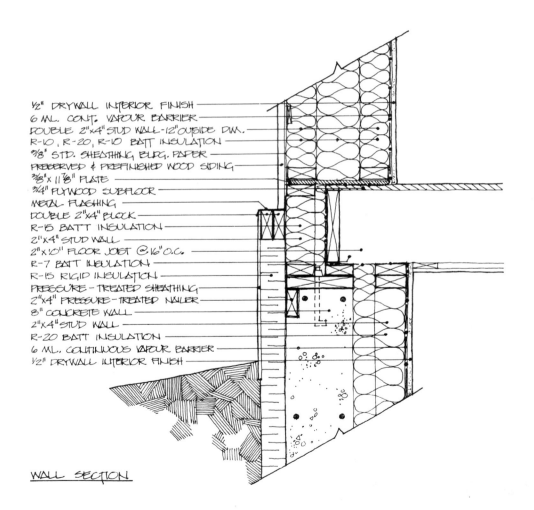

½" DRYWALL INTERIOR FINISH
6 ML. CONT. VAPOUR BARRIER
DOUBLE 2"x4" STUD WALL - 12" OUTSIDE DIM.
R-10, R-20, R-10 BATT INSULATION
⅜" STD. SHEATHING BLDG. PAPER
PRESERVED & PREFINISHED WOOD SIDING
⅜" x 11⅞" PLATE
¾" PLYWOOD SUBFLOOR
METAL FLASHING
DOUBLE 2"x4" BLOCK
R-15 BATT INSULATION
2"x4" STUD WALL
2"x10" FLOOR JOIST @ 16" O.C.
R-7 BATT INSULATION
R-15 RIGID INSULATION
PRESSURE-TREATED SHEATHING
2"x4" PRESSURE-TREATED NAILER
8" CONCRETE WALL
2"x4" STUD WALL
R-20 BATT INSULATION
6 ML. CONTINUOUS VAPOUR BARRIER
½" DRYWALL INTERIOR FINISH

WALL SECTION

Pasqua House
Regina, Sask.

Designer/builder: Enercon Building Corporation
Date completed: Februrary, 1979
Size of house: 1760 sq. ft.
Latitude: 50° 25′N
Heating degree-days: 10806 (°F) 5920 (°C)
Hours bright sunshine: 2264
Design temperature: -29°F (house built to -33°F)

Conservation techniques: This is a super-insulated house. Double 2 x 4 stud walls with a 2¹/₂″ gap between walls allowed a 9¹/₂″ cavity. With an added R8 sheathing, the walls are insulated to a total of R40. Fibreglass batts (R52) were used in the ceiling. The foundation has R15 of extruded polystyrene. A continuous 6 mil poly vapour-barrier was placed on the inside of the inner wall. Infiltration has been measured at approximately .1 changes per hour. An Enercon air-to-air heat exchange makes up the ventilation air. Exhaust air which feeds the heat exchanger comes from bathrooms, kitchen and electric clothes dryer. Non south-facing windows have manually operated internal shutters with an R15 polystyrene core (R18 plus). Shutters are either sliding in-frame or interior hinged-door type. Small fans (up to 100 cfm) move air from the second floor to the first; air returns up the stairwell. There is an air-lock vestibule at the entrance to reduce the inflow of cold air.

Air-to-air heat exchanger is connected with the furnace/duct system

Passive solar features: This is a direct gain house, with a solarium opening to the living room. It consists of 150 sq. ft. of vertical south-facing windows. A 3¹/₂ ft. overhang shades the windows in summer. Shuttering for the main window area consists of a three-layer aluminized-mylar dacron-filled curtain (R10) between the glazings. Operation is either manually controlled or automatic. A small isolated 24 hour cycle, thermal storage system consists of 500 gallons of containerized water in a basement room.

Operation: The system has two thermostats. The thermostat in the solarium activates a 400 cfm fan (at 75°F) and moves air from the top of the solarium to the storage. The house thermostat calls on the storage when required. The second stage operates the auxiliary heat (as necessary). A humidistat is used to control the fresh air heat-exchanger. Operation of the system (including fans which move the air around the house) is estimated to cost $40 per year.

Back-up: Back-up energy is supplied by a 4 kw electric heater in the duct line from the storage to the house. A Pre-way wood burning fireplace is within the living room. It uses outside air for combustion, has airtight glass doors and a heat circulating system that dumps heat into the solarium.

Performance: The heat load of the house (at -33°F) is 17,000 BTU/hr with the shutters closed, 26,000 BTU/hr with the shutters open. Over a year, solar gain is estimated to supply 30-40 per cent. Internal gains account for an additional 20-30 per cent. 30 to 40 per cent is supplied by the electrical back-up. The total monitored heating requirement was 7,200 kwh per year (25 million BTU). The temperature has hovered between 18 and 22°C throughout the year. The highest recorded temperature has been 25°C. (The house has no air-conditioning, but is closed up on hot days.) Of equal significance is the occupants' subjective evaluation of the house as a living place. "Super comfort" and "lovely living" describe the controlled environment that is draft free, with higher temperature walls, controlled humidity, and is quiet and bright. Cost of the building, excluding land, ran to about $43 per sq. ft., estimated to be about 10 per cent more than conventional housing of similar quality in that region.

Saskatchewan Conservation House
Regina, Saskatchewan

Designer: Grolle Architect and Engineer Ltd.
Date Completed: December 1977
Size of house: 188 m²
Latitude: 50° 30'N
Heating degree-days: 10806 (°F), 6000 (°C)
Hours bright sunshine: 2264
Design temperature: -29°F

Conservation techniques: This is a super-insulated house incorporating many important conservation features. It was built in a cube shape with no basement.

Insulation: The walls are insulated to R40 with fibreglass. They are 12″ thick and consist of two separate walls; one of 2 x 4 studs, separated with a gap from a 2 x 6 wall. The floor and attic (R30 and R60) are insulated with cellulose fibre.

Vapour Barrier: A 6 mil polyethylene airtight vapour barrier was used throughout. All seams between sheets were caulked, as were vent pipes, door and window frames, as well as between floors, walls and ceilings. "Polypans" were used behind exterior wall electrical outlets. An air exchange rate of 5 per cent per hour was achieved (non-ventilated).

Heat-exchange ventilation: To provide adequate ventilation (one-half change per hour), an air-to-air heat exchanger was installed. Stale air (including from the dryer) is exhausted, exchanging its heat with fresh incoming air, which is circulated through the duct system.

Hot-water exchange: Heat from draining hot water is recaptured by a waste water heat recovery unit. A temporary holding tank for waste water pre-heats the hot water supply tank.

Air-locks: Air locks are used at both entrances. Insulated steel thermal doors (R14) are weatherstripped.

Appliances: Energy-efficient kitchen appliances are used throughout. A water-conserving toilet and constant temperature water taps save water. Task lighting is used in the house. The thermostat has an automatic night set-back.

Passive solar features: There are 11.9 m² of window area facing 21° west of south (6.4 per cent of heated floor area). The first floor living room windows have hinged exterior shutters raised by manually operated motors. The shutters have 4″ of polystyrene (R22). Other windows have insulated panels which slide between an outer single-glazed window and an inner double-glazed casement. They retract into a cavity in the wall. No additional thermal mass was built into the house. An overhang (plus the shutters) keeps out the summer sun.

Active solar heating: 17.8 sq. m. (192 sq. ft.) of vacuum-tube collector panels provide the remaining required heat. They are set at an angle of 70° and face 21° west of south. Storage is in a 2,800-gallon steel tank. When fully charged, it will carry all the house's space and water heating needs for 10 to 15 days. It should be noted that the solar system is for demonstration. The house has a minimum heat load that does not justify a solar system.

Back-up: Electrical back-up is designed to be used during the off-peak hours (11 pm. to 7am.) of electrical demand. The system consists of two 3 kw heaters in the domestic hot water tank and in the main waterline from the solar storage tank.

Performance: From October 1978 to March 1979, the house was run in a passive mode with electric backup. The total electrical energy consumption was 35.6 Giga joules. For average year conditions with average usage the net space heating requirement would be 13.2 Giga joules. It is anticipated that with further work on the house (tight shutter seals etc.) the net space heating demand will be reduced to about 5 Giga joules per year, about 5 million BTU.

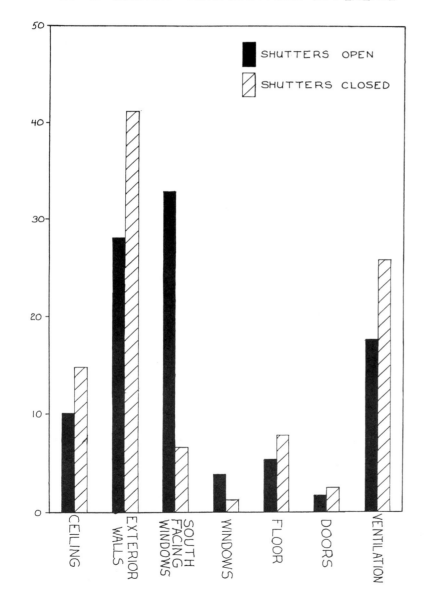

HEAT LOSSES
55°C DESIGN TEMPERATURE DIFFERENCE

■ SHUTTERS OPEN

▨ SHUTTERS CLOSED

% OF TOTAL HEAT LOSS

CEILING / EXTERIOR WALLS / SOUTH FACING WINDOWS / WINDOWS / FLOOR / DOORS / VENTILATION

EXTRA COST FOR ENERGY CONSERVING FEATURES
(2 STOREY HOUSE – 94 m² PER FLOOR)

	MATERIALS	LABOUR
AIR TIGHT VAPOUR BARRIER	150	300
AIR TO AIR HEAT EXCHANGER	300	100
WINDOW SHUTTERS 15 sq.m at $50/m²	600	150
EXTRA INSULATION		
WALLS (R7.3 m² °C/W instead of R2.1)	670	50
CEILING (R10.6 m² °C/W instead of R6.16)	300	50
FLOOR (R5.4 m² °C/W instead of R2.1)	120	50
EXTRA FRAMING FOR WALLS	300	300
EXTRA FOUNDATION TO SUPPORT WALLS $50/m²	250	250

TOTALS $2690 + 1250 = $3940

NET SPACE HEATING REQUIREMENTS REGINA LOCATION
HOUSES OF EQUIVALENT FLOOR AREA

PRE-1975 STANDARD HOUSE — 140 GJ/YR.

1979 STANDARD HOUSE — 80 GJ/YR.
CONSTRUCTED TO MINIMUM INSULATION
REQUIREMENTS

SASKATCHEWAN CONSERVATION HOUSE — 13.2 GJ/YR.
WITH NO CONTRIBUTION FROM ACTIVE
SOLAR SYSTEM
ASSUMING AVERAGE YEAR AND AVERAGE
OCCUPANCY CONDITIONS

Saratoga House
Saskatoon, Sask.

Designer/builder: Concept Construction
Date completed: August 1979
Size of house: 1240 sq. ft.
Latitude: 52° 10'N
Heating degree-days: 10,870 (°F), 6077 (°C)
Hours bright sunshine: 2367
Design temperature: -30°F, -34°C

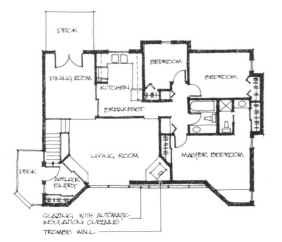

Conservation techniques: The frame walls are constructed with 2 x 6 studs, 24" on centre. Fibreglass insulation between studs plus 2" of extruded polystyrene on the outside insulate to R30. The ceiling is insulated with R50 fibreglass batts. The foundation basement is made with preserved wood and has R28 fibreglass insulation. A continuously sealed 4 mil poly vapour barrier was used throughout. Exterior wall electrical outlets were placed in polypans to ensure a continuous air-vapour barrier. Ventilation is controlled with a counter-flow air-to-air heat exchanger, replacing stale, humid, indoor air with fresh, preheated, outdoor air. Non south-facing windows are triple-glazed. A four-foot overhang shades the south glazing in the summer.

Interior view of mass-wall and insulating shutter

Passive solar features: There are 200 sq. ft. of south-facing glazing. The glazing is double-pane 5 mm plate glass with the glazings 8" apart. Approximately 35 sq. ft. is window area, allowing for direct solar gain. The additional glazed area (165 sq. ft.) consists of a mass-wall. The concrete wall is 9½" thick, poured as a slab on the subflooring and hoisted erect with a crane. Vents with dust filter and one-way flaps are 4 x 12" air registrars located every 4-5 ft. and placed 6" from the top and bottom of the walls. Shuttering of the entire glazed area consists of four-layer aluminized-nylon inflating curtain placed between the glazings.

Operation: The insulating curtain operates either manually or automatically, controlled by a freon tube thermostat. The system is set for either summer or winter mode, depending on whether the sun is to be admitted or repelled. The motor and curtain come with a guarantee for the lifetime of the house.

Back-up: Back-up energy is supplied by individually controlled electric baseboard heaters. There is also an airtight Jotal #6 wood stove. A passive solar water preheat system is incorporated within the mass-wall. Four inch PVC pipe runs through the wall, and heat (via thermosyphon) a tank placed above the wall. The solar-heated tank is in series with the electric water heater.

Performance: The house heat loss at -30°F is 20,500 BTU when the house is shuttered. Back-up requirements are 8-10 MBTU per year. Internal gain will supply about 14 MBTU while solar supplies the rest or 50 per cent of the yearly requirement. The system has no air-conditioning, but with shutters in place there is a 4°F rise in indoor temperature throughout the day when the outdoor temperature is 35°F higher than the indoor temperature. The cost of construction of this stock house was $45 per sq. ft. A comparable (conventional) house in the region would cost approximately $43 per sq. ft.

MacDonald House
Toronto, Ontario

design/builder: owner-built
date completed: summer, 1979
size of house: 1800 sq. ft.
latitude: 43°39'N
heating degree-days: 6827 (°F), 4082 (°C)
hours of bright sunshine: 1846
design temperature: 1°F, -17°C

Conservation Techniques: This is a retrofitted urban bungalow (800 sq. ft., plus basement) converted to 1800 sq. ft. During renovation it was made airtight, and super-insulated. The house incorporates direct gain passive features. The original home was double brick (R4). Five inches of SM styrofoam was installed on the exterior using a track system with exterior aluminum siding for a new wall with R30. The ceiling has fibreglass batts with cellulose blown on top for a total of R50 to R60. The new slab floor has R15 underneath. A vapour barrier of 6 mil poly was installed wherever possible. The house was painted throughout with 2 coats of Glidden Insulaid®. New double-pane windows were installed throughout, with minimum window area to the east, west and north. An air-lock entry was installed with insulated steel doors.

Passive Solar Features: This direct gain system consists of 200 sq. ft. of vertical south-facing windows. Windows are double-pane with a 1 inch air gap, manufactured by Pella. Mass is contained in a 1000 sq. ft. slab floor of 4-to 6-inch-thick concrete. The east and west walls to either side of the windows are 10 inch block, faced on the interior with brick and insulated on the exterior. The floor in front of the windows is covered with brown ceramic tiles. A central partition hearth is masonry construction. In addition the original house is double-brick with the mass inside of the exterior insulation. A temporary shuttering system consists of 2-inch foam panels that are manually friction fitted to windows at night.

Back-up: A gas furnace supplies back-up heating. At night the system is shut down and house temperatures may drop to 60°F. During the day the furnace fan runs continuously on low speed, distributing air around the house through ceiling air returns and oversized ducts. The high speed fan operates when the furnace is running or manually when there is excess solar gain. A Jotul wood-stove sits in a masonry hearth. Air can be drawn from above and fed into the air-distribution system.

Active solar system: A Sun Master evacuated-tube solar water heater has been supplied by Solartech. It consists of 42 sq. ft. of panel, a 40 gallon preheater tank and an 89 gallon storage tank.

Performance: The new house is calculated to require 50 Million BTU per heating season. 15 MBTU will come from the south-facing windows and 15 MBTU from internal gains. The house requires 20 MBTU from the gas back-up. The old (smaller) house required 71 MBTU per year, or 90,000 BTU/ft²/season, compared to the new house's requirement of 27,000 BTU/ft²/season. Problems of inadequate shutters and excessive air-leakage (discovered during a pressure test) are being corrected.

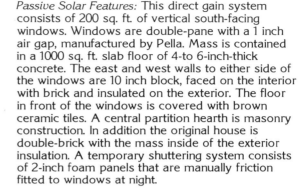

Ecology House
Toronto, Ont.

Designer/builder: Energy Probe and 50 volunteers
Date completed: Spring 1980
Size of house: 5,000 sq. ft. (retrofit)
Latitude: 43° 39'N
Heating degree-days: 6827 (°F), 4082 (°C)
Hours bright sunshine: 1846
Design temperature: 1°F, -17°C

Conservation techniques: This retrofit in downtown Toronto is a demonstration of urban conservation techniques, and so includes a wide range of examples. The house is double-brick (originally R3.9). The north wall is now R24 with extruded polystyrene nailed to the brick and covered with a fibre-reinforced stucco (Gemite). The attic is insulated to R52 with fibreglass and the roof has had a second stud installed to allow a total R40 of fibreglass batts. The basement is insulated to R10 with exterior mounted polystyrene. The east and west wall were insulated from the inside with R20 fibreglass to maintain the brick facade. Throughout the house, where possible, a continuously sealed (with acoustical sealant) 6 mil vapour barrier was installed. All windows were double-glazed and a variety of moveable insulation techniques are used for night-time insulation. These include IS mylar curtains, Window Quilt, handmade hinged shutters of rigid fibreglass (R18) and Watershed honeycomb windows.

Passive solar features: The principal passive solar heating feature is the retrofit Trombe wall (mass-wall) on the south side (oriented 9° east of south). Its gross area is 1325 sq. ft. and is made with thermopane tempered glass. The brick wall, stained a dark brown, is 9″ thick and contains 1000 cu. ft. The space between the glazing and the brick is 18″ to allow for easy access. Night-time shuttering is by two sections of hand-pulled three-ply aluminized-mylar curtains that were custom made. A third floor greenhouse also aids in heating. A dormer was removed and replaced with 168 sq. ft. of SDP double-walled acrylic (angle is 56°). Excess heat is mechanically drawn to a basement 173 cu. ft. rock-bed storage. Hand-operated rigid fibreglass hinges close off the greenhouse. The greenhouse is hydroponic, to reduce the weight.

Back-up: Back-up heating is by a 64,000 BTU gas furnace that feeds directly to the rock storage. A woodburning stove, connected to a fireplace, is on the first floor. A solar system, for domestic hot water, consists of three workshop-built panels.

Other features: The house contains a number of energy and resource conservation features. A greenhouse attached to the west wall, contains 148 sq. ft. and is insulated to R28 on the back wall and ceiling and R20 on the west wall. The foundation is made with R10 thermal blocks. 250 gallons of water add to the thermal mass. A door connects the greenhouse directly to the kitchen. An owner-built grey water system has a triple-filter feed into the greenhouse soil beds. A MullToa composting toilet handles human and kitchen wastes. Energy-efficient appliances, water-saver shower heads and other conservation systems are demonstrated. The house has been designed and built by a large group of volunteers. It's open to the public. Library and meeting facilities are also available. It is located at 12 Madison Avenue, in Toronto.

Performance: Before the retrofit the house had an average yearly heating demand of 609 million BTU. The 'after' yearly heat load is estimated to be 162 MBTU. The mass-wall should supply 75 MBTU and the two greenhouses a total of 29 MBTU for a solar gain of 104 MBTU. The auxiliary heat from the gas furnace is estimated to be 58 MBTU (a 90 per cent reduction from the original house).

Super-insulating the third floor

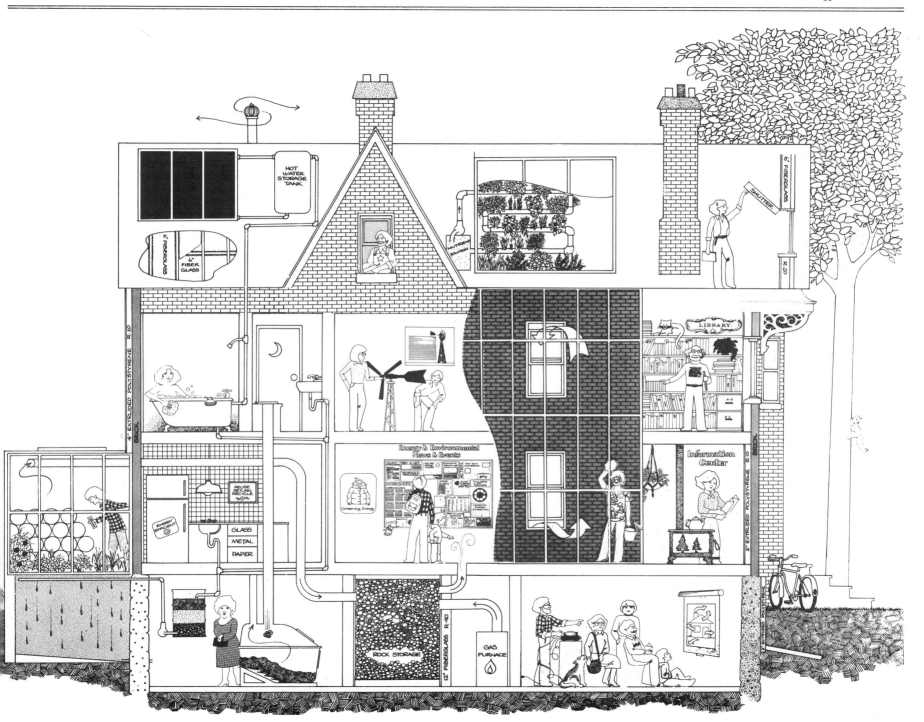

Braun-McCollam House
Amherst Island, Ontario

Designer/builder: McCollam-Braun
Date of occupancy: December 1978
Size of House: 1550 sq. ft.
Latitude: 44°30′N
Heating degree-days: 4266 (°C)
Hours of bright sunshine: 2113
Design temperature: -13°F, -25°C

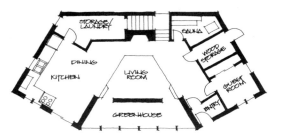

GROUND FLOOR PLAN

Conservation techniques: The walls were constructed with 2 x 6 studs, with cedar strip exterior; total insulating value of R23. The ceiling is R30 of fibreglass batts. The foundation has R16. Extensive weather-stripping and caulking ($150 worth) was used throughout. Most windows are draft-free sealed thermopane units. Cold rooms with insulated doors and walls are on the north side (sauna and pantry); there is an air-lock entrance.

Passive Solar features: This is a direct gain house. The main collection area is a livingroom/greenhouse with 275 sq. ft. of vertical thermal-pane glass. In addition there is 50 sq. ft. of glass facing SW and 25 sq. ft. facing SE. Mass is contained in 420 cu. ft. of limestone and mortar; a 3″ thick floor and 12″ interior walls. In addition there is a 30″ thick fireplace unit. A 36″ overhanging balcony provides shade for the south, SE, and SW faces. Shuttering for the windows is manual using 2″ urethane boards. Ventilation of the house is through four casement windows, summer-screened doors and two 8″ roof-mounted wind turbines. The lakeside location keeps the house cool, while specific features include the overhangs which shade the summer sun, and 2000 gallons of water stored in the crawl space.

Back-up: Back-up is provided by a Riteway Model 2000 wood burning stove. The centrally located fireplace is double-dampered and contains a heatilator unit. An interior woodbox holds 225 cu. ft. of wood.

Performance: From December 1, 1978 to May 1979, one and a half cords of wood were burned. No other back-up was used (wood was 50 per cent red cedar and 50 per cent ash). Generally the house was maintained between 66° and 68°F during the day. At night it would reach a minimum of 58-60°F. The house was unoccupied for seven days in January without providing back-up heat; a low of 44°F was reached. The house has reached 80°F on a couple of the hottest days in August. Seventy per cent of the south-facing glass is on the first floor. That, combined with a small stairwell on the north side, has ensured that the house experiences very little temperature stratification between the two stories.

Hedges House
Stella, Ontario

designer/builder: Kip and Bill Hedges
date completed: June 1979
size of house: 2,000 sq. ft.
latitude: 44°30'N
degree-days: 4266 (°C)
hours of bright sunshine: 2113
design temperature: -13°F, -25°C

Conservation Techniques: This is a massive passive solar house constructed with locally collected beach stone. Fibreglass insulation is framed to the outside of the masonry wall, insulated to R22. The ceiling insulation is R23, below grade is insulated to R14. A vapour barrier was placed between the stone and the insulation.

Passive Solar Features: There is 275 sq. ft. of due south-facing vertical glass. The glazing runs the two stories and is double-glazed. A two-foot overhang provides some shading, while a skylight at the peak of the house provides a ventilation exit and light. A total of 110 tons of stone and cement went into the house. It is located in the 17-inch perimeter walls and in an interior fireplace/chimney which runs up the middle of the house. The south window area is insulated at night with styrofoam panels pushed into place.

Back-up: The only back-up to the solar system is an airtight wood-burning stove. In an average winter they would require four cords of wood, gathered from locally fallen trees, and from the wood lot. With no back-up, the average night-time temperature drop in the house from December to February was 3°C.

Coté-McIntyre House
Kirks Ferry, Québec

designer: Bruce D. Gough
builder: contracted by D'arcy Coté
date completed: September 1978
Size of house: net 1925 sq. ft.,
    plus 1058 sq. ft. basement
latitude: 45°32'N
degree-days: 8700 (°F) 4670 (°C)
hours of bright sunshine: 1995
design temperature: -13°F, -25°C

Conservation Techniques: This is a super-insulated house. The basic wall construction is 2 x 6 stud wall, 24 inches on centre. 2 x 2 furring runs horizontally 24 inches on centre, on standoffs exterior to the stud wall. This allows two R20 friction fit Fibreglass batts to run perpendicular to each other, providing a total of R40. A 6 mil polyethylene vapour barrier was lapped and caulked. No electrical fixtures or outlets were mounted on the exterior walls in order to maintain the integrity of the air-vapour barrier. The ceiling is insulated to R55, the basement wall to R20. Where the second floor connection meets the wall there is 5 inches of styrofoam and R12 batts. The vapour barrier was wrapped around the floor platform and caulked to the inside of the wall studs.

Passive Solar Features: 260 sq. ft., or 91 per cent of the total window area of the building is located on the south wall, which is oriented 15° east of south. Because of the large south-facing window area (13.2 per cent of the floor area) additional mass was provided. Quarry tiles were used as a floor finish and block masonry surrounds the Heatilator firebox. Over 26,000 lbs. of drywall were used in the wall and ceiling finish. Exterior walls have two layers, totalling 1³/₈ inches. All partition walls and ceilings have a single ⁵/₈-inch layer. The total thermal capacity of all the interior materials is calculated to be 16,000 BTU/°F (excluding all basement materials). The storage-to-glass ratio is 60 BTU/°F/sq.ft. of south glass. All windows are double-glazed Pella units. Ten of the 25 units are casement-type for ventilation.

Back-up: The auxiliary heating system consists of an 18 kw forced-air electric furnace. It has perimeter floor supply and return from the ceiling of the second floor. There is a 38-inch Heatilator double-wall steel fireplace set in masonry in the interior of the house. Outside air is supplied for combustion. The furnace return air is drawn through the air-jacket surrounding the firebox. The furnace fan may be operated independently of the furnace heat.

Performance: The house has a heat loss factor of 461.8 BTU/°F-hr (243.5 W/°K) At the design temperature of -13°F the heat loss is 39,253 BTU/hr. (11.5 kw) without any movable insulation. Over the year internal gain and passive solar contribute 13,000 kwh, or 45 per cent of the gross heat load. Future plans include thermal shades for the windows; a counterflow air-to-air heat exchanger to preheat intake air (ductwork is already in place); and a grey water heat exchanger to preheat the cold water supply to the hot water tank (the plumbing has been split to accommodate this). Estimated additional cost for extra insulation, air-tight vapour barrier, extra drywall, plumbing, etc., is $3000. This includes materials and direct and supervisory labour.

North-east view of Coté house

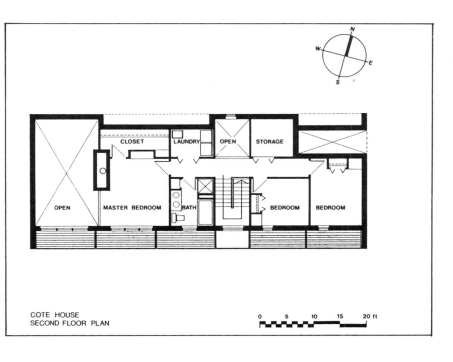

COTE HOUSE
SECOND FLOOR PLAN

0 5 10 15 20 ft

CLOSET LAUNDRY OPEN STORAGE

OPEN MASTER BEDROOM BATH BEDROOM BEDROOM

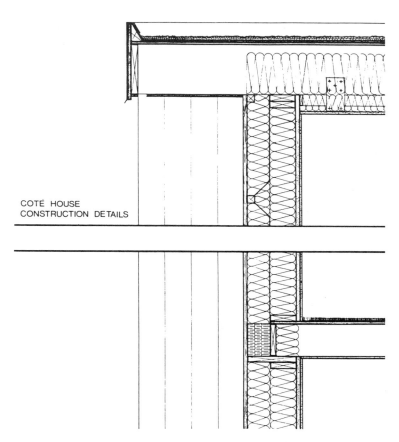

COTÉ HOUSE
CONSTRUCTION DETAILS

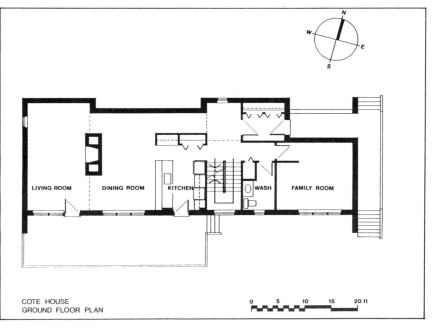

COTE HOUSE
GROUND FLOOR PLAN

0 5 10 15 20 ft

LIVING ROOM DINING ROOM KITCHEN WASH FAMILY ROOM

Sawyerville House
Sawyerville, Québec

designer/builder: Allen Drerup White
date completed: December 1979
size of house: 2388 sq. ft. (heated)
latitude: 45°N
degree days: 8252 (°F), 5242 (°C)
hours bright sunshine: 1902
design temperature: -22°F, -30°C

**Water preheat tank
sitting on the top of the
rock-bed storage**

Conservation Techniques: This is a super-insulated passive hybrid solar house. The walls are constructed to ensure 1) minimum thermal bridging from the interior to the exterior; 2) R30 insulation; 3) continuous vapour barrier throughout. The basement walls are insulated in the same manner. The ceiling insulation ranges from R56 to R65. A 10 mil poly vapour barrier was used throughout. An air-to-air heat exchanger is used to preheat ventilation air. The house is bermed to the north and west 14 feet. Conifers are to the north while a variety of deciduous trees have been planted on the south.

Passive Solar Features: There are 384 sq. ft. of south-facing windows. 126 sq. ft. are at 75° (the solarium); the rest are vertical. All are thermopane units. The thermal mass consists of the house materials, a brick wall within the solarium and a rock storage that is centrally located within the house. It occupies 280 cu. ft., has ¾ to 1½" stones and a heat storage capacity of 196,000 BTU/°F. House air is extracted through the sauna (which functions as a hot air plenum) and into the top of the rock storage. The flow is reversed to heat the house. An ADW reversing damper with an (almost) standard distribution system is used.

Back-up: a 10-kw electric furnace provides the back-up. A Fisher Goldilocks wood-burning stove is in the wall between the living area and the sauna, to heat both areas. In this way wood-burning heat is drawn through the sauna plenum and into the rock storage. The stove is fed outside air for combustion.

Performance: The electric furnace is used as a back-up, with wood and solar being the primary heating source. The annual back-up (non-solar) required is approximately 20 million BTU, the greatest loss being through the non-shuttered windows. When shutters are installed, the heat load is expected to be cut in half. During an average winter day the furnace fan would come on in the early morning (5 a.m.).

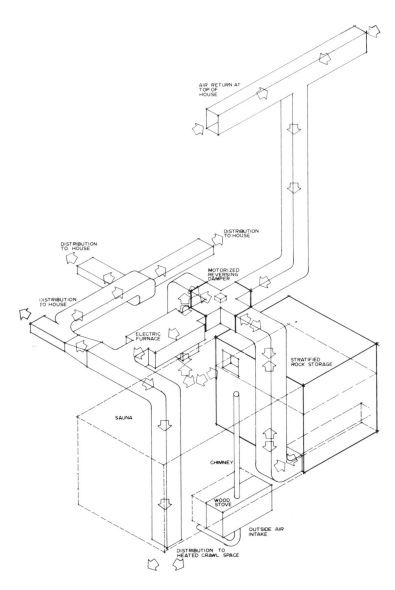

QUEBEC COUNTRY HOUSE

HYBRID AIR / ROCK THREE MODE SYSTEM

Labels on diagram:

AIR RETURN AT TOP OF HOUSE

DISTRIBUTION TO HOUSE

DISTRIBUTION TO HOUSE

DISTRIBUTION TO HOUSE

MOTORIZED REVERSING DAMPER

ELECTRIC FURNACE

STRATIFIED ROCK STORAGE

SAUNA

CHIMNEY

WOOD STOVE

OUTSIDE AIR INTAKE

DISTRIBUTION TO HEATED CRAWL SPACE

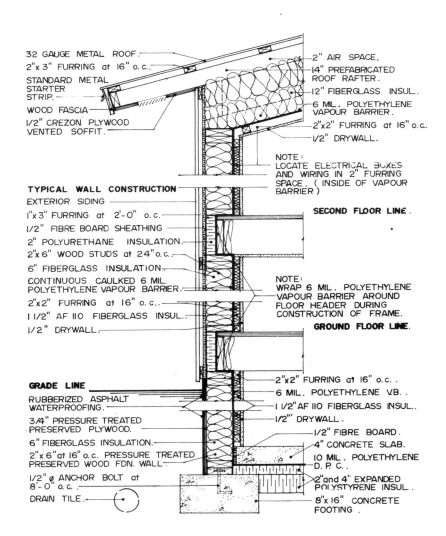

32 GAUGE METAL ROOF.
2"x 3" FURRING at 16" o.c.
STANDARD METAL STARTER STRIP.
WOOD FASCIA
1/2" CREZON PLYWOOD VENTED SOFFIT.

2" AIR SPACE.
14" PREFABRICATED ROOF RAFTER.
12" FIBERGLASS INSUL.
6 MIL. POLYETHYLENE VAPOUR BARRIER.
2"x2" FURRING at 16" o.c.
1/2" DRYWALL.

NOTE:
LOCATE ELECTRICAL BOXES AND WIRING IN 2" FURRING SPACE. (INSIDE OF VAPOUR BARRIER)

TYPICAL WALL CONSTRUCTION
EXTERIOR SIDING
1"x 3" FURRING at 2'-0" o.c.
1/2" FIBRE BOARD SHEATHING
2" POLYURETHANE INSULATION.
2"x 6" WOOD STUDS at 24" o.c.
6" FIBERGLASS INSULATION.
CONTINUOUS CAULKED 6 MIL. POLYETHYLENE VAPOUR BARRIER.
2"x2" FURRING at 16" o.c.
1 1/2" AF 110 FIBERGLASS INSUL.
1/2" DRYWALL.

SECOND FLOOR LINE.

NOTE:
WRAP 6 MIL. POLYETHYLENE VAPOUR BARRIER AROUND FLOOR HEADER DURING CONSTRUCTION OF FRAME.

GROUND FLOOR LINE.

GRADE LINE
RUBBERIZED ASPHALT WATERPROOFING.
3/4" PRESSURE TREATED PRESERVED PLYWOOD.
6" FIBERGLASS INSULATION.
2"x 6" at 16" o.c. PRESSURE TREATED PRESERVED WOOD FDN. WALL.
1/2" ø ANCHOR BOLT at 8'-0" o.c.
DRAIN TILE.

2"x2" FURRING at 16" o.c.
6 MIL. POLYETHYLENE V.B.
1 1/2" AF 110 FIBERGLASS INSUL.
1/2" DRYWALL.
1/2" FIBRE BOARD.
4" CONCRETE SLAB.
10 MIL. POLYETHYLENE D. P. C.
2" and 4" EXPANDED POLYSTYRENE INSUL.
8"x 16" CONCRETE FOOTING.

TYPICAL WALL SECTION (WOOD FOUNDATION)

The Nasonworth House
Fredericton, N.B.

Designer: Mike Start — Design Workshop Ltd.
Initiator: Verne Ireton
Date Completed: April 1979
Size of house: 1385 sq. ft. gross, 1266 sq. ft. net
Latitude: 45° 52′N
Heating degree-days: 8671 (°F), 4700 (°C)
Hours bright sunshine: 1748
Design temperature: -10°F, -23°C

Conservation techniques: This is a well-insulated, air-tight house. Walls are constructed with 2 x 6 studs on 16″ centres. They are sheathed with 1½″ of SM styrofoam for a nominal rating of R30. The ceiling has R40 of loose cellulose insulation. A continuous 6 mil air-vapour barrier was installed. An exhaust-gas heat-exchanger with a 50 cfm fan provides 0.3 air changes per hour. Air is exhausted from the kitchen and bathroom through the unit and is controlled by a humidistat. There are no windows to the north, 50 sq. ft. to the east and 55 sq. ft. to the west. The foundation is back filled as high as possible, and air-lock "mud-rooms" are used in both entries.

Passive solar features: This is a direct gain system. The south wall has 238 sq. ft. of sealed double-paned glass. A grill on the inclined glazing allows the winter sun in, but blocks it in the summer. Interior, hinged insulating shutters are manually operated and cover all but 10.5 sq. ft. The shutters are made with styrofoam-filled hollow-core doors. The added mass to the house totals 13,140 lbs. A 4″ concrete floor slab runs in front of the windows, and is covered with quarry tile, totalling 6480 lbs. A concrete block bench in front of the windows contains an additional 2500 lbs. The north wall of the living room is brick faced (3600 lbs.) and the stairwell contains 560 lbs. of brick.

Back-up: Back-up energy is supplied by a series of three 2 kw electric elements in a warm-air heater. Two elements come on upon demand from the thermostat and the third comes on at an outside temperature of -4°C (25°F). The furnace includes a two-speed fan, operating continuously at low speed, switching to high speed when the furnace is heating. Return air is collected at the high point of the house. A wood stove has also been installed.

Performance: The total heat loss of the house at the -10°F (-23°C) design temperature is 18,000 BTU/hr, with the shutters closed. Internal gain is estimated to be 3400 BTU/hr. The solar portion is about 50 per cent of the heat load. It is currently being monitored. Cost of the building (excluding land) was $34.66 per square foot, comparable to similar construction in the area.

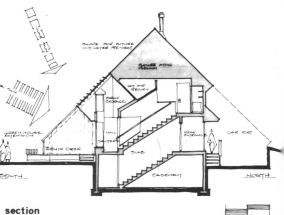

section

Sun Glow I
Western New York State

designer/builder: Allen Drerup White/owner-built
date completed: Spring 1980
size of house: 1000 sq. ft.
latitude: 43°N
degree-days: 7286°F
hours of bright sunshine: 2025
design temperature: -30°F

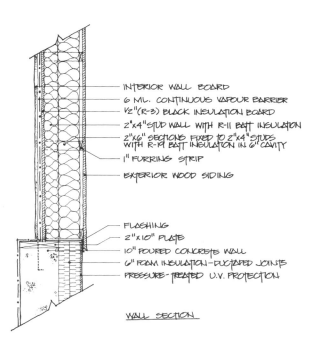

INTERIOR WALL BOARD
6 ML. CONTINUOUS VAPOUR BARRIER
½" (R-3) BLACK INSULATION BOARD
2"x4" STUD WALL WITH R-11 BATT INSULATION
2"x6" SECTIONS FIXED TO 2"x4" STUDS WITH R-19 BATT INSULATION IN 6" CAVITY
1" FURRING STRIP
EXTERIOR WOOD SIDING

FLASHING
2"x10" PLATE
10" POURED CONCRETE WALL
6" FOAM INSULATION—DUCTAPED JOINTS
PRESSURE-TREATED U.V. PROTECTION

<u>WALL SECTION</u>

Conservation techniques: This is a well-insulated owner-built house with an attached greenhouse. The walls are double-wall construction. A standard 2 x 4 supporting stud wall contains R11 fibreglass batts. A 6"-curtain wall is mounted on the exterior of that wall, adding an additional R19. Including the siding and insulating board, the wall is R35. There is an air-lock entrance. Domestic hot water comes from a flash hot water heater.

Passive solar features: There is a 180 sq. ft. greenhouse on the south side of the house. Orientation is 15° east of south. It is connected to the house via a 10-inch-thick concrete wall, which has both a doorway and operable vents for access and air/heat exchange. The foundation and interior of the first floor walls are 10-inch poured concrete, containing 50 cubic yards. Two-inch styrofoam shutters are applied at night to all windows, including the greenhouse glazing.

Performance: The heat loss of the house at -30°F is 21,000 BTU when the shutters are in place. A small wood-burning stove is the only back-up. During the summer the greenhouse glazing will be shaded and the mass of the concrete will be used to keep the house cool.

The following firms or individuals may be contacted for further information. Please remember that they are extremely busy professionals, many of whom are in the business of designing/building energy-efficient houses. Only serious enquiries should be addressed to them.

Schindler House

WoodCraft Industries
P.O. Box 839
Dawson Creek, B.C. V1G 4H8
(604) 782-3722

Kitsun Housing Co-op
Cooper Greenhouse

Solar Applications and Research
3683 West 4th Avenue
Vancouver, B.C. V6R 1P2
(604) 872-1429

Pasqua House

Enercon Ltd.
2073 Cornwall Street
Regina, Sask. S4P 2K6
(306) 585-0022

Saskatchewan Conservation House

Office of Energy Conservation
Saskatchewan Mineral Resources
Regina, Saskatchewan

Saratoga House

Concept Construction Ltd.
2-271 2nd Avenue S.
Saskatoon, Saskatchewan S7K 1K8

MacDonald House

Rob MacDonald
c/o Faculty of Environmental Studies
York University
Toronto, Ont.
(416) 667-6453

Ecology House

Energy Probe
12 Madison Ave.
Toronto, Ont.
(416) 967-0577

Hedges House

Bill Hedges
Stella, Ont.
(613) 389-9868

Coté-McIntyre House

Bruce Gough
75 Sparks St., Suite 302
Ottawa, Ont. K1B 5A5

Sawyerville House
Sun Glow I

Allen Drerup White
334 Parliament St., Studio 505
Toronto, Ont. M5A 1K8
(416) 863-1762

Nasonworth House

Design Workshop Ltd.
48 Bonaccord Ave.
Moncton, N.B. E1C 5K7
(506) 855-1990

Access

Sources for follow-up information;
includes bibliography, product catalogue,
and solar organizations.

Introduction

Sources of information and access to the appropriate hardware are critical ingredients in the construction or retrofitting of the well-tempered house. The following pages should help connect you with sources.

The Bibliography annotates books that are widely available. Many will provide in-depth information on specific aspects of energy-efficient building.

The Product Catalogue lists the manufacturers and distributors of hard-to-get components. Before ordering any equipment write to the manufacturer or distributor for additional information or price revisions. It would be an impossible task to include all companies working in this field, though we have endeavoured to provide as comprehensive a list as possible. The omission of a company does not imply a negative opinion of their product.

The Organization section lists both key government and non-government sources of information. It includes a list of North American Solar Energy Chapters.

Bibliography

The following titles will serve as a useful introduction to various aspects of energy-efficient housing.

Energy-Efficient Housing

The following books deal with the many varied aspects of energy-efficient home design, ranging from general presentations to specific construction details.

An Air-to-Air Heat Exchanger for Residences *Extension Division, University of Saskatchewan, Saskatoon, Sask. S7N 0W0, $1.00*

This pamphlet is for the do-it-yourselfer and those wishing to learn more about air-to-air heat exchangers. Contains detailed information on how to build a low-cost counter-flow heat exchanger for residential use.

Builders Guide to Energy-Efficiency in New Housing *HUDAC, Ontario Ministry of Energy, 1980, 135 pages, $6.00: available from HUDAC, 15 Toronto Street, Toronto, Ont. M5C 2E3*

This book is meant to set before the building trades the options and economics of energy-efficient new house construction. It covers design, airtightness, insulation, domestic hot water and lighting. Unfortunately it falls below the state-of-the-art of superinsulated houses. For example the best insulated wall strategy presented was R25 (RSI 4.38), and there is virtually no mention of shutters, air-to-air heat exchangers and the sizing of south-facing windows.

The Conservation of Energy in Housing *Central Mortgage and Housing Corp., 1977, 145 pp.*

This extensive document provides guidelines for planning, building, and landscaping for thermal efficiency, with an emphasis on existing buildings. Topics covered include: principles, building sites, building envelope, space heating, energy conservation opportunities.

A Design and Construction Handbook for Energy-Saving Houses *Alex Wade, Rodale Press, 1980, 432 pages*

Alex Wade, co-author of *30 Energy Efficient Homes,* takes the reader through preparation (site selection, materials, tools, working with contractors, etc.) and through all construction operations. 11 inspiring owner-built homes, a detailed list of recommended sources and a complete set of working drawings for one of Wade's houses are also included.

Earth Sheltered Housing Design; Guidelines, Examples and References *Van Nostrand Reinhold Co., 1978, 310 pp.*

This is a must book for anyone contemplating building an underground house. Written for homeowners and architects, it presents design considerations and tools covering site planning, architectural design, energy use, structural design, water-proofing and insulation building codes, and goes on to present 17 existing houses from both warm and cold climate areas.

Energy-Efficient: Technical Guidelines *Canadian Electrical Association, 1979, 51 pp.*

This booklet, distributed by Electrical Utilities, presents their version of an energy-efficient home program. Predictably they take a soft stance. Part of the requirements are R20 walls (new construction) or R12 (retrofit). Other requirements are equally soft, and nowhere does the book suggest night-shutters or south-facing windows that will make a house more efficient. It contains an interesting "penalties and merit points system" for assessing a house, new or retrofit.

From The Walls In *Charles Wing, Atlantic Monthly Press, 1979, 217 pages, $12.95*

This book is all about the retrofit; improving the energy-efficiency of existing homes. Wing cares about the subject and carefully explains to the reader the why's and how's of dealing with older houses. Excellent, clearly presented information on doors, windows, insulation, vapour barriers and weatherstripping.

The Fuel Savers *D. Scully et. al., Total Environmental Action Inc., 1978, 59 pp., $3.75*

This book, well-written and illustrated, is subtitled *A Kit of Solar Ideas for Existing Homes.* It presents 20 specific projects, from shutters and insulating curtains, to passive solar retrofit and solar water heaters. Each project is discussed with regard to principles, variations, advantages and disadvantages, and economics.

Keeping the Heat In *Energy, Mines and Resources, Ottawa, 1976, 98 pp. Free*
Subtitled *How to re-insulate your home to save energy and money (and be comfortable too)*, this is an excellent general introduction on how to assess your house and re-insulate. Has well-illustrated "how to" sections.

Low-Cost Energy Efficient Shelter: for the Owner and Builder *ed. Eugene Eccli. Rodale Press. 1976, 399 pp.*
This is an excellent manual for designing and building efficient housing. It provides details on how to reduce the first costs of building a home and how to design to lower your operating expenses. It covers a wide range of approaches from window strategies, site planning, lighting, appliances and water heating.

Low Energy Passive Solar Housing Handbook *University of Saskatchewan, 1979, 38 pp. $5.00 from Division of Extension and Community Relations, University of Saskatchewan, Saskatoon, Sask.*
This excellent booklet looks at methods of reducing the energy needs of (mainly) new housing. It examines air-tightness, insulation and shuttered south-facing windows as the three approaches to creating a super-insulated building. It contains many drawings of wall construction (to insulate to R40) and the installation of continuous air/vapour barriers.

Seal Your House Before Re-Insulating *Saskatchewan Science Council, 1979, 15 pp. Free: Office of Energy Conservation, Sask. Mineral Resources, Regina, Sask.*
This pamphlet presents the why's and how-to's of sealing a house as the critical first step before re-insulation. It examines attics, basements, doors, windows, vents, electrical outlets and other sources of air and (therefore) heat loss.

30 Energy Efficient Houses...You can build *Alex Wade, et. al., Rodale, 1977, 309 pp.*
Thirty well-designed, energy-efficient solar houses are presented with clear drawings, plans, photographs and descriptions. The houses present a wide and inspiring range of innovative possibilities.

Underground Designs *Malcolm Wells, 1977, 87 pp. Available from Malcolm Wells, P.O. Box 1149, Brewster, MA, 02631.*
This book presents the plans and illustrations of 18 of Wells' underground designs. (Not all have been built.) There are sections on site, structure, building codes, waterproofing, etc.

Window Design Strategies to Conserve Energy *S. Hastings, R. Grenshaw, National Bureau of Standards, USA, 1977, 210 pp.*
This publication looks at windows from six functions: solar heating, daylighting, shading, insulation, air-tightness and ventilation. Thirty-nine strategies are examined to make these functions more energy-efficient.

Passive Solar Heating

The following books deal directly with the principles of passive solar heating for both houses and greenhouses and their potential application.

Natural Solar Architecture: a passive primer *David Wright, Van Nostrand Reinhold Co., 1978, 245 pp.*
This book nicely outlines the A-B-C's of solar thermal phenomena, illustrates some of the concerns of passive solar design and provides some inspiration. A fun book to read.

Passive Solar Catalogue *David Bainbridge, Passive Solar Inst., 1978, $6.00, Available from PSI, P.O. Box 722, Davis, CA, 95616*
This book contains three major sections: a primer to passive solar heating; a survey of twelve examples; a catalogue listing of components.

The Passive Solar Energy Book *Ed Mazria, Rodale Press, 1979, 421 pp.*
This book, using a clear and effective format, presents details of designing passive solar heated buildings. The principles are explained, examples given and detailed step-by-step design tools and methods are presented. It will help calculate heat-loss, heat-gain and system performance. Note that some of the sizing data would lead to oversized systems in Canadian climates.

Passive Solar Heating in Canada

Bruce Gough, Conservation and Renewable Energy Branch, EMR, Ottawa, 1979, 160 pp.
This is a background paper that looks at the architectural, technical and economic implications of passive solar heating for Canada. The paper covers design, planning, performance, materials and building standards.

Residential Passive Solar Heating

Cuplinskas et. al., Ontario Ministry of Energy, 1980. 158 pp. From: Ont. Government Books, 880 Bay St., Toronto
This is the result of a study to assess the potential of passive solar heating systems and to develop simple manual design aids. It generally takes a conservative stance towards energy-efficient building, but does offer some useful insights.

The Solar Greenhouse Book

ed. J. McCullagh. Rodale Press, 1978, 328 pp.
This is probably the best book on designing and building an energy-efficient greenhouse. It covers a wide range of approaches, including freestanding, attached, and pit solar greenhouses. It also covers the management of a solar greenhouse from both the plants and energy perspectives.

The Survival Greenhouse *James DeKorne, Peace Press, 1978, 165 pp.*
An Eco-System Approach to Home Food Production, this book describes greenhouse basics, photoperiod, carbon dioxide, hydroponics, greenhouse management, aquaculture and wind generators. The book concentrates on the self-maintaining pit greenhouse built and operated by DeKorne.

General Energy

The following books provide a good introduction to the principles and implementation of energy-conserving practices.

The Autonomous House Report

Nick Nicholson, The Ayer's Cliff Centre for Self-Sufficiency, 1980, three volumes.
There are three volumes to this report of Nicholson's latest work which involves the building of an autonomous house. Features of the house include: earth sheltering, passive solar heating, site-built air-type collector, salt storage tubes, photovoltaic power, a greenhouse and a hot tub.

Basic Guidelines for Energy Conservation in Community Planning and Building Design *1979, 65 pp.*

This booklet is a clear introduction to energy-efficient and passive solar heating. It covers the design of buildings, their siting, landscaping, and community design and planning. The booklet contains a number of recommendations and useful appendices, such as looking at the economics of different wall and window strategies.

The Canadian Wood Heat Book

Gordon Flagler, Deneau and Greenberg Ltd., 1979, 280 pp.
This is a guide and catalogue for wood heating. It discusses the selection of a wood-heating appliance and its safe usage. It examines wood supply techniques, from harvesting to storing. The catalogue lists and describes almost 300 wood-burning units as well as accessories such as chain saws, chimneys and wood splitters.

Energy-Efficient Community Planning *James Ridgeway, The JG Press Inc., 1978, 218 pp.*

Subtitled *A Guide to Saving Energy and Producing Power at the Local Level,* this book looks at the comprehensive energy conservation policies initiated in four American towns and cities. It also discusses initiatives taken by four other communities in wind power, wood power, energy audits and energy from wastes.

Home Energy for the Eighties

R. Wolfe et. al., Garden Way, 1979, 257 pp., $14.50
This book covers energy conservation, solar heating, wind power, water power and wood heat. Each section contains a primer on the subject, followed by a catalogue of manufacturers and suppliers of equipment. While the advice in the primer slips occasionally, the catalogue offers a fascinating glimpse of the state-of-the-commercial-art.

New Inventions in Low-Cost Solar Heating *William A. Shurcliff, Brick House Publishing, Co., 1979, 290 pp.*
The *100 Daring Schemes Tried and Untried* is a collection of Shurcliff's and others' ideas on new approaches to solar heating. The systems include hybrid, active, storage, domestic hot water. A bonus are some humorous essays on the field.

Solar Heating Catalogue No. 2 *Energy, Mines and Resources, Ottawa, 1978, 120 pp. $2.00*
This catalogue (now over two years old) is still the best source of solar equipment manufacturers in Canada. It contains a yellow pages section by province and a product guide which lists and describes systems, components and parts and materials.

The Solar Home Book *B. Anderson, Cheshire Books, 1976, 293 pp.*
This is a classic introductory book to solar heating systems, both active and passive. It explains how the systems work, describes several good examples and presents many useful charts and tables.

The Solar Water Heater Book
R. Bryenton, et. al., Renewable Energy in Canada. 1980, 128 pp., $6.95. Available from REIC, 415 Parkside Drive, Toronto M6R 2Z7
Subtitled *A Practical Guide to Building and Installing Your Own System,* this is a well-illustrated step-by-step guide to building solar water heating systems, using a system that has been successfully operated throughout Canada and the United States. It requires common household tools and utilizes readily available materials.

Solplan 2 *R. Kadulski et. al., The Drawing Room Graphic Services, 1978, 40 pp., $3.00*
Solplan 2 examines solar energy for existing homes and looks at retrofit houses for passive and active solar heating. It contains a series of worksheets that will let you calculate the potential contribution solar can make to your house.

Catalogue of Products

This section will present the components and products available on the market today that will make the job of building the well-tempered house all the easier. In addition, the various qualities to look for are discussed. A knowledge of these qualities will help you choose the product most appropriate for your needs. We recommend that you refer to the primer and appendix sections to learn more about the choices available. The products to consider include insulation, glazing, efficient windows and doors, back-up heating systems, sealants, vapour barriers, caulking and weather-stripping.

Some components are so widely available that it would be impossible to list all their sources. Others are more difficult to find because they are relatively new and not established in the market place. Sources for these products are listed below. They include air-to-air heat exchangers, moveable insulation (night-time shutters), water-conserving showerheads, etc.

Further information on these and other products (including do-it-yourself projects) is available in some of the books listed in the bibliography.

There will be many products and retail outlets which we have not listed. We apologize to the entrepreneurs who are putting their resources into this field, and to our readers for our incomplete list. We hope that you will keep us informed of activity in your region, so that subsequent editions and publications will accurately reflect the state of the art.

Conservation Gadgets

The following groups provide access to many of the products which can result in lower fuel and water consumption in the home.

Condecor Products Ltd.
40 Main Street N.
Halton Hills, Ont. L7G 3G8
(416) 877-5566
Condecor supplies insulating wall sections which range from R12 to R50. They are attached to masonry or concrete walls. The interlocking sections are urethane-based and come either unfinished or finished (cement surface).

Conservation Unlimited
Box 215
Canning, N.S. B0P 1H0
(902) 582-3562
Conservation Unlimited distribute *Saver Shower* low-water-use shower heads, water saving faucet aerators and toilet water savers.

Dalen Products Ltd.
201 Sherlake Drive
Knoxville, Tennessee
U.S.A. 37922
Dalen manufactures *Solarvent®*, an automatic greenhouse window ventilator. This self-powering unit will open a venting window (up to 9 lbs., up to 20 lbs. with counter-balance spring) at 68°F to 75°F then close it automatically, thus preventing overheating.

Energy House
P.O. Box 185, Station G
Toronto, Ont. M4M 3G7
(416) 690-6846
Energy House distributes *Saver Shower* showerheads which reduce flow rates from 5 to 8 gallons per minute to 1.8 gallons per minute while maintaining a forceful-feeling shower. They also distribute faucet water-savers and toilet water savers.

EPU Educational Products Unlimited
5250 Ferrier Street, Suite 802
Montreal, Que. H4P 1L4
(514) 342-2663
EPU markets the *NOVA* flow-controlled showerhead. This reduces a shower's flow from 4 to 7 gallons to 1.7 gallons of water per minute. They also carry low-volume faucet aerators and water-saving toilet dams. "EPU Marketing Inc." (same address) carry the *Energy Button* that increases the life of incandescent bulbs 100 times by halving their light output (and energy use).

Insulok Systems
3325 North Service Rd., Unit 12B
Burlington, Ont. L7N 3G2
(416) 335-5557
Insulok is a wall-insulating system which consists of a slotted rigid foam insulation board that has a metal furring channel installed. The board and the furring channel are mechanically fastened to masonry or concrete walls. Dry wall can then be fastened to the metal channel.

Sun of Man Solar Systems
Drawer W.
Bethel Island
California, U.S.A. 94511
(415) 684-3362
They manufacture the *Solarsyphon Diode®*, a valve which prevents backsyphoning in a thermosyphon solar water heater. It allows the storage container to be placed in any relationship to the collector provided the container inlet (hot) is above the collector outlet (hot). Minimum rise is 1/4 inch per foot of horizontal run.

Sparfil
Case Postale No. 9
Delson, Que. J0L 1G0
(514) 632-7531
Sparfil manufactures insulating concrete blocks with R factors from R8 to R23. They are stacked dry and coated on both sides with surface bonding cement. The blocks have up to a four-day thermal lag. Also distributed by **Thermal-Block**
Box 430, Mount Forest, Ontario N0G 2L0
(519) 323-2626.

Weather Energy Systems Inc.
39 Barlows Landing Rd.
Pocasset, Massachusetts
U.S.A. 02559
(617) 563-9337
WES Inc. manufactures the *Plexus 1* system which controls airflow in passive/hybrid solar spaceheating systems. Heat is used, stored or vented as determined by pre-programming. Controls up to three fans and five dampers from eight thermostats. *Plexus 3* is a simple fan that operates proportionately with the temperature. It is reversible and can be used with a greenhouse/sunspace and a house.

Moveable Insulation

The following companies manufacture and/or distribute systems for minimizing heat loss through windows at night.

A.A. Beaulieu

P.O. Box 341
Edmundston, N.B. E3V 3K9
(506) 735-4771
A.A. Beaulieu manufactures doors and windows. They supplied the shutters used in the Nasonworth passive solar house in New Brunswick. The shutters are made of veneer-faced doors insulated with S.M. rigid insulation, 1³/₈ inches thick.

Ener-Gard

1409 Wallace Rd.
Oakville, Ont. L6L 2Y1
(416) 827-8777
Ener-Gard distributes the *Heatcool* interior storm window system. Various mechanisms are used to seal the edges, including: double-sided adhesive tape, magnetic seal (available with or without self-storing roller), and velcro attachment. The systems are sold pre-assembled or as a kit form. Also available from
Heatcool, Inc., *P.O. Box 21196, Eugene, OR 97402.*

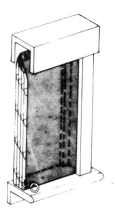

Appropriate Technology Corporation

P.O. Box 975
Brattleboro, VT 05301
(802) 257-1773

Canadian Gem Instruments

3060 Lakeshore Rd. W.
P.O. Box 403
Oakville, Ont.
(416) 827-6446
Canadian Gem distributes the *Window Quilt®* insulating shade made by Appropriate Technology Corp. The core is aluminized polyester plastic film which acts as a heat reflector and vapour barrier. The film is surrounded by insulating fibre-fill, the outer surfaces are covered with a fabric. The unit is bonded in a quilt pattern. The sides and bottom are all sealed. Combined with double glazing it provides R5.2 insulation.

IS Insulating Shade Company Inc.

P.O. Box 282
Branford, CT 06405
(203) 481-2337
IS manufactures and sells the *IS High "R"®* Shade. The shade is made up of five layers of plastic film which, when pulled down, separate to form dead air space. The interior is made of metalized film, the room side of vinyl. A wooden or plastic guide frame ensures sealed edges. The shade is installed on the interior of the window, like a conventional unit. Combined with double glass, a five-layer unit insulates to R15.

National Marketing Group

31 Eward Place
Waterloo, Ont. N2L 4E5
(519) 884-2602
National Marketing are the Canadian Sales agents of *Martin Processing Inc.'s* U-V stabilized aluminized mylar, used as a reflective surface for insulating shutters and curtains.

Passive Solar Products Ltd.

2234 Hanselman Avenue
Saskatoon, Sask. S7L 6A4
Passive Solar Products manufacture a moveable insulating curtain. It consists of four layers of metallized fabric, that self-inflates to create dead air spaces. The curtain is motor-driven. This can be supplied as a complete package, including glass. Operation may be performed by manual switching or automatic.

Patry Products Inc.

10 Stonefield Crescent
West Hill, Ont. M1E 4J5
(416) 282-1771
Patry Products distribute a line of solar shading systems, operated either manually, by motor or automatically. One of the models, the *Dual Shade,* is a two-layer shade with a reflective film, air gap, and see-through woven fabric. It can be used in the winter (R1.75) and as a sun-screen in the summer.

Shutters, Inc.

110 E. 5th St.
Hastings, Minnesota
U.S.A. 55033
Shutters, Inc. manufactures *Thermafold Shutters* for sliding glass doors. Mounted on the outside, they are operated from the inside via a crank. Made specially for sliding glass doors, they provide a total of R9.9. Can be easily retrofitted.

Solar Energy Components Inc.

212 Welsh Pool Rd.
Lionville, PA.
U.S.A. 19353
(215) 644-9017
SECO manufactures *Thermo-Shade®* thermal barriers which are an attractive roll-down insulating shade. Automatically or manually operated, it is made with hollow PVC slats. Provides R7 with double pane windows. The units are also distributed by **Solace Energy Centres** *2425 Main St., Vancouver, B.C.*

Sunflake

625 Goddard Ave.
P.O. Box 676
Ignacio, Colorado
U.S.A. 81137
(303) 563-4597
Sunflake manufactures a sliding urethane insulating panel. The panel rests in a pocket beside the window (behind the wall) and slides out when required. It comes as a system (complete with window) and provides R16. (The hidden pocket when empty provides R16 as well.) The system can be used for both 2 x 4 and 2 x 6 construction. They produce a power-driven shuttered skylight system.

Sun Quilt Corporation

P.O. Box 374
Newport, NH
U.S.A. 03773
Sun Quilt manufactures a moveable quilt-type insulation. It comes in various R-values (average R6) and is made of a waterproof nylon with a urethane vapour barrier, stuffed with a polyester/cotton blend. It is an automatic system, activated by light or heat and is intended for large glassed areas, including greenhouses. Installed costs range between $5 and $8 per square foot.

Thermal Technology Corp.

P.O. Box 130
Snowmass, Colorado
U.S.A. 81654
(303) 963-3185
Thermal Technology manufactures an automatic insulating *Curtain Wall®*. Designed for large window-areas (south face, greenhouse, etc.), it mounts on the inside or between glazings. An expanding four-layer aluminized nylon curtain offers R9 to R12 insulation. Automatic operation can be reversed for summertime and has a manual override. Costs for standard units range from $4 per sq. ft. and up. Standard sizes range from 8 x 8 ft. to 13 x 20 ft.

Window Insulation Specialists Co.

1662 Bonhill Rd., Unit 15
Mississauga, Ont. L5T 1E1
(416) 671-2242
Window Insulation Specialists distributes *Thermo Shutter,* an interior-mounted insulated shutter. It incorporates a rigid insulation core within a solid basswood frame. There is a metal foil layer on either side of the polyurethane core. Other products carried include set-back thermostats, Heat Cheater®, and Sun-Gard window film. Thermo Shutters are also distributed by **Window Insulation Co.** *2700 Paulus Street, Montreal, Que. H4S 1G1 (514) 336-2445 and* **Insul Shutter Inc.** *Box 338, Silt, Colorado USA 81652.*

Heat Exchangers

A prerequisite for super-insulated air-tight homes, heat exchangers are available from the following groups.

Advanced Idea Mechanics

P.O. Box 48
Hyde Park, Ont. N0M 1Z0
(519) 473-0638
Advanced Idea Mechanics distribute the *Mitsubishi Lossnay* air-to-air heat exchange ventilators. Made of specially treated paper, the units are capable of exchanging both sensible heat (temperature) and latent heat (humidity).

Enercon Industries Ltd.

2073 Cornwall Street
Regina, Sask. S4P 2K6
(306) 585-0022
Enercon manufactures a residential-size counter-flow air-to-air heat exchanger for recapturing heat in ventilation air. The unit can recover up to 90 per cent of the heat energy of exhausted air, is self-draining and has a variable speed fan control.

Dick VanEe

R.R. #3
Saskatoon, Sask.
S7K 3J6
Dick VanEe manufactures an air-to-air heat exchanger for ventilation and humidity control. The unit measures 17.5 x 24 x 90 inches, has a nominal flow of 80 cfm with a recovery ratio of 0.75. The system cost, including fans and ductwork, is approximately $350. A custom-built heat exchanger for indoor pools is also available.

Glazing Materials

The following companies distribute materials which can be employed for windows, collectors and greenhouses.

Allied Plastics

4461 Chesswood Dr.
Downsview, Ont. M3J 2C2
(416) 630-5600
Allied Plastics manufactures a dome skylight that is energy-efficient. It provides double glazing (acrylic) and rigid vinyl frames with a thermal break.

Chemacryl

73 Richmond St. W.
Toronto, Ont.
(416) 869-0013
Manufactures *SDP* double-skinned acrylic, a poly-carbonate material with good thermal and light transmission characteristics. The material is widely used for greenhouses.

Chemplast Inc.

2450 Dunwin Dr., Units 6 & 7
Mississauga, Ont. L5L 1J9
(416) 828-2100
Chemplast distributes a number of glazings for use in solar collectors or glazing for greenhouses. These products include: *Llumar Weatherable Film®, Polyester Film, Teflon®* solar film (used as an inner glazing).

Convenience Products Ltd.

307 Bering Ave.
Toronto, Ont. M8Z 3A5
(416) 239-3523
Convenience Products distribute 3M Products, including *Scotchtint®* window insulation film and adhesive weather strip.

Energy Systems Company

167 Dolomite Dr.
Downsview, Ont. M3J 2N1
(416) 663-5701
Energy Systems distribute *Solar Film®*, a centralized temperature setback for all electrically heated homes, and *Coroplast* window sheeting. Coroplast is a double-walled polypropylene translucent sheet. It can be taped or installed using a plastic extrusion. Added to an existing window it adds R2.44.

Graham Products Ltd.

Box 2000
Inglewood, Ont. L0N 1K0
(416) 457-5290
Graham Products manufactures *Excelite®*, a fibreglass reinforced polyester glazing. Excelite is translucent and so it diffuses sunlight. This is of benefit in many window applications and for greenhouses. The panels are also used as coverings for solar panels (85 to 90 per cent transmittance). A sister organization, **Graham Fibreglass Ltd.** *300 Main St., Erin, Ont. N0B 1T0,* manufactures a new fibreglass insulation.

Homesworth Corp.

54 Cumberland St.
Brunswick, Maine
U.S.A. 04011
Homesworth manufactures and distributes *Sun Saver* thermal shutter kits. Common household tools and skills are used to cut and mount these rigid, hinged shutters onto existing windows. Sun Savers with double-glazing insulate to approximately R5.5.

NRG Energy Designs & Products Inc.

P.O. Box 1753
Cornwall, Ont. K6H 5V7
(613) 933-5249
NRG are glazing fabricators for the *SDP Acrylite* double-wall sheets. They sell other components for passive systems, such as *Kalwall* storage tubes. They are presently in design stages of a night-time insulation and thermosyphon solar and wood domestic hot water system that they hope to manufacture.

Watershed Energy Systems Ltd.

108 Liberty Street W.
Toronto, Ont. M6K 3C4
(416) 536-6884
Watershed manufactures a *Honeycomb* window glazing. These are double-glazed windows with a horizontal honeycomb of *Teflon®* film between the glazings. They can be used anywhere as a glazing; skylights, clerestories, mass-walls, greenhouses, etc. The glazing unit is approximately $3\frac{1}{2}$ inches thick. It offers over twice the insulation of standard double thermal panes. The units are also used as efficient glazing for solar collectors.

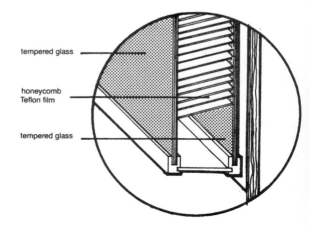

tempered glass

honeycomb
Teflon film

tempered glass

Energy Stores

There are a number of multi-purpose store-front and mail-order houses which carry a wide range of energy related products. The following stores carry a large line of goods related to energy-efficient and passive solar design.

Access Books

Development Education Centre
121 Avenue Road
Toronto, Ont. M5R 2G3
(416) 964-6560
Access Books, formerly *Island Universe Books,* offers a wide range of books on renewable energy, technology and the environment. They have a bookroom as well as a mail-order catalogue, available free.

Conservation Store

477 Dupont St.
Toronto, Ont.
This is a store-front operation that sells literature and components dealing with various aspects of energy conservation. Products include weatherstripping, set-back thermostats, water-saver showerheads, etc.

Highlands Energy Centre

RR #2
Orangeville, Ont.
(519) 941-5041
Highlands carry a range of energy conservation products and various renewable energy systems; including water saving devices, wood stoves and solar heating equipment.

Prometheus Energy Components

7773 Yonge St.
Thornhill, Ont. L3T 2C4
(416) 881-3369
Prometheus sells literature and components for energy conservation and renewable energy systems. Products include solar and wood heating equipment, wind generators and conservation items such as Window Quilt thermal shutters, thermostat set-backs and blowers. They have a mail-order catalogue for a refundable $1.50.

Solace Energy Centres

2425 Main Street
Vancouver, B.C. V5T 3E1
(604) 879-5258
Solace Energy Centres distribute systems and components for solar, wood, wind, water and energy conservation. They distribute *Coroplast* window sheeting, *Thermoshade,* a roll-up thermal barrier, *IS High "R" Shade,* a roll-up shade device.

Solar Usage Now, Inc.

Box 306
Bascom, Ohio
U.S.A. 44809
The Sun Catalog ($2) is the mail-order supermarket of the solar business. Their approximately 300-page catalogue is worth it, if only to look at all the paraphernalia that is currently available. Items include components and systems for active and passive solar heating, energy conservation and even some solar toys.

Solerco Ltd.

4732 Thimens Boulevard
Saint Laurent, Montreal
Quebec H4R 2B2
(514) 337-2252
Solerco offers a mail-order service for solar heating systems, components and literature. They are distributors for the *Kalwall* line which includes *Kalwall Sun-Lite*® fibreglass cover panels, and *Kalwall Solar Storage,* fibreglass thermal storage tubes used in direct gain, waterwall or isolated storage systems. They also carry *Excelite* glazing, *Solarvent* automatic greenhouse vent, *Heat Cheater* temperature set back devices, sealants, controls, publications and miscellaneous components.

Zomeworks Corp.

P.O. Box 712
Albuquerque, New Mexico
U.S.A. 87103
(505) 242-5354
Zomeworks carry a number of items of interest, including *Skylid*® *Louvers;* self-contained insulated aluminum louvers for use under skylights which open and close in response to the sun. *Beadwall*® *Panels;* a double-glazing system which automatically pumps styrofoam beads between glass for night-time insulation. *Nightwall Clips;* magnetic clips which hold bead-board insulating panels directly to a window pane. *Direct Gain Passive Water Heaters;* a seasonally adjustable reflector that directs sunlight into the house and onto a 66-gallon water tank.

Sources of Information

Obtaining information from individuals and groups involved in the field is a valuable means of finding out what is happening in your area. No need duplicating mistakes which have already been made; contact the following people.

General Information

Conservation and Renewable Energy Branch
Energy, Mines and Resources Canada
580 Booth St., Ottawa, Ont.
K1A 0E4

National Solar Heating and Cooling Information Centre
P.O. Box 1607
Rockville, MD 20850

The Enersave "Heatline"
Call free of charge in Canada:
1 (800) 267-9563
British Columbia: 112 (800) 267-9563
Yukon and N.W.T.: collect (613) 995-1801

Solar Energy Project
National Research Council
Montreal Road,
Ottawa, Ont.
K1A 0R6

Solar Energy Societies

Solar Energy Society of Canada Inc.
Suite 303, 870 Cambridge Street,
Winnipeg, Manitoba
R3M 3H5
(204) 284-3076

American Section of the International Solar Energy Society
American Technological University
P.O. Box 1416, Kileen, Texas 76541

Chapters of SESCI

Sesci Newfoundland
c/o A.P. VanCraeynest
P.O. Box 9600,
Virginia Park Plaza
St. John's, Nfld. A1A 3C1

Sesci Nova Scotia
c/o John Young
Community Assoc. of Canada,
P.O. Box 211,
Halifax, N.S. B3J 2M4

Sesci Prince Edward Island
P.O. Box 1041,
Charlottetown, P.E.I.
C1A 7M4

Sesci New Brunswick
P.O. Box 1114, Station 'A',
Fredericton, N.B.
E3B 5C6

Sesci Region du Quebec
Ecole Polytechnique
C.P. 6079, Succ. 'A',
Montreal, P.Q. H3C 3A7

Sesci Eastern Ontario
R.R. #3
Dalkeith, Ontario
K0B 1E0

Sesci Hamilton
c/o S. Mendiratta
Mohawk College of Applied Arts
and Technology
Fennell Avenue and West 5th.,
Box 2034,
Hamilton, Ontario
L8N 3T2

Sesci Kawartha
611 Weller Street
Peterborough, Ontario
K9J 4W8

Sesci Kent
c/o Wilson Kerr
#807-150 Mary Street,
Chatham, Ontario
N7L 4V2

Sesci Mississauga-Oakville
c/o T. Gruner
2222 Belfast Crescent
Mississauga, Ontario
L5K 1N9

Sesci Ottawa
c/o Algonquin College
Physics Department
Lees Avenue,
Ottawa, Ontario
K1S 0C5

Sesci Sarnia
c/o W. Himmelman
1034 Lombardy Drive
Sarnia, Ontario
N7S 2E2

Sesci Simcoe County
c/o Georgian College
   Technology Building
401 Duckworth Street
Barrie, Ontario
L4M 3X9

Sesci South Central Ontario
16 Crescent Street
Kitchener, Ontario
N2H 1H8

Sesci Southwest Ontario
P.O. Box 2220, Station 'A',
London, Ontario
N6A 4E3

Sesci Thunder Bay
c/o E.J. Tymura
Hilldale Road
Thunder Bay, Ontario
P7B 5N1

Sesci Toronto
P.O. Box 396, Station 'D',
Toronto, Ontario
M6P 3J9

Sesci Windsor-Essex
c/o Edgar Scrutton
Box 74A, R.R. #4,
Amherstburg, Ontario
N9V 2Y9

Sesci Manitoba
c/o Mrs. A. Olson
237 Lanark Street
Winnipeg, Manitoba
R3N 1L3

Sesci Northern Saskatchewan
c/o Rob Dumont
Dept. Mechanical Engineering
U. of Saskatchewan
Saskatoon, Saskatchewan
S7N 0W0

Sesci Regina
P.O. Box 3959
Regina, Saskatchewan
S4P 3R9

Sesci Swift Current
416 Hayes Drive
Swift Current, Saskatchewan
S9H 4H9

Sesci Calgary
c/o Prof. T.G. Lee
Faculty of Environmental
   Design
University of Calgary
Calgary, Alberta
T2N 1N4

Sesci Northern Alberta
P.O. Box 11062
Edmonton, Alberta
T5J 3K4

Sesci British Columbia
c/o Richard Kadulski
504 Davie Street,
Vancouver, B.C.
V6B 2G4

Sesci Okanagan Region
Box 2321
Kelowna, B.C.
V1X 6A5

Sesci Vancouver Island
P.O. Box 6003
Victoria, B.C.
V5T 2V9

Sesci Northwest Territories
c/o Mr. C. Jalkotzy
Box 9, Site 11,
Yellowknife, N.W.T.
X1A 2N1

Chapters of the American Section

Alabama Solar Energy Association
Dr. Don Wallace
University of Alabama
P.O. Box 1247
Huntsville, Alabama 35807

Arizona Solar Energy Association
Don Osborn
Arizona Solar Energy Research Commission
State Capitol
Phoenix, Arizona 85301

Northern California SEA
David Richards
250 Evandale Ave. #3
Mountain View, CA 94043

Colorado Solar Energy Association
Rachel Snyder
P.O. Box 5272-TA
Denver, Colorado 80217

Eastern New York Solar Energy Assn.
Ronald Stewart
P.O. Box 5181
Albany, New York 12205

Georgia Solar Energy Association
Dr. J. Richard Williams
Associate Dean of Research
College of Engineering
Georgia Institute of Technology
Atlanta, Georgia 30332

Hoosier Solar Energy Association, Inc.
James O. Johnson
Johnson Ritchhart & Associates, Inc.
227 West 11th Street
Anderson, Indiana 46016

Kansas Solar Energy Association
Donald R. Stewart
1202 South Washington
Wichita, Kansas 67211

New England SEA
Drew Gillett
Cambridge, Mass. 02142

**Metropolitan New York
Solar Energy Assn.**
Kurt J. Wasserman
P.O. Box Z
Port Jervis, New York 12771

Michigan Solar Energy Assn.
Edward J. Kelly, Jr.
201 East Liberty Street
Ann Arbor, Michigan 48104

Mid-Atlantic Solar Energy Assn.
Linda Knapp, Director
2233 Grays Ferry Avenue
Philadelphia, PA 19146

Minnesota Solar Energy Association
Peter Pfister
P.O. Box 171
Minneapolis, Minnesota 55440

Mississippi Solar Energy Assn.
Dr. Pablo Okhuysen
225 West Lampkin Road
Starkville, Mississippi 39759

MO-ARK Solar Energy Association
Box 1643
Jefferson City, Missouri 65102

Nebraska Solar Energy Association
Dr. Bing Chen
University of Nebraska
Department of Electrical Technology
60th & Dodge Streets
Omaha, Nebraska 68182

New England Solar Energy Assn.
Tom Minnon, Executive Director
P.O. Box 541
Brattleboro, Vermont 05301

New Mexico Solar Energy Assn.
P.O. Box 2004
Santa Fe, New Mexico 87501

Northern California SEA
Marshal Merriam
University of California-Berkeley
Material Science
Berkeley, California 94720

North Carolina Solar Energy Assn.
Leon Neal
P.O. Box 12235
Research Triangle Park
North Carolina 27709

Northern Illinois Solar Energy Assn.
James A. Hartley
P.O. Box 1592
Aurora, Illinois 60507

Ohio Solar Energy Association
Joseph Barbish, Chairman
13125 Dorothy Drive
Chesterland, Ohio 44026

Ohio Solar Energy Assn.
Bruce Austin
Wright State University
Dayton, Ohio 45433

Oklahoma Solar Energy Assn.
Dr. Bruce V. Ketcham
Solar Energy Laboratory
University of Tulsa
Tulsa, Oklahoma 74104

Pacific Northwest Solar Energy Assn.
Dr. Douglas R. Boleyn, P.E.
17610 Spring Hill Place
Gladstone, Oregon 97027

South Central Illinois Solar Energy Assn.
Earl G. Powell
637 Eccles
Hillsboro, Illinois 62049

Southern California Solar Energy Assn.
Ildiko Demeter, Executive Director
San Diego City Hall
202 C Street
San Diego, California 92101

Tennessee Solar Energy Assn.
Joe Hultquist, Executive Director
P.O. Box 127
Kodak, Tennessee 37764

Texas Solar Energy Assn.
Russell E. Smith, Executive Director
1007 South Congress, Suite 348
Austin, Texas 78704

Virginia Solar Energy Assn.
John W. Spears
PRC Energy Analysis Company
7600 Old Springhouse Road
McLean, Virginia 22102

Wisconsin Solar Energy Assn.
Ernest Rogers
6704 Spring Grove Court
Middleton, Wisconsin 53562

Appendix
Background information including climatic data, material characteristics and a glossary.

Introduction

As a close reading of the book will demonstrate, conflicts exist as to what data, measures and numbers are relevant in designing and constructing energy-efficient houses. All of the data included in the charts and appendices is subject to the many assumptions governing the desired end result. In most cases we have attempted to define the assumptions made. In some charts the data is compiled to reflect the relative importance and performance of materials.

The data included will give the designer and builder the basic tools required to judge the performance of a building with a degree of accuracy. Actual performance data will probably alter by as much as ± 10 per cent. Use the design tools as general rules of thumb.

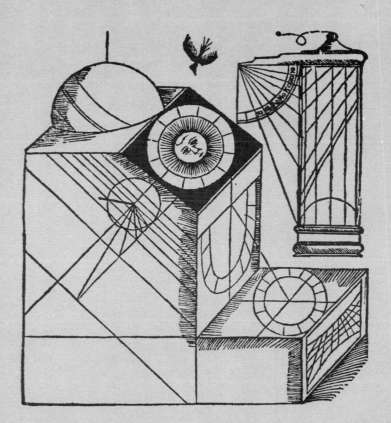

Climatic Data

Degree Days (D-D) — Degree day information can be used to determine the annual heating requirements of buildings. A degree-day accrues for every degree the average outside temperature is below 65°F (18°C) for a 24 hour period.

Average Daily Temperature (Temp.) — The temperatures listed (in °F and °C) are the average daily temperature by month.

Hours of bright sunshine (sunlight) — Averaged over several years the number of hours of bright sunshine can be used with clear day radiation figures to determine requirements for glazing and storage facilities.

Solar Noon — Solar noon refers to the time when the sun is at its greatest azimuth, for any given location and month. These figures were calculated for the 21st day of each month assuming standard time in each time zone. To accommodate day-light savings time subtract one hour.

Heat loss through a double glazed window — In calculating the heat loss through a double glazed window several assumptions have been made. We have assumed that the window has an R value of 1.8 (.31) averaged over a 24 hour period. The second set of figures accounts for the use of an R12 value for 12 hours during the evenings (shuttered windows). Units are BTU ft^{-2} day^{-1} and MJ m^{-2} day^{-1}.

Listed beside each city is the *design temperature* (in °F and °C) and the *latitude* of that city. The design temperature for any given location refers to the probable minimum temperature which will occur during the heating season. The design temperature will only be exceeded for less than 1% of the year.

Yellowknife, N.W.T. -49°F -45°C 62°28′N

	Units	J	F	M	A	M	J	J	A	S	O	N	D	Total
D-D	°F	2601	2223	2048	1399	783	320	137	227	599	1073	1741	2317	15,468
	°C	1445	1235	1138	777	435	178	76	126	333	596	967	1287	8,593
Temp.	°F	-19.4	-14.3	-1.4	17.9	39.2	53.9	60.8	57.4	44.3	29.8	6.5	-10.8	
	°C	-28.6	-25.7	-18.6	-7.8	4.0	12.2	16.0	14.1	6.8	-1.2	-14.2	-23.8	
Sunlight	hrs	60	110	175	235	283	302	299	261	125	90	47	30	2,017
Sol. Noon	MST	12.45	12.48	12.42	12.32	12.31	12.33	12.40	12.37	12.27	12.19	12.19	12.32	at 21st day
Heat loss Window	Btu	1165	1097	925.3	668	384	188	96.0	141.3	316	509.3	820	1050.7	
	MJ	13.23	12.46	10.51	7.59	4.36	2.13	1.09	1.60	3.59	5.78	9.31	11.90	
Shuttered Window	Btu	670.1	630.9	532.1	394.1	220.8	108.1	55.2	81.3	181.7	292.8	471.5	542.8	
	MJ	7.61	7.16	6.04	4.47	2.51	1.22	0.63	0.92	2.06	3.33	5.35	6.16	

Whitehorse, Yukon -45°F -43°C 60°43′N

	Units	J	F	M	A	M	J	J	A	S	O	N	D	Total
D-D	°F	2055	1599	1438	985	625	323	243	336	575	985	1468	1908	12,550
	°C	1143	881	798	543	338	171	125	176	307	537	812	1048	6,879
Temp.	°F	-2.0	8.2	18.1	31.8	44.7	54.3	57.4	54.0	46.0	33.3	15.8	3.6	
	°C	-18.9	-13.2	-7.7	-0.1	7.1	12.4	14.1	12.3	7.8	0.7	-9.0	-15.8	
Sunlight	hrs	42	81	160	230	267	271	250	225	134	96	48	21	1,825
Sol. Noon	PST	1.11	1.14	1.08	12.58	12.57	1.01	1.06	1.03	12.53	12.45	12.45	12.58	at 21st day
Heat loss Window	Btu	933.6	796.8	664.8	482.4	309.6	182.7	141.3	186.7	293.3	462.7	696.0	858.7	
	MJ	10.6	9.05	7.55	5.48	3.52	2.07	1.60	2.12	3.33	5.25	7.90	9.75	
Shuttered Window	Btu	536.8	458.2	382.3	277.4	178.0	105.0	81.3	107.3	168.7	266.0	400.2	493.7	
	MJ	6.10	5.20	4.34	3.15	2.02	1.19	0.92	1.22	1.92	3.02	4.55	5.61	

Victoria, B.C. 20°F -7°C 48°30′N

	Units	J	F	M	A	M	J	J	A	S	O	N	D	Total
D-D	°F	840	718	691	504	341	204	136	140	225	462	663	775	5,699
	°C	467	375	378	282	191	108	61	65	122	247	358	427	3,076
Temp.	°F	37.3	40.5	42.4	47.4	53.4	58.1	61.5	60.9	57.1	50.0	43.2	39.6	
	°C	2.9	4.7	5.8	8.6	11.9	14.5	16.4	16.1	13.9	10.0	6.2	4.2	
Sunlight	hrs	70	98	150	198	277	276	338	287	209	139	81	60	2,183
Sol. Noon	PST	12.25	12.28	12.22	12.23	12.22	12.26	12.31	12.28	12.18	12.10	12.10	12.23	at 21st day
Heat loss Window	Btu	409.3	366.7	341.3	274.7	194.7	132.0	86.7	94.7	145.3	240.0	330.7	378.7	
	MJ	4.65	4.16	3.88	3.12	2.21	1.50	.98	1.08	1.65	2.73	3.76	4.30	
Shuttered Window	Btu	235.4	210.8	196.3	157.9	111.9	75.9	49.8	54.4	83.6	138.0	190.1	217.7	
	MJ	2.67	2.39	2.23	1.79	1.27	.86	.57	.62	.95	1.57	2.16	2.47	

Vancouver, B.C. 16°F -9°C 49°11'N

	Units	J	F	M	A	M	J	J	A	S	O	N	D	Total
D-D	°F	862	723	676	501	310	156	81	87	219	456	657	787	5,515
	°C	484	383	377	272	174	85	35	40	114	245	358	440	3,007
Temp.	°F	36.3	40.0	42.5	48.1	54.3	59.5	63.4	62.7	57.6	50.1	42.9	38.9	
	°C	2.4	4.4	5.8	8.9	12.4	15.3	17.4	17.1	14.2	10.1	6.1	3.8	
Sunlight	hrs	49	92	131	164	246	244	303	241	183	119	69	46	1,887
Sol. Noon	PST	12.23	12.26	12.20	12.10	12.09	12.13	12.18	12.15	12.05	11.57	11.57	12.10	at 21st day
Heat loss Window	Btu	423	373	340	265	182	113	61	71	139	239	335	388	
	MJ	4.80	4.24	3.86	3.01	2.07	1.28	.69	.81	1.58	2.71	3.81	4.41	
Shuttered Window	Btu	243	215	196	153	105	65	35	41	80	137	192	223	
	MJ	2.76	2.44	2.23	1.74	1.19	.74	.40	.47	.91	1.56	2.18	2.53	

Grande Prairie, Alta. -38°F -39°C 55°11'N

	Units	J	F	M	A	M	J	J	A	S	O	N	D	Total
D-D	°F	1976	1554	1426	847	449	240	135	193	426	778	1319	1747	11,090
	°C	1095	861	790	469	249	133	75	107	236	431	731	968	6,144
Temp.	°F	0.9	9.6	18.6	36.9	50.0	56.7	60.8	58.7	50.3	39.5	20.6	8.2	
	°C	-17.3	-12.4	-7.4	2.7	10.0	13.7	16.0	14.8	10.2	4.2	-6.3	-13.2	
Sunlight	hrs	75	106	162	214	270	276	300	259	176	139	83	62	2,122
Sol. Noon	PST	1.07	1.10	1.04	12.54	12.53	12.57	1.02	12.59	12.49	12.41	12.41	12.54	at 21st day
Heat loss Window	Btu	894.7	778.7	885.3	414.7	240	150.7	96	124	236	380	632	797.3	
	MJ	10.2	8.8	10.1	4.7	2.7	1.7	1.1	1.4	2.7	4.3	7.1	9.1	
Shuttered Window	Btu	514.6	447.9	378.8	238.5	138.1	86.7	52.2	71	135.8	218.6	363.6	458.7	
	MJ	5.8	5.1	4.3	2.7	1.6	0.9	0.6	0.8	1.5	2.5	4.1	5.2	

Prince George, B.C. -33°F -36°C 53°53'N

	Units	J	F	M	A	M	J	J	A	S	O	N	D	Total
D-D	°F	1612	1319	1122	747	468	279	236	251	444	747	1110	1420	9,755
	°C	925	685	623	422	265	152	102	135	245	413	626	795	5,388
Temp.	°F	10.7	20.8	28.3	39.1	49.0	55.4	58.9	56.7	49.7	40.4	26.9	18.3	
	°C	-11.8	-6.2	-2.1	3.9	9.4	13.0	14.9	13.7	9.8	4.7	-2.8	-7.6	
Sunlight	hrs	54	89	139	187	255	256	279	245	158	104	60	39	1,865
Sol. Noon	PST	12.23	12.26	12.20	12.10	12.09	12.13	12.18	12.15	12.05	11.57	11.57	12.10	at 21st day
Heat loss Window	Btu	764	629.3	529.3	385.3	253.3	168.0	121.3	150.7	244.0	368.0	548.0	662.7	
	MJ	8.68	7.15	6.01	4.38	2.88	1.91	1.38	1.71	2.77	4.18	6.22	7.53	
Shuttered Window	Btu	439.3	361.9	304.4	221.6	145.7	96.6	69.8	86.6	140.3	211.6	315.1	381.0	
	MJ	4.99	4.11	3.46	2.52	1.65	1.10	0.79	0.98	1.59	2.40	3.58	4.33	

Edmonton, Alta. -29°F -34°C 53°40'N

	Units	J	F	M	A	M	J	J	A	S	O	N	D	Total
D-D	°F	1810	1520	1330	765	400	222	74	180	411	738	1215	1603	10,268
	°C	1016	806	727	421	222	109	47	82	215	388	666	890	5,589
Temp.	°F	2.7	10.3	18.9	37.3	49.5	56.0	61.0	57.9	49.5	39.6	22.0	9.8	
	°C	-16.3	-12.1	-7.3	2.9	9.7	13.3	16.1	14.4	9.7	4.2	-5.6	-12.3	
Sunlight	hrs	103	113	171	237	286	291	316	293	187	165	100	94	2,356
Sol. Noon	PST	12.45	12.48	12.42	12.32	12.31	12.33	12.40	12.37	12.27	12.19	12.19	12.32	at 21st day
Heat loss Window	Btu	870.4	769.1	654.5	409.2	246.6	160.0	93.3	134.6	246.6	378.6	613.2	775.8	
	MJ	9.89	8.73	7.43	4.65	2.80	1.82	1.06	1.53	2.80	4.30	6.96	8.81	
Shuttered Window	Btu	499.9	441.8	375.9	235.0	141.6	91.9	53.6	77.3	141.6	217.4	352.2	445.6	
	MJ	5.11	5.02	4.27	2.67	1.61	1.04	0.61	0.88	1.61	2.47	4.0	5.06	

Kamloops, B.C. -16°F -27°C 50°40'N

	Units	J	F	M	A	M	J	J	A	S	O	N	D	Total
D-D	°F	1314	1057	818	462	217	102	22	40	189	546	894	1138	6,799
	°C	742	543	458	272	128	41	11	20	106	298	495	642	3,756
Temp.	°F	21.5	30.8	39.5	49.4	58.2	65.2	70.0	68.3	59.4	47.9	36.1	27.6	
	°C	-5.8	-0.7	4.2	9.7	14.6	18.4	21.1	20.2	15.2	8.8	2.3	-2.4	
Sunlight	hrs	50	84	152	166	225	225	298	270	189	113	56	32	1,860
Sol. Noon	PST	12.11	12.14	12.08	11.58	11.57	12.01	12.06	12.03	11.53	11.45	11.45	11.58	at 21st day
Heat loss Window	Btu	619.4	496	380	248	130.5	37.3	—	—	114.6	268	424.9	538.1	
	MJ	7.03	5.63	4.32	2.81	1.48	0.42	—	—	1.30	3.04	4.83	6.11	
Shuttered Window	Btu	356	284.8	218.2	142.4	75.0	21.4	—	—	65.8	153.9	244.2	309.3	
	MJ	4.04	3.24	2.48	1.62	0.85	0.24	—	—	0.75	1.75	2.77	3.51	

Calgary, Alta. -27°F -33°C 51°66'N

	Units	J	F	M	A	M	J	J	A	S	O	N	D	Total
D-D	°F	1575	1379	1268	798	477	291	109	186	402	719	1110	1386	9,703
	°C	899	719	691	439	269	150	65	97	221	383	619	793	5,345
Temp.	°F	12.3	18.6	24.3	38.0	48.8	55.7	61.7	59.4	51.2	42.2	27.3	18.4	
	°C	-10.9	-7.4	-4.3	3.3	9.3	13.2	16.5	15.2	10.7	5.7	-2.6	-7.6	
Sunlight	hrs	99	121	156	196	237	240	317	278	188	166	116	44	2,158
Sol. Noon	PST	12.47	12.50	12.44	12.34	12.33	12.37	12.42	12.39	12.29	12.21	12.21	12.34	at 21st day
Heat loss Window	Btu	742.7	658.7	582.7	400	256	164	84	114.7	224	344	542.7	661.3	
	MJ	8.4	7.5	6.6	4.5	2.9	1.9	.95	1.3	2.5	3.9	6.2	7.5	
Shuttered Window	Btu	427	378.7	335	230	147.2	94.3	48.3	65.9	128.8	197.8	312	380.3	
	MJ	4.8	4.3	3.8	2.6	1.7	1.1	.54	.75	1.5	2.2	3.5	4.3	

Medicine Hat, Alta. -29°F -34°C 50°00'N

	Units	J	F	M	A	M	J	J	A	S	O	N	D	Total
D-D	°F	1696	1344	1203	665	348	148	36	66	300	603	1076	1441	8,926
	°C	934	739	659	361	189	79	17	34	157	324	588	593	4,674
Temp.	°F	10.2	17.4	26.2	42.7	53.8	61.0	68.4	66.1	55.7	45.6	29.2	18.4	
	°C	-12.1	-8.1	-3.2	5.9	12.1	16.1	20.2	18.9	13.2	7.6	-1.6	-7.6	
Sunlight	hrs	91	118	149	199	256	261	342	292	188	165	105	86	2,252
Sol. Noon	MST	12.35	12.38	12.32	12.22	12.21	12.25	12.30	12.27	12.17	12.09	12.09	12.23	at 21st day
Heat loss Window	Btu	770.6	674.6	557.3	337.3	189.3	93.3	—	25.3	164	298.7	517.3	661.3	
	MJ	8.75	7.66	6.33	3.83	2.15	1.05	—	.29	1.86	3.39	5.88	7.51	
Shuttered Window	Btu	443.1	387.9	320.5	194.0	108.9	53.7	—	14.57	94.3	171.7	297.5	380.3	
	MJ	5.03	4.41	3.64	2.20	1.24	.61	—	.17	1.07	1.95	3.38	4.32	

Regina, Sask. -33°F -36°C 50°26'N

	Units	J	F	M	A	M	J	J	A	S	O	N	D	Total
D-D	°F	1965	1687	1473	804	409	201	78	93	360	741	1284	1711	10,806
	°C	1094	914	817	441	234	97	29	46	198	394	697	959	5,920
Temp.	°F	0.9	6.2	17.0	38.0	51.0	59.5	66.0	64.3	52.8	41.5	22.6	8.8	
	°C	-17.3	-14.3	-8.3	3.3	10.6	15.3	18.9	17.9	11.6	5.3	-5.2	-12.9	
Sunlight	hrs	98	101	156	210	271	253	337	293	194	169	96	83	2,261
Sol. Noon	MST	1.09	1.12	1.06	12.56	12.55	12.59	1.04	1.01	12.51	12.43	12.43	12.56	at 21st day
Heat loss Window	Btu	894.6	824	680	400	226.6	113.3	26.6	49.3	202.6	353.3	605.3	789.3	
	MJ	11.2	9.4	7.7	4.5	2.6	1.3	0.3	0.6	2.3	4.0	6.9	9.0	
Shuttered Window	Btu	514.4	473.8	391	230	130.3	65.1	15.3	28.3	116.5	203.1	348.1	453.9	
	MJ	5.8	5.4	4.4	2.6	1.5	0.7	0.2	0.3	1.3	2.3	4.0	5.2	

Prince Albert, Sask. -42°F -41°C 53°12'N

	Units	J	F	M	A	M	J	J	A	S	O	N	D	Total
D-D	°F	2103	1763	1559	867	446	219	81	136	414	797	1368	1872	11,630
	°C	1204	987	883	489	265	119	45	74	234	436	753	1073	6,562
Temp.	°F	-5.9	1.6	13.2	35.1	49.1	57.8	63.8	61.2	50.4	39.1	19.3	2.5	
	°C	-21	-16.8	-10.4	1.7	9.5	14.3	17.6	16.2	10.2	3.9	-7.0	-16.3	
Sunlight	hrs	94	115	168	212	259	258	303	269	170	143	80	72	2,145
Sol. Noon	CST	1.15	1.18	1.12	1.02	1.01	1.05	1.10	1.07	12.57	12.49	12.49	1.02	at 21st day
Heat loss Window	Btu	985.3	835.3	730.6	438.6	252.0	136.0	56.0	90.6	234.6	385.3	649.3	873.3	
	MJ	11.19	10.05	8.29	4.98	2.86	1.54	0.63	1.02	2.66	4.37	7.37	9.91	
Shuttered Window	Btu	565.5	509.0	420.1	252.2	144.9	78.2	31.6	52.1	134.9	221.5	373.5	506.1	
	MJ	6.42	5.78	4.77	2.86	1.64	0.88	0.36	0.59	1.53	2.51	4.23	5.70	

Saskatoon, Sask. -35°F -37°C 52°07'N

	Units	J	F	M	A	M	J	J	A	S	O	N	D	Total
D-D	°F	2034	1626	1462	828	410	163	50	90	383	693	1269	1705	10,713
	°C	1139	936	829	445	233	97	30	54	204	402	714	994	6,077
Temp.	°F	-0.5	6.2	17.4	38.1	51.3	60.0	66.4	64.0	52.8	41.8	22.5	8.0	
	°C	-18.1	-14.3	-8.1	3.4	10.7	15.6	19.1	17.8	11.6	5.4	-5.3	-13.3	
Sunlight	hrs	99	129	192	225	279	280	341	294	207	175	98	84	2,403
Sol. Noon	CST	1.19	1.22	1.16	1.06	1.05	1.09	1.14	1.11	1.01	12.53	12.53	1.06	at 21st day
Heat loss Window	Btu	913.3	824.0	647.6	398.6	222.6	106.6	21.3	53.3	202.6	349.3	606.6	800	
	MJ	10.37	9.36	7.35	4.53	2.53	1.21	.24	.61	2.30	3.97	6.89	9.09	
Shuttered Window	Btu	525.2	473.8	387.9	229.2	128	61.3	12.3	30.7	116.5	200.9	348.8	460	
	MJ	5.96	5.38	4.41	2.60	1.45	.70	.14	.35	1.32	2.28	3.96	5.22	

Swift Current, Sask. -36°F -34°C 50°20'N

	Units	J	F	M	A	M	J	J	A	S	O	N	D	Total
D-D	°F	1800	1469	1366	787	449	210	68	108	370	684	1142	1562	10,015
	°C	991	809	742	429	242	110	33	54	194	370	648	860	5,482
Temp.	°F	6.9	12.9	21.3	38.7	50.5	58.6	65.7	63.8	53.2	43.0	25.3	14.5	
	°C	-13.9	-10.6	-5.9	3.7	10.3	14.4	18.7	17.6	11.8	6.1	-3.7	-9.7	
Sunlight	hrs	95	115	149	207	264	260	342	293	193	167	106	85	2,276
Sol. Noon	CST	1.23	1.26	1.20	1.10	1.09	1.13	1.18	1.15	1.05	12.57	12.57	1.10	at 21st day
Heat loss Window	Btu	814.6	734.7	622.7	390.7	233.3	125.3	30.7	56.0	197.3	333.3	569.3	713.3	
	MJ	9.25	8.34	7.07	4.44	2.65	1.42	0.35	0.64	2.24	3.79	6.47	8.10	
Shuttered Window	Btu	468.4	422.4	358.0	224.6	134.2	72.1	17.6	32.2	113.5	191.7	331.4	410.2	
	MJ	5.32	4.80	4.07	2.55	1.52	0.82	0.20	0.37	1.29	2.18	3.76	4.67	

Brandon, Man. -31°F -35°C 49°50'N

	Units	J	F	M	A	M	J	J	A	S	O	N	D	Total
D-D	°F	2059	1682	1496	815	438	155	44	83	351	688	1258	1782	10,871
	°C	1144	934	831	453	234	86	24	46	195	382	699	989	6,037
Temp.	°F	-1.4	4.4	16.3	36.7	49.8	60.2	66.0	63.8	53.0	42.1	22.5	7.1	
	°C	-18.6	-15.3	-8.7	2.6	9.9	15.7	18.9	17.7	11.7	5.6	-5.3	-13.8	
Sunlight	hrs	106	127	164	200	239	235	300	269	188	160	84	85	2,157
Sol. Noon	CST	12.51	12.54	12.48	12.38	12.37	12.41	12.46	12.43	12.33	12.25	12.25	12.38	at 21st day
Heat loss Window	Btu	926.4	847.2	688.8	417.6	242.4	103.2	26.4	55.2	149.2	345.6	607.2	811.2	
	MJ	10.52	9.62	7.82	4.74	2.75	1.17	.30	.63	2.26	3.93	6.90	9.21	
Shuttered Window	Btu	532.6	487.2	396.1	240.1	131.2	55.9	14.2	29.8	107.8	187.2	328.9	439.4	
	MJ	6.05	5.53	4.50	2.73	1.49	.64	.16	.34	1.23	2.13	3.74	5.00	

Winnipeg, Man. -31°F -35°C 49°50'N

	Units	J	F	M	A	M	J	J	A	S	O	N	D	Total
D-D	°F	2008	1719	1465	813	405	147	38	71	322	683	1251	1757	10,679
	°C	1126	953	810	441	236	76	21	38	175	356	674	983	5,889
Temp.	°F	-0.9	3.7	17.4	38.0	51.1	61.7	67.5	65.6	54.6	43.8	24.0	7.4	
	°C	-18.2	-15.7	8.1	3.3	10.6	16.5	19.7	18.7	12.6	6.6	-4.4	-13.7	
Sunlight	hrs	112	139	170	209	246	259	311	276	183	158	81	86	2,230
Sol. Noon	CST	12.43	12.46	12.40	12.30	12.29	12.33	12.38	12.35	12.25	12.17	12.17	12.30	at 21st day
Heat loss Window	Btu	917.7	856.5	674.0	399.6	226.4	30.8	6.16	31.9	178.5	322.3	586.1	807.2	
	MJ	10.42	9.73	7.65	4.54	2.57	.35	.07	.36	2.03	3.66	6.66	9.17	
Shuttered Window	Btu	527.8	492.5	387.6	229.8	129.4	48.3	3.8	18.4	102.6	185.4	337.0	464.2	
	MJ	5.99	5.59	4.40	2.61	1.47	.55	.04	.21	1.16	2.10	3.83	5.27	

Thunder Bay, Ont. -29°F -33°C 48°25'N

	Units	J	F	M	A	M	J	J	A	S	O	N	D	Total
D-D	°F	1792	1557	1380	876	543	237	90	133	366	694	1140	1597	10,405
	°C	1017	877	749	469	301	131	47	71	204	371	616	893	5,746
Temp.	°F	5.6	8.4	22.3	36.0	46.4	55.8	63.2	61.2	53.2	43.4	29.3	13.9	
	°C	-14.7	-13.1	-5.4	2.2	8.0	13.1	17.3	16.2	11.8	6.3	-1.5	-10.1	
Sunlight	hrs	116	149	185	205	235	258	302	251	173	116	80	92	2,162
Sol. Noon	CST	1.07	1.10	1.04	12.54	12.53	12.57	1.02	12.59	12.49	12.41	12.41	12.54	at 21st day
Heat loss Window	Btu	830	793	608	426	287	162	66	90	197	327	515	720	
	MJ	9.43	9.01	6.91	4.84	3.26	1.84	0.75	1.02	2.24	3.71	5.35	8.18	
Shuttered Window	Btu	478	457	350	245	168	93	37	52	113	188	296	414	
	MJ	5.43	5.19	3.98	2.78	1.91	1.06	0.42	0.59	1.28	2.14	3.35	4.70	

The Pas, Man. -36°F -38°C 53°N

	Units	J	F	M	A	M	J	J	A	S	O	N	D	Total
D-D	°F	2232	1853	1624	969	508	228	59	127	429	831	1440	1981	12,281
	°C	1253	1026	913	554	322	130	40	74	237	439	766	1098	6,852
Temp.	°F	-10.4	-3.3	10.1	31.3	47.3	58.3	63.6	60.5	49.4	37.9	15.9	-0.6	
	°C	-23.6	-19.6	-12.2	-.4	8.5	14.6	17.6	15.8	9.7	3.3	-8.9	-18.1	
Sunlight	hrs	103	129	172	217	277	263	301	246	147	120	63	70	2,108
Sol. Noon	CST	12.55	12.58	12.52	12.42	12.41	12.45	12.50	12.47	12.37	12.29	12.29	12.42	at 21st day
Heat loss Window	Btu	1045	950	772	489	276	129	59	100	248	401	695	915	
	MJ	11.9	10.7	8.8	5.6	3.1	1.5	.67	1.1	2.8	4.6	7.9	10.4	
Shuttered Window	Btu	601	547	444	281	159	74	34	58	143	231	399	526	
	MJ	6.8	6.2	5.0	3.2	1.8	.84	.39	.66	1.6	2.6	4.5	5.9	

Sault Ste. Marie, Ont. -18°F -28°C 46°29'N

	Units	J	F	M	A	M	J	J	A	S	O	N	D	Total
D-D	°F	1605	1484	1302	801	503	215	99	111	310	575	953	1404	9,362
	°C	882	814	713	435	269	111	49	56	163	309	519	770	5,090
Temp.	°F	13.1	12.6	22.6	38.1	48.7	58.6	64.0	63.5	55.8	46.6	33.3	20.5	
	°C	-10.5	-10.8	-5.2	3.4	9.3	14.8	17.8	17.5	13.2	8.1	0.7	-6.4	
Sunlight	hrs	74	114	160	186	246	265	288	258	159	121	62	66	1,999
Sol. Noon	CST	12.49	12.52	12.46	12.36	12.35	12.39	12.44	12.41	12.31	12.23	12.23	12.36	at 21st day
Heat loss Window	Btu	731.3	737.9	604.7	398.3	257.1	125.2	53.3	59.9	162.5	285.0	462.2	632.7	
	MJ	8.31	8.38	6.87	4.52	2.99	1.42	0.61	0.68	1.85	3.24	5.25	7.19	
Shuttered Window	Btu	420.3	424.1	347.6	228.9	147.8	71.9	26.6	34.5	93.4	163.8	265.7	363.7	
	MJ	4.77	4.82	3.95	2.59	1.68	0.82	0.30	0.39	1.06	1.86	3.02	4.13	

Churchill, Man. -42°F -41°C 58°45'N

	Units	J	F	M	A	M	J	J	A	S	O	N	D	Total
D-D	°F	2558	2277	2130	1569	1153	675	360	375	681	1082	1620	2248	16,728
	°C	1414	1262	1187	871	630	359	194	204	366	590	902	1234	9,213
Temp.	°F	-17.7	-16.0	-4.5	12.2	27.8	42.9	53.6	52.7	42.3	30.2	10.5	-7.3	
	°C	-27.6	-26.6	-20.2	-11.0	-2.3	6.0	12.0	11.5	5.7	-1.0	-11.9	-21.8	
Sunlight	hrs	78	130	183	196	182	234	285	234	104	63	45	55	1,789
Sol. Noon	CST	12.27	12.30	12.24	12.14	12.13	12.17	12.22	12.19	12.09	12.01	12.01	12.14	at 21st day
Heat loss Window	Btu	1141.5	1118.8	965.7	743.2	535.4	334.3	191.8	203.7	342.3	503.4	765.9	1002.9	
	MJ	12.96	12.70	10.96	8.44	6.08	3.79	2.17	2.31	3.88	5.71	8.69	11.39	
Shuttered Window	Btu	656.4	643.4	555.3	427.4	307.9	192.2	110.3	117.5	196.8	289.5	440.4	576.8	
	MJ	7.45	7.30	6.30	4.85	3.49	2.18	1.25	1.33	2.23	3.28	5.00	6.55	

North Bay, Ont. -22°F -30°C 46°22'N

	Units	J	F	M	A	M	J	J	A	S	O	N	D	Total
D-D	°F	1680	1463	1277	780	400	120	37	90	267	608	990	1507	9,219
	°C	956	823	725	444	248	87	37	62	176	343	564	853	5,318
Temp.	°F	8.9	12.0	22.3	37.8	50.2	60.5	65.0	62.7	54.4	44.5	30.5	15.0	
	°C	-12.8	-11.0	-5.4	3.2	10.1	15.8	18.3	17.0	12.6	6.9	-0.8	-9.4	
Sunlight	hrs	97	130	158	188	231	246	267	226	158	115	59	70	1,945
Sol. Noon	CST	12.27	12.30	12.24	12.14	12.13	12.17	12.22	12.19	12.09	12.01	12.01	12.14	at 21st day
Heat loss Window	Btu	788.0	746.7	609.3	402.7	237.3	100.0	40.0	70.7	181.3	313.3	500.0	706.7	
	MJ	8.9	8.5	6.9	4.6	2.7	1.1	0.45	0.8	2.1	3.6	5.7	8.0	
Shuttered Window	Btu	453.1	429.3	350.4	231.5	136.5	57.5	23.0	40.6	104.3	180.2	287.5	406.3	
	MJ	5.1	4.9	4.0	2.6	1.6	0.65	0.26	0.46	1.18	2.0	2.1	4.6	

Windsor, Ont. -1°F -18°C 42°16'N

	Units	J	F	M	A	M	J	J	A	S	O	N	D	Total
D-D	°F	1231	1080	1055	526	252	51	5	14	113	363	732	1102	6,529
	°C	691	606	520	295	141	29	3	8	64	204	411	618	3,590
Temp.	°F	24.3	25.8	34.2	46.8	57.2	67.9	72.1	70.4	63.4	52.9	39.8	28.4	
	°C	-4.3	-3.4	1.2	8.2	14.0	19.9	22.3	21.3	17.4	11.6	4.3	-2.0	
Sunlight	hrs	77	97	126	162	229	247	277	258	191	163	82	71	1,980
Sol. Noon	EST	12.43	12.46	12.40	12.30	12.29	12.33	12.38	12.35	12.25	12.17	12.17	12.30	at 21st day
Heat loss Window	Btu	582.7	562.7	450.7	282.7	144.0	1.3	—	—	61.3	201.3	376.0	528.0	
	MJ	6.62	6.39	5.12	3.21	1.64	0.02	—	—	0.70	2.29	4.27	6.00	
Shuttered Window	Btu	335.0	323.5	259.1	162.5	82.8	0.8	—	—	35.3	115.8	216.2	303.6	
	MJ	3.80	3.67	2.94	1.85	0.94	0.01	—	—	0.40	1.32	2.46	3.45	

Chicoutimi, Que. -26°F -32°C 48°25'N

	Units	J	F	M	A	M	J	J	A	S	O	N	D	Total
D-D	°F	1997	1721	1486	943	535	217	107	172	395	720	1120	1762	11,175
	°C	1099	946	816	514	287	112	54	88	210	390	612	969	6,097
Temp.	°F	5.6	9.1	22.3	37.3	49.2	60.3	65.8	63.3	54.7	44.3	31.2	13.4	
	°C	-14.7	-12.7	-5.4	2.9	9.6	15.7	18.8	17.4	12.6	6.8	-0.4	-10.3	
Sunlight	hrs	96	115	156	181	213	221	235	215	144	109	63	74	1,822
Sol. Noon	EST	11.55	11.58	11.52	11.42	11.41	11.45	11.50	11.47	11.37	11.29	11.29	11.42	at 21st day
Heat loss Window	Btu	832	785.3	609.3	409.3	250.7	102.7	29.3	62.7	177.3	316	490.7	728	
	MJ	9.4	8.9	6.9	4.6	2.8	1.2	0.3	0.71	2.0	3.6	5.6	8.3	
Shuttered Window	Btu	478.6	451.8	350.5	235.5	144.2	59.1	16.9	36.0	102.0	181.8	282.3	418.8	
	MJ	5.4	5.1	4.0	2.7	1.6	0.7	0.2	0.4	1.2	2.1	3.2	4.8	

Toronto, Ont. -3°F -19°C 43°40'N

	Units	J	F	M	A	M	J	J	A	S	O	N	D	Total
D-D	°F	1233	1119	1013	616	298	62	7	18	151	439	760	1111	6,827
	°C	688.0	621.7	502.8	343.2	165.6	34.4	3.9	10	83.4	243.9	422.2	617.2	3,792.8
Temp.	°F	24.1	25.2	33.1	45.6	55.3	66.6	71.3	69.9	62.6	52.2	40.7	28.8	
	°C	-4.4	-3.8	0.6	7.5	13.2	19.2	21.8	21.1	17	11.8	4.8	-1.8	
Sunlight	hrs	78	105	139	170	220	257	287	254	198	154	84	75	2,026
Sol. Noon	EST	12.28	12.32	12.26	12.16	12.15	12.19	12.24	12.21	12.11	12.03	12.03	12.16	at 21st day
Heat loss Window	Btu	588.3	570.7	483.3	298.7	168.7	20.0	—	—	72.0	210.7	364.0	522.7	
	MJ	6.65	6.48	5.28	3.39	1.85	0.23	—	—	0.82	2.34	4.13	5.93	
Shuttered Window	Btu	336.6	328.2	267.6	171.8	93.6	11.5	—	—	41.4	121.2	209.3	300.6	
	MJ	3.82	3.73	3.04	1.95	1.06	0.13	—	—	0.47	1.38	2.39	3.41	

Montreal, P.Q. (City) -15°F -26°C 45°35'N

	Units	J	F	M	A	M	J	J	A	S	O	N	D	Total
D-D	°F	1510	1328	1138	657	288	54	16	28	165	496	864	1355	7,899
	°C	829	728	622	355	151	27	8	14	84	266	470	743	4,297
Temp.	°F	16	18.4	29.5	44	56.4	66.3	70.9	68.7	60.5	50.2	37.2	21.7	
	°C	-8.9	-7.6	-1.3	6.7	13.6	19.1	21.6	20.4	15.8	10.1	2.9	-5.7	
Sunlight	hrs	93	109	156	171	220	241	264	238	180	140	70	77	1,959
Sol. Noon	EST	12.05	12.08	12.02	11.52	11.51	11.55	12.00	11.57	11.47	11.39	11.39	11.52	at 21st day
Heat loss Window	Btu	693.3	661.3	513.3	320	154.6	22.6	—	—	100	237.3	410.7	617.3	
	MJ	7.87	7.51	5.83	3.63	1.76	.27	—	—	1.13	2.70	4.66	7.01	
Shuttered Window	Btu	398.6	380.2	295.1	184	88.9	13.0	—	—	57.5	136.4	236.2	354.9	
	MJ	4.53	4.32	3.35	2.08	.99	.14	—	—	.65	1.55	2.68	4.03	

Ottawa, Ont. -17°F -27°C 45°25'N

	Units	J	F	M	A	M	J	J	A	S	O	N	D	Total
D-D	°F	1624	1441	1231	708	341	90	25	81	222	567	936	1469	8,735
	°C	899	778	654	371	181	44	10	28	123	290	499	796	4,673
Temp.	°F	12.3	14.9	26.5	42.1	54.4	64.7	69.2	66.7	58.3	47.6	34.5	18.2	
	°C	-10.9	-9.5	-3.0	5.6	12.4	18.2	20.7	19.3	14.6	8.7	1.4	-7.7	
Sunlight	hrs	96	115	150	175	231	245	277	243	171	138	76	78	1,995
Sol. Noon	EST	12.14	12.17	12.11	12.01	12.00	11.59	12.09	12.06	11.56	11.48	11.48	12.01	at 21st day
Heat loss Window	Btu	742.7	708	553.3	345.3	181.3	44.0	—	17.3	129.3	272	446.7	664	
	MJ	8.42	8.02	6.32	3.91	2.01	0.50	—	0.20	1.50	3.11	5.12	7.52	
Shuttered Window	Btu	427.0	407.1	318.2	198.6	104.3	25.3	—	10.0	74.4	156.4	256.8	381.8	
	MJ	4.84	4.62	3.61	2.26	1.18	0.29	—	0.11	0.84	1.78	2.92	4.34	

Montreal, Que. -15°F -26°C 45°35'N

	Units	J	F	M	A	M	J	J	A	S	O	N	D	Total
D-D	°F	1540	1370	1150	700	300	50	10	40	180	530	890	1370	8,130
	°C	865	757	636	369	168	38	7	20	106	269	471	765	4,471
Temp.	°F	15.4	16.4	28.0	41.6	55.6	65.6	70.4	68.2	59.6	48.0	35.2	20.7	
	°C	-9.2	-8.7	-2.2	5.3	13.1	18.7	21.3	20.1	15.3	8.9	1.8	-6.3	
Sunlight	hrs	79	102	145	167	203	222	244	223	170	126	69	61	1,811
Sol. Noon	EST	12.05	12.08	12.02	11.52	11.51	11.55	12.00	11.57	11.47	11.39	11.39	11.52	at 21st day
Heat loss Window	Btu	701.3	688	533.3	352	165.3	32.0	—	—	112.0	266.7	437.3	630.7	
	MJ	7.96	7.81	6.06	4.00	1.88	0.36	—	—	1.27	3.03	4.97	7.16	
Shuttered Window	Btu	403.3	395.6	306.7	202.4	96.1	18.4	—	—	64.4	153.3	251.5	362.6	
	MJ	4.58	4.49	3.48	2.30	1.08	0.21	—	—	0.73	1.74	2.85	4.12	

Sherbrooke, Que. -22°F -30°C 45°24'N

	Units	J	F	M	A	M	J	J	A	S	O	N	D	Total
D-D	°F	1541	1352	1139	693	349	100	24	63	231	526	868	1366	8,252
	°C	918	835	697	438	249	91	49	76	188	337	536	828	5,242
Temp.	°F	14.7	16.6	27.7	41.3	53.6	63.5	68.1	65.5	57.7	47.5	35.5	20.0	
	°C	-9.61	-8.55	-2.39	5.16	12.0	17.5	20.05	18.61	14.16	8.61	1.94	-6.66	
Sunlight	hrs	83	103	141	171	218	238	264	234	174	140	71	65	1,902
Sol. Noon	EST	11.59	12.02	11.56	11.46	11.45	11.49	11.54	11.51	11.41	11.33	11.33	11.46	at 21st day
Heat loss Window	Btu	710.7	685.3	537.3	356.0	192.0	60.0	—	33.3	137.3	273.3	433.3	640.0	
	MJ	8.07	7.78	6.10	4.04	2.18	0.68	—	0.38	1.56	3.10	4.92	7.27	
Shuttered Window	Btu	408.6	394.1	309.0	204.7	110.4	34.5	—	19.2	79.0	157.2	249.2	368.0	
	MJ	4.64	4.47	3.51	2.32	1.25	0.39	—	0.22	0.89	1.78	2.83	4.18	

Edmunston, N.B. -20°F -29°C 47°23'N

	Units	J	F	M	A	M	J	J	A	S	O	N	D	Total
D-D	°F	1707	1454	1285	821	445	176	52	106	315	630	995	1520	9,511
	°C	938	798	704	446	238	91	26	53	166	340	543	834	5,177
Temp.	°F	9.4	12.7	23.0	36.9	50.2	59.7	65.4	62.8	54.3	44.0	31.5	15.9	
	°C	-12.6	-10.7	-5.0	2.7	10.1	15.4	18.6	17.1	12.4	6.7	-0.3	-8.9	
Sunlight	hrs	102	122	150	179	217	226	245	232	174	135	84	89	1,955
Sol. Noon	EST	12.45	12.48	12.42	12.32	12.31	12.35	12.40	12.37	12.27	12.19	12.19	12.32	at 21st day
Heat loss Window	Btu	781.1	737.2	599.9	414.6	237.3	110.6	34.7	69.3	182.6	319.9	486.6	694.5	
	MJ	8.87	8.37	6.81	4.71	2.70	1.26	0.39	0.79	2.07	3.63	5.53	7.89	
Shuttered Window	Btu	449.5	424.2	345.2	238.5	136.5	63.7	19.9	39.9	105.1	184.1	280.0	399.6	
	MJ	5.11	4.82	3.92	2.71	1.55	0.72	0.23	0.45	1.19	2.09	3.18	4.54	

Quebec City, Que. -18°F -28°C 46°50'N

	Units	J	F	M	A	M	J	J	A	S	O	N	D	Total
D-D	°F	1695	1495	1276	814	427	140	41	82	286	613	984	1517	9,372
	°C	919	810	692	441	232	76	22	45	155	332	533	823	5,080
Temp.	°F	11.1	12.9	24.1	37.9	51.1	61.3	66.6	64.0	55.6	45.0	32.4	16.6	
	°C	-11.6	-10.6	-4.4	3.3	10.6	16.3	19.2	17.8	13.1	7.2	.22	-8.6	
Sunlight	hrs	93	105	138	173	217	224	240	218	155	124	68	74	1,829
Sol. Noon	EST	12.33	12.30	12.36	12.42	12.41	12.45	12.50	12.47	12.37	12.29	12.29	12.42	at 21st day
Heat loss Window	Btu	758.5	734.5	585.2	401.2	225.3	89.3	18.7	53.3	165.3	306.6	474.5	685.2	
	MJ	8.61	8.34	6.65	4.56	2.56	1.01	0.21	0.61	1.88	3.48	5.39	7.78	
Shuttered Window	Btu	436.4	422.6	336.7	230.8	129.6	51.4	10.7	30.7	95.1	176.4	273	394.2	
	MJ	4.96	4.8	3.82	2.62	1.47	.58	0.12	0.35	1.08	2.0	3.1	4.48	

Fredericton, N.B. -17°F -27°C 45°57'N

	Units	J	F	M	A	M	J	J	A	S	O	N	D	Total
D-D	°F	1541	1379	1172	753	406	141	78	68	234	592	915	1392	8,671
	°C	833	737	635	418	235	80	21	39	147	315	489	750	4,699
Temp.	°F	16.1	17.5	27.6	39.5	51.0	60.9	66.6	64.5	56.1	46.1	35.1	20.9	
	°C	-8.8	-8.1	-2.4	4.2	10.6	16.1	19.2	18.1	13.4	7.8	1.7	-6.2	
Sunlight	hrs	103	118	141	160	201	203	234	218	166	140	85	91	1,860
Sol. Noon	EST	12.38	12.41	12.35	12.25	12.24	12.28	12.33	12.30	12.20	12.12	12.12	12.25	at 21st day
Heat loss Window	Btu	692	673	539	380	227	95	19	47	159	292	439	628	
	MJ	7.9	7.6	6.1	4.3	2.6	1.1	0.2	0.5	1.8	3.3	5.0	7.1	
Shuttered Window	Btu	398	389	311	220	131	109	11	27	92	169	253	363	
	MJ	4.5	4.4	3.5	2.5	1.5	1.2	0.1	0.3	1.1	1.9	2.9	4.1	

Rimouski, Que. -17°F -27°C 48°27'N

	Units	J	F	M	A	M	J	J	A	S	O	N	D	Total
D-D	°F	1617	1421	1278	850	542	221	106	153	358	657	963	1448	9,614
	°C	888	779	700	462	291	114	53	78	189	355	525	794	5,228
Temp.	°F	12.5	14.7	23.7	36.6	47.4	58.4	62.7	60.6	53.2	43.7	33.0	18.8	
	°C	-10.8	-9.6	-4.6	2.6	8.6	14.7	17.1	15.9	11.3	6.5	0.6	-7.3	
Sunlight	hrs	62	81	124	166	182	206	206	194	159	103	59	43	1,585
Sol. Noon	EST	12.05	12.08	12.02	11.52	11.51	11.55	12.00	11.57	11.47	11.39	11.39	11.52	at 21st day
Heat loss Window	Btu	738.6	710.4	590.6	417.3	273.3	126.7	69.3	98.7	197.3	324	465	655.2	
	MJ	8.5	8.1	6.7	4.7	3.1	1.4	0.8	1.1	2.2	3.7	5.3	7.4	
Shuttered Window	Btu	424.7	408.6	339.6	240	157.3	83.9	39.9	56.7	113.5	186.3	267.6	376.4	
	MJ	4.8	4.6	3.9	2.7	1.8	1.0	0.5	0.6	1.3	2.1	3.0	4.3	

St. John, N.B. -11°F -24°C 45°20'N

	Units	J	F	M	A	M	J	J	A	S	O	N	D	Total
D-D	°F	1370	1229	1097	756	490	249	109	102	246	527	807	1194	8,219
	°C	790	721	640	447	286	135	49	62	145	308	472	722	4,709
Temp.	°F	19.3	20.2	29.4	39.4	49.3	56.6	62.8	63.0	57.2	48.0	30.6	24.3	
	°C	-7	-6	-1.5	4.1	9.6	13.7	17.1	17.2	19.9	8.9	-0.8	-4.3	
Sunlight	hrs	99	118	143	160	202	199	218	204	163	138	88	87	1,819
Sol. Noon	EST	12.35	12.38	12.32	12.22	12.21	12.25	12.30	12.27	12.17	12.09	12.09	12.22	at 21st day
Heat loss Window	Btu	649.3	637.3	514.6	381.3	249.3	152	69.3	66.7	144	266.7	405.3	582.7	
	MJ	7.37	7.2	5.9	4.3	2.8	1.7	0.8	0.76	1.6	3.0	4.6	6.6	
Shuttered Window	Btu	372.8	366	295.5	219	143.2	87.3	39.8	38.3	82.7	153.1	232.7	334.6	
	MJ	4.23	4.16	3.36	2.49	1.63	0.99	0.45	0.43	0.94	1.74	2.64	3.80	

Nappan, Nova Scotia -9°F -23°C 45°46'N

	Units	J	F	M	A	M	J	J	A	S	O	N	D	Total
D-D	°F	1415	1293	1160	810	503	224	61	92	268	551	823	1250	8,450
	°C	776	708	634	440	269	116	30	46	140	296	447	684	4,586
Temp.	°F	19.4	19.4	27.6	38.0	48.8	57.9	64.5	63.2	56.4	47.2	37.6	24.7	
	°C	-7.0	-7.0	-2.4	3.3	9.3	14.4	18.1	17.3	13.6	8.4	3.1	-4.1	
Sunlight	hrs	86	105	125	152	194	202	239	211	163	120	76	74	1,747
Sol. Noon	AST	12.27	12.30	12.24	12.14	12.13	12.17	12.22	12.19	12.09	12.01	12.01	12.14	at 21st day
Heat loss Window	Btu	647.9	647.9	538.6	399.9	255.9	134.7	46.6	63.9	154.6	277.3	405.3	577.3	
	MJ	7.36	7.36	6.12	4.54	2.9	1.53	.53	.73	1.76	3.15	4.6	6.55	
Shuttered Window	Btu	372.6	372.6	309.7	230.0	147.2	77.4	26.8	36.8	88.9	159.5	233.1	331.9	
	MJ	4.23	4.23	3.52	2.61	1.67	0.88	0.30	0.42	1.01	1.81	2.65	3.77	

Charlottetown, P.E.I. -8°F -22°C 46°19'N

	Units	J	F	M	A	M	J	J	A	S	O	N	D	Total
D-D	°F	1380	1274	1169	813	496	204	40	53	198	518	804	1215	8,164
	°C	767	714	657	470	292	126	27	37	130	290	441	672	4,623
Temp.	°F	20.2	19.8	27.1	37.3	48.6	58.4	66.3	65.3	58.2	48.5	38.7	26.2	
	°C	-6.6	-6.8	-2.7	3.0	9.2	14.7	19.1	18.5	14.6	9.2	3.7	-3.2	
Sunlight	hrs	83	105	137	156	199	215	244	220	180	133	72	59	1,803
Sol. Noon	AST	12.23	12.26	12.20	12.10	12.09	12.13	12.18	12.15	12.05	11.57	11.57	12.10	at 21st day
Heat loss Window	Btu	637.3	642.7	545.3	409.3	258.7	128.0	22.7	36.0	130.7	260	390.7	557.3	
	MJ	7.2	7.26	6.16	4.63	2.92	1.45	0.26	0.41	1.48	2.94	4.41	6.30	
Shuttered Window	Btu	366.5	369.5	331.6	245.5	148.7	73.6	13.0	20.7	75.1	149.5	124.6	320.5	
	MJ	4.14	4.18	3.75	2.75	1.68	0.83	0.14	0.23	0.85	1.69	1.41	3.62	

Halifax, N.S. 0°F -18°C 44°39'N

	Units	J	F	M	A	M	J	J	A	S	O	N	D	Total
D-D	°F	1213	1122	1030	742	487	251	58	54	180	457	710	1074	7,361
	°C	676	628	582	419	278	133	37	30	105	251	391	593	4,123
Temp.	°F	26.3	26.1	32.2	40.6	49.5	58.0	65.0	64.4	60.0	51.2	42.2	31.0	
	°C	-3.1	-3.2	0.1	4.7	9.7	14.4	18.3	18.0	15.5	10.6	5.6	-0.5	
Sunlight	hrs	91	117	144	162	201	202	219	222	179	157	92	87	1,873
Sol. Noon	AST	12.25	12.28	12.22	12.12	12.11	12.15	12.20	12.17	12.07	11.59	11.59	12.12	at 21st day
Heat loss Window	Btu	556	558	477	365	247	133	40	48	107	224	344	493	
	MJ	6.31	6.34	5.42	4.14	2.80	1.51	.45	.54	1.21	2.54	3.90	5.60	
Shuttered Window	Btu	320	321	275	210	141	77	23	27	61	129	198	284	
	MJ	3.63	3.64	3.12	2.38	1.60	.87	.26	.31	.69	1.46	2.24	3.22	

Corner Brook, Nfld. -10°F -24°C 48°58'N

	Units	J	F	M	A	M	J	J	A	S	O	N	D	Total
D-D	°F	1358	1283	1212	885	639	333	102	133	324	643	873	1194	8,978
	°C	744	703	663	482	345	176	51	67	171	347	475	653	4,877
Temp.	°F	22.6	20.8	26.8	35.5	44.6	53.7	62.4	61.4	54.1	44.8	37.7	27.7	
	°C	-5.2	-6.2	-2.8	1.9	7.0	12.0	16.8	16.3	12.2	7.1	2.8	-2.6	
Sunlight	hrs	not available												
Sol. Noon	AST	12.33	12.36	12.30	12.20	12.19	12.23	12.28	12.25	12.15	12.07	12.07	12.20	at 21st day
Heat loss Window	Btu	605.3	629.3	549.3	433.3	311.9	190.6	74.6	87.9	185.3	309.3	410.6	537.3	
	MJ	6.87	7.14	6.23	4.92	3.54	2.1	0.84	0.99	2.1	3.51	4.66	6.1	
Shuttered Window	Btu	348.0	361.8	315.8	249.1	179.3	109.6	92.9	50.5	106.5	177.8	236.1	308.9	
	MJ	3.95	4.11	3.58	2.82	2.03	1.24	0.48	0.57	1.21	2.0	2.68	305.0	

Sydney, N.S. -1°F -18°C 46°10'N

	Units	J	F	M	A	M	J	J	A	S	O	N	D	Total
D-D	°F	1262	1206	1150	840	567	276	62	71	219	518	765	1113	8,049
	°C	696	664	633	475	320	158	41	41	130	283	413	605	4,459
Temp.	°F	24.0	22.1	27.7	35.9	45.8	55.4	64.3	64.1	57.1	48.0	39.6	29.3	
	°C	-4.4	-5.5	-2.4	2.2	7.7	13.0	17.9	17.8	13.9	8.9	4.2	-1.5	
Sunlight	hrs	81	106	126	161	204	222	251	225	168	139	74	67	1,824
Sol. Noon	AST	12.11	12.14	12.08	11.58	11.57	12.01	12.06	12.03	11.53	11.45	11.45	11.58	at 21st day
Heat loss Window	Btu	586.7	612.0	537.1	423.0	296.5	168.0	49.3	52.0	145.3	266.7	378.7	516.0	
	MJ	6.66	6.55	6.10	4.86	3.36	1.91	0.56	0.59	1.65	3.03	4.80	5.86	
Shuttered Window	Btu	337.3	351.9	309.0	246.1	170.2	96.6	58.4	29.9	83.6	153.3	217.7	296.7	
	MJ	3.83	4.00	3.51	2.80	1.93	1.10	0.32	0.34	0.95	1.74	2.47	3.37	

St. John's, Nfld. 3°F -15°C 47°37'N

	Units	J	F	M	A	M	J	J	A	S	O	N	D	Total
D-D	°F	1262	1170	1187	927	710	432	186	180	342	651	831	1113	8,991
	°C	674	629	634	507	387	229	98	91	184	337	435	599	4,804
Temp.	°F	26.3	25.2	28.8	35.3	43.3	52.0	60.5	60.9	54.0	46.0	39.3	31.3	
	°C	-3.2	-3.8	-1.8	1.8	6.3	11.1	15.8	16.1	12.2	7.8	4.1	-0.4	
Sunlight	hrs	64	76	89	116	158	188	213	184	145	111	62	52	1,458
Sol. Noon	AST	12.11	12.14	12.08	11.58	11.57	12.01	12.06	12.03	11.53	11.45	11.45	11.58	at 21st day
Heat loss Window	Btu	556	570.7	522.7	436	329.3	213.3	100	94.7	186.7	293.3	382.7	486.3	
	MJ	6.31	6.48	5.94	4.95	3.74	2.42	1.14	1.08	2.12	3.33	4.35	5.56	
Shuttered Window	Btu	319.7	328.2	300.6	250.7	189.4	122.7	57.5	54.5	107.4	168.7	220.1	281.4	
	MJ	3.63	3.73	3.41	2.85	2.15	1.39	.65	.62	1.22	1.92	2.50	3.20	

U.S. climatic data

Includes: latitude; design temperature (°F); monthly average daily temperature in °F (Ave. Temp.); average daily radiation on a horizontal surface in BTU/day-sq.ft. (Sol. Rad.) and degree-days based on 65°F (D-D)

Astoria, Oregon 46° 12' 27°F

		J	F	M	A	M	J	J	A	S	O	N	D	Total
Solar Rad.	Btu	338	607	1008	1402	1839	1753	2008	1721	1322	780	414	295	
Ave. Temp.	°F	41.3	44.7	46.9	51.3	55	59.3	62.6	63.6	62.2	55.7	48.5	43.9	
D-D	°F	772	613	611	459	357	222	138	111	146	338	537	691	4995

Lander, Wyo. 42° 48' -16°F

		J	F	M	A	M	J	J	A	S	O	N	D	Total
Solar Rad.	Btu	786	1146	1638	1988	2114	2492	2438	2121	1713	1302	837	695	
Ave. Temp.	°F	20.2	26.3	34.7	45.5	56.0	65.4	74.6	72.5	61.4	48.3	33.4	23.8	
D-D	°F	1494	1179	1045	687	396	163	7	23	244	632	1050	1383	8303

Bismark, N. Dak. 46° 47' -24°F

		J	F	M	A	M	J	J	A	S	O	N	D	Total
Solar Rad.	Btu	587	934	1328	1668	2056	2174	2306	1929	1441	1018	600	464	
Ave. Temp.	°F	12.4	15.9	29.7	46.6	58.6	67.4	76.1	73.5	61.6	49.6	31.4	18.4	
D-D	°F	1730	1464	1187	657	355	116	29	37	227	598	1098	1535	9033

Madison, Wis. 43° 08' -9°F

		J	F	M	A	M	J	J	A	S	O	N	D	Total
Solar Rad.	Btu	565	812	1232	1455	1745	2032	2046	1740	1444	993	556	496	
Ave. Temp.	°F	21.8	24.6	35.3	49.0	61.0	70.9	76.8	74.4	65.6	53.7	37.8	25.4	
D-D	°F	1417	1207	1011	573	266	79	10	30	137	419	864	1287	7300

Blue Hill, Mass. 42° 13' -4°F

		J	F	M	A	M	J	J	A	S	O	N	D	Total
Solar Rad.	Btu	555	797	1144	1438	1776	1944	1882	1622	1314	941	592	482	
Ave. Temp.	6F	28.3	28.3	36.9	46.9	58.5	67.2	72.3	70.6	64.2	54.1	43.3	31.5	
D-D	°F	1178	1053	936	579	267	69	0	22	108	381	690	1085	6368

Medford, Oreg. 42° 23' 21°F

		J	F	M	A	M	J	J	A	S	O	N	D	Total
Solar Rad.	Btu	435	804	1260	1807	2216	2440	2607	2262	1672	1043	559	346	
Ave. Temp.	°F	39.4	45.4	50.8	56.3	63.1	69.4	76.9	76.4	69.6	58.7	47.1	40.5	
D-D	°F	862	627	552	381	207	69	0	0	77	326	624	822	4547

Boise, Idaho 43° 34' 4°F

		J	F	M	A	M	J	J	A	S	O	N	D	Total
Solar Rad.	Btu	519	885	1280	1814	2189	2377	2500	2149	1718	1128	679	457	
Ave. Temp.	°F	29.5	36.5	45.0	53.5	62.1	69.3	79.6	77.2	66.7	56.3	42.3	33.1	
D-D	°F	1169	868	719	453	249	92	0	0	135	389	762	1054	5890

New York, N.Y. 40° 46' 11°F

		J	F	M	A	M	J	J	A	S	O	N	D	Total
Solar Rad.	Btu	539	791	1180	1426	1738	1994	1939	1606	1349	978	598	476	
Ave. Temp.	°F	35.0	34.9	43.1	52.3	63.3	72.2	76.9	75.3	69.5	59.3	48.3	37.7	
D-D	°F	995	904	753	456	153	18	0	0	39	263	561	908	5050

Boston, Mass. 42° 22' 6°F

		J	F	M	A	M	J	J	A	S	O	N	D	Total
Solar Rad.	Btu	506	738	1067	1355	1769	1864	1860	1570	1268	897	536	443	
Ave. Temp.	°F	31.4	31.4	39.9	49.5	60.4	69.8	74.5	73.8	66.8	57.4	46.6	34.9	
D-D	°F	1113	1002	849	534	236	42	0	7	77	315	618	998	5791

Portland, Maine 43° 39' -5°F

		J	F	M	A	M	J	J	A	S	O	N	D	Total
Solar Rad.	Btu	566	874	1329	1528	1923	2017	2096	1799	1429	1035	591	508	
Ave. Temp.	°F	23.7	24.5	34.4	44.8	55.4	65.1	71.1	69.7	61.9	51.8	40.3	28.0	
D-D	°F	1373	1218	1039	693	394	117	15	56	199	515	825	1237	7681

Caribou, Maine 46° 52' -18°F

		J	F	M	A	M	J	J	A	S	O	N	D	Total
Solar Rad.	Btu	497	862	1360	1496	1780	1780	1898	1676	1255	793	416	399	
Ave. Temp.	°F	11.5	12.8	24.4	37.3	51.8	61.6	67.2	65	56.2	44.7	31.3	16.8	
D-D	°F	1745	1546	1342	909	512	201	85	133	354	710	1074	1562	10173

Rapid City, S. Dak. 44° 09' -9°F

		J	F	M	A	M	J	J	A	S	O	N	D	Total
Solar Rad.	Btu	688	1032	1504	1807	2028	2194	2236	2020	1628	1179	763	590	
Ave. Temp.	°F	24.7	27.4	34.7	48.2	58.3	67.3	76.3	75.0	64.7	52.9	38.7	29.2	
D-D	°F	1361	1151	1045	615	357	148	32	24	193	500	891	1218	7535

Cleveland, Ohio 41° 24' 2°F

		J	F	M	A	M	J	J	A	S	O	N	D	Total
Solar Rad.	Btu	467	682	1207	1444	1928	2103	2094	1841	1410	997	527	427	
Ave. Temp.	°F	30.8	30.9	39.4	50.2	62.4	72.7	77.0	75.1	68.5	57.4	44.0	32.8	
D-D	°F	1101	977	846	510	223	49	0	9	60	311	636	995	5717

St. Cloud, Minn. 45° 35' -17°F

		J	F	M	A	M	J	J	A	S	O	N	D	Total
Solar Rad.	Btu	633	977	1383	1598	1859	2003	2088	1828	1369	890	545	463	
Ave. Temp.	°F	13.6	16.9	29.8	46.2	58.8	68.5	74.4	71.9	62.5	50.2	32.1	18.3	
D-D	°F	1690	1439	1181	663	331	106	32	53	225	570	1068	1535	8893

East Lansing, Mich. 42° 44' 2°F

		J	F	M	A	M	J	J	A	S	O	N	D	Total
Solar Rad.	Btu	426	739	1086	1250	1733	1914	1885	1628	1303	892	473	380	
Ave. Temp.	°F	26.0	26.4	35.7	48.4	59.8	70.3	74.5	72.4	65.0	53.5	40.0	29.0	
D-D	°F	1277	1142	986	591	287	70	13	33	140	455	813	1175	6982

Sault Ste. Marie, Mich. 46° 28' -12°F

		J	F	M	A	M	J	J	A	S	O	N	D	Total
Solar Rad.	Btu	489	844	1336	1559	1962	2064	2149	1768	1207	809	392	360	
Ave. Temp.	°F	16.3	16.2	25.6	39.5	52.1	61.6	67.3	66.0	57.9	46.8	33.4	21.9	
D-D	°F	1587	1442	1302	846	499	224	109	126	298	639	1005	1398	9475

Fairbanks, Alaska 64° 49' -53°F

		J	F	M	A	M	J	J	A	S	O	N	D	Total
Solar Rad.	Btu	66	283	861	1481	1806	1971	1703	1248	700	324	104	20	
Ave. Temp.	°F	-7.0	0.3	13.0	32.2	50.5	62.4	63.8	58.3	47.1	29.6	5.5	-6.6	
D-D	°F	1240	1089	1082	858	685	471	149	296	612	1163	1857	1190	10692

Schenectady, N.Y. 42° 50' -5°F

		J	F	M	A	M	J	J	A	S	O	N	D	Total
Solar Rad.	Btu	488	753	1027	1272	1553	1688	1662	1495	1125	821	436	357	
Ave. Temp.	°F	24.7	24.6	34.9	48.3	61.7	70.8	76.9	73.7	64.6	53.1	40.1	28.0	
D-D	°F	1349	1207	1008	597	233	40	0	19	137	456	792	1212	7050

Glasgow, Mont. 48° 13' -25°F

		J	F	M	A	M	J	J	A	S	O	N	D	Total
Solar Rad.	Btu	573	966	1438	1741	2127	2262	2415	1985	1531	997	575	428	
Ave. Temp.	°F	13.3	17.3	31.1	47.8	59.3	67.3	76.0	73.2	61.2	49.2	31.0	18.6	
D-D	°F	1683	1408	1119	597	312	113	14	30	244	574	1086	1570	8690

Seattle, Wash. 47° 27' 28°F

		J	F	M	A	M	J	J	A	S	O	N	D	Total
Solar Rad.	Btu	283	521	992	1507	1881	1910	2111	1688	1212	702	386	239	
Ave. Temp.	°F	42.1	45.0	48.9	54.1	59.8	64.4	68.4	67.9	63.3	56.3	48.4	44.4	
D-D	°F	831	655	608	411	242	99	34	40	147	384	624	763	4838

Great Falls, Mont. 47° 29' -20°F

		J	F	M	A	M	J	J	A	S	O	N	D	Total
Solar Rad.	Btu	524	869	1370	1621	1971	2179	2383	1986	1536	985	575	421	
Ave. Temp.	°F	25.4	27.6	35.6	47.7	57.5	64.3	73.8	71.3	60.6	51.4	38.0	29.1	
D-D	°F	1311	1131	1008	621	359	166	24	50	273	524	894	1194	7555

Spokane, Wash. 47° 40' -2°F

		J	F	M	A	M	J	J	A	S	O	N	D	Total
Solar Rad.	Btu	446	838	1200	1865	2104	2226	2480	2076	1511	845	486	279	
Ave. Temp.	°F	26.5	31.7	40.5	49.2	57.9	64.6	73.4	71.7	62.7	51.5	37.4	20.5	
D-D	°F	1243	988	834	561	330	146	17	28	205	508	879	1113	6852

Clear day radiation on south-facing vertical surface

		JAN	FEB	MAR	APR	MAY	JUN	JUL	AUG	SEP	OCT	NOV	DEC
43°N	Btu	1806	1877	1668	1228	922	814	906	1187	1612	1801	1769	1684
	MJ	20.5	21.3	18.9	13.9	10.5	9.24	10.3	13.4	18.3	20.4	20.0	19.1
45°N	Btu	1746	1865	1709	1297	998	888	980	1251	1645	1792	1709	1592
	MJ	19.8	21.1	19.4	14.7	11.3	10.1	11.1	14.2	18.7	20.3	19.4	18.1
47°N	Btu	1668	1952	1746	1359	1070	964	1049	1309	1679	1776	1631	1484
	MJ	18.9	21.0	19.8	15.4	12.1	10.9	11.9	14.8	19.0	20.2	18.5	16.8
49°N	Btu	1573	1838	1776	1421	1143	1037	1125	1373	1704	1751	1538	1373
	MJ	17.9	20.9	20.2	16.1	13.0	11.8	12.8	15.6	19.3	20.0	17.5	15.6
51°N	Btu	1467	1812	1801	1477	1212	1106	1194	1426	1725	1736	1435	1228
	MJ	16.6	20.6	20.4	16.8	13.8	12.6	13.6	16.2	19.6	19.6	16.3	13.9
53°N	Btu	1350	1778	1824	1532	1296	1182	1263	1479	1741	1695	1316	1053
	MJ	15.3	20.2	20.7	17.4	14.6	13.4	14.3	16.8	19.8	19.2	14.9	11.9
55°N	Btu	1208	1730	1835	1582	1352	1251	1327	1527	1743	1645	1175	856
	MJ	13.7	19.6	20.8	18.0	15.3	14.2	15.1	17.3	19.8	18.7	13.3	9.7

This measures the sunlight striking a vertical surface on a clear day on the 21st of each month. It is measured in BTU ft^{-2} day^{-1} and MJ m^{-2} day^{-1} for every two degrees of latitude between 43° and 55°N. These data can be used for calculating the maximum energy collected by a south-facing window for any day.

Solar radiation data through vertical glass

Data accumulated for ten Canadian cities accounts for the average solar radiation on a daily basis (by month) which will pass through a double-glazed window oriented in several directions. The figures are collected for vertical windows and assume a glass coefficient of .75. Data are extracted from An Analysis of Solar Radiation Data for Selected Locations in Canada, Climatological Studies, Canada (1978). Units are BTU ft^{-2} day^{-1} and MJ m^{-2} day^{-1}.

This information can be used to determine the maximum possible solar contribution by month. The data for south, 60°, is for a south-facing, 60° sloped surface (i.e. greenhouse).

Vancouver, B.C.

Orientation	Units	JAN	FEB	MAR	APR	MAY	JUN	JUL	AUG	SEP	OCT	NOV	DEC
South	Btu	330.2	550.3	716.7	759.2	780.1	712.3	789.8	832.1	864.6	633.1	377.7	291.2
	MJ	3.75	6.25	8.14	8.6	8.86	8.09	8.97	9.45	9.82	7.19	4.29	3.08
S-E	Btu	250.1	425.3	583.8	681.5	776.6	739.5	838.2	808.3	749.3	503.6	289.7	207.8
	MJ	2.84	4.83	6.63	7.74	8.82	8.4	9.52	9.18	8.51	5.72	3.29	2.36
East	Btu	123.3	234.2	382.1	521.3	688.5	702.6	787.2	681.5	523.0	296.7	147.0	98.6
	MJ	1.40	2.66	4.34	5.92	7.82	7.98	8.94	7.74	5.94	3.37	1.67	1.12
S-W	Btu	269.4	460.5	657.7	765.1	876.1	839.1	920.1	887.5	802.1	533.6	306.4	217.5
	MJ	3.06	5.23	7.47	8.69	9.95	9.53	10.45	10.08	9.11	6.06	3.48	2.47
West	Btu	139.1	263.3	452.6	623.4	818.0	848.8	901.6	773.1	572.3	321.4	160.2	106.5
	MJ	1.58	2.99	5.14	7.08	9.29	9.64	10.24	8.78	6.5	3.65	1.82	1.21
South, 60°	Btu	350.4	612.8	870.8	1037.2	1198.4	1156.1	1271.4	1206.3	1100	726.4	408.5	285.3
	MJ	3.98	6.96	9.89	11.78	13.61	13.13	14.44	13.7	12.5	8.25	4.64	3.24

Suffield, Alta.

Orientation	Units	JAN	FEB	MAR	APR	MAY	JUN	JUL	AUG	SEP	OCT	NOV	DEC
South	Btu	834.7	1053.1	1186.9	958.0	825.9	772.2	870.8	949.2	976.5	965.1	749.3	704.4
	MJ	9.48	11.96	13.48	10.88	9.38	8.77	9.89	10.78	11.09	10.96	8.51	8.00
S-E	Btu	628.7	847.0	1033.7	955.3	916.6	893.7	989.7	987.0	905.1	790.7	577.6	521.3
	MJ	7.14	9.62	11.74	10.85	10.41	10.15	11.24	11.21	10.28	8.98	6.56	5.92
East	Btu	299.4	474.6	690.3	773.1	855.0	894.6	971.2	849.7	650.7	448.2	268.6	221.0
	MJ	3.40	5.39	7.84	8.78	9.71	10.16	11.03	9.65	7.39	5.09	3.05	2.51
S-W	Btu	658.6	843.5	1016.1	915.7	862.8	860.9	973.8	956.2	855.8	762.5	567.0	542.4
	MJ	7.48	9.58	11.54	10.40	9.80	9.76	11.06	10.86	9.72	8.66	6.44	6.16
West	Btu	321.4	471.9	670.1	725.5	790.7	857.6	954.5	811.8	595.2	422.6	260.6	235.0
	MJ	3.65	5.36	7.61	8.24	8.98	9.74	10.84	9.22	6.76	4.80	2.96	2.68
South, 60°	Btu	829.4	1106.8	1383.3	1300.5	1267.9	1260.9	1401.8	1370.9	1232.7	1079.5	773.1	696.4
	MJ	9.42	12.57	15.71	14.77	14.40	14.32	15.92	15.57	14.00	12.26	8.78	7.91

Edmonton, Alta.

Orientation	Units	JAN	FEB	MAR	APR	MAY	JUN	JUL	AUG	SEP	OCT	NOV	DEC
South	Btu	675.5	929.2	1142.5	1034.8	860.5	785.8	857.8	901.4	911.3	878.3	659.7	526.3
	MJ	7.67	10.55	12.97	11.75	9.77	8.92	9.74	10.23	10.35	9.97	7.49	5.95
S-E	Btu	503.6	734.3	968.8	999.8	933.1	876.3	946.3	892.8	809.6	708.6	499.9	391.6
	MJ	5.72	8.34	11.00	11.35	10.59	9.95	10.74	10.14	9.19	8.04	5.67	4.44
East	Btu	229.8	411.4	635.2	783.2	857.8	857.1	910.6	738.9	559.9	342.9	292.4	159.1
	MJ	2.61	4.67	7.21	8.89	9.74	9.74	10.34	8.39	6.36	4.46	2.64	1.80
S-W	Btu	534.9	768.6	997.8	981.9	880.9	839.3	913.9	905.3	805.6	706.6	514.4	406.1
	MJ	6.07	8.73	11.33	11.15	10.00	9.53	10.38	10.28	9.15	8.02	5.84	4.61
West	Btu	252.9	441.1	663.2	769.3	801.0	807.6	873.6	750.8	551.4	390.9	244.3	169.7
	MJ	2.87	5.01	7.53	8.73	9.09	9.17	9.92	8.52	6.26	4.44	2.77	1.92
South, 60°	Btu	658.3	951.6	1280.4	1341.9	1267.2	1226.3	1316.7	1259.3	1121.3	960.1	663	509.1
	MJ	7.47	10.80	14.54	15.24	14.39	13.92	14.95	14.3	12.73	10.90	7.53	5.78

Swift Current, Alta.

Orientation	Units	JAN	FEB	MAR	APR	MAY	JUN	JUL	AUG	SEP	OCT	NOV	DEC
South	Btu	855.8	1096.2	1244.8	958.2	814.9	753.5	851.9	927.8	972.7	989.2	766.0	709.2
	MJ	9.72	12.45	14.14	10.88	9.26	8.56	9.68	10.54	11.05	11.24	8.70	8.06
S-E	Btu	652.5	880.9	1096.9	978.0	910.7	875.0	974.7	968.8	902.1	805.7	586.4	531.6
	MJ	7.41	10.01	12.46	11.12	10.34	9.94	11.07	11.00	10.25	9.15	6.66	6.04
East	Btu	312.4	501.9	756.8	808.3	849.9	884.2	964.8	839.3	649.8	459.0	276.0	233.1
	MJ	3.55	5.70	8.60	9.18	9.65	10.04	10.96	9.53	7.38	5.21	3.14	2.65
S-W	Btu	668.3	889.5	1083.7	916.6	856.5	844.6	963.5	956.2	864.4	789.8	587.7	545.5
	MJ	7.59	10.10	12.31	10.41	9.73	9.59	10.94	10.86	9.82	8.97	6.68	6.20
West	Btu	324.9	509.8	774.9	740.3	794.4	855.2	958.9	828.1	610.8	445.1	276.7	243.0
	MJ	3.69	5.79	8.80	8.41	9.02	9.71	10.89	9.41	6.94	5.06	3.14	2.76
South, 60°	Btu	848.6	1142.4	1417.8	1285.8	1249.4	1225.7	1369.0	1341.2	1227.6	1105.5	788.5	698.7
	MJ	9.64	12.98	16.10	14.60	14.19	13.92	15.55	15.23	13.94	12.56	8.96	7.94

Winnipeg, Man.

Orientation	Units	JAN	FEB	MAR	APR	MAY	JUN	JUL	AUG	SEP	OCT	NOV	DEC
South	Btu	878.7	1134.5	1192.6	949.3	794.4	750.1	795.6	869.7	877.6	783.6	591.6	662.3
	MJ	8.97	12.88	13.54	10.63	9.02	8.52	9.04	9.87	9.96	8.91	6.72	7.52
S-E	Btu	674.9	915.2	1050.6	939.7	864.4	863.7	902.0	906.6	822.8	640.5	461.5	499.2
	MJ	7.66	10.39	11.93	10.67	9.81	9.81	10.24	10.29	9.34	7.27	5.24	5.67
East	Btu	326.2	525.6	725.0	767.3	797.0	865.7	884.2	789.2	597.6	367.8	223.2	205.3
	MJ	3.10	5.97	8.23	8.71	9.05	9.83	10.04	8.97	6.78	4.17	2.53	2.33
S-W	Btu	680.8	917.2	1034.4	897.2	830.3	834.7	871.6	890.1	760.9	630.6	454.9	505.8
	MJ	7.73	10.41	11.74	10.19	9.43	9.48	9.90	10.11	8.68	7.16	5.16	5.74
West	Btu	330.8	526.9	709.8	720.4	759.4	833.3	847.9	771.3	538.8	358.5	217.9	223.8
	MJ	3.75	5.98	8.06	8.18	8.62	9.46	9.63	8.76	6.12	4.07	2.47	2.54
South, 60°	Btu	872.3	1183.3	1362.3	1258.2	1216.8	1224.9	1273.2	1257.3	1112.7	889.5	618.6	655.7
	MJ	9.90	13.44	15.47	14.29	13.82	13.91	14.46	14.28	12.63	10.10	7.03	7.44

Montreal, Quebec

Orientation	Units	JAN	FEB	MAR	APR	MAY	JUN	JUL	AUG	SEP	OCT	NOV	DEC
South	Btu	652.4	862.9	849.9	742.3	644.5	630.6	678.2	700.6	769.5	688.8	476.1	473.5
	MJ	7.41	9.80	9.65	8.43	7.32	7.16	7.70	7.96	8.74	7.82	5.41	5.38
S-E	Btu	495.9	677.5	736.3	746.2	728.4	721.1	773.3	735.0	723.1	569.2	376.4	361.9
	MJ	5.63	7.69	8.36	8.47	8.27	8.19	8.78	8.35	8.21	6.46	4.27	4.11
East	Btu	234.2	383.0	505.8	614.8	700.0	728.4	763.4	659.0	540.8	346.7	194.1	167.7
	MJ	2.66	4.35	5.74	6.98	7.95	8.27	8.67	7.48	6.14	3.94	2.20	1.90
S-W	Btu	512.4	717.8	752.2	715.8	690.1	715.2	751.5	725.1	690.7	561.3	367.8	367.8
	MJ	5.82	8.15	8.54	8.13	7.84	8.12	8.53	8.23	7.84	6.37	4.18	4.18
West	Btu	247.0	418.0	522.3	581.8	658.4	720.5	737.6	644.5	511.1	338.8	187.5	190.8
	MJ	2.81	4.75	5.93	6.61	7.48	8.18	8.38	7.32	5.80	3.85	2.13	2.17
South, 60°	Btu	690.7	960.2	1057.9	1056.0	1022.3	1054.6	1116.7	1040.7	1009.7	807.0	520.4	499.2
	MJ	7.84	10.9	12.0	11.99	11.61	11.98	12.68	11.82	11.47	9.16	5.91	5.67

Toronto, Ont.

Orientation	Units	JAN	FEB	MAR	APR	MAY	JUN	JUL	AUG	SEP	OCT	NOV	DEC
South	Btu	719.4	880.5	892.8	812.7	648.9	621.6	675.3	745.8	783.6	720.2	441.1	502.8
	MJ	8.17	10.00	10.14	9.23	7.37	7.06	7.67	8.47	8.90	8.18	5.01	5.71
S-E	Btu	567.0	736.1	819.7	841.8	729.9	725.5	800.4	810.4	750.2	601.4	355.8	398.8
	MJ	6.44	8.36	9.31	9.56	8.29	8.24	9.04	9.21	8.52	6.83	4.04	4.53
East	Btu	302.0	461.4	603.1	711.4	712.3	744.9	811.8	738.7	376.9	376.4	199.9	205.2
	MJ	3.43	5.24	6.85	8.68	8.09	8.46	9.22	8.39	6.60	4.28	2.27	2.33
S-W	Btu	571.4	725.5	781.0	753.7	714.1	705.3	762.5	771.3	725.5	590.8	352.2	312.7
	MJ	6.49	8.24	8.87	8.90	8.11	8.01	8.66	8.76	8.24	6.71	4.00	4.46
West	Btu	305.5	453.5	562.7	651.6	692.1	722.9	766.0	649.1	555.6	365.4	196.4	200.4
	MJ	3.47	5.15	6.39	7.40	7.86	8.21	8.70	7.94	6.31	4.15	2.23	2.28
South, 60°	Btu	751.9	962.4	1083.9	1157.4	1045.2	1044.3	1142.9	1135.0	1043.4	854.9	489.6	529.2
	MJ	8.54	10.93	12.31	13.15	11.87	11.86	12.98	12.89	11.85	9.70	5.56	6.01

Fredericton, N.B.

Orientation	Units	JAN	FEB	MAR	APR	MAY	JUN	JUL	AUG	SEP	OCT	NOV	DEC
South	Btu	716.7	928.0	891.8	735.2	639.2	638.3	642.7	728.8	782.5	713.2	510.5	550.3
	MJ	8.13	10.53	10.12	8.25	7.26	7.24	7.29	8.27	8.88	8.09	5.79	6.25
S-E	Btu	548.5	760.2	812.7	744.0	705.2	709.6	700.0	741.3	701.7	601.3	416.4	427.0
	MJ	6.23	8.63	9.23	8.45	8.01	8.06	7.95	8.42	7.47	6.83	4.73	4.85
East	Btu	258.8	450.8	576.7	615.4	674.4	703.5	675.3	644.5	450.8	369.8	220.1	198.1
	MJ	2.94	5.11	6.55	6.41	7.66	7.99	7.67	7.32	5.12	4.19	2.50	2.24
S-W	Btu	553.8	751.0	753.7	692.9	667.4	716.7	711.4	725.5	690.3	572.3	389.2	418.2
	MJ	6.29	8.53	8.56	7.87	7.58	8.14	8.08	8.24	7.84	6.50	4.42	4.75
West	Btu	262.4	439.4	518.6	560.0	626.9	716.7	695.9	627.8	508.0	343.4	199.0	191.1
	MJ	2.98	4.99	5.81	6.36	7.12	8.14	7.90	7.13	5.77	3.90	2.26	2.17
South, 60°	Btu	751.1	1017.9	1083.9	1036.3	995.0	1058.4	1043.4	1070.7	996.7	835.6	556.5	574.1
	MJ	8.53	11.56	12.31	11.77	11.30	12.02	11.85	12.16	11.32	9.49	6.32	6.52

Ottawa, Ont.

Orientation	Units	JAN	FEB	MAR	APR	MAY	JUN	JUL	AUG	SEP	OCT	NOV	DEC
South	Btu	693.0	952.7	1009.1	782.8	692.1	646.2	677.1	744.0	775.7	707.0	463.1	530.1
	MJ	7.87	10.82	11.46	8.89	7.86	7.34	7.69	8.45	8.81	8.03	5.26	6.02
S-E	Btu	556.5	788.9	899.0	781.9	768.7	751.9	783.6	788.9	733.5	592.6	368.9	420.9
	MJ	6.32	8.96	10.21	8.88	8.43	8.54	8.90	8.96	8.33	6.73	4.19	4.48
East	Btu	310.8	497.5	641.9	641.0	735.2	763.4	776.6	699.1	552.1	362.7	193.7	229.2
	MJ	3.53	5.65	7.29	7.28	8.35	8.67	8.82	7.94	6.27	4.12	2.20	2.58
S-W	Btu	560.7	803.0	882.3	747.5	749.5	733.3	752.0	748.4	692.7	570.6	363.6	429.6
	MJ	6.37	9.12	10.02	8.49	8.51	8.33	8.54	8.50	7.87	6.48	4.13	4.88
West	Btu	313.7	511.1	627.8	604.3	714.5	742.9	743.5	653.1	508.5	344.1	189.5	234.4
	MJ	3.56	5.81	7.13	6.86	8.12	8.44	8.44	7.42	5.78	3.91	2.15	2.66
South, 60°	Btu	710.6	1015.7	1196.0	1110.8	1102.2	1090.9	1127.3	1113.4	1017.7	830.8	511.8	543.5
	MJ	8.07	11.53	13.58	12.62	12.52	12.39	12.80	12.65	11.56	9.44	5.81	6.17

Halifax, N.S.

Orientation	Units	JAN	FEB	MAR	APR	MAY	JUN	JUL	AUG	SEP	OCT	NOV	DEC
South	Btu	582.4	737.6	820.2	676.9	600.5	612.2	615.5	715.8	785.8	734.3	529.6	417.4
	MJ	6.61	8.38	9.31	7.69	6.82	6.95	6.99	8.13	8.92	8.34	6.01	4.74
S-E	Btu	448.4	613.5	735.6	658.4	622.7	661.7	638.6	715.8	739.6	610.2	418.7	324.2
	MJ	5.09	6.97	8.35	7.48	7.07	7.51	7.25	8.13	8.40	6.93	4.75	3.68
East	Btu	231.1	384.9	523.7	545.5	581.8	653.8	608.2	620.1	561.9	373.1	218.6	163.1
	MJ	2.62	4.37	5.95	6.19	6.61	7.42	6.91	7.04	6.38	4.24	2.48	1.85
S-W	Btu	472.2	615.5	719.8	661.7	652.4	717.8	709.9	755.5	721.1	598.9	416.0	332.2
	MJ	5.36	6.99	8.17	7.51	7.41	8.15	8.06	8.58	8.19	6.80	4.72	3.77
West	Btu	250.3	516.8	511.1	735.2	832.9	734.9	706.6	674.2	541.5	363.2	216.6	169.7
	MJ	2.84	4.40	5.80	6.26	7.09	8.35	8.02	7.66	6.15	4.12	2.46	1.93
South, 60°	Btu	620.1	816.2	1013.7	948.3	934.4	1021.6	1000.5	1073.1	1038.1	867.1	584.4	445.1
	MJ	7.04	9.27	11.51	10.77	10.61	11.60	11.36	12.19	11.79	9.85	6.64	5.05

Using the Sun Path Chart

The sun path chart is a useful tool in determining the solar potential for any given site. Used properly, the chart can assist in site planning and the appropriate positioning of collector surfaces.

The chart traces the movement of the sun across the sky throughout the months of the year, as viewed from a particular location. Trees, buildings and other objects can be transposed onto the chart enabling one to evaluate shadowing problems which might arise over the heating season.

The vertical and horizontal axis of the chart portray the altitude and azimuth of the sun's movement during the year. Using the same matrix, the surrounding objects can be traced over the sun path chart.

Standing in the location of the proposed collection area, face directly to the south. Using either a compass or a transit, determine the location of any obstructions in degrees from south. Plot the objects on the chart.

From the same location determine the height of the same objects, using either a clinometer or a protractor to guage the angle from the top of the obstruction above the horizon. Plot the height of the objects onto the sun path chart.

By joining the points which have been plotted onto the chart one obtains an outline of the various obstructions in relation to the collecting surface. By shading in the outlines one can then calculate the impact of the objects in shadowing the collector.

The figures transposed on the chart relate the percentage of sunlight falling on a surface each hour of the day. Using these figures the percentage of the daily radiation shaded by obstructions can be determined.

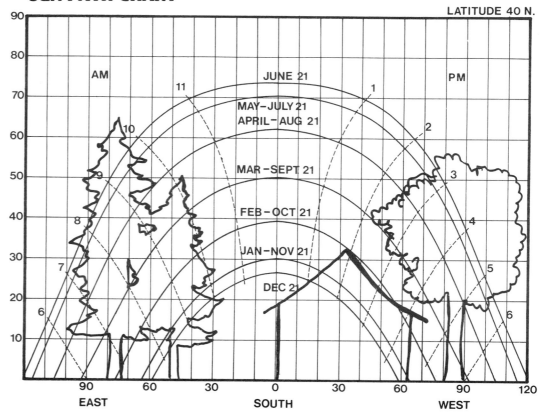

SUN PATH CHART

SUN PATH CHART

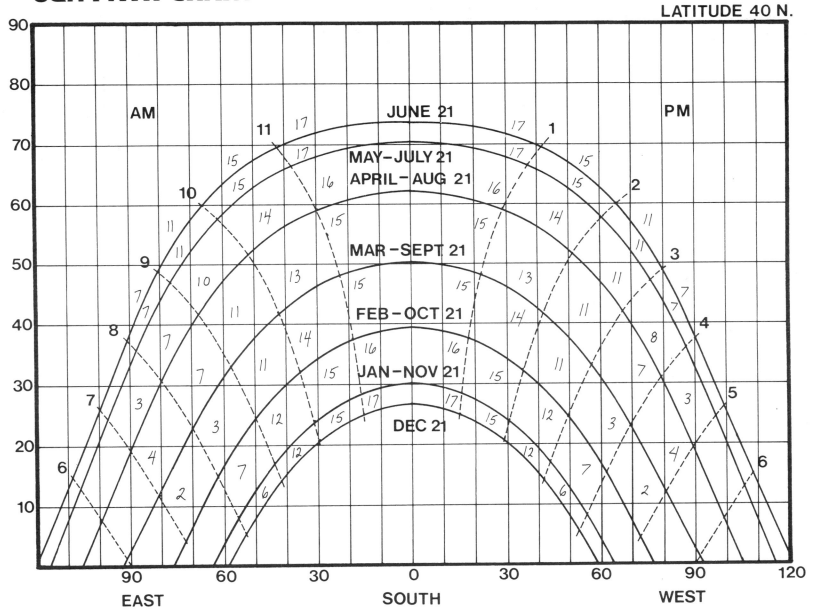

LATITUDE 40 N.

AM JUNE 21 PM

MAY–JULY 21
APRIL–AUG 21

MAR–SEPT 21

FEB–OCT 21

JAN–NOV 21

DEC 21

EAST SOUTH WEST

SUN PATH CHART

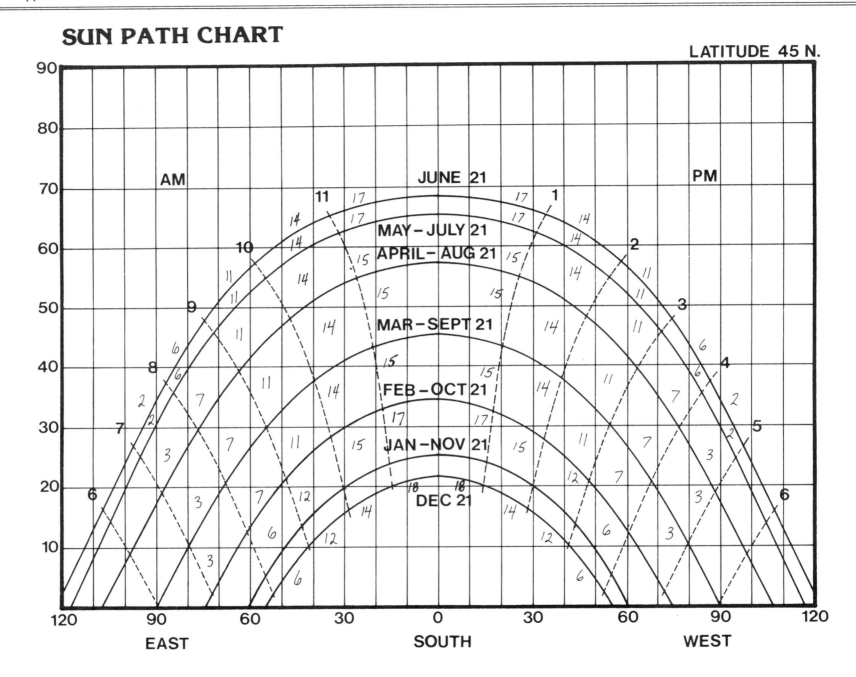

LATITUDE 45 N.

SUN PATH CHART

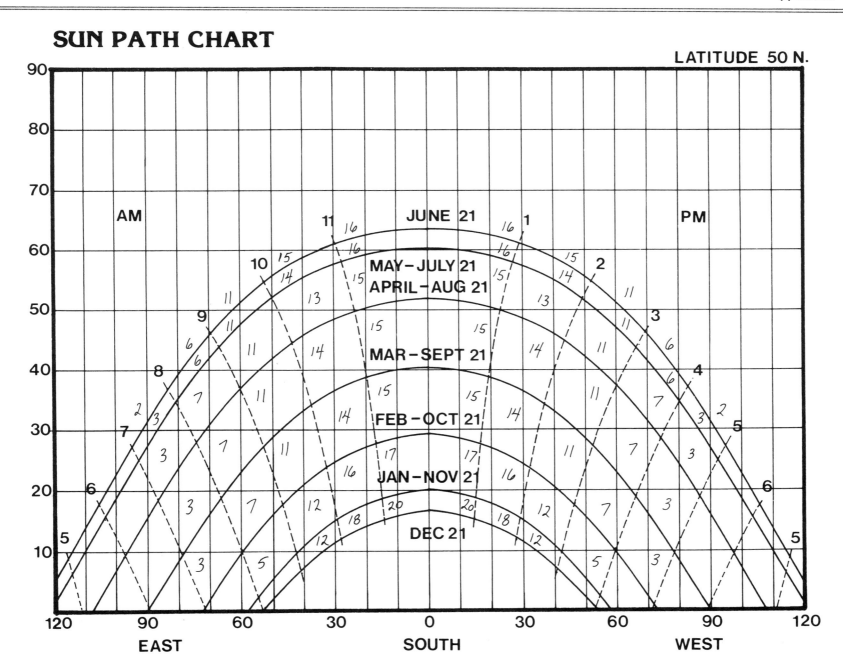

LATITUDE 50 N.

SUN PATH CHART

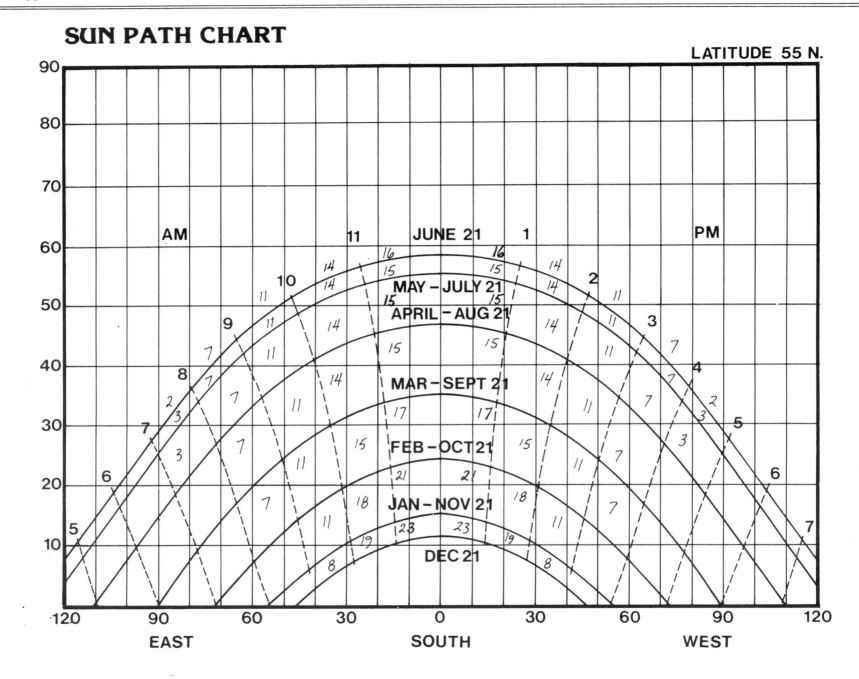

LATITUDE 55 N.

AM   11   JUNE 21   1   PM

MAY – JULY 21

APRIL – AUG 21

MAR – SEPT 21

FEB – OCT 21

JAN – NOV 21

DEC 21

120   90   60   30   0   30   60   90   120

EAST   SOUTH   WEST

Permeance Ratings of Common Building Materials

Material	Average Perm Rating	
	$_{85}$/Ns (10^{-11})	grain/hr ft² (in. Hg)
Vapour Barriers		
1 mil. aluminum foil	0.00	0.00
6 mil. polyethylene	0.34	0.06
4 mil. polyethylene	0.46	0.08
2 mil. polyethylene	0.92	0.16
1 mil. polyester	4.0	0.69
Asphalt kraft paper	4.3	0.74
Paint and Wallpaper		
1 coat latex vapour barrier paint	3.4	0.59
vinyl wallpaper	5.7	0.99
2 coats oil based paint on plaster	11	1.90
3 coats latex paint on wood	57	9.90
ordinary wallpaper	115	20.00
Insulation		
25mm (1") polyurethane	5.7	0.99
25mm (1") extruded styrofoam (blue)	3.5	0.60
25mm (1") beadboard	23	4.0
100mm (4") urea formaldehyde	52	9.0
100mm (4") cellulose	172	29.9
100mm (4") fibreglass	172	29.9
Other Materials		
13mm (½") plywood CDX	2.9	0.17
100mm (4") brick	5.7	0.99
200mm (8") concrete block	11	1.90
19mm (¾") wood	17	2.90
6.8kg (15 lb.) tarpaper	103	17.90
plaster	115	20.00
drywall	287	49.90

Permeance Ratings

The permeance value of a material relates to the ability of the material to allow or restrict the flow of water vapour through the surface. The lower the perm rating the more effective the material is in restricting any moisture passage. Materials with a perm rating of less than 6×10^{11} kg/ns (1 grain/hr. ft²) are considered sufficient to protect a structure from damage caused by the diffusion of water vapour.

The inside surface of houses should be made as tight as possible to restrict the flow of. moisture into insulated cavities. Yet in almost all applications some moisture will find its way past the interior surface. To prevent any long-term damage to the structure of the house this moisture must be allowed to pass easily through the exterior surface of the dwelling. A rule of thumb suggests that the exterior surface of a wall or ceiling section should be at least five time as permeable as the interior surface. However, vapour carried by air leakage is probably the largest single source of moisture problems. The inside should be air-tight, while the exterior should permit some leakage. A good air-vapour barrier combination will ensure no moisture problems.

Properties of Solids and Liquids

Material	Specific Heat Btu/lb. °F	X	Density lb/ft³	=	Heat Capacity Btu/ft³-°F	Thermal Conductivity Btu hr/ft²°F
Adobe	0.24		106		25.44	0.3
Building Brick	0.20		133		26.60	0.4
Cement	0.16		120		19.20	0.017
Concrete	0.23		140		32.20	0.54
Fireclay brick	0.19		112		22.17	0.58
Gypsum	0.25		78		20.20	0.25
Sand	0.19		95		18.06	0.19
Stone (quarried)	0.20		170		34.00	
Wood (average)	0.52		47		24.44	0.102-0.063
Water	1.00		62.5		62.5	0.348

Thermal Resistance Values of Common Building Materials

Many purchasers of new cars have discovered that claims regarding fuel efficiency have been exaggerated. Similarly, claims made by agencies and manufacturers concerning the 'R' values of insulation materials don't necessarily reflect the actual operating results. In addition, ensuring that the material is used properly is an important factor. As many people drive their cars with a "lead foot," thereby drastically reducing gas mileage, the improper installation and "operation" of insulating materials can reduce the effectiveness of insulating properties by as much as 50 per cent. A lack of attention to the installation of a vapour barrier, inadequate ventilation and the choice of inappropriate materials may all result in less than satisfactory performance. And as an automobile will lose its power over the course of its lifetime, so can the 'R' value of some insulation materials slowly degrade. The shrinkage of blown-in-place foams, outgassing of the florocarbon expanding agent in rigid foams, settling and even small animals looking for nesting materials, will all decrease the performance of an insulated cavity.

The following chart has taken advantage of some of the long term results acquired with insulating materials in arriving at realistic 'R' values. Proper use and installation is the key to success!

Material	R/inch	RSI/mm
Insulation		
Fibreglass batt	3.17	.022
Rock wool batt	3.32	.023
Fibreglass loose (blown)	2.16	.015
Fibreglass loose (poured)	3.03	.021
Rock wool loose (blown)	2.74	.019
Rock wool loose (poured)	3.03	.021
Cellulose (blown)	3.61	.025
Cellulose (poured)	3.46	.024
Vermiculite	2.31	.016
Polystyrene (loose)	2.88	.020
Expanded Polystyrene	3.89	.027
Extruded Polystyrene	4.62	.032
Polyurethane (rigid or foamed)	6.06	.042
Fibreglass sheathing	4.47	.031
Urea Formaldehyde	2.60	.018
Wood fibre	3.32	.023
Wood shavings	2.45	.017
Cork	3.75	.026
Glass fibre roof board	4.04	.028
Mineral aggregate board	2.60	.018
Compressed strawboard	2.02	.014
Fibreboard	2.74	.019
Cladding Materials		
Fibreboard siding	.45-.57 (³/₈″)	.10-.08 (9.5mm)
Softwood lapped siding		
drop —	.80 (³/₄″)	.14 (18mm)
bevel —	.80-1.0 (¹/₂″-³/₄″)	.14-.18 (12-19mm)
Plywood	.57 (³/₈″)	.10 (9mm)
Wood shingles	1.0	.17
Brick	.30-.42 (4″)	.053-.074 (100mm)
Stucco	.20 (1″)	.001 (25mm)
Metal clapboard with backing	1.40	.246

Material	R/inch	RSI/mm
Sheathing Materials		
Softwood plywood	1.25	.008
Mat-formed particleboard	1.25	.008
Insulating fibreboard	2.45	.017
Gypsum sheathing	.89	.006
Sheathing paper	.06	.0004
Polyethylene vapour barrier	—	—
Roofing Materials		
Asphalt roll roofing	.15	.026
Asphalt shingles	.44	.078
Wood shingles	.97	.170
Structural Materials		
Softwood lumber	1.25	.008
Cedar logs and lumber	1.33	.009
Concrete		
— high density	.06	.0004
— medium density	.19	.001
— low density	1.00	.006
Concrete Block (3 oval core)		
— sand and gravel aggregate	1.14 (8″)	.20 (200mm)
	1.25 (12″)	.22 (300mm)
— cinder aggregate	1.70 (8″)	.30 (200mm)
	1.87 (12″)	.33 (300mm)
— lightweight aggregate	1.99 (8″)	.35 (200mm)
	2.27 (12″)	.40 (300mm)
Common Brick		
— clay or shale	.40 (4″)	.07 (100mm)
— concrete mix	.28 (4″)	.05 (100mm)
Interior Finishing Materials		
Gypsum board	.45 (1/2″)	.08 (13mm)
Gypsum plaster (sand)	.10 (1/2″)	.018 (13mm)
(lightweight)	.32 (1/2″)	.05 (13mm)
Plywood	.40 (1/4″)	.07 (7.5mm)
Hardboard	.18 (1/4″)	.032 (6mm)
Fibreboard	2.39 (1″)	.42 (25mm)
Drywall	.45 (1/2″)	.08 (13mm)

Material	R/inch	RSI/mm
Flooring Materials		
Maple or Oak flooring	.68 (3/4″)	.12 (19mm)
Pine or Fir	.97 (3/4″)	.17 (19mm)
Plywood	.80 (5/8″)	.14 (16mm)
Wood Fibre Tiles	1.12 (1/2″)	.21 (13mm)
Tile or Linoleum	.08 (1/8″)	.014 (3mm)
Carpeting		
— with fibre underlay	2.10 (average)	.37
— with foam underlay	1.31 (average)	.23
Windows (including air films)		
Single glass	.85	.15
Double glass (sealed units)		
1/4″ airspace	1.53	.27
1/2″ airspace	1.70	.30
3/4″ airspace	1.89	.33
Triple glass (sealed units)		
1/4″ airspace	2.15	.38
1/2″ airspace	2.78	.49
3/4″ airspace	2.84	.50

Glossary

Active Solar — Solar heating systems requiring the use of conventional energy sources to circulate heat from collectors to storage to the living space; implies pumps or fans and controls in the system.

Air Barrier — A carefully installed covering of the interior of a structure to minimize the uncontrolled passage of air into and out of a dwelling; most commonly a continuously sealed 6 mil. polyethylene sheet.

Airtight — The use of sound construction practices resulting in an air change rate in a structure of less than .1 changes per hour.

Air-to-Air Heat Exchanger — A means of extracting much of the heat from stale air that is exhausted from a building. While the stale air is removed from a building, fresh air is drawn in. Concurrently the heat is transferred from the exhausted air to the incoming air.

Awning Windows — Vertically hinged windows which allow for an airtight seal.

Berm — A mound of earth or other material situated to divert winds away from a building.

Casement Windows — A window hinged on the vertical side to open outwards; good installation can provide an airtight seal.

Caulking — A variety of materials which are used to seal fixed and moveable construction joints to prevent infiltration.

Chimney Effect — The pressure caused by the upward movement of heated air; as air is heated it naturally rises and is replaced by cooler air.

Clerestories — Vertical windows built into a wall built into the roof structure allowing for passive gain and natural illumination.

Conduction — The movement of heat through a material by molecular agitation.

Convection — The transfer of heat energy by the motion of fluids which are carrying the heat; fluids can be either liquids or gases.

Defenestration — The act of throwing an object out of a window; ie. junk, cheating husbands/wives, glossaries with bad jokes.

Degree Days — An indicating factor of the relative severity of the heating season in any given area. Refers to the difference between a base temperature (68°F or 18°C) and the average daily temperature.

Design Temperature — The lowest temperature to be expected during the heating season; the time at which the heat loss from a building is at its maximum rate.

Dew Point — The temperature at which water vapour will condense as warm, moist air is cooled.

Direct Gain — The living space is heated by solar radiation entering the structure through south-facing windows. Passive solar heating.

Glazing — A covering of transparent or transluscent material which allows light to enter a structure. While permitting solar gain to a space, glazing also slows the flow of heat to the exterior. Commonly used materials include glass, plastics and fibreglass. Simply stated, a greater number of layers of any material employed will result in reduced heat loss.

Infiltration — The uncontrolled movement of air into a structure through cracks and holes in the shell of a building.

Internal Gain — The heat produced in the interior of a dwelling from the operation of lights, appliances and water heating systems.

Mass-Wall — Sunlight is intercepted from the living spaces by a thermal storage wall — either water or masonry — which acts as the thermal storage for the house. Also called a Trombe wall. Passive solar heating.

Passive Solar — Solar heating systems which operate on natural thermal processes.

R (RSI) value — The value attributed to a given material to determine its insulating properties. The higher the R the greater the resistance a material has to heat transfer; the inverse of the materials conductivity.

Radiation — The direct transfer of energy through space.

Relative Humidity — The humidity expressed as a percentage of the maximum possible humidity at a given temperature.

Retrofit — The thermal improvement of an existing house or structure.

Stratification — Natural convections resulting in the accumulation of the hottest material at the top of a container/house.

Sun Space — Passive solar heating wherein the solar collection is performed in an area adjacent to the living space; usually used in reference to an attached greenhouse/atrium.

Super-Insulation — Construction practices resulting in a minimal heat load for a building, i.e. R40 walls and R60 ceilings, air-tight construction and south-facing shuttered windows.

Thermal Break — An air space or insulating material which prevents the direct coupling of a cold surface to a heated surface.

Thermal Bridge — The direct coupling in a wall assembly from the interior to the exterior; although a wall cavity may house R20, there is a thermal bridge directly across a stud.

Thermal Mass — The amount of heat storage capacity available in a given material or assembly. Thermal mass will absorb excess heat generated during the day and store it until the ambient temperature drops; most commonly water, concrete or rocks.

Thermosyphon — The convective circulation of a fluid (water or air) through natural thermal processes; as warm fluid rises it is displaced by cooler, denser fluids from the same system.

Vapour Barrier — A material which restricts the flow of water vapour from one side to another. Most commonly aluminum foil, plastic, or paints with a low permeability. Used in wall assemblies. The materials, if properly installed, double as air barriers.

Ventilation — Outside air which is mechanically drawn into a structure either through the use of a fan, air-to-air heat exchanger, or by opening a window.

Weather stripping — Thin sections of a material which are used to prevent air leakage around operable windows and doors. Most commonly metal strips, vinyl, or foam gasketing.

CONVERSION TABLES

Multiply	by	To Obtain
feet	0.3048	metres
inches	25.4	millimetres
square feet	0.0929	square metres
gallon (Imp.)	4.55	litres
gallon (U.S.)	3.79	litres
litre	0.001	cubic metres
cubic feet	0.0283	cubic metres
pounds	0.4535	kilogram
lb/cubic foot	16.03	kg/cubic metre
Btu	1054.35	Joules
Btu	0.0002929	Kilowatt-hours
Joule/sec.	1	Watt
Btu/hr	0.293	Watt
Btu/ft²/day	.0113	MJ/m²/day
Btu/hr/ft²/°F	5.679	W/m²/°C

Multiply	by	To Obtain
metres	3.2808	feet
millemetres	0.0393	inches
square metres	10.76	square feet
litre	0.2197	gallon (Imp)
litre	0.2638	gallon (U.S.)
cubic metres	1,000	litres
cubic metres	35.33	cubic feet
kilogram	2.204	pounds
kg/cubic metre	.0623	lb/cubic foot
Joules	.0009485	Btu
Kilowatt-hours	3,414.4	Btu
Watt	1	Joule/sec
Watt	3.412	Btu/hr
MJ/m²/day	88.05	Btu/ft²/day
W/m²/°C	.1760	Btu/hr/ft²/°F

Index

Acknowledgements

Editor

Rick Wilks

Illustration

Vilnis Lucs (Primer)
Paul Kerman (Survey, Conference)

Cover

Valdis Lapsa
(also thanks for the camera, copier
and car)

Photographs

Photographs from the Fairview Conference were supplied by the speakers. All
other photographs by Robert Argue,
except:

Page 174 N.B. Power
Page 175 Danny

Research and Production

Anne MacInnes
Jane McNulty
Karen Englander
The Allen Drerup White office
Annick Press Ltd.
Brian Marshall, for his substantial con-
tribution to the research and produc-
tion of this title.
Peter Meridew and his students at Ryer-
son Polytechnical Institute, Toronto for
compiling much of the weather data in
the Appendix.
Barbara Eidlitz
Sylvia Argue

Renewable Energy in Canada would also
like to thank the following for their
generous support of the production of
this book.

The Samuel and Saidye Bronfman Family Foundation
Laidlaw Foundation

Author

Robert Argue has been actively involved in environmental issues for the last ten years. Since 1974 his greatest area of interest has been the emerging solar heating field. This involvement has lead to numerous travels throughout North America to gain first-hand knowledge of the people and their projects. He has furthered his experience with work on the construction and documentation of Ecology House, an urban retrofit demonstration, and by installing a solar water heating system in his house in Toronto.

Mr. Argue's writing or co-author credits include *The Sun Builders; A People's Guide To Solar, Wind and Wood Energy In Canada, Solar Heating Catalogue #1, Renewable Energy Resources; A Guide To The Literature, Canada's Renewable Energy Resources; An Assessment of Potential.*

Other activities include conducting solar construction workshops, solar tours and classroom sessions on renewable energy strategies. He also works as a consultant for government and business in the solar heating field.

Mr. Argue holds a Masters degree in Environmental Studies from York University.